# Fire
# and
# Water

## Other Works by Ralph D. Sawyer
### Published by Westview Press

*The Tao of War: The Martial Tao Te Ching*

*Sun-tzu's Art of War*

*The Complete Art of War*

*The Seven Military Classics of Ancient China*

*Sun Pin: Military Methods*

*One Hundred Unorthodox Strategies: Battle and Tactics of Chinese Warfare*

*The Tao of Spycraft: Intelligence Theory and Practice in Traditional China*

# Fire and Water

## The Art of Incendiary and Aquatic Warfare in China

*Ralph D. Sawyer*

*With the collaboration of*
*Mei-chün Lee Sawyer*

**Westview**
PRESS
A Member of the Perseus Books Group

Copyright © 2004 by Ralph D. Sawyer

Published in the United States of America by Westview Press, A Member of the Perseus Books Group, 5500 Central Avenue, Boulder, Colorado 80301–2877, and in the United Kingdom by Westview Press, 12 Hid's Copse Road, Cumnor Hill, Oxford OX2 9JJ.

Find us on the world wide web at www.westviewpress.com

Westview Press books are available at special discounts for bulk purchases in the United States by corporations, institutions, and other organizations. For more information, please contact the Special Markets Department at the Perseus Books Group, 11 Cambridge Center, Cambridge, MA 02142, or call (617) 252–5298, (800) 255–1514 or email j.mccrary@perseusbooks.com.

Library of Congress Cataloging-in-Publication Data

Sawyer, Ralph D.
    Fire and water : the art of incendiary and aquatic warfare in China / Ralph D. Sawyer ; with the collaboration of Mei-Chun Lee Sawyer.
        p. cm.
Includes bibliographical references and index.
    ISBN 0-8133-4065-9 (hardcover : alk. paper)
    1. Military art and science--China. 2. Floods—China. 3. Fires—China. 4. Defensive (Military science). 5. Offensive (Military science). 6. Riverine operations—China. I. Sawyer, Mei-chÉun. II. Title.
U31.S375 2003
355'.00951—dc22

                                                              2003017362

The paper used in this publication meets the requirements of the American National Standard for Permanence of Paper for Printed Library Materials Z39.48–1984.

Set in 11 Point Galliard by the Perseus Books Group

10    9    8    7    6    5    4    3    2    1

# Contents

*Preface*                                                                      *ix*

## INCENDIARY WARFARE

1 Fire                                                                           3
   Fires and Fire Fighting, 4
   Combustion, Ignition, and Incendiary Warfare, 6
   Early Incendiary Activity, 9
   Sun-tzu's Concepts and Doctrine, 15

2 The Warring States                                                            23
   Methods of Attack and Defense, 29
   Mining, 33
   Theoretical Developments, 35
   Early Escalation and Reaction, 41

3 Post–Warring States Developments                                              49

4 Theoretical Developments                                                      77
   Targeting Provisions, 101

5 Methods, Weapons, and Techniques                                             109
   Assault Devices, 112
   Animal Delivery Systems, 115
   Theoretical Texts and Considerations, 122
   Action at a Distance, 128
   Hurled Incendiary Bombs, 133

Special Operations, 134
Gunpowder-Era Incendiaries, 139

6  Wind, Smoke, and Issues of Defense                    149
   Smoke, 164
   Defense Against Incendiary Attack, 172
   Incendiary Measures in Defense, 177
   Incendiaries in Mining and Counter-mining, 191

7  Riverine Warfare                                      195
   Riverine Theory and Fundamental Incendiary
      Practices, 199
   Incendiaries in Riverine Clashes, 210
   Riverine Incendiary Targets, 223
   Defense Against Riverine Incendiary Attack, 234

# AQUATIC WARFARE

8  Water                                                 241
   Defensive Employment, 244
   Defense Against Flooding, 253
   Early Aquatic Warfare, 256
   Rain and Natural Inundation, 265

9  Aquatic Attack                                        275
   Theory, 275
   Successful Practice, 285
   Stalemates and Failure, 296
   Reversals and Compounded Disaster, 306
   Aquatic Ram, 308
   Theft of Water, 314

10  Negating Water Sources                               317
    Extraordinary Measures, 329

Poison, 333
Detecting Poison and Locating Sources, 339

11 Illustrative Sieges 343
The Siege of Yü-pi (Jade Cliff), 348
Hou Ching and the Siege of Chien-k'ang, 351
The Clash at Ch'eng-tu, 357
The Siege of T'ai-yüan, A.D. 1126, 359
The Siege of Te-an, A.D. 1127–1132, 361
The Siege of Te-an, A.D. 1206–1207, 363
The Siege of Hsiang-yang, A.D. 1206–1207, 366

Notes 373
Bibliography of Chinese Materials 421
Suggested Further Reading 423
Index 427

# Preface

Long before gunpowder's epochal discovery in China, incendiary and aquatic warfare, the only two modes capable of inflicting inestimable and uncontrollable damage once initiated, had appeared and proliferated. It is their theory, tactics, and methods, rather than the gunpowder-based explosives and tubed weapons that came to dominate from the fourteenth century onward, already masterfully charted in Joseph Needham's monumental "The Gunpowder Epic," that form the focus of our brief work.

In tracing their development and adoption over the centuries, recourse has been equally to the virtually continuous tradition of theoretical military texts and actual battlefield practices as they may be glimpsed in China's extensive historical writings, particularly the *Twenty-five Dynastic Histories,* Ssu-ma Kuang's comprehensive overview entitled the *Tzu-chih T'ung-chien,* and of course its subsequent, if somewhat inferior, continuation through the Sung. However, although the theoretical material has perhaps been comprehensively arrayed, for every battle cited in illustration, many more, often not unimportant clashes, could have been recounted.

Since academic sinologists generally deprecate warfare's role in traditional China, often viewing it as a mere barbarous intrusion into a glorious cultural and political edifice rather than a transforming and ever present factor of horrific impact, we have (apart from the military writings) de-emphasized translation, simplified names and titles wherever possible, and dispensed with our usual textual and philological comments to make the work more accessible to a broader audience. Nevertheless, extensive footnotes have been provided which not only briefly identify the sources for readers with expertise in Chinese, but also amplify the textual material itself with additional examples and historical comments.

We would like to acknowledge the ongoing interest and support provided by Steve Catalano, Senior Editor, and Holly Hodder, Publisher, at Westview Press; Max Gartenberg's unstinting advice; Diane Harper's insights into horses and their capabilities; Penny Gardiner's efforts; Dr. Margaret Rappaport for ruminations on fire; and the assistance of Philip Cho and Miao Yung-yi in locating and acquiring essential and obscure materials over the years. Once again, we are pleased to have Lee T'ing-rong's calligraphy for our cover. Finally, as previously, while I am responsible for the writing, military texts, theorizing, and conclusions, Mei-chün has contributed immeasurably through our joint examination of a wide variety of historical records.

*Ralph D. Sawyer*
*Winter, 2002*

*RalphSawyer.com*

# INCENDIARY WARFARE

Because of its unimaginable impact, fire has always been the weapon of the downtrodden and outnumbered. Single arrows have little effect unless they slay commanders or political leaders, but a flaming shaft launched with equal effort may ignite a major conflagration. So too the embers stolen or carried by a subversive agent creeping about a silent city in the dead of night, virtually overwhelmed by the many potential targets about. Even "incendiary thieves" who sneak into encampments under the cover of darkness can wreck great havoc merely by igniting the enemy's provisions and flammable stores, paving the way for a devastating attack.

Fire can also be envisioned in a purifying role, the basis of meditative techniques, as one of the fundamental elements (conceived as phases in China), and even the foundation of religious beliefs and cultural myths.[1] Its unpredictability frightens, its awesome destructiveness terrifies.[2] Its ability to rapidly change, spread erratically, and inflict great pain induces panic even as efforts to combat it exacerbate the chaos. Accordingly, it was employed in crucial analogies, likening evil to a fire burning on the plains that can't be approached or extinguished[3] or asserting that "military weapons are like fire. If you don't put the fire aside, you will burn yourself."[4] Thus even the mere prospect of coming under incendiary attack induced Li Yu to surrender in the T'ang.[5]

Not surprisingly, fire came to be employed to test discipline and assess the impact of rewards and punishments, producing the conclusion that unlike combat, rewards alone are insufficient to ensure compliance, that only the threat of severe punishment will motivate action.[6] Three such tests appear in the Warring States work known as the *Han Fei-tzu,* the most famous being introduced by a hypothetical dialogue between the remarkable king of Yüeh, Kou Chien, and his high official Chung:[7]

> "I would like to attack the state of Wu. Is it possible?"
> "Yes, it is. Our rewards are generous and trusted, our punishments severe and certain. If you would like to ascertain this, why not conduct a test by setting a fire in a palace room?"
> The king had a fire set in one of the palace rooms but no one went to put it out. An order was then issued which stated that anyone who died while fighting the fire would be rewarded equally with having died fighting the enemy.[8] Anyone who fought the fire but didn't perish would be rewarded comparable to achieving victory over the enemy. And anyone who failed to fight the fire would be punished as if they had surrendered or fled.
> The number of people who smeared their bodies with mud, donned wet clothes, and went into the fire amounted to three thousand on the left and three thousand on the right. From this the king knew they had certainly attained sufficient power to be victorious.[9]

The challenges posed by fire were so severe that soldiers who willingly braved the flames garnered instant fame and struck terror in their enemies, just as one small band of soldiers did by wrapping themselves in wet hemp to turn the battle against superior Jurchen aggressors.[10]

## FIRES AND FIRE FIGHTING

In China, as in all pre-modern civilizations, the populace employed open or minimally contained fires for cooking, heating, lighting, and various essential processes such as drying goods, smoking meat and fish, burning fields, and fumigating buildings. While essential to the evolution of civilization and crucial in colder climates, the deleterious effects were manifold and the people's acquaintance with smoke ubiquitous. Moreover, especially during the dry seasons and when the winter winds blew, their thatched roofs made even common mud huts susceptible to fire. Close structural packing in the limited space of fortified towns naturally fostered its rapid spread, and since the smallest fire could easily engulf a city, draconian regulations regarding the lighting and use of fires were promulgated and enforced.

The *Han Fei-tzu*, in elucidating the *Tao Te Ching*'s insights into the difficulty of affecting things and processes once they have grown and become established—and thus the necessity for taking preemptive action while affairs might easily be managed—adduces an illustration centered upon fire and water. Speaking about dikes and stoves, it observes that even the smallest gap can foster disaster. Just as the minute holes created by ants and burrowing bugs in massive riverside embankments can quickly become so enlarged by the pressurized water that they crumble, so the insignificant flame flickering through a cracked stove can set a mansion afire.[11]

The dozen or so conflagrations documented in the *Tso Chuan* testify to the difficulty of controlling, much less extinguishing, urban fires once they attained even minimally substantial proportions. Many noteworthy fires were initiated by lightning strikes, a form of Heavenly retribution deemed particularly baleful when palaces or ancestral temples were struck, though the loss of key granaries and storehouses affected the populace more severely, both directly and then indirectly as new taxes were imposed to compensate for the government's losses.[12]

In the absence of pumps and hoses, well-organized brute-force efforts remained the only recourse for combating fires and preventing disorder and looting. Most actions were necessarily preventive, focused upon removing flammable materials from the fire's path, soaking and draping structures with wet hides and cloths, applying a layer of mud, or spreading sand rather than actually trying to extinguish the fire. Even under the direction of the legendary administrator Tzu Ch'an, the state of Cheng was unable to do more than remove valuables, keep public order, pray, compensate people for their losses, and initiate rebuilding.[13]

A conflagration in Chin at the end of the third century, which followed a summer of evil omens, five inches of hail, and severe flooding in six provinces, saw priceless military treasures, including Liu Pang's fabled sword, destroyed when the royal armory burned. Their inability to cope with the quickly spreading fire, partly because officials tried to prevent the theft of potentially dangerous weapons, may be realized from the extent of the destruction, enough weapons to equip two million soldiers having been consumed.[14] Early the next century, a fire in Hopei consumed three districts, destroying more than 7,000 dwellings and killing an astonishing 15,000 people.[15]

The advantage of launching incendiary attacks against structures confined within walled cities or troops caught in encampments was inescapably apparent. Although some strikes were no doubt thwarted by basic defensive measures or by quickly extinguishing the incendiaries on impact, others succeeded in inflicting nearly total destruction. To cite just two examples from among hundreds, a night attack in 301 A.D. mounted by the rebel leader Li Te on Chao Hsin's field army reportedly killed 80 to 90 percent of the 10,000 men caught in the encampment.[16] In one of the numerous internecine conflicts that beset China in the sixth century A.D., Eastern Wei besieged the major city of Chin-yung (Luo-yang), then part of Western Wei. The Eastern Wei commander eventually ordered an incendiary attack that reportedly consumed 70 to 80 percent of all the structures within and immediately about the city.[17]

## COMBUSTION, IGNITION, AND INCENDIARY WARFARE

True incendiary warfare consists of deliberately using fire to achieve tactical or strategic objectives, destroying defenses, eliminating material resources, and slaying men more effectively than with ordinary arrows and shock weapons. Although not a focal topic in early Greek and Roman military history, from the Warring States onward it became a crucial part of Chinese theory and practice.[18] However, despite fire's often voracious tendency to flare and spread, starting fires at crucial moments amidst the stress and uncertainty of battle was never simple or certain.

Prior to the discovery and perfection of gunpowder, enemy targets could only be ignited by putting adequate quantities of burning material against or in close proximity to them for sufficient time. The employment of simple accelerants such as sesame oil and lard improved the likelihood of success, but highly combustible straw and dry bamboo would also produce an intense localized blaze. All of them could provide the heat energy required to achieve combustion, a fact intuitively realized though not explicitly conceptualized. Wind was understood to immensely facilitate the process and augment the effects, but be detrimental at the incipient stage if it should blow too strongly or change direction suddenly.

The dual but distinctive perspectives of chemistry and thermodynamics explain the difficulties encountered in starting fires and the surprising eruption of conflagrations. Although limitations of space preclude an extensive contemplation of combustion, a few words about the mysteries of fire are warranted.[19] Briefly, things "burn" or are oxidized when a material (fuel) is raised to the ignition point in the presence of oxygen so that combustion occurs, releasing heat, gas, particles, and light. Substances vary in their combustibility, the temperature at which the reaction becomes self-sustaining as the heat being released adequately warms the contiguous material. Some substances require very high heat energy to combust or, like candle wax, may even be endothermic, requiring a continuous input of external energy to decompose.[20] They therefore cannot be destroyed by "fire" unless burned in conjunction with (strongly) exothermic materials, creating immense difficulties should they constitute important military targets.

As anyone who has ever tried to light a campfire, burn brush, or use a real charcoal grill quickly learns, strong winds thwart ignition because they disperse the gaseous materials and carry away the heat energy required to attain the combustion temperature. However, once ignition has been achieved, most materials of military value decompose exothermically, rapidly volatilizing nearby material components to the necessary gaseous state, at which time strong oxygenation not only becomes advantageous, but necessary. Thus high winds fan the flames and quickly turn a small blaze into an unstoppable, all consuming firestorm.

The speed of chemical reactions, including combustion, rapidly increases with both rising temperature and pressure, accounting for objects burning more readily on hot summer days and in confined spaces (assuming adequate oxygen intake), as well as to flare up and achieve frightening size. Dry conditions also favor the tactical use of incendiaries because water, as Chinese phase theory postulates, and fire are antagonistic. Low moisture content being essential, hydroscopic substances, including some of the nitrates found in gunpowder, absorb water and therefore burn poorly, if at all.

Substances that burn extremely rapidly but without "exploding" when unconfined, often with sparking, hissing, and the evolution of large quantities of gas, are said to deflagrate. (They may weakly explode if contained, such as in heavy resin-coated paper balls or bamboo tubes, but are distinguished from true explosives, which detonate with a pressure wave that propagates at supersonic speeds.) Because of the rapidity of the wave front and high temperatures generated, such substances provide ideal materials for advanced incendiary warfare, and in fact the speed sometimes needs to be tempered to achieve a longer burn effect.

The remarkable mixture known as gunpowder deflagrates when all the components are present in less than the proper proportions, roughly 75 percent nitrate, 15 percent sulfur, and 10 percent charcoal, with the type of charcoal surprisingly affecting the burn rate. Even when perfectly balanced, only weak explosive effects will be achieved unless the mixture has undergone such a thorough process of pre-grinding, sifting, premixing, mixing, wetting, pressing or rolling, and finally grinding that a uniform, fine powder with high surface area results whose combustion properties are said to approach those of a compound rather than a composite mixture.[21] Centuries of painful experience and experimentation were required to evolve the craft knowledge and production techniques necessary to maximize black powder's explosiveness, enabling it to provide the requisite force for cannon and bombs.[22]

Since gunpowder's chief component, the nitrate salts, liberates oxygen when decomposing in the presence of the heat generated by the burning sulfur, combustion will continue even in the absence of atmospheric sources. This critical feature allows it to be confined in sealed containers ranging from resin-coated layers of paper through bamboo tubes and iron casings. Thus, in the realm of incendiary warfare, small gourds of oil that might not be effective can be replaced by paper tubes of black powder that will burn until exhaustion and produce much higher temperatures.

Since the key variables within the already mentioned need to apply sufficient heat to the target are oxygen supply, the incendiary's temperature, and length of time on target, hotter materials can achieve localized ignition much more quickly. Moreover, although liquids such as sesame oil volatize readily and can spread, in contrast to gunpowder-based devices, they may be extinguished by the wind or burn out without setting the target on fire. However, since gunpowder didn't become a viable operational option until well into the Sung, the first 1500 years of Chinese incendiary warfare relied upon a variety of common and esoteric substances, including petroleum distillates, to achieve ever increasing destruction.

## EARLY INCENDIARY ACTIVITY

The earliest historical recountings of incendiary attacks depict the victors pummeling the vanquished in post-conquest expressions of rage. When the self-proclaimed righteous Chou troops proceeded to the secondary Shang capital of Ch'ao-ko subsequent to the battle of Mu-yeh in 1035 B.C., they set it ablaze, explaining how King Chou was able to immolate himself in the Deer Tower despite being cloaked in jade.[23] In 771 B.C., reputedly facilitated by the Chou king having rendered the border warning system ineffective through treating it as a plaything for his concubine's amusement, so-called barbarian invaders burned and plundered the Chou capital of Ch'eng-chou. Coerced by these ongoing steppe threats, the next Chou king moved the capital eastward to Luo-yang, a watershed event that not only bifurcates the Chou era but essentially marks the end of their remnant authority over the feudal states.

Even the Warring States era symbolically closed with Hsiang Yü's vengeful plundering and burning of Hsien-yang, the Ch'in capital, contrary to Liu Pang's promise to preserve it as an inducement to end armed resistance. The ensuing conflagration reportedly continued unabated for three months and rendered the capital so uninhabitable that Hsiang Yü was forced to return east to rule.[24] He thus shortsightedly abandoned this strategic city to three surrendered Ch'in generals who were expected to function as a bulwark against Liu Pang, then ironically being exiled to the fertile bastion of Szechuan.

Although remains at Erh-li-t'ou, reputedly the last capital of the Hsia, and earlier sites show that fire's vengeful employment certainly predates the Shang dynasty, the first recorded incendiary attack, one deliberately undertaken to deprive the enemy of provisions, dates to 718 B.C. By then incessant strife had long wracked the state of Chin, having been engendered in 745 B.C. when Huan-shu, the uncle of the newly enthroned ruler, was enfeoffed in Ch'ü-wo, a secondary city whose size and economic might exceeded that of the capital.[25] Huan-shu's virtuous policies and personal charisma attracted the people's allegiance and thus inevitably cast him in the role of a royal competitor. The situation was exacerbated by the other fiefs being comparatively smaller and the state's military forces being dispersed among the feudal lords rather than concentrated in the capital of Yi.

Even though he neither initiated nor participated in the rebellion, hoping to bring him to the capital, Huan-shu's adherents murdered the legitimate ruler in 739 B.C. However, the local populace blocked his entry into Yi and established a new ruler instead. When Huan-shu died in 732, his son (Duke Chuang) attacked the capital and slew the ruler, but the inhabitants again managed to repulse the aggressors and establish a new duke. However, when the latter died in his sixth year, Duke Chuang exploited the momentary instability to strike again only to be forced back to Ch'ü-wo by a coalition of feudal lords. Although accounts differ, forces deputed by the Chou king apparently played a key role.

In reprisal for Duke Chuang's attacks, shortly after ascending the throne the new duke of Chin took advantage of the instability caused by the coalition attack on Ch'ü-wo (and apparently Duke Chuang's death) to burn the immature grain standing in the latter's fields. The following year he exploited the resulting hunger and deprivation to mount a victorious attack, compelling Duke Chuang's son, known as Duke Wu, to seek peace. However, Ch'ü-wo continued to strengthen and ultimately displaced the Chin ruling line through political machination and a series of military actions in Duke Wu's 37th year.

According to the sparse chronicle known as the *Ch'un Ch'iu (Spring and Autumn Annals)*, the next incendiary attack dates to 705 B.C., when the duke of Lu set fire to Hsien-ch'iu, a place generally identified by later commentators as an area of fields within the state of Lu itself.[26] One explanation suggests the duke deliberately had the fires set as part of a massive hunting expedition in order to startle the game and drive them toward the hunters. (Royal hunts were still sometimes employed to train warriors in coordinated maneuver and deployment, though force size had already grown too unwieldy for them to encompass more than a few core units.) However, others identify Hsien-ch'iu as a town in the contiguous state of Ch'u and term the event a *"huo kung"* or "incendiary assault."[27] Moreover, Ho Yen-hsi, one of the ten important commentators on Sun-tzu's *Art of War,* right at the beginning of the chapter entitled "Incendiary Warfare" asserts that this incident marks the beginning of incendiary warfare

Incendiary techniques were next tactically employed in 698 B.C. when a multi-state coalition under Sung's leadership struck Cheng in reprisal for an attack two years earlier. (Attacks and reprisals offset by one to three years, such as between Chin and Ch'in, often defined interstate relationships during the Spring and Autumn period.) The coalition burnt the important Chü Gate before penetrating the eastern suburbs, seizing various areas, and even dismantling the ancestral temple in order to acquire rafters for their own gates.[28]

As this incursion shows, city gates were prime targets, especially in the earliest era.[29] Being constructed from wood and therefore susceptible to both fire and shock, they constituted the only weakness in the otherwise massive earthen walls which often exceeded thirty feet in width and twenty in height. Moreover, they not only controlled physical access but also functioned symbolically, demarking the outer realm from the inner sanctum of defined community.

Within the city, palaces and ancestral temples, the state's most symbolically charged structures, were commonly targeted.[30] As neither entailed any great tactical value, their burning vented anger and hatred while visibly impressing the reality of defeat upon the vanquished. Markets were eventually included among these punitive targets, presumably because they functioned as the center of economic and social activity.[31] However, being temporary and normally permitted by regulation only on specific days, they were readily moved to new locations, minimizing the disruptive effects.

In the midst of the seventh century B.C., several steppe peoples adopted incendiary techniques, eventually becoming avid practitioners as they increasingly targeted the immobile assets of China's sedentary civilization throughout the imperial period. In 649 B.C., a conjoined force of six steppe groups attacked the royal army and penetrated the old Chou capital of Ch'eng-chou by setting fire to the east gate. In a momentous development, the peripheral states of Ch'in and Chin both dispatched rescue forces which evicted the invaders, after which the duke of Chin futilely attempted to broker peace talks among the parties.[32]

Greater frequency and scope in incendiary attacks came to mark the sixth century, part of an ongoing increase in exploiting unorthodox and non-shock weapons. For example, in breaking off diplomatic relations in 578 B.C., Chin's emissary upbraided Ch'in for having burned two border towns, attacking nearby farmers, and killing and making prisoners of the local inhabitants.[33] A decade later, when Ch'u invaded Cheng in reprisal for Cheng having attacked its ally, the minor state of Ts'ai, a Cheng emissary pleaded with Ch'u to understand the precarious nature of their pivotal position.[34] He emotionally charged Ch'u with having wantonly burned their outer strongpoints before pummeling the city so severely that every family lost a member and the populace lacked any refuge.

Even allowing for exaggeration in the emissary's harangue, it is clear that incendiary attacks were being effectively employed in a tactical mode prior to mounting citadel assaults. Thus, at one point in the internal strife besetting the remnant Chou state, in 516 B.C. dissident forces in control of the royal city rebounded from an earlier defeat by burning a loyalist bastion, compelling the latter's forces to flee.[35] The objective of such assaults was no longer mere penetration but vanquishing the enemy by first incinerating their cities rather than destroying them post-conquest.[36]

Just after Sun-tzu's era, early in the fifth century the king of Yüeh attacked the state of Wu while its ruler, Fu Ch'ai, was away convening the feudal lords. The campaign penetrated as far as the capital of Ku-su where they burned the suburbs before withdrawing just when Wu's army returned.[37] Meanwhile, while passing by the state of Sung en route back from the convocation, Fu Ch'ai preemptively burned the northern suburbs to preclude an ambush by it and possibly Ch'i.[38]

Fire's first recorded defensive employment also dates to this era when forces ensconced at Lin-ch'iu attempted to thwart the duke of Lu's attack by setting his assault wagons ablaze in 502 B.C. However, the invaders successfully extinguished the fires with wet hemp cloths before going on to destroy the walls, prompting the defenders to flee.[39] The next year the rebel Yang Hu exploited fire's inherent ability to threaten and confuse when, while under attack by royal Lu forces, he deliberately set the main city gate afire to frighten and thwart the attackers.[40] Yang then exploited the ensuing consternation to mount a counter-attack before fleeing to Ch'i.

An interesting dialogue attributed to 479 B.C. records a potential usurper declining to burn the state's storehouses because it would deprive him of critical materials needed after wresting control of the throne.[41] This incident clearly shows that incendiary measures had become readily adopted options, even if only as an adjunct to more traditional martial practices, and were often purely destructive. (Ironically, a later text suggests he was advised to burn the storehouses to preclude their seizure by other parties who might then employ the contents to attract new adherents, as in fact happened.)[42] However, only a single *Tso Chuan* account—one which illuminates not only late Spring and Autumn warfare practices but also the effectiveness of ruses and deception—actually portrays a combatant deliberately choosing to inflict extensive incendiary destruction.

In the winter of 555 B.C., a coalition force under the leadership of the marquis of Chin invaded powerful Ch'i by employing the state of Lu as a springboard.[43] Ch'i not only suffered an initial defeat, but ruses and tricks clearly designed to magnify the size of Chin's forces—multiple flags, dummies in chariots, and dragging brush—terrified the marquis of Ch'i into abandoning his forces on a moonless night. After his armies also hastily retreated, Chin's forces easily pressed forward, scoring repeated victories until they reached Ch'in-chou where they "hewed down the catalpa trees around Yung Gate."

A day later "they burned Yung Gate together with the western and southern quarters. Liu Nan and Shih Juo led the armies of the feudal lords in burning the trees and bamboo around Shen-ch'ih. On the sixth, they burned the eastern and northern quarters and Fan Yang assaulted Yang Gate." Within a few more days they had advanced in both the east and south and finally pursued the vanquished Ch'i army right back to the capital of Lin-tzu where they torched the outer suburbs before withdrawing, ending the first campaign known to have heavily exploited fire, at least punitively.[44]

While the *Tso Chuan* and *Kuo Yü*, the two texts depicting the history of the Spring and Autumn period,[45] thus preserve vestiges of an ever increasing employment and scope to incendiary measures, they remain sparse, only some twenty episodes among several hundred battles reported in varying detail. Moreover, the terms employed to describe these incidents are invariably *huo* (fire, to set fire to) and *fen* (to burn) rather than *shao* (to burn, set afire) or *huo kung* (incendiary attack), neither of which appears at all. Such paucity inevitably prompts questions as to whether incendiary techniques were rarely employed or had already become so commonplace that they didn't merit special mention, especially as a late *Kuan-tzu* chapter asserts that during Duke Huan's reign as hegemon, Ch'u extensively burned Cheng.[46] Other sources, including Sun-tzu's focal chapter on incendiary warfare, must therefore be studied for insights into late Spring and Autumn period practices.

## SUN-TZU'S CONCEPTS AND DOCTRINE

Warfare in Sun-tzu's era, the last decades of the Spring and Autumn period, had been escalating in both scope and intensity for more than a century as the powerful preyed upon the weak and extinctions and annexations radically altered the political geography. The twelfth chapter of the traditionally received *Art of War (Sun-tzu Ping-fa)*, entitled "Incendiary Attacks," being followed by the infamous final section on spycraft, has been comparatively neglected over the ages. However, it constitutes not only the first enunciation of incendiary measures but also the theoretical underpinning for later explications of objectives and techniques and a touchstone for most focal chapters in T'ang and later military writings. Moreover, it was well known to Three Kingdoms commanders such as Ts'ao Ts'ao and Chu-ko Liang, who dramatically exploited incendiary assaults to wrest decisive victories, thereby initiating the true age of incendiary warfare. Being extremely brief, the entire text may be translated as follows:[47]

There are five types of incendiary attack: The first is to incinerate men, the second to incinerate provisions, the third to incinerate supply trains, the fourth to incinerate armories, and the fifth to incinerate formations.[48]

Implementing an incendiary attack depends on the proper conditions. Equipment for incendiary attacks should be fully prepared before required. Launching an incendiary attack has appropriate seasons, igniting the fire proper days. As for the seasons, it is the time of the dry spell; as for the day, when the moon is in *chi, pi, yi,* or *chen*. When it is in these four lunar lodges, these are days when winds will arise.

In general, in incendiary warfare you must respond to the five changes of fire:

If fires are started within, then you should immediately respond from without.

If fires are ignited but their army remains quiet, then wait, do not attack.

If they flare into a conflagration and you can follow up, then do so; if you cannot, then desist.

If the attack can be launched from outside without relying on inside assistance, initiate it at an appropriate time.

If fires are ignited upwind, do not attack downwind.

Winds that arise in the daytime will persist, those that arise at night will cease.

Now the army must know the five changes of fire in order to defend against them at astrologically appropriate times. Thus using fire to aid an attack is enlightened, using water to assist an attack is powerful. Water can be used to sever, but cannot be employed to seize.

Now if someone is victorious in battle and succeeds in attack but does not exploit the achievement, it is disastrous and his fate should be termed "wasteful and tarrying." Thus it is said that the wise general ponders it, the good general cultivates it.

If it is not advantageous, do not move. If objectives cannot be attained, do not employ the army. Unless endangered, do not engage in warfare.

The ruler cannot mobilize the army out of personal anger, the general cannot engage in battle because of personal frustration. When it is advantageous, move; when not advantageous, stop. Anger can revert to happiness, annoyance can revert to joy, but a vanquished state cannot be revived, the dead cannot be brought back to life.

Thus the unenlightened ruler is cautious about it, the good general respectful of it. This is the Tao for bringing security to the state and preserving the army intact.

Even the most cursory reading immediately reveals that the conceptualization of incendiary warfare had already reached a sophisticated stage, doubtlessly premised upon experience and contemplation, but a major disjuncture marks the chapter's two halves. However, before we explore these issues more fully, some comments should be ventured upon the individual lines beginning with the five objectives, which may be reduced to simply men and materials. The latter encompasses provisions (in the form of stockpiles and supply trains) and weapons (in armories or centralized warehouses), the former men in encampments and deployed for battle. However, there is no mention of attacking cities or citadels, presumably because the walls would present a formidable, non-flammable exterior and Sun-tzu advocated avoiding siege mounted assaults unless absolutely necessary.

Incinerating the enemy's provisions and supplies would immediately plunge their forces into difficulty even though late Spring and Autumn armies extensively relied upon plundering and foraging to sustain their campaigns. Moreover, Sun-tzu's cognizance of war's debilitating economic effects led him to emphasize efficiency and the avoidance of prolonged campaigns. However, damaging an army's logistical support would not only impact them directly as starvation quickly weakened the men, but secondarily foster illness and dispirit while requiring further, sustained efforts at resupply. Given the enormous effort required to transport provisions and the considerable discomfiture experienced by the populace, successful incendiary attacks thus had ramifications far beyond simply debilitating a campaign army to the point where they might be overwhelmed or compelled to withdraw.

Subsequent battlefield history would show that launching incendiary attacks against encamped soldiers could accomplish three objectives: the immediate killing and wounding of enemy combatants, incineration of supplies, and creation of readily exploited chaos. Protected only by wooden palisades or an outer ring of wagons rather than the massive earthworks erected about cities, encampments were both vulnerable and accessible. If the troops could be trapped through containment measures and surprise, the first of these could easily be accomplished simply by targeting the camp as a whole.

The incineration of formations, synonymous with troops deployed on the battlefield, became feasible and worthwhile only with the advent of large field armies. The chariot warriors of the late Shang and early Chou, whether fighting individually or accompanied by squads of loosely attached troops, were too few and highly dispersed for incendiary arrows to achieve discernible effects. Even setting the terrain alight, as frequently seen in later centuries under conducive conditions, would have limited impact against small numbers of inherently more mobile forces. However, as infantry forces grew to tens of thousands and the number and therefore density of chariots escalated to 1,000 or more at the famous Spring and Autumn battles of Ch'eng-p'u, Yao, Pi, and Chi-fu, incendiary attacks directed against battlefield forces could prove both disruptive and effective.[49]

The second paragraph commences by emphasizing the need for wind and dryness, two situational factors thereafter regarded as fundamental. However, in contrast to his emphasis on human agency found earlier in the text, certain days determined by lunar references are somehow correlated with the wind's onset. This is puzzling because (as later theorists would assert) seasonal conditions and wind shifts in monsoon-affected areas such as northern China can be expected with a certain degree of reliability, but blowing winds cannot be pegged to individual days.[50] However, the admonition to be especially prepared at these moments which concludes the third section not only reflects belief, but would also become essentially self-fulfilling with the book's increasing dissemination. Interjecting the observation that "winds that arise in the daytime will persist, those that arise at night will cease" further emphasizes the wind's importance to any attack's effectiveness.

The second section also includes an injunction to prepare the equipment required for incendiary attacks well in advance even though it would have consisted of little more than torches, straw, and incendiary arrows in his era. However, as warfare escalated and became more complex, ad hoc tactical operations were increasingly doomed to failure. Thus Warring States texts such as the *Six Secret Teachings* contain lists of essential equipment and admonitions to be prepared for more unconventional situations, such as crossing bodies of water.

The "five changes of fire" in the third paragraph essentially correlate five situational developments with normative responses. The first three may be reduced to the basic rule that incendiary attacks should be exploited if and when opportunity allows. Thus, conflagrations ignited by subversive agents (and accidental fires), equally with successful external incendiary strikes, may be expected to produce the surprise and chaos necessary for a follow-on attack. However, if the enemy maintains order and discipline in the face of the flames and smoke, their defenses will have been insufficiently compromised to undertake an assault.

Neither the fourth situation, simply a warning not to endanger your troops by maneuvering downwind of a fire, nor the fifth require further comment. However, the first—"If fires are started within, then you should immediately respond from outside"—provides at least indirect evidence that subversive agents were already torching cities and camps, presumably in coordination with pre-poised assaults. The historical texts indicate that such operatives sometimes effected the subjugation of well-defended cities, causing the Mohists (who viewed them as the greatest threat) to promulgate rules prohibiting soldiers from abandoning their posts even in the face of massive conflagrations.

Within the context of national survival, the second half of the chapter unfolds extremely fundamental operational principles but makes absolutely no reference to incendiary techniques. As they are self-explanatory, the question as to why they are appended to a chapter ostensibly focusing on incendiary warfare—in fact, the only chapter in which incendiary measures are advanced—deserves pondering. Two explanations have been proposed: either the passages continue the specific theme and should be narrowly understood with reference to the employment of incendiary measures or the bamboo strips containing them simply became misplaced and should perhaps belong to the first chapter, "Initial Estimations."

Proponents of the first view suggest that the character of incendiary warfare, being dramatically different in inflicting widespread, indiscriminate destruction and extremely painful wounds, caused it to be viewed as particularly heinous and completely contrary to the ancient or virtuous practice of warfare. Moreover, employing incendiary techniques would cause such extreme suffering among the people that no subsequent policy could ameliorate their hatred. Accordingly, the second half of the text is viewed as asserting that these unusual measures should only be employed when forces become endangered and action becomes unavoidable, but then they should be fully exploited because of their high cost to humanity.[51] Furthermore, the argument that these strips have been misplaced, that they belong in the first chapter, is inverted by claiming that their inclusion here, rather than in "Initial Estimations," proves their highly specific nature.

Certainly the admonition to fully exploit every success simply reiterates the third section's concrete injunctions to follow up with infantry measures. However, this may be the very reason later editors appended such seemingly general pronouncements here rather than in the first section, particularly if they symmetrically concluded the book in the absence of the last section on "Employing Spies." Even the idea of not striking unless endangered well accords with the era's military situation because any external action, even if successful and profitable, could severely debilitate the state both physically and economically, as earlier chapters of the *Art of War* pointedly show. Nothing could be more generally applicable than the statement "If it is not advantageous, do not move; if objectives cannot be attained, do not employ the army."

In addition, although voices such as Mo-tzu's would soon begin to decry not only warfare's carnage and waste, but also the rampant excesses of rampaging armies, there is no evidence that in Sun-tzu's era or the Warring States, despite the promulgations of prohibitions, anyone condemned incendiary warfare as particularly brutal or inhuman. Being destructive and pernicious doesn't necessarily mean it was viewed as something distinctive, equivalent to the pariah of atomic weapons.

Despite the generally laconic nature of the *Art of War,* the final lines of the chapter's first half—"Thus using fire to aid an attack is enlightened, using water to assist an attack is powerful. Water can be used to sever, but cannot be employed to seize"—tend to suggest that an equally lengthy section on water assaults has been lost. Contrary to any negative implications, the author obviously believed incendiary warfare techniques to be effective and therefore concluded that their employment is enlightened, perhaps because it obviates any need to mount risky frontal attacks. Moreover, while powerful inundations can isolate and even destroy an enemy, fire can be employed to expeditiously seize their position.[52] In addition, flooding requires lengthy effort to channel the water source and time to debilitate the enemy, but incineration proceeds rapidly and therefore accords with the *Art of War*'s emphasis upon avoiding protracted engagements. On the downside, everything of value might be destroyed, including vital foodstuffs which could reduce the logistical burden and valuables needed to reward the troops.[53]

More broadly, Sun-tzu was the first to articulate the fundamental concept of the unorthodox and orthodox, the former being the employment of forces in situationally unexpected ways, accomplished by maneuver and concentrated firepower, the latter proceeding in measured fashion according to commonly accepted tactical principles.[54] Yet he never identified incendiary attacks as unorthodox, nor did many military thinkers thereafter.

Configuration of terrain, a second concept no doubt preexistent but first systematically conceived and explicated in the *Art of War*, would subsequently become an important factor in assessing the possibilities for mounting an incendiary attack. Although wind and dry conditions remain essential, terrain marked by heavy vegetation, natural obstructions, and difficult contours which constrain movement ensure maximum impact. Thus valleys and precipitous, enclosed terrains such as Heaven's Pit and Heaven's Well invariably constitute fatal ground for any fire attack, while so-called accessible or open terrain is totally inappropriate and any incendiary assault likely to be ineffective.[55]

# 2

# The Warring States

The remnants of the work known as the *Book of Lord Shang (Shang-chün Shu)*, attributed to, and possibly in substantial part derived from the hand of, the famous Legalist reformer and proponent Shang Yang, include two passages which indicate incendiary techniques were being employed in mid-to-late-fourth-century B.C. warfare. (Shang Yang wielded power as minister in Ch'in from 359 to 338 B.C., thereafter briefly in Ch'u.) In common with the Mohists, he advocated the ruthless imposition of measures designed to deny the enemy all materials of possible utility in conducting a siege, especially flammable ones. Thus, even as efforts were underway to store provisions and deploy traps, pitfalls, and obstacles, whatever could not be dismantled and transported away had to be burned.[1] When attacking, miners working in teams of eighteen on each side of the citadel or town were also to tunnel under the walls, erect wooden supports, and then set them ablaze.[2]

Although Mo-tzu was active at the end of the fifth century, the highly disparate military chapters in the extant work bearing his name, though possibly incorporating practices and pronouncements from earlier times, certainly date to the middle to late Warring States period. Badly fragmented, sometimes repetitious, and often cryptic, in contrast to the

*Shang-chün Shu* or *Wei Liao-tzu,* which confine themselves to fundamental issues and questions of feasibility, they preserve the first known expositions of defensive techniques.[3] Moreover, unlike the many pronouncements embedded in the philosophical chapters, particularly those advocating "universalized love," which were alternately condemned by proponents of Confucianism and ignored by the intellectual world at large, they were highly valued by military thinkers through the centuries. Not only were Mohist methods commonly employed to withstand sieges, but they were also incorporated into military treatises such as the T'ang dynasty's *T'ai-pai Yin-ching* and the military compendia initiated with the Sung dynasty's *Wu-ching Tsung-yao.*[4]

Mo-tzu became well known for opposing warfare, for vehemently condemning the waste and carnage wrought as men destroyed each other with "water, fire, poison, and drugs."[5] To mitigate human suffering and discourage aggressive behavior he developed the science and technology of defense, traveling widely with his personal band of disciples to deter aggressors and assist victims by implementing them. (A famous story found in the *Mo-tzu* depicts him dissuading the king of Ch'u from attacking Sung by expounding how his defensive methods would thwart any assault device conceived by the era's most brilliant innovator.) However, in concord with his view that "in defending a city, severely wounding the enemy is the top priority,"[6] the Mohists imposed draconian strictures upon the besieged populace while implementing brutal, externally directed techniques. Traps and enticements augmented the lethality of the defenses and picked troops sallied forth to exploit temporary reversals once strong countermeasures had been successfully executed.

Although important dictums are scattered among the thematic chapters, four chapters document the core measures necessary for survival: "Responding to the Enemy," "Banners and Flags," "Orders and Commands," and "Miscellaneous Defensive Measures."[7] However, even they are premised upon the city being fundamentally defensible, whereas five situations in which there is an imbalance between the population and the city's size, or an absence of essential materials, are not: "The city is large, the populace few; the city is small, the populace numerous; the people are numerous but provisions scarce; the market is far outside the city; or livestock and stores are outside the city while the wealthy live in the suburbs."[8]

Mo-tzu deemed fourteen factors to be crucial:

> If our city walls and moats are well maintained, defensive equipment complete, firewood and grain adequate, upper and lower ranks in accord, and we also have the prospect of rescue forces from the feudal lords on all four sides, these can be relied upon. Nevertheless, even though the defenders excel, there are still circumstances in which they cannot prevail. If the ruler employs them for defense but is incapable of directing them, then it is as if they cannot mount any defense. Only if the defenders excel and the ruler respectfully employs them can a successful defense be mounted.
>
> In general, to defend a besieged state the walls must be thick and high, ditches and moats deep and wide, towers prominent and protected, defensive equipment excellent and advantageous, firewood and foodstuffs sufficient to sustain three months or more, people numerous and selected,[9] officials and people of rank harmonious, high ministers with records of achievement and labor many, and the ruler trusted and righteous so that the myriad people take unlimited pleasure in him.
>
> In addition their ancestral graves and funeral mounds lie within, the resources of the mountains, forests, grasslands, and marshes are sufficiently profitable, the terrain is difficult to attack but easy to defend, there is deep enmity toward the enemy but a great feeling of appreciation for the ruler's accomplishments, and the rewards are clear and trusted while the punishments are strict and amply fearsome. Only when these fourteen are complete and the people are in harmony with the ruler can the city be defended. If a single one of the fourteen is lacking, even those who excel at defense will be unable to preserve the city.[10]

The requirements for several months of provisions should particularly be noted since besieged cities often failed to take vigorous action until too late, until starvation reduced them to gruesome, even cannibalistic practices.[11]

During the Warring States period military reconnaissance and border security became vital to ensuring imminent incursions would not go undetected. The Mohist military writings describe a number of external observation and control measures designed not only to accomplish this purpose but also to deny enemy agents freedom of movement in the immediate countryside. Vital passages and byways are to be strictly controlled,[12] coded flags and fires signal the approach and position of aggressor forces. All passage in and out of the city, as well as movement within it, was severely constrained, based upon personal knowledge and appropriate passes and tallies. People were scrutinized for their character and threat potential, presumably with an eye to denying them access or imprisoning them.[13] The fidelity of all personnel involved in security work, whether within the city or outside, would be ensured through holding their family members hostage.[14] However, they were not incarcerated but instead given preferential treatment, including superior food and wine, to encourage loyalty as much as guarantee it.[15]

Although the Mohists have a selfless, highly beneficent image due to their vaunted efforts to rescue the beleaguered and preserve the endangered, their practices actually mandated the ruthless control of every aspect of civic life. Strict discipline and thoroughgoing adherence to the rules were required, infractions and violations were punished severely. Minor offenses would not only implicate immediate family members but could also entangle the clan and anyone linked to the offender through the military squad, work unit, neighborhood association, or other group established for the express purpose of mutual surveillance and guarantee. Execution in more or less painful form was generally prescribed for offenses ranging from simply disobeying the regulations through subversion and rebellion, the chief threats to the city.[16]

At the approach of an enemy force certain ritual actions were to be undertaken, including the taking of prognostications, but any rumors that might be sparked by omens quashed.[17] More importantly, a thoroughgoing policy of denial had to be effected, though the requisite range of implementation varies among the chapters.[18] At a minimum all obstructions within bowshot that might be exploited as cover, including any low walls or embankments, had to be reduced. Usable materials within 100 paces such as stone, metal, sand, and especially wood (which the enemy might employ for siege machines and incendiaries) had to be removed and brought into the city to deny them to the enemy and for their potential use.[19] Whatever might not be removed in time, including permanent structures and large timbers, had to be burnt despite pleas to the contrary. All the nearby livestock also had to be gathered, slain, and processed.[20] However, the people were to be compensated for any losses and whatever might be confiscated, including provisions and materials, at prevailing prices.

Mounting an effective defense required that every aspect of staffing and supply be carefully organized. Essential materials not only had to be stockpiled, but also appropriately dispersed throughout the city. Specified quantities of critical items were to be always kept atop the walls, including water in various sized containers, caltrops, heavy stones, charcoal, cauldrons, and stoves. The city's wells and stoves were similarly regulated in number and position, and wide roads constructed to facilitate internal movement. Specialized units, designated by appropriately symbolic flags, were responsible for the various logistical and defensive functions, whether by type (such as wood, fire, water, stone, or sand) or function, including halberdiers and cavalry. Both ordinary and unique weapons were employed to defend the fortifications, especially those whose long shafts allowed them to be brought to bear against attackers before they could crest the wall or wield their own weapons.[21] Strict organization and discipline were to prevail, every aspect of life within the besieged city was to be controlled. While probably more prescriptive than actualized, through implementing these measures the Mohists believed 4,000 defenders could successfully fend off 100,000 attackers.[22]

Subversion and rebellion constituted the main human threats, but fire, whether accidental or deliberate, could quickly result in irreversible disaster. Fires for cooking and illumination were therefore strictly regulated, stoves had to be placed outside the dwellings and prohibitions, some seasonal, decreed when they could be lit and extinguished. Not unexpectedly, extremely severe penalties were imposed for deliberately starting a fire, whether as a matter of personal revenge or part of an attempt to cause chaos and undermine the city's defenses, but also lesser ones for accidentally igniting a blaze.[23] Moreover, to preclude the enemy from exploiting any defensive gaps should a fire arise, only designated personnel were to respond, none of the officers controlling public security being permitted to abandon their posts to provide assistance.[24] Silence was also to be maintained to minimize the disorder and chaos.

Incendiary attacks were clearly a major concern to the Mohists during the Warring States period even though there is virtually no mention of their employment or impact beyond the burning of ancestral temples in the famous chapters such as "Against Aggressive Warfare" and "Moderation in Expenditure" which condemn the violent conflicts increasingly plaguing their age. However, their prevalence can be inferred from the extensive preparations detailed in the military chapters. All flammable structures, exposed wooden surfaces, external palisades, and stockpiles of materials and provisions were to be rendered fireproof by covering with mud, the only effective material available.[25]

In general a minimum thickness of two inches was specified, particularly for moving items such as gate leaves, but sometimes as much as five, coincidentally adding considerable weight to the protected structure. Cracks were to be well sealed and the interior of gates and passageways even tiled over to ensure their imperviousness to flames, as well as to create a killing zone for gassing invaders. Finally, defensive equipment exploiting incendiary power should have the key support components, such as beams and suspension ropes, similarly coated in mud to preclude premature incineration and retard the effects of enemy fire attacks.

Although gates were clearly the most accessible to direct incendiary attack and almost invariably targeted, arrows could deliver simple incendiaries onto targets ranging from defensive wooden structures atop the walls to dwellings and buildings within the wall's immediate interior. Therefore, every structure within this range either had to be removed or protected with mud covering and the storage of flammables was invariably prohibited. Some passages specify an implementation range of 50 paces, others 100 paces, and still others simply require that these protective measures be applied throughout the city, no doubt on the premise that any small fire, however ignited, might become a major conflagration. While these discrepancies may result from different composition dates with the longer ranges reflecting the increased power of bows and crossbows over the period, there seems to have been no concern about trebuchet hurled incendiary devices, such as pots of flaming oil. This remains puzzling because oils were widely employed for lamps, torches, and cooking in this era and large burning logs were being hurled in defense. However, whether boiling or flaming, oil apparently would not become part of the incendiary repertoire until the Han period.[26]

## METHODS OF ATTACK AND DEFENSE

Generals who remained mindful of Sun-tzu's condemnation of those who impatiently ordered their men to "swarm over the walls like ants" and therefore sought to undertake well-planned, constrained sieges had but limited possibilities. Defenders who had no prospect for rescue by external forces might be starved out; simple incendiaries might be employed against the town and the wall-mounted defenses; the walls and gates could be directly attacked, including with rams and incendiaries, in the hopes of breaching them; or lengthy, difficult mining operations could be mounted. The Mohists in fact identified some twelve categories of attack, largely dependent upon the type of equipment being employed.[27] Though the terms are somewhat nebulous, they include direct attacks upon the walls with various types of ascension ladders, including large folding or raisable ladders mounted on movable carts; filling in moats and building earthen ramps prior to mounting a direct assault; flooding; mining; and other ways of approaching the walls without being decimated. However, incendiary attacks are not mentioned, though their employment was feared and expected as an integral part of these techniques.

Fire's destructive power was in fact extensively employed in both attack and defense in the Warring States period, having become an essential tool even though often unspecified in contemporary battle accounts. Aggressors targeted the gates, defensive structures, and interior of the city itself with incendiaries, whether delivered by arrows or directly placed against them. The defenders employed the vantage point of high fortifications to rain down burning planks, hot charcoal, boiling water, arrows, sand, stone, and various noxious materials, and also constructed fiendish devices designed to trap and incinerate the aggressors, though their very complexity raises questions about their feasibility. However, a more indirect utilization of fire had also evolved, being seen primarily in attempts to undermine the walls and in countermeasures which employed heat-generated noxious agents to incapacitate and kill. It is with these chapters that presumably reflect actual practices and technological expertise that the true employment of incendiary measures becomes visible.

In addition to the hot water and discrete projectiles, ablaze or not, poured down upon the invaders, larger and more complex incendiary devices were fabricated and deployed. Among the most effective must have been the *lei-t'a,* a coarse mat that was suspended by mud-covered ropes and set alight before being released.[28] As described, the width and height should each be twelve feet, and it should be constructed from cords plaited over a horizontal beam. The crossbeam itself should be suspended by ropes well soaked in mud for protection against fire, but attached to the beam's ends by iron hooks.[29] The cords in the mat may have been infused with some flammable substance so that they would burn more rapidly, although dry rushes would also burn quite hot once well lit. Suspended just over the side of the wall, it would be set alight before being dropped to overspread any invaders attempting an ascent. Its accelerating weight would certainly have knocked them off their scaling ladders and its flexibility likely covered them with an inescapable sheet of fire. Nevertheless, it was not employed alone, but in conjunction with arrows, sand, and stones, though naturally not hot water.

In contrast to the mat's massive size, another wheelbarrow-like device dumped smaller pieces of burning firewood upon their heads. Termed a *huo-tsu* or *ch'uan-t'ang*, it was constructed by essentially affixing a long box between two wagon wheels (presumably allowing it to pivot on the axle) and protecting the interior with mud so that kindling and small faggots might be fully ignited before dumping.[30] Hollowed-out logs filled with burning charcoal were also hurled by trebuchet, allowing the enemy to be attacked at greater distance from the walls, whatever their approach method.[31] And while there seem to be vestiges of other incendiary devices,[32] more important is the admonition to exploit their disruptive effects by having courageous warriors drop down or sally forth and strike them, much as Sun-tzu advocated in "Incendiary Warfare."

Mo-tzu also advised the creation of two traps whose slaying power derived from fire. One was internal, exploiting the passage area within the *t'u-men* or "sally port" embedded in the wall, the other external, being incorporated in an exterior palisade.[33] The premise underlying the former's employment as a device of last resort was that the invaders had successfully repelled the defenders' outward thrust and penetrated the passageway. One of these sally ports was to be constructed every 100 paces[34] around the wall's perimeter, the passageway within it sealed with mud, and the ceiling tiled to prevent any leakage of air or water. Quick closures whose dimensions exactly fit the openings were to be fabricated from large wheels onto which appropriately sized boards were attached and then mudded over as protection against fire. Once the enemy penetrated this limited area, they were to be employed to tightly seal off both the internal and external entrances before noxious gasses from moxa burning in stoves emplaced four to five feet to the interior would be forced into the chamber by pipe-connected bellows.[35] The fatal effects of this terrifying entrapment would almost certainly deter their surviving comrades from rashly entering another breach.

Two sections describe the complex nature of an entrapment named "the slayer," essentially a constricted passageway which can be blocked and set afire, killing the men inside.[36] In fact, in order to ensure they were slain, additional sequential measures were implemented, all under command of the drums. The descriptions differ slightly and despite yeoman effort over the centuries, some of the terms remain opaque, precluding a precise technical translation. However, from the two descriptions it is clear that a solid wooden palisade was to be erected from whatever diameter timbers might be available by cutting them to a uniform length of ten feet and then securely burying them, presumably some three feet deep, resulting in a height of perhaps seven feet and a width of ten feet, somewhat too massive and high for soldiers to simply clamber over. (The uniform height of the poles also allowed troops to patrol the top.) Wide gates[37] should be interspersed every twenty paces and be distinguished by unusual flimsiness, ensuring that they could be breached by the enemy. Exterior walls, ten feet thick, were also appended to the trap, no doubt to contain any breakout.[38]

Once the gates were breached and enemy troops surged in, the exits were blocked and set afire, trapping the soldiers. Thereafter, troops stationed on either side of the gate would attack them in a coordinated manner on signal with the incendiaries already provided ready to hand baskets of flammable material having been hung from iron hooks every four feet and stoves to ignite them and provide burning coals emplaced every five paces. If the enemy somehow managed to avoid the fires or extinguish the flames and remount an attack, a second wave of incendiaries would be employed. In either case, any aggressors who managed to escape would certainly flee in terror and spread panic among the invading army, probably prompting its localized withdrawal. Once in movement and therefore vulnerable, "death-defying" warriors would sally forth from the gate area and more massive numbers of troops from the citadel itself then follow on to thoroughly pummel them, again in accord with Sun-tzu's dictum to exploit opportunities created by incendiary attacks.

## MINING

The usual measures found worldwide in antiquity were employed by miners who necessarily reinforced the ceiling and walls with posts and beams to preclude their premature collapse, though while always wrapping them in rags presumably treated with some sort of accelerant, such as oil or lard. Once they completed excavating the area under a targeted section of wall, the posts would then be set ablaze. Assuming the fires received sufficient oxygen, a not insignificant problem, they would eventually collapse under the weight of the massive earthen fortifications, causing the wall directly above to buckle and crumble. Well-poised invaders would immediately exploit the gap and resulting chaos to surge into the city and overwhelm the stunned defenders, though numerous internal obstructions might still be expected.

Mo-tzu's counter-methods were premised upon intensively observing the enemy's activities from high lookout towers in order to detect any evidence of excavations, such as new earthen mounds or sudden turbidity in moat or river water. These visual efforts were to be supplemented with a virtual network of listening wells positioned every five paces around the wall's interior, excavated to a minimum depth of fifteen feet or three feet below the water line. Guards, whose task was facilitated by large earthen jars fashioned specifically for the purpose with thin leather membranes stretched over the mouths, were posted at the bottom to carefully listen for any indication of enemy tunneling. Once detected, these multiple wells would allow a fairly accurate determination of the tunnel's location preliminary to mounting countermeasures.

The Mohist military writings detail two different approaches for thwarting miners. If the enemy were just commencing their tunneling efforts outside the wall, but within drop or throw reach, a simple but direct incendiary attack could be effected by dropping burning faggots down into the mouth, assuming it was uncovered or not otherwise protected by fireproof materials.[39] However, once they were working underneath the walls—whether to undermine them or cut a tunnel into the city itself—incendiary measures had to be abandoned to avoid setting the pillars ablaze and thereby achieving the invader's very objective.

Surprisingly, but consonant with their use of incendiary-based techniques, the Mohists advocate employing poison smoke to thwart the aggressors rather than directly engaging them with elite warriors or flooding them out. Moreover, there is no suggestion that the gas attack be followed up with an infantry assault that might in turn easily penetrate the enemy's lines. On the contrary, they advise employing essentially negative or "collapsing" defensive methods should enemy forces be encountered in the tunnels, no doubt to minimize any risk of the latter breaching the counter-mines and thereby accessing the city itself. (A large shield, with holes for gas pipes and thrusting spears that could block the passageway in an emergency, was to be prepared and the soldiers were to be equipped with specialized short weapons for close combat in confined spaces, if absolutely unavoidable.)[40]

Effecting a smoke attack required precise, complex measures, including the excavation of a counter-mine from the nearest listening well so as to intercept the enemy's tunnel. The walls and ceiling of this counter-mine had to be reinforced with large posts and beams, all fully protected against fire with a coating of mud[41] while ensuring that there were no leaks of either water or air. When the enemy was finally encountered, poison smoke from artemesia burnt in kiln-like stoves (capable of higher heat) at the bottom of the listening well would be forced by bellows through an ingenious piping system laid into the tunnel.[42]

Additional protective measures were taken at the mouth of the well and the bellows generally operated from above, thus requiring only minimal staffing at the bottom once the actual gassing process commenced. Moreover, caution had to be exercised to prevent the gas from leaking backward or upward, inflicting severe misery upon those engaged in the task of active defense. Once the enemy's workers had died or fled, the area was to be secured and patrols mounted to ensure it would not be revitalized or the tunnel system otherwise exploited to enter the city.

## THEORETICAL DEVELOPMENTS

Although an increasing tendency toward employing fire as a tactical and punitive weapon can perhaps be discerned in Spring and Autumn historical sources, those charting the Warring States, an era when cities and armies were repeatedly exterminated, unexpectedly contain only a handful of references to incendiary activity.[43] Even these are minimal in nature, much in contrast to archeological evidence of fierce fires having ravaged many Warring States cities, the heavy damage concentrated around the gates proof they were not accidental. Conversely, the Warring States classic military writings suggest an increasingly intense and widespread employment of incendiary measures. Although the technology remained primitive, they were becoming equally indispensable to attacking and defending fortified towns.

Apart from the era's most famous incendiary event—T'ien Tan's dramatic utilization of "fire-oxen" to escape extermination—only Yüeh Yi's burning of Ch'i's palaces and temples following the conquest of Lin-tzu[44] and Pai Ch'i's burning of Ch'u's royal tombs,[45] both manifest expressions of vengeance and domination, receive prominent mention. However, Hsiang Yü's vengeful burning of the Ch'in capital, Hsien-yang, which reportedly lasted for three months and rendered it un-inhabitable, symbolically ended the Warring States in a blaze of fire.

The *Wu-tzu,* a work attributed to Wu Ch'i (440–361 B.C.) but almost certainly compiled after his death, codified the conditions for employing incendiary attacks as simply the presence of wind and heavy vegetation: "If the enemy makes camp in a wild marsh or fields dense with heavy tangles of grass and stalks, should violent winds repeatedly arise, you can burn the fields and destroy them."[46] Then, in the mid-fourth century B.C., Sun Pin—reputedly a lineal descendant, but certainly the inheritor of Sun-tzu's thought and writings—added further constraints:[47]

> If the enemy is downwind in an area abundant with dry grass, one where the soldiers of their Three Armies would not have anywhere to escape, you can mount an incendiary attack.
>
> When there is a frigid fierce wind, abundant vegetation and undergrowth, and firewood and grass for fuel already piled up while their earthworks have not yet been prepared, in such circumstances you can mount an incendiary attack.[48]

Sun Pin not only reaffirmed Wu Ch'i's identification of wind and vegetation as critical factors but also echoed Sun-tzu's emphasis on exploiting incendiary attacks rather than simply being satisfied with the intermediate destructive results, as would often happen: "Use the flames to confuse them, loose arrows like rain. Beat the drums and set up a clamor to motivate your soldiers. Assist the attack with strategic power. These are the tactics for incendiary warfare." A fragment apparently preserved in the T'ang dynasty *T'ung Tien* indicates that one mission for the cavalry (which did not play a significant military role until the end of the Warring States period) should be "incinerating accumulated stores and emptying out market lanes."[49] Apart from reflecting the urban warfare shift marking the Warring States period, by exploiting the cavalry's mobility to expand the scope of incendiary warfare these tactics fully cohere with Sun-tzu's concept of strategic power.

Thereafter, field commanders who suddenly encountered strong winds and heavy, dry vegetation, whether individually or in combination, would almost automatically ponder the potential advantages of employing incendiary techniques and be forced to avoid situations conducive to its employment. Although Sun-tzu never suggested any measures for defending against them, Sun Pin was acutely aware of the danger of incendiary attacks and therefore outlined a method for protective encirclement:

> When your ditches and ramparts have already been completed, construct another outer ring of ditches and moats. Every five paces pile up firewood, being certain to equalize the quantities in each pile. A designated number of attendants should be assigned to them. Order men to make linked *chevaux-de-frise*; they must be light and sharp. If it is windy, avoid. . . . If the vapors from the fire overspread you and engaging in battle will not result in victory, stand down and retreat.[50]

Unfortunately, the bamboo strips are too badly damaged to determine what actions Sun Pin advised for windy conditions, but he almost certainly warned against deploying in exposed positions, such as in front of external palisades. The wood piles were probably intended to provide ready material for backfires in the event of an incendiary attack and for mounting an active defense out beyond the camp's essential perimeter. However, even with such extensive preparations circumstances might still prove adverse, compelling a tactically advantageous retreat.

The *Six Secret Teachings (Liu T'ao)*, nominally attributed to Lü Shang, better known as the T'ai Kung—the famous commander, advisor, and strategist who reportedly played a crucial role in the Chou's ascension and conquest over the Shang—but actually compiled late in the Warring States period, discusses several concrete measures for extricating oneself from an incendiary attack:

King Wu asked the T'ai Kung: "Suppose we have led our troops deep into the territory of the feudal lords where we encounter deep grass and heavy growth which surround our army on all sides. Our Three Armies have traveled several hundred *li;* men and horses are exhausted, and have halted to rest. Taking advantage of the extremely dry weather and a strong wind, the enemy ignites fires upwind from us. Their chariots, cavalry, and elite forces are firmly concealed in ambush to our rear. Our Three Armies become terrified, scatter in confusion, and run off. What can be done?"

The T'ai Kung replied: "Under such circumstances use the cloud ladders and flying towers to look far out to the left and right, to carefully investigate front and rear. When you see the fires arise, then set fires in front of our own forces, spreading them out over the area. Also set fires to the rear. If the enemy comes, withdraw the army and take up entrenched positions on the blackened earth to await their assault. In the same way, if you see flames arise to the rear, you must move far away. If you occupy the blackened ground with our strong crossbowmen and skilled soldiers protecting the left and right flanks, you can also set fires to the front and rear. In this way the enemy will not be able to harm you."

King Wu asked: "Suppose the enemy has set fires to the left and right, and also to the front and rear. Smoke covers our army, while their main force appears from over the blackened ground. What should we do?"

The T'ai Kung said: "In this case (assuming you have prepared a burnt section of ground) disperse the Martial Attack chariots to form a fighting barrier on all four sides, and have strong crossbowmen cover the flanks. This method will not bring victory, but will also not end in defeat."[51]

The formulation of normative tactical methods for escaping from dire situations provides concrete evidence that field armies were being increasingly targeted for incendiary attacks, particularly under windy conditions.[52] In this incident, because exhaustion had severely compromised their mobility, backfires had to be employed prior to attempting an entrenched defense. However, these measures can only be temporary because, as Sun Pin pointed out, "Thoroughly incinerated terrain being deadly ground, it can be attacked."[53] Nevertheless, often being the only possibility they persisted over the centuries, even appearing as late as the Ming dynasty *Ts'ao-lü Ching-lüeh*:

> When the army is deployed in the wilds, should you happen to encounter fire, cut down the grass and reeds to the sides of the army and in accord with the wind's direction burn them in advance on the left or right, front or back. Then shift the army onto the burned over terrain, assuming a strict formation in order to wait the enemy.[54]

Ho Liang-ch'en provided the final formulation, suggesting slight variations in the army's response, though the fundamentals remained unchanged:[55]

> If, after entering the enemy's borders, you happen to encounter places with heavy vegetation while it's the dry season and dusk is approaching, you must first clear away the vegetation in front of your encampment. If the enemy should start fires upwind, you should order your troops to remain silent and unmoving and set fire to the grass in front of the encampment so that the two fires will intersect.
>
> When the grass has fully burned and they observe your army remaining quiet despite the fires, they will be doubtful and not dare advance. They will then grow fearful and unstable, and being unstable will certainly retreat. Quickly order your poisonous crossbowmen and other wielders of spiritual implements to rely upon the darkness to establish ambushes along any routes they must traverse, providing them with a secret signal. At the right moment they should rise up from the eight corners, thunder their drums, and attack in irregular fashion so that the enemy does not know where to flee. This is referred to as employing the enemy's fires against them.

The most famous case of surviving through backfires arose not in the Warring States period, but a century afterward during Li Ling's valiant but doomed struggle against overwhelming odds. A dramatic episode that would be retold across the centuries, it constitutes a definitive moment in incendiary history, one naturally recalled by anyone trapped in heavy vegetation.[56] In command of a mere 5,000 infantry, Li ventured far out into the northern steppe in a vainglorious strike at the Hsiung-nu, whose leader, the Shan-yü, confronted him with 30,000 cavalry. However, the Shan-yü quickly increased the number to 80,000 when the Han troops fought viciously in their initial encounter, decimating the Hsiung-nu with mass crossbow fire.

Hopelessly outnumbered, Li was compelled to withdraw back toward the border, fighting numerous running battles and incurring heavy casualties on a daily basis. His dwindling forces, most of whom had already suffered one or more wounds, still fought so resolutely that the Shan-yü erroneously concluded Li must be deliberately drawing them into a trap or that massive reinforcements would shortly appear. (He was eventually informed of Li's isolation by a disaffected scout.) However, in following the ancient route from Dragon City, Li was compelled to pass through deep valleys whose mountainside vantage points allowed the enemy to rain arrows down upon them.

The incendiary clash unfolded when the Han forces negotiated a large marsh with extensive vegetation that the Hsiung-nu naturally exploited by igniting fires upwind. However, Li thwarted the attack by resorting to the classic *Liu-t'ao* tactic of setting backfires and thus preserved his remnant forces. Thereafter, though they were bottled up in the valley, they continued to struggle resolutely, finally taking advantage of the nearby woods. However, as their 500,000 arrows had been exhausted and the situation seemed hopeless, Li created a diversion so that a few men might escape before surrendering himself, much to the emperor's ire. He then suffered undying condemnation rather than the praise his heroic ac-

complishments, achieved with few men and limited resources, should have garnered.

## EARLY ESCALATION AND REACTION

Recognizing the fear and chaos that conflagrations evoke, the
earliest theoreticians conceived of incendiary strikes as preliminary to heavy missile fire and zealous follow-on attacks.
Destroying materials and provisions would physically and
emotionally weaken the enemy, rendering them vulnerable to
attack and possibly compelling their withdrawal after protracted stalemates or prolonged campaigns.[57] Moreover, coincident with the emergence of gunpowder, from the late
Sung onward incendiary attacks were increasingly viewed as
capable of wresting decisive victory by themselves because
armies subjected to them often crumbled out of sheer
terror.[58] It was even thought that campaign armies moving
through the countryside should not waste their efforts on inconsequential cities, but instead focus on destroying the crucial ones in order to sever any hope of resistance.[59]

From the inception of conflict, fire seems to have been employed in a vengeful fashion, to destroy and thereby punish
the vanquished long before being conceptualized as a tactical
tool. Even though the victor thus sacrificed profits and engendered undying animosity, numerous burned cities and ruined
citadels attest to its frequency even in prehistoric times, to the
widespread venting of anger and hatred. (Given that armies
depended upon foraging and expected to plunder for rewards,
this destructive behavior was highly inimical to any form of
self-interest.) Thus, while capable of thwarting superior enemies and seizing advantage at long range, incendiary attacks
have inevitably been associated with uncontrolled and uncontrollable destruction, equally depriving the aggressor and victim of buildings, material goods, and provisions that might
have been advantageously used by both.

Post-conquest burning was also deliberately implemented
as part of systematic sack-and-pillage measures designed to
deprive the enemy of potential resources for future conflict.

Especially practiced by such steppe powers as the Jurchen and Mongols when withdrawing in late spring to avoid the insufferable heat, rampant burning was also intended to psychologically impress the populace, to terrorize them into not resisting future incursions and thereby spare themselves further afflictions.[60] However, because vital provisions and essential shelter were extensively destroyed, the inhabitants perished in large numbers through starvation and the illnesses consequent to increased exposure to the weather.

The rapid escalation of warfare in China during the Spring and Autumn and Warring States periods witnessed the multiplication of forces, widespread practice of sieges, catastrophic devastation, and even the decimation of entire towns. Some Warring States thinkers accordingly concluded that violence and conflict, whether brought about by desire and the increasingly fierce competition for material goods or simply innate, were inherent to the human condition and therefore inescapable. The quest to survive, to dominate one's enemies and even friends became all-consuming, attesting to the veracity of Sun-tzu's conclusion that "Warfare is the greatest affair of state, the basis of life or death, the Tao to survival or extinction." Accordingly, the great general Wu Ch'i condemned one powerful ruler for consigning his people to death by failing to adequately prepare against their enemies.

Under these circumstances many believed that warfare should be coopted by the virtuous in the service of humanity and that it must be undertaken solely to alleviate the suffering brought on by oppression and restore a semblance of order so that "All under Heaven" might pursue their lives in tranquility and security. Moreover, Sun-tzu had earlier premised military affairs upon subjugating other states without actually engaging in armed combat and thereby realizing the ideal of complete victory:

> The highest realization of warfare is to attack the enemy's plans; next is to attack their alliances; next to attack their army; and the lowest is to attack their fortified cities. Thus one who excels at employing the military subjugates other

people's armies without engaging in battle, captures other people's fortified cities without attacking them, and destroys other people's states without prolonged fighting. He must fight under Heaven with the paramount aim of preservation. Thus his weapons will not become dull and the gains can be preserved. This is the strategy for planning offensives.[61]

In Sun-tzu's view, whenever possible, victory should be achieved through diplomatic coercion, thwarting the enemy's plans and alliances, and frustrating their strategy. Only if an enemy threatens the state with military action or refuses to acquiesce without being brutalized into submission should the government resort to armed combat. Even when exercising this option, every military campaign should focus upon achieving maximum results with minimum risk and exposure, limiting as far as possible the destruction to be inflicted and suffered, preserving as much as possible.[62] Paradoxically, the actual practice of Chinese warfare proved exactly opposite, frequently marked by rape and destruction, burning and pillaging, and the slaughter of untold numbers. Despite the *Art of War*'s definitive influence on subsequent military thought, rarely did it approach Sun-tzu's ideal.

In fact, Southern Sung's invasion of Northern Wei saw an unusual incident unfold in A.D. 450 in which the commander actually tried to preserve the target, though not necessarily the populace, complete. Wang Hsüan-mo, who reportedly suffered from the flaws of greed and arrogance, hoped to enormously profit by easily capturing Hua-t'ai and therefore rejected advice to incinerate the town whose structures were largely fabricated from highly flammable reeds. Realizing their vulnerability, the inhabitants quickly dismantled their dwellings and moved underground to outlast the siege. Over the intervening three months Wang contemptuously mistreated the thousands of volunteers flocking to join him, undermining the army's spirit. Then, learning that a massive army was coming forth, he fled in terror but was intercepted and crushed in a decisive battle which cost 10,000 casualties, dispersed his remaining forces, and saw all his war materials confiscated or destroyed.[63]

Troubled by these developments, voices were also raised against this escalating brutality and wanton devastation, remnants of which are preserved in various Warring States texts. In a chapter which purportedly reprises the benevolent and righteous behavior characterizing the legendary sage leaders when they rectified disorder and extirpated evil, the *Ssu-ma Fa* asserts that the following edict was issued after charging the enemy with their crimes, praying, and setting out the campaign's objectives:

> When you enter the offender's territory, do not do violence to their gods; do not hunt their wild animals; do not destroy their earthworks; do not set fire to their buildings; do not cut down forests; do not take their six domesticated animals, grains, or implements.
>
> When you see their elderly or very young, return them without harming them. Even if you encounter adults, unless they engage you in combat, do not treat them as enemies. If an enemy has been wounded, provide medical attention and return him.[64]

Subsequently, the *Wu-tzu* more brusquely admonished: "Wherever your army goes, do not cut down the trees, destroy houses, take the grain, slaughter the animals, or burn their supplies. Thus you will show the populace that you do not harbor vicious intentions. Accept those who seek to surrender and settle them."[65] Thereafter, the *Six Secret Teachings (Liu-t'ao)*, even though now couching the campaign in far more realistic terms without any trappings of ritualized denunciation and righteous posturing, still advocated a policy of restraint to avoid antagonizing the people and differentiate oneself from those targeted for extirpation:

> Do not set fire to what the people have accumulated, do not destroy their palaces or houses. Do not cut down the trees at grave sites or altars. Do not kill those who surrender

nor slay your captives. Instead, show them benevolence and righteousness, extend your generous Virtue to them. Cause their people to say "the guilt lies with one man." In this way the entire realm will then submit.[66]

Such prohibitions were obviously intended to counter such late Warring States' excesses as Pai Ch'i's reported slaying of 400,000 surrendered prisoners after the battle of Ch'ang-p'ing in 260 B.C. However, despite prohibitions directed to burning, only after incendiary warfare proliferated in the Three Kingdoms period were questions raised about its particularly vicious nature. Tradition (but no contemporary evidence) holds that Chu-ko Liang, sometimes identified as the progenitor of the incendiary assault, felt his life would be shortened for having employed them. Nearly fifteen centuries later in the Ming dynasty, when cannon and early gunpowder weapons were already coming into common use, the military writings betray an increased consciousness of fire's all-consuming, fierce power, often phrased in terms of the so-called five phases: "Now the employment of fire is the fiercest among the five phases. The ancients knew its basic nature was fierce and could not be withstood."[67]

Though there was some sentiment that incendiary warfare was neither righteous nor humane,[68] the plight of people caught in incinerated war zones was rarely noticed except in the odd historical dialogue. Even the anonymous Ming dynasty *Ts'ao-lü Ching-lüeh* simply reiterated the classic prohibitions against allowing the troops to engage in cruel and destructive behavior, including burning their walls and houses, incinerating their forests and trees.[69] Accordingly, over the centuries native commanders and invasion leaders who sought to minimize popular opposition and attract the allegiance of the people ostensibly constrained their troops by promulgating severe rescripts similar to those first uttered in the Warring States period.[70]

Nevertheless, in its discussion of incendiary theory the late military compendium known as the *Wu-pei Chih,* which stands at the very conclusion of China's incendiary tradition, discerned eight situations in which the author deemed incendiary assaults would be inappropriate. Even though some of them clearly entail unreasonable risk, others impinge upon broader questions of humanity:[71]

> When you encounter the funeral mounds of ancient emperors and kings, temples to former sages and worthies, capitals, or important village crossroads, employing fire to attack them would not be the thought of one who respects the Tao nor the mind of one who would be humane to the people and is the first prohibition.
>
> If you are obstructed to the fore by dense woods so that if you advance there isn't any place which can be occupied, while to the rear the army backs against rivers or marshes so there isn't any route for a quick retreat, and you are being pressed close to the barriers of your own encampment while the army is not yet properly deployed, so if you employ an incendiary attack you fear you will be burned as well, this is the second prohibition.
>
> There is no greater disaster than the wind's indications still being uncertain, advantages of terrain not yet achieved, and a fierce wind extinguishing any flames. Incendiary attacks are mounted by first occupying difficult terrain and predicting the wind's direction, so this is the third prohibition.
>
> If the enemy's troops want to surrender but haven't had any opportunity, finally taking advantage of the wind to launch an incendiary attack in which the fire consumes even jade and precious stones would be the fourth prohibition.
>
> If their army includes a courageous and wise general whom you plan to employ, you must plot to capture him alive, so this is the fifth prohibition.
>
> When you are suspicious that enemy soldiers who have already surrendered will rebel and you therefore slay them, you will lose the minds of the soldiers just as when Pai Ch'i buried the troops from Chao. Nothing is more inhumane, so it is the sixth prohibition.
>
> When brigands who have already been defeated continue to plunder and pillage our people in order to enhance their power, you must think up unorthodox plans. To cast away the

fate of the people by not rescuing them but instead employ incendiary attacks against the rebels while claiming that you didn't know it was inhumane, this is the seventh prohibition.

When the first sprouts have just grown and scaly insects have begun to sting, burning the naked earth would greatly harm all life, thereby diminishing benevolence and virtue. This is the eighth prohibition.

In concluding, Mao Yüan-yi states: "Neither ghosts nor spirits will be able to fathom the subtle plans of someone who respects these eight and assembles like flying clouds and birds congregating, nor will they discern the mysteriousness of their transformations if they strike like lightning and pound like thunder."

# 3

# Post–Warring States Developments

The first systematic employment of incendiary warfare for strategic purposes occurred during the long struggle that forged the Han dynasty. Without the campaign of harassment which targeted Hsiang Yü's provisions and supplies with both incendiary and conventional attacks, Hsiang might have prevailed after nearly annihilating Liu Pang, progenitor of the Han, in the debacle at P'eng-ch'eng. However, other Han incidents became far more famous, eclipsing even the destructive rampages that saw millenarian factions such as the Yellow Turbans indiscriminately burn government structures, storehouses, and ordinary huts alike.

Numerous instances of employing incendiary traps are mentioned in the historical records, some sprung successfully, others anticipated and balked, but the military texts have traditionally recognized Han Hsin's destruction of Chang Han as the first.[1] Han initially feigned defeat in two successive battles, prompting Chang to speak of him as contemptuously as Lung Chü would prior to being overwhelmed by the water ram. Even though warned of a trap, Chang vigorously pursued him into Ch'en-ts'ang Gorge where Han exploited a strong east wind to set numerous fires while simultaneously blocking the entrance with piles of stones. Chang's entire contingent reportedly perished, though he extricated himself by abandoning his horse and clambering up over the cliffs.

Incendiary measures were also employed for special operations long before the clandestine methods that would be described in subsequent military manuals. For example, in A.D. 73 Pan Ch'ao, although accompanied by only thirty soldiers, had been entrusted with the military aspects of a diplomatic mission to the Western Region designed to keep the steppe peoples submissive and mutually isolated. At first the king of Shan-shan treated them well, but then his demeanor suddenly changed, prompting Pan to conclude that emissaries from the powerful Hsiung-nu were no doubt nearby. Immediately after confirming his suspicions, without the ambassador's approval (since he would certainly hesitate and cower, allowing the mission to leak out) he roused his few men into preemptively acting to balk any steppe alliance and avoid being taken prisoner by the Hsiung-nu.

That night they traversed the thirty *li* (ten miles) between the camps in darkness, whereupon Pan deployed his drums to the enemy's rear, away from the wind, and dispersed his remaining men with their powerful crossbows in ambush outside their tents. He then exploited the strong wind to set their tents afire and drum the attack, causing the panic and confusion necessary to slay some 30 of the enemy even as the remaining 100 perished in the fires. The next day Pan shocked the king of Shan-shan and his own ambassador with the emissary's head, thereby coercing a promise of submissive loyalty.[2]

More than a century earlier, in 36 B.C., a Han expedition against the brutal Hsiung-nu leader Chih-chih under Ch'en T'ang's direction ventured out onto the steppe with several prongs amounting to 40,000 men. Despite lacking imperial authority for the campaign, Ch'en resolutely pressed forward after forging the necessary edict, compounding his capital offenses. With the help of local guides and disaffected tribal people, they reached and surprised the Shan-yü at his recently fortified city.

After preliminary posturing and skirmishes, Ch'en set fire to the outer wooden defenses, driving the warriors back within the security of their earthen walls, before again employing a multisided incendiary assault as part of a concerted attack. Incendiaries were employed yet again against the core citadel where the Shan-yü and his consorts took refuge and fought on tenaciously. Han crossbows coupled with the incendiary attack's ferocity soon proved overwhelming, resulting in complete victory and the extermination of a bloodthirsty nemesis.[3]

However, the Western Region was always considered an area apart from China proper, a virtual no man's land inhabited by various "barbaric" peoples and warlike nomads. Conversely, over the centuries China's civilized core has traditionally, though simplistically, been conceptualized as divisible into two broad regions falling north and south of one of the three great rivers essentially running east to west: the Yellow, the Huai, and finally the Yangtze. Fundamentally distinguished by their agricultural practices, the north was commonly regarded as a millet- and wheat-based culture, whereas the south stressed rice and aquaculture. Some of these distinctions blurred, others were exacerbated as waves of northerners migrated to the south to escape steppe threats and barbarian conquests over the centuries, but defining prejudices still lingered.

Encompassing a large plains area bordered by mountains, desert, and the steppe, the north was conducive to chariot, cavalry, and infantry maneuvers. In contrast, the area southward toward the Yangtze, known as a region of half-naked barbarians, being crisscrossed by rivers and streams and pockmarked by lakes and marshes, thwarted chariot expeditions and rendered infantry movements difficult. Not unexpectedly, it early on became an area of boats and riverine warfare, of naval combat rather than dusty clashes fought on relatively open fields. In the T'ang, Hsü Tung characterized the dichotomy:

> The west and north are conducive to soldiers and horses, the east and south have the convenience of boats and oars.

The west and north are cold and miserable and lack copper and iron, while the east and south are hot and humid, their bows and crossbows rot away. The middle terrain has the five weapons in abundance and various trees and is conducive to bows and horses, boats and oars. These are their appropriate differences. Thus "the state of Yen lacks armor, Ch'in lacks bamboo shafts for their weapons, while the Hu lack bows and chariots."

Even in the drier northern areas, the towns and cities which came to comprise the chief targets for military campaigns initially developed beside the rivers and lakes and then flourished as boats increasingly facilitated the transport of goods and people. From the Chou dynasty onward China's topography compelled the integration of naval tactics into campaign strategies, yet military histories of China have generally ignored aquatic warfare except for a handful of specialized works. As well as facilitating logistical support in general, an aspect that stimulated the construction of canals from the Warring States onward, rivers were exploited for amphibious assaults and with lakes quickly came to be the arena for naval engagements. Major campaigns in the Warring States period already turned on amphibious conflicts; Ch'in mounted a large-scale naval effort and even invaded the south along five different rivers with a force said to number 200,000; and naval craft developed from the Han onward, including for limited use at sea, primarily along the upper coast since the littoral waters north of the Yangtze were characterized as far calmer.

Nevertheless, it wasn't until the Three Kingdoms period and the rapid escalation of conflict in the Yangtze watershed that incendiary warfare emerged as a decisive factor. This sudden fluorescence is often attributed to its advantageousness in riverine combat, but land warfare also benefited from its utilization in several crucial battles. The first of these is known as the Battle of Kuan-tu, though in actuality the critical blow was struck slightly northeast preliminary to the main conflict in the most famous incendiary raid in Chinese history, one which destroyed the enemy's provisions and thereby reversed an apparently inevitable outcome.[4]

While Ts'ao Ts'ao was vanquishing his many challengers from A.D. 197 through 198, the powerful military aristocrat Yüan Shao gained control of much of the north and amassed a force of perhaps 150,000, of which 100,000 infantry, 10,000 cavalry, and 8,000 elite barbarian cavalry would be employed in his forthcoming southern campaign. Little unified and constantly suffering from a shortage of provisions, Yüan Shao's armies were tired after three years of nearly constant warfare while Ts'ao Ts'ao's troops remained animated. Moreover, to reach Ts'ao's bastion at Hsü-ch'ang, he had to penetrate the latter's Yellow River perimeter defenses and also defeat a primary holding force at Kuan-tu, yet he still decided to attack.

Rather than seeking a swift, essentially preemptive victory, Yüan secured his rear and proceeded in measured fashion, apparently ensuring a continuous flow of supplies by employing 10,000 wagons for transport. He also neutralized external threats with judicious alliances and improved the army's command and control, but generally neglected the cavalry's maneuver capabilities and chose to concentrate his overwhelmingly superior forces rather than segment them for multiple strikes. Conversely, still threatened by Liu Piao and Chang Hsiu, embattled Ts'ao Ts'ao could only field 30,000 men who were precariously close to starvation. However, his advisors discerned critical flaws in Yüan Shao's character, including greed, ignorance, cowardice, jealousy, and suspiciousness.

Ts'ao Ts'ao dispatched 20,000 troops to Li-yang, deployed numerous small contingents to key areas and strong points on the flanks and rear, including the famous ford at Mengchin, and positioned 10,000 soldiers at Kuan-tu. Chang Hsiu fortuitously shifted his allegiance to Ts'ao Ts'ao, Liu Piao chose to remain neutral, and other groups either joined as allies or stood by, though Sun Ts'e's assassination precluded any immediate support from the east. Ts'ao Ts'ao therefore chose to mount his primary defense at Kuan-tu, south of the

Chi River, to compel Yüan's forces to cross it, just as Sun-tzu had advised. (Ts'ao Ts'ao was an astute student of the classic military writings, often said to be the *Art of War's* first editor and commentator.) When Liu Pei renounced his nominal allegiance and became a threat in the east at the end of 199, Ts'ao Ts'ao quickly vanquished him with a lightning strike, compelling him to flee to Yüan Shao.

In the second month, 200, Yüan Shao finally launched his southern offensive with perimeter strikes that saw Ts'ao Ts'ao withdraw from Li-yang, but also one of Yüan's generals vanquished in a collateral action at Pai-ma. Exemplifying his frequent use of varying and imaginative tactics, Ts'ao Ts'ao managed to ambush the pursuing forces to gain another surprising victory. Yüan Shao then gingerly attempted to exploit his numerical advantage by deputing secondary forces in maneuver down through the west, Liu Pei striking toward the capital while a second force proceeded in a smaller arc. Perhaps because their numbers were insufficient, both were summarily defeated by highly motivated troops under Ts'ao Jen and others.

Seeking a decisive confrontation, Yüan then moved the bulk of his forces south in the eighth month, by which time Ts'ao Ts'ao's situation had deteriorated further. Although suffering constant shortages, increasing defections among his own and allied troops, and even the risk of subversion, Ts'ao Ts'ao maintained his defensive posture because retreat would mean extinction. Fortunately, the six-month standoff was resolved when one of Yüan's frustrated commanders defected and provided detailed knowledge of their supply depot roughly 40 *li* to the north where some 10,000 wagons and an equal number of troops were concentrated, but no perimeter defenses or scouting operations had been undertaken. Ts'ao Ts'ao immediately mounted a night assault with 5,000 disguised cavalry flying the enemy's banners. Proceeding by an indirect route and deflecting all challenges by claiming they had been sent to reinforce the camp against sudden attack, they mounted an incendiary attack and then exploited the succeeding chaos to slaughter the defenders and complete the destruction.

Yüan Shao found himself in a dilemma: whether to immediately attack Kuan-tu en masse since its defenses had been significantly depleted, or dispatch a large force to rescue the supply depot and vanquish the attackers. Essentially he attempted both, ordering a massive, direct assault on Kuan-tu (despite having failed to reduce it for some six months) while also dispatching cavalry to the supply depot. Aware of the latter's imminent arrival, Ts'ao Ts'ao concentrated upon the task of destruction before defeating the onrushing reinforcements and then hastening back. Meanwhile, realizing he was doomed for failing to overrun the bastion at Kuan-tu, the assault commander simply surrendered with all his troops and equipment. Ts'ao Ts'ao then counterattacked Yüan Shao's remaining, dispirited troops and achieved total victory. Yüan barely escaped with just 800 men while his forces suffered upwards of 70,000 casualties.

Basking in victory and confident of his power, Ts'ao Ts'ao soon undertook the ill-fated campaign that concluded with the infamous Battle of Red Cliffs.[5] Having solidified his hold on the north and northeast, the despotic leader intended to move south to launch a primary attack on Sun Ch'üan (who controlled Wu in the southeast), Liu Pei (who was then an insignificant ally of Sun Ch'üan), and others in the area of the ancient state of Ching. Prior to the actual battle he deployed some secondary forces to fragment Sun Ch'üan's power, but the thrust of the campaign was simply the direct movement of both naval and infantry forces down the Yangtze River. Because he thus mobilized superior, experienced forces, the debacle at Red Cliffs has traditionally been attributed to a number of factors, but the crux is simply that Sun Ch'üan's commanders effectively exploited the devastating power of an incendiary attack while Ts'ao Ts'ao made two unimaginable errors.

The Battle of Red Cliffs can be characterized as a naval engagement only because boats rather than chariots were involved. Despite an overwhelming superiority in numbers—perhaps 150,000 to 30,000—Ts'ao Ts'ao failed to seize the initiative, choosing instead to ensconce his forces in port after suffering minor naval setbacks. Not only did he abandon the aggressor's role, but he also sacrificed his mobility by lashing his hundreds of vessels together and then erecting wooden catwalks about them and his land encampments on the northern side of the Yangtze River at Ch'ih Pi. Presumably intended to facilitate training and accommodating the northern troops who were beset by illness and found the rocking motion uncomfortable, these catwalks were quickly noticed when archers commenced practicing upon them.

Immediately realizing that a fire started among them would rapidly spread throughout the hundreds of closely packed wooden boats, Huang Kai advised Chou Yü, Wu's commanding general, to mount an incendiary attack. The carefully planned assault employed ten large vessels filled with combustible materials soaked in oil and a number of small, swift boats intended for the troops to escape, and was made possible by the key ruse of a feigned surrender which allowed their unimpeded approach. (Although stealthy nighttime guerrilla attacks employing small boats might have accomplished their objective, the amount of combustible materials would have been minimal and the effects uncertain, while a large force would certainly have been detected and possibly thwarted.) Employing a number of sizable vessels ensured the massive conflagration would entail heavy losses and allow pre-positioned forces to inflict massive casualties in the resulting confusion.

Even though Ts'ao Ts'ao must have been familiar with Sun-tzu's warning against peace talks and proffered surrenders being exploited to induce negligence and laxity, he permitted himself to be persuaded that Huang wanted to surrender and should be allowed to approach with his forces. However, fidelity and credibility having long been abandoned except among Confucian pedants while dramatic betrayals were common in his era, Huang's surrender should have been accepted at some distant location where his forces could not have posed a threat. Ts'ao Ts'ao's arrogance and complacency have long been cited to explain his negligence, but while they were probably a factor, the abject surrender of

Liu Piao's substantial, primarily naval forces somewhat earlier created a basis for confidence. Being severely outnumbered, why wouldn't Huang have been mesmerized by the prospect of great rewards in the face of an early, watery death?

Ts'ao Ts'ao's defeat has also been attributed to relying upon newly captured naval forces or upon his own sailors' inadequate experience and training. However, this merely reiterates in another form the simplistic belief that the environments north and south of the Yangtze differ so radically that the northerners could not adjust to the terrain's food, climate, lifestyle, and tactical requirements. Men from the north may have found the south surprisingly moist and luxuriant, but it was neither a harsh nor fundamentally adverse environment and probably a great improvement over their own dusty villages.

Furthermore, even if the loyalty of the newly surrendered forces, some 70,000 predominately sailors, may have been questionable (particularly if Ts'ao Ts'ao neglected measures to win their allegiance), subsuming enemy armies intact was a long-established practice. After being integrated into Wei's hierarchy, they would certainly have been supervised and controlled by Ts'ao Ts'ao's officers. In addition, merely adequate (rather than exemplary) performance would have sufficed to vanquish Chou Yü's insignificant navy even though the latter was more spirited and unified.

Ts'ao Ts'ao's original troops were hardly unfamiliar with naval requirements or completely lacking in experience. Realizing the vital role of naval forces, the great general had in fact trained them for some six months on an artificial lake, prompting unfounded criticism that the environmental conditions weren't sufficiently severe or realistic because the lake lacked noticeable currents. (The main objectives would have been training the men in unified rowing and the coordinated maneuvering of vessels in order to execute some sort of rudimentary tactics since navigating under sail along the Yangtze, by then commonplace, could prove unreliable in actual combat.) Even though Ts'ao Ts'ao had originally come downstream and Liu Pei and Wu's forces upstream, the engagement primarily unfolded in a limited area by forces opposing each other across the river, no doubt trying to exploit the current's force where possible, but not a clash in which one force gained an insurmountable advantage by attacking downstream from the outset.

It has also been suggested that Ts'ao Ts'ao's army was exhausted from extensive campaigning and forced marches. Nevertheless, they had neither just arrived nor was this a land battle requiring strength and endurance, just the incineration of immovable wooden structures. Simplistic accounts frequently state that Liu Pei exploited the wind to initiate the conflagration, but a more careful examination indicates that the wind had not originally been severe but had fortuitously grown stronger so that they were able to employ their sails to gather momentum prior to impact. Moreover, as Ts'ao Ts'ao had set the time for Huang's surrender, the aggressors can hardly be credited with having anticipated and exploited the wind's sudden onset.[6]

Ts'ao Ts'ao's performance in the ensuing debacle certainly belies his reputation for acumen and valor because he simply fled without making any attempt to gather his remnant forces, inspire a valiant defense, or otherwise thwart the enemy's advance such as by igniting counter-fires. Apart from the horrendous casualties incurred by fire, drowning, and enemy blades at Red Cliffs, thousands of weak and sick troops perished on the road and were slaughtered by the southern forces as his disorganized rabble fled for their lives. Even the heavens themselves turned vengeful by inundating them with torrential rains, making the roads impassable. Yet, when rescue forces arrived, he still sped off virtually alone without rallying his troops.

Several, no doubt largely fabricated dialogues preserved in the *San-kuo Chih* show that strategic analysis, founded upon sound military intelligence, made Ts'ao Ts'ao and his opponents battle for Ching, a crucial crossroads whose agricultural productivity could sustain a major army. The large number of troops committed to the conflict indicates its importance, while Ts'ao Ts'ao's defeat virtually ensured the empire would be sundered into three for decades. The hundreds of boats and tens of thousands of men also show the integral role and necessity of naval forces in campaigns around and south of the Yangtze River. Kuan Yü, who would eventually be apotheosized as the god of war, had charge of Liu Pei's naval forces but took no real part, while Chu-ko Liang, another famous hero from the period, played at most a minor role as strategist and counselor. Ambition marked all the participants on both sides, but Sun Ch'üan realized the need to at least temporarily employ potential enemies who would otherwise willingly divide up the empire. It was an age subsequently envisioned in greatness, one that produced romanticized warriors and heroic stories but ultimately couldn't survive the success that victory brings.

Before the era ended Liu Pei would also be overwhelmed by an incendiary attack (even though he had employed one himself at Tso-ma-k'u) because encampments established alongside rivers, particularly those linked with wooden or fenced walkways, docking structures, and closely moored ships, presented targets accessible by water. Among the several major disasters spawned by laxity, the destruction of Shu's armies through incendiary attack near the end of the Three Kingdoms period, ending their military power and dooming them to extinction, stands out.

The ongoing conflict between Liu Pei in Shu and Sun Ch'üan of Wu, who had been infuriated by Liu's seizure of Yi, was further exacerbated by Liu's forcible retention of the area between them known as Ching-chou which he had secured by dispatching Kuan Yü to consolidate their position against Wu while attempting to encroach upon Wei's territory following Ts'ao Ts'ao's defeat at Ch'ih Pi. In A.D. 219 Liu Pei's forces managed to project their power even further northward by seizing Han-chung. Meanwhile, in the seventh month Wu and Wei clashed in the Huai-nan region, presenting Kuan Yü with an opportunity to attack the city of Fan-ch'eng. Heavy rains in the eighth month fortuitously inundated Wei's encampments, forcing Yü Chin to surrender with seven armies totaling some 40,000 men. Kuan Yü then besieged Fan-ch'eng and attacked the companion city of Hsiang-yang on the southern bank of the Han River. (Much contested in future centuries, these twin cities were crucial to any military progress north or south, but apparently not yet linked.) Due to his luck and the numerous inhabitants flocking to his allegiance, Kuan Yü had momentum and looked invincible, but in moving northward inadvertently left a vacuum to his rear.

Prudence dictated mounting a preventive defense against possible Wu perfidy, but Kuan Yü focused all his efforts on the assault, thereby providing Ts'ao Ts'ao with an opportunity to cajole Wu into launching an unexpected strike. Sun Ch'üan foolishly responded with a secret letter of agreement that Ts'ao Ts'ao creatively employed to stimulate resolve among Fan-ch'eng's beleaguered defenders and foster doubt and consternation in Kuan Yü's camp. However, wary of Kuan Yü's strength, rather than immediately undertaking a strike, the Wu commander Lü Meng opted to subvert his wariness. Feigning illness, he arranged for the appointment of a sub-commander (Lu Hsün) who sent laudatory letters of admiration which exploited Kuan Yü's vanity and put him so at ease that he failed to undertake any defensive preparations.

This idyllic rapport was shattered when a pretext for initiating military action was found in Kuan Yü having appropriated provisions from Wu's storehouses to feed the 40,000 northern prisoners who apparently hadn't yet been integrated into Shu's armies. By concealing most of the troops within their ships, dressing the sailors as normal boatmen, and then having them actually man the oars and poles, Lu Hsün cleverly cloaked his assault on Ching-ling as a fleet of ordinary commercial vessels moving upriver. Traveling day and night, they overwhelmed all the lookouts posted along the river and achieved complete surprise when they suddenly appeared on target. Most of the startled local commanders, including at the fortified city of Ching-ling, surrendered without fighting. Venturing further westward, Lu seized Yi-ling and subdued the local people, thereby cutting off Kuan Yü's retreat into Yi and exposing him to the promised northern strike which never materialized since Ts'ao Ts'ao withheld his forces while his enemies decimated each other.

In a classic manipulative effort, Wu's commander-in-chief Lü Meng then implemented a conspicuously humanitarian policy in the newly occupied territory. He treated the populace and surrendered soldiers so well that spies returned with glowing reports which severely undermined Shu's enmity and fighting spirit. Bereft of external support from even nearby Shu generals, Kuan Yü also experienced a high rate of desertion among his officers and men as he moved to a more advantageous position. In the twelfth month he was finally captured and killed, an ignominious fate for the much glorified warrior who would subsequently be apotheosized as the god of war.

Why Liu Pei didn't dispatch a supportive force remains an open question, but as a result of these victories Wu now controlled all of southern Ching-chou. The next year another important Shu general defected to Ts'ao-Wei, further reducing Shu's terrain. However, Sun Ch'üan's campaign, while increasing the territory under their immediate control, thwarted Shu from achieving a substantial victory over their main enemy, Ts'ao-Wei, and thereby further weakening it. Even though the captured troops increased Wu's total strength somewhat, by undermining their natural ally they were forced to shoulder the full burden of defending Chingchou. No doubt intended as another step in empire building, their gullible impetuousness contravened the geostrategic reality of tripart division.

Infuriated by the perfidious slaughter of his longtime comrade and commander, Liu Pei promptly prepared a massive campaign to exact revenge and recover Ching-chou. In 221, after declaring himself emperor, Pei commenced his attack in the seventh month with at least 100,000 troops. Even though Sun Ch'üan, expecting retribution, had prepared extensive defenses along the Yangtze River, the onslaught quickly achieved several victories, forcing Lu Hsün to withdraw and undertake a persisting defense. In addition, the campaign benefited from Wei again refraining from attacking either belligerent, but was perhaps ill-fated by Chang Fei's assassination at the start.

Wu adopted the classic strategy of allowing the invader to penetrate the interior by pulling back more than a 100 miles from their border onto relatively flat terrain before finally making a resolute stand, thereby avoiding combat amidst winding mountain corridors while stretching out Shu's supply lines and dispersing their forces.[7] After deliberately refusing battle for some six months despite virulent taunts and provocations, Lu then exploited Shu's enervation, frustration, and dispirit by first launching nighttime incendiary attacks against the forty camps which had been dispersed amidst the woods and heavy vegetation along both sides of the Yangtze River to escape the interminable heat, then exploiting the chaos and isolation of the various contingents with fervent follow-on strikes. The dry, oppressive conditions ensured the vegetation around the camps, as well as any supplies within them and their boats, would readily ignite, while the fires spread rapidly since Lu had initiated the attacks under windy conditions. (Yeh Meng-hsiung's subsequent assertion that the attackers employed bundles of reeds and grass infused with saltpeter and sulfur lacks substantiation while the employment of chemical accelerants would have been unnecessary.)[8]

Despite well-prepared ambushes to the flanks and rear, Liu Pei managed to escape with a very small contingent, in part by setting their provisions ablaze to thwart pursuit. However, the majority of Shu's troops perished and their ships and supplies were largely destroyed while another Shu field commander, finding himself isolated in the north, despicably opted to surrender rather than intercede with a flank attack. Liu Pei's poor exercise of field command and undertaking of an ill-advised campaign that became moribund because he failed to initiate such unorthodox tactics as sending fire ships downriver to exploit the dry conditions doomed the expedition and any hopes for further expansion.[9]

The Three Kingdoms period also witnessed a classic city siege when the great strategist Chu-ko Liang led a force of some 40,000 troops northward to attack Ch'en-ts'ang in the twelfth month of A.D. 228.[10] However, more than a year earlier Ts'ao Chen of Wei had anticipated that Chu-ko Liang, having been frustrated on his previous incursion route, would mount his next invasion in this area and therefore had the city fortified, though it was apparently defended by only 1,000 under Hao Chao. After the usual provocatory remarks, Shu's forces attacked from all four sides with mobile ladders whose height allowed archers perched atop to shoot down into the city. Under their cover ordinary portable ladders and ropes were then employed to ascend the walls. However, the defenders employed incendiary arrows to burn the ladders and troops, the bodies of those who had succeeded in mounting the wall even falling into the city.[11]

Chu-ko Liang then used assault wagons to attack the four sides but they were all destroyed by large stones lashed together and hurled by trebuchet. He next turned to building earthen mounds but was countered when Hao increased the height of the interior walls. Frustrated, he finally undertook a clandestine tunneling effort from the area of the mounds, no doubt assuming it would go undetected since they were already moving earth about and his troops would be able to surge into the heart of the city. However, they were stymied when Hao had several transverse trenches cut to intercept the approaching miners. Even though no rescue forces had yet approached, Chu-ko Liang was forced to withdraw after twenty days of unremitting attacks because his provisions were running low. However, he did manage to defeat a Wei army sent out to exploit their retreat.

Although Chu-ko Liang was closely associated with incendiary warfare, even baselessly credited by later tradition with conceiving the incendiary attack at Ch'ih Pi, the reconstructed *Chu-ko Liang Ping-fa* contains only one indirect reference (in "Chün Ling") to incendiaries—the need to soak the cloth covers being employed on the boats to extinguish arrows and torches in water. Nevertheless, several Ming stories and even military manuals such as the *Huo-lung Shen-ch'i Ch'en-fa* focus on Chu-ko Liang's supposed employment of incendiary techniques in decisive battles.[12]

More reliably, one of Shu's northern campaigns resulted in a standoff along the Wei River when Ssu-ma Yi adopted a persisting strategy in view of Shu's well-known logistical difficulties and steadfastly refused to engage in battle despite being badly insulted. Chu-ko Liang then supposedly resolved their supply problem by reportedly inventing his famous wooden horses and oxen, no doubt some sort of wheelbarrow with a single wheel that subsequent generations quickly imbued with highly mythical mechanical properties, including self-propulsion.

Frustrated by his strategy's failure, Ssu-ma Yi went on the offensive, driving Chu-ko Liang back but also being lured forward himself. Chu-ko Liang then reportedly established an incendiary ambush amidst a nearby valley through which they had to retreat with primitive (non-explosive) mines and grass huts filled with flammables. Somewhat hesitant, Ssu-ma Yi still followed him in and—tactical embellishments aside— became trapped when the incendiaries were ignited by troops emplaced above. Just when he and his son were about to perish, an unexpected torrential downpour damped the fires sufficiently for them to escape.[13]

During his southern campaign of suppression mounted shortly after Liu Pei's demise, Chu-ko Liang deliberately had heavy, highly flammable reed palisades set up about his encampment to lure Meng Huo into mounting a nighttime incendiary attack. When Meng indeed struck, he encountered an empty camp just before being ambushed by encircling forces.[14] Chu-ko Liang thus exploited the common recognition of incendiary possibilities to trap and defeat his opponent.

A battle of wits arose during one of Chu-ko Liang's northern thrusts when it became clear that Shu's armies had run short of supplies. Wei's commander tried to trap them into seizing a contrived line of supply wagons which were actually filled with highly flammable dry grass. However, Chu-ko Liang anticipated his tactics and frustrated the plot by setting them aflame before mounting a pincer attack and scoring a localized victory.[15]

Another unfounded incident recorded in the *Yün-ch'ou Kang-mu* presumably shows Chu-ko Liang's tactical influence. Retreating before Teng Ai's superior forces, Chiang Wei proceeded in ordered and measured fashion, placing his provisions to the fore, infantry in the middle, and cavalry at the rear.[16] Teng therefore suspected he was plotting an ambush and forbade his generals to pursue them. Further reconnaissance confirmed his suspicions because Chang's troops had dispersed piles of firewood throughout an upcoming valley which could be ignited once Teng's army irreversibly entered it. (Being an unorthodox technique, it may have been a deliberately transparent ploy, one designed to scare off pursuers rather than intended for execution.)

Nearly two centuries later when China was divided into northern and southern kingdoms, Lu Hsün inherited a religiously based popular rebellion in A.D. 402 that initially burgeoned before finally stagnating amidst the interminable chaos in 410. Subsequently pushed out of the Yangtze valley, down through the lakes and rivers of Kuang-tung, Lu battled on until finally perishing in northern Vietnam in the fourth month of 411. His defeat was accomplished through throwing "pheasant tail torches"—apparently their first historical mention—onto his remaining ships, setting them ablaze and inducing his suicide.[17]

Six centuries earlier than the "swallow's tail torch" described in the Sung dynasty *Wu-ching Tsung-yao,* this precursor was similarly named after a bird and presumably fabricated from reeds with some sort of metal head. The defining characteristic was a tail fanning out like a pheasant's plumage at maximum display, immensely increasing the flammable area in comparison with the "iron-beaked fire goose" also depicted in the *Wu-ching Tsung-yao,* which had an incendiary compound dispersed through the tail. However, it's unknown if this early version was dipped in an accelerant such as sesame oil or was simply dry, though the tail's large area would ensure maximum oxygenation and a swiftly spreading fire even if unimproved.

Some commanders who experimented with incendiary techniques at the beginning of their careers subsequently employed them as the decisive element in crucial battles and regularly resorted to them in difficult circumstances. For example, early in the fragmented, war-weary fifth century, Liu Yü, an Eastern Chin commander who assiduously nurtured his power until establishing the Southern Sung in 420 by defeating Hou Chin (a Ch'iang state) and Southern Yen, often utilized them to defeat superior enemies. As early as 402, while serving as a subcommander in Huan Hsüan's forces during their campaign to seize Chien-k'ang, Liu witnessed an incendiary attack that destroyed a flotilla of vessels and isolated the government's forces.[18]

After usurping the emperorship late in 403, Huan Hsüan had an opportunity to slay Liu Yü, whose majestic demeanor clearly forewarned potential danger, but retained him to ensure the empire could be consolidated. However, Liu and several other "righteous" commanders who sought to restore the Chin imperial family eventually initiated an undermanned but multipronged campaign. Despite their contingents numbering only a few thousand each, they quickly gained some minor victories prior to the crucial battle to retake Chien-k'ang (Nan-ching) at nearby Fu-chou mountain where 20,000 troops blocked their advance while patiently waiting for the rebel's fervor to abate before engaging them.

The conspirators were quick, used the pretense of hunting expeditions to shuffle men in and out of cities, and excelled in heroic leadership, Liu Yü personally directing his troops by fighting in the forefront with strength and courage. He also dispatched older and weaker troops to deploy numerous flags throughout otherwise undefended areas, an antique ruse designed to convey the impression that vast forces had already occupied the mountain's perimeter that in fact prompted Huan to deplete his core defenses to reinforce the periphery.

Relying upon the fierce northwestern wind, Liu then struck Huan's main army by mounting an incendiary attack whose "fire and smoke reached Heaven." Seeing his troops crumble and certain he was fated to be overthrown by his valiant enemies because he had offended the people and angered the spirits, Huan precipitously abandoned Chien-k'ang. A small but determined contingent thus unexpectedly defeated a well-entrenched, superior force, in large part through their ready utilization of incendiary techniques.[19]

Liu Yü's coalition pursued Huan Hsüan back to Hsünyang, scoring several victories en route, almost always against superior forces. Although outnumbered at least two to one (20,000 to 10,000) in their final clash in the fifth month, they were again victorious by concentrating their forces, employing swiftness and surprise, and utilizing incendiary measures. Moreover, Huan repeated the ancient error of maintaining a fleet of escape boats, thereby undermining the army's courage and resolve. The second commander, Liu Yi, simply had the ships burned to cut off their escape before assaulting the city and shattering the enemy, though Huan managed to flee only to be assassinated not long thereafter.[20] Even Liu Yü's subsequent success in the suppressive campaign mounted against Liu Yi, whose jealousy caused him to rebel nearly a decade later in 412, was partly due to Yü's army burning all of Yi's boats prior to attacking the nearby city, precluding movement up river.[21]

Several clashes between Ma Sui and T'ien Yüeh in the T'ang show how experienced commanders well versed in military studies from an early age routinely employed incendiary and aquatic measures.[22] Part of the multi-year conflict which unfolded roughly between 781 and 784 in China's north and northeast as the powerful military governors who emerged in the aftermath of An Lu-shan's rebellion clashed with the new emperor Te-tsung over the hereditary preservation of their dictatorial authority, it ultimately saw T'ien Yüeh assassinated when the members of the rebel alliance suffered reversals and fell to fighting each other. Some perished, but others, as well as many generals and subcommanders, were readmitted to the imperial fold and confirmed in their positions, effectively continuing the policy long implemented to defuse An Lushan's rebellion.

T'ien Yüeh, who was actually T'ien Ch'eng-ssu's nephew but would eventually be designated to succeed Ch'eng-ssu because of his age, courage, talent, and military knowledge, entered the stage in 776 when he was deputed with 5,000 troops in an effort to sustain the rebel general Li Ling-yao, then under attack by government forces in the vital crossroads of Pien-chou.[23] However, this first foray turned disastrous because he was vanquished by government forces under Ma Sui and Li Chung-ch'en and lost some 80 percent of his forces. Despite barely escaping, he managed to avoid further imperial punishment.

After inheriting Ch'eng-ssu's power upon the latter's demise, T'ien Yüeh was prodded into revolting when an imperial inspector who found he had amassed an army of some 70,000 ordered 40,000 returned to agricultural status. Under the guise that they were being deprived of their livelihood, T'ien—who would repeatedly excel at motivating men in difficult situations—successfully stimulated the troops into undertaking a revolt. Moreover, to preclude other, opportunistic provincial armies from thwarting his bold thrust to power (as they had his uncle's earlier attempt), T'ien forged alliances with such kindred spirits as Li Wei-yüeh (who had sought to wrest recognition as Li Pao-ch'en's successor) and the beleaguered regional governor Li Na, son of Li Cheng-yi.

T'ien immediately attempted to solidify his position by expanding eastward. After establishing a blocking force at Han-tan, he dispatched a secondary force to attack Hsing-chou and besieged Lin-ming himself. Although both moves were stubbornly resisted, he ignored advice to move quickly and thereby avoid becoming entangled in lengthy sieges or exposed to counter-attack. Ma Sui, one of the three generals in command of a punitive force numbering some 80,000 troops, immediately employed a dated but still effective psychological ploy to successfully induce arrogance and laxity. In accord with classic military doctrine and the famous example of Lu Hsün subverting Kuan Yü's watchfulness during the Three Kingdoms period, Ma sent a highly respectful letter implying that he feared T'ien Yüeh. However, once the desired effect had been achieved, Ma's forces suddenly struck the secondary force at Han-tan.

In addition to sending Li Wei-yüeh, T'ien personally led a rescue force to Han-tan but was successfully repelled by one of Ma's subcommanders, after which Ma employed "fire wagons" to incinerate the wooden palisades erected by another small force and overwhelm them. After resting his troops for five days, Ma then advanced against T'ien's position at Lin-ming, engaged the rebels in intense fighting, and inflicted a severe defeat in which the casualties exceeded 10,000 men. Although the threat of siege at Hsing-chou was thus ended, T'ien managed to retreat and, bolstered by reinforcements from Li Na and Li Wei-yüeh, establish an encampment across the Huan River, resulting in their respective forces assuming a confrontational posture some thirty *li* apart.

When Ma found they were unable to cross a key bridge over the Chang River which was being strongly defended by troops ensconced behind a projective wall, he resorted to the historically effective but labor-intensive technique of manipulating the water level sufficiently to allow passage. Several hundred wagons loaded with sacks of earth were linked by iron chains and lowered into the river to temporarily dam the flow, allowing the army a brief interval to cross en masse. After establishing a position directly opposite T'ien across the intervening Huan River, Ma tried to provoke a quick battle. However, fully aware of Ma's limited logistical support, T'ien opted for an attritional approach and therefore ordered his men to ignore every taunt and challenge.

To manipulate them and lure the troops out of their fortifications, Ma had three bridges constructed over the Huan River, shifted his encampment close to T'ien's position, and continued highly visible attempts to provoke an engagement. However, in the middle of night he clandestinely dispatched all but a 100 cavalry along the river down to Wei-chou, T'ien's bastion, retaining the 100 to mimic the continued residence of a massive army within the encampment through noise, fires, and the semblance of flurried activity. After they had all successfully set out, Ma then quickly quieted the camp and had the cavalry concealed in the nearby countryside.

Learning of the impending strike against Wei-chou only after they had proceeded about ten *li*, T'ien rushed forth with 40,000 cavalry, crossing the bridges en route. Upon catching up to the marchers, he exploited a strong, favorable wind to set fire to the vegetation and set up a great clamor and drumming, just as Sun Pin had advised. However, Ma quickly had his forces clear away all the loose vegetation for some 100 paces around (rather than setting backfires which might have burned toward them) to create a firebreak. Frustrated at the fires petering out rather than incinerating the enemy and causing exploitable consternation, T'ien's formerly enthusiastic troops suffered a sudden deflation of spirit, providing an opportunity for the 5,000 elite troops deployed as a vanguard to not only halt the onslaught but penetrate T'ien's advancing lines as well.

This sudden success encouraged the other commanders, who had been withdrawing, to reverse course and strike, inflicting heavy losses. T'ien then hastily tried to retreat, but found the bridges had all been burned and their escape route cut off. Coming under swift attack by the concealed cavalry force, confined and in turmoil, they failed to mount an effective defense and were decimated. Twenty thousand reportedly died, many drowning in the river, though T'ien managed to flee back to Wei-chou with just 1000 men. However, due to long-standing differences with the other commander, Li Pao-chen, the imperial forces failed to exploit the opportunity and immediately inflict a fatal blow upon the then vulnerable city.

By the time Ma and Li arrived on site some ten days later, T'ien had again stabilized his forces sufficiently to mount a stalwart defense and prevent the city's collapse. Ma cut off the water, causing fear and consternation, but to little avail. Meanwhile, the political situation grew more complicated as Wang Wu-chün, who had assassinated Li Wei-yüeh, and others, such as Chu T'ao and even Chu Tz'u (who initially submitted but would subsequently mount a revolt from within the capital) felt insufficiently rewarded or otherwise threatened by the emperor and joined in a rebellious, feudal-like allegiance.[24] The next major clash between Ma Sui and T'ien Yüeh then occurred in 782 when Chu T'ao and Wang Wu-chün came in force to relieve Wei-chou.

Coincidentally, Chu and Wang's forces arrived on the same day as a supplementary government force under Li Huai-kuang. Chu immediately deployed his troops and began perspicaciously establishing his encampment against possible sudden attack. The latter in fact materialized when Li Huai-kuang insisted upon striking the supposedly unprepared enemy rather than resting his troops as Ma Sui and the *Art of War* counseled. (Fragmented authority and the lack of a supreme commander often plagued T'ang campaign forays, resulting in disjointed tactics and contrary operations.)

Li's assault initially achieved rapid penetration, causing Chu's defenses to crumble, but the elated imperial troops then began plundering the encampment, contrary to good discipline. Wang immediately led 2,000 experienced cavalry in a charge that easily bisected Li's army, throwing them into confusion. Chu's forces quickly exploited the opportunity to counterattack, and even pushed them into the large transport canal to their rear where many drowned and others perished while flailing about.

Ma Sui managed to rescue the situation and withdraw the remnant troops to the safety of their encampment. However, Chu and Wang then blocked the canal, causing the water to flow into an old riverbed, thereby cutting the imperial forces off from their supply lines and paths of retreat. Confronted by a camp inundated by three feet of water overnight, Ma Sui resorted to the subterfuge of false rapprochement by openly confessing to Chu T'ao that he had erred in trying to suppress them and promising to persuade the court to confirm and even augment their authority. Accepting these protestations and promises over Wang's objections, Chu naively released Ma's army from their confinement, allowing his resurgence another day.

Several well-known battles which arose during An Lu-shan's rebellion just decades earlier, fracturing the dynasty's power, illustrate the imaginative ways in which incendiary techniques, by exploiting confined spaces and surprise, were employed in the T'ang to achieve victory. An Lu-shan's rebellion, which entailed nearly eight years of intermittent but often intense fighting between A.D. 755 and 763, fatally segmented imperial authority when standing border forces had to be summoned and new, regional military commands were established whose independence would finally precipitate the dynasty's collapse. Operational forces ranged from 30,000 to 150,000 men, casualties numbered in the tens of thousands, and entire field armies were virtually annihilated as the balance of power repeatedly shifted. Although the actual fighting was confined to two main corridors, the localized destruction and depopulation was immense and collateral revolts that exploited the chaos severely impacted the land.

Initially successful, the rebellion ultimately crumbled because it was so plagued by internal dissension that its first three leaders were murdered; failed to consolidate conquered territory, compelling the reconquest of previously vanquished towns; and not only lacked broad support, especially south of the Yangtze, but antagonized the aggrieved populace through brutal and rapacious practices. In contrast, to encourage submission the emperor consciously implemented such an all-encompassing policy of leniency that vicious enemies were often allowed to retain power and dominate important areas. Many disenchanted rebels were reconverted to nominal allegiance, but control of the realm was increasingly lost to de facto regional military rulers such as T'ien Ch'eng-ssu, a former An Lu-shan subordinate.

Prior to the rebellion, powerful regional military administrators with unique authority to stem barbarian challenges had been created and the militia system basically abandoned in favor of a professional force capable of enduring lengthy border assignments. Some of the troops were destitute commoners, others were drawn by the appeal of military life, including mercenaries, former convicts, and foreign peoples, especially skilled barbarian fighters. These units were often commanded by non-Chinese officers such as the Korean Ko-shu Han, the Khitan Li Kuang-pi, and An Lu-shan, said to be of mixed Sogdian and Turkish parentage. Because they served almost continuously in relatively isolated areas, their troops were invariably more loyal to them than to the nebulous emperor.

One of three powerful military governors, An Lu-shan had gained control of some 200,000 troops in three contiguous northern administrative areas through his achievements, both real and contrived, in suppressing barbarian threats, and become highly honored by the emperor and his beguiling consort, Yang Kuei-fei. Before acting, he accumulated supplies, retained surrendered barbarian cavalry, and assiduously planned. When he finally struck, decades of relative peace and the absence of credible security forces within the realm allowed him to quickly penetrate to the secondary capital of Luoyang and seize the vital transportation center of Pien. However, to preserve troop strength and induce surrenders, he shortsightedly retained local officials in their posts, leaving only minimal forces and a few overseers to ensure their compliance and loyalty.

Once their advance toward Ch'ang-an and other areas was blunted, most of the nominally submissive northern towns forcibly reverted their allegiance to the T'ang and even spontaneously raised troops to eliminate the rebels, compelling An to urgently divert valuable resources to retake his base of operations between Fan-yang and Luo-yang. After initial rebel success, primarily under Shih Ssu-ming's direction, imperial troops scored several noteworthy victories and successfully withstood other rebel onslaughts. However, the rebellion's dwindling prospects were revitalized when Tsui Ch'ien-yu scored a dramatic victory over Ko-shu Han just outside the crucial pass of T'ung-kuan following a several-month standoff when the emperor was misled into ordering Ko-shu to engage the invaders in a decisive battle despite the latter's adamant opposition. Unable to await further erosion in the enemy's spirit, Ko-shu abandoned his unassailable position to launch the ill-fated assault that saw roughly 150,000 imperial troops perish when the rebels lured his forces into the constricted corridor between the mountains to the south and Yellow River to the north, immobilized, and then decimated them.

Although the highly experienced Ko-shu had deployed a 30,000-man advance element followed by a massive 100,000-man main force, he strangely chose to exercise command from the north bank of the Yellow River where he retained an additional 30,000 troops. To manipulate the T'ang commanders, the rebels sent forth a limited force that deliberately crumbled under the initial attack and fled. Deeming them cowardly and incompetent, T'ang troops elatedly pursued them only to be viciously ambushed by heavy logs, boulders, and dense archery fire from the mountains. Ko-shu immediately ordered a break-out with their felt-covered wagons, but it was thwarted by a rebel incendiary assault employing dozens of flaming wagons filled with grass and faggots. Blinded by the heavy smoke, the confused T'ang troops fired wildly, killing many of their comrades.[25] When the smoke finally cleared toward dusk, the rebels launched a fervent cavalry attack from the rear, shattering the main force. Ko-shu's soldiers fled into nearby ravines and jumped into the river where many drowned. Others were trampled, and only 8,000 survived the sustained attacks from both front and rear.

Hard on Ko-shu's fiery defeat in the sixth month of 756, the remaining defenses east of Ch'ang-an evaporated and Emperor Hsüan ignominiously fled to Szechuan, leaving his son, the future Su-tsung, who quickly usurped the throne, to eventually confront the rebels. Newly reanimated, An's forces quickly moved to exploit the awesomeness of their success in the north, where the withdrawal of key imperial armies created a vacuum and numerous adherents and formerly vacillating officials raced to join the cause. Shih Ssu-ming mounted a generally successful offensive which retook most of the north, though he also encountered several defeats, including at the famous siege of T'ai-yüan, where the resourceful Li Kuang-pi and just 10,000 men withstood a four-pronged attack by 100,000 rebel troops.

An Lu-shan's assassination by his son An Ch'ing-hsü adversely affected the rebellion's command unity and prompted numerous re-defections. Moreover, although the rebels held considerable territory, it was highly circumscribed because their thrusts to the east and south had long been stymied and their Western invasion had only carried them as far as Ch'ang-an itself. The first T'ang attempt in the autumn of 756 to retake Ch'ang-an had produced only an ignominious debacle at Ch'en-t'ou-hsieh because Fang Kuan, an old but inexperienced civil official, had been entrusted with overall command and seconded by two men with no combat experience. A staunch believer in the sagely practices of antiquity, Fang naively deployed 2,000 oxen-powered chariots flanked by infantry and cavalry units before ordering the northern and central armies to effect a measured advance. The rebels reacted with a great tumult of drums and shouts while raising clouds of dust, startling the oxen and confusing the columns. Incendiary attacks then set the chariots afire, terrifying the oxen and creating a panicked mêlée in which many soldiers were trampled. A follow-on, concerted attack inflicted heavy casualties amounting to some 40,000. Two days later Fang's southern army suffered another horrendous defeat, possibly from relying upon similar methods, though details of his deployment remain unknown.[26]

# 4

# Theoretical
# Developments

Although incendiary warfare practices multiplied and became widespread in the Three Kingdoms period before subsequently proliferating, the first military manual to discuss their theory and depict actual techniques and delivery devices was Li Ch'üan's *T'ai-pai Yin-ching,* datable to about A.D. 750, or roughly the middle T'ang dynasty. Li frequently quotes the classic Warring States military writings, including Sun-tzu's *Art of War* for which he is one of the ten well-known commentators, though not without frequently pointing out their datedness and limitations. Despite lacking historical examples, the several chapters devoted to incendiary warfare became highly influential, being incorporated virtually unaltered into most of the military compendia compiled in succeeding centuries.

Somewhat surprisingly, the *T'ai-pai Yin-ching* is marked by a thoroughgoing acceptance of metaphysical perspectives already vociferously eschewed by the classic military writings and thus a tendency to conceptualize within a proto-scientific system heavily imbued with *yin* and *yang*.[1] Although the core military chapters are both rational and precise, the work also incorporates extensive material on ceremony, divination, and prognostication amounting to more than 40 percent of the entire text. Moreover, despite founding his theory of incendiary attacks upon Sun-tzu's classic statement, unlike later texts which shed baseless constraints, Li strangely limits their initiation to the presence of a prevailing southerly wind and Sun-tzu's lunar lodges:[2]

> The classic states that "using fire to aid an attack is enlightened." When the weather is dry and parched; the encampment's huts are fashioned from reeds or bamboo; or they have piled hay, grain, and the army's provisions among dry grass or withered undergrowth; and the moon is in the lodges of *chi*, *pi*, *yi*, or *chen* at dusk, prepare equipment for the five incendiary attacks, exploit the south wind, and burn them."

Although numerous theories, none sustainable, had already been advanced to support the idea that seasonal winds would wax particularly strong on these days, such artificial limitations also make incendiary attacks highly predictable.[3] Certain unanswered questions also arise, including whether an attack might be mounted when the wind isn't southerly or the army's deployment places them in a disadvantageous position with respect to the wind and enemy.

At first reading it would seem that Li Ch'üan had accepted the *Art of War's* five categories of incendiary attack, but Sun-tzu based his enumeration more upon objectives than method, whereas Li's five attacks primarily target provisions and supplies, only secondarily structures, and never men. However, among the methods sketched for attacking enemy encampments, the text describes what might be termed "animal delivery systems" which range from deer and pigs to wild chickens and sparrows. Yet, despite aggressively employing fire both offensively and defensively, it includes virtually nothing on protective countermeasures apart from burning the brush around cities and some simple extinguishing methods.

The *T'ung Tien*, completed by Tu Yu in the early years of the ninth century, was one of the first encyclopedic works ever compiled in China. Encompassing material on a wide variety of subjects presumably of interest to administrators, the general discussions and selected principles are illustrated with historical incidents prior to A.D. 755. It also incorporates a moderately long section devoted to military issues that, even though buried amidst much material of little interest to strategists and commanders, came to comprise a virtual manual in itself, essentially the second T'ang dynasty martial work. Moreover, unlike the seven classic military writings, including the text known as *Questions and Replies* attributed to the early T'ang general Li Ching but probably compiled from unknown sources considerably later, it not only discusses concepts and operational tactics, but concretely illustrates them with actual battles as well, initiating a practice imitated by subsequent military compendia.[4]

Although Tu Yu generally based his ruminations upon the classic military texts, especially the *Art of War, Wu-tzu,* and *Liu-t'ao,* he also incorporated extensive material from the *T'ai-pai Yin-ching,* another practice assiduously copied thereafter.[5] His chapters on incendiary and aquatic warfare and the attack and defense of cities, including the primary engines and techniques, all derive from Li Ch'üan's work, though somewhat expanded with actual examples adduced in support. However, he simply cites Sun-tzu's chapter in its entirety to introduce his section on historical incendiary attacks, but does add one lunar lodge to the list of appropriate times for launching them.[6]

Of particular import is Tu's citation of a historical incident marking a new realization that incendiary warfare might be exploited for strategic rather than simply tactical ends. Although only briefly summarized in the *T'ung Tien,* sufficient information has been preserved in the *Sui Shih,* the official history of the Sui dynasty, to provide an expanded recounting of the events.[7] The Sui was founded in A.D. 581 by Yang Chien, an influential general who usurped the Northern Chou throne before proceeding to reunify China for the first time in roughly three centuries. The remarkable effort through which this incipient power then conquered Ch'en to the south, its last indigenous opponent, in a virtual replay of Chin extinguishing Wu not only implemented many traditional Chinese tactical concepts, but in fact epitomized Sun-tzu's conceptualization of ruthless, efficient warfare.

Lacking the resources to conduct a multi-front campaign but threatened by formidable enemies in every direction, Yang Chien (Sui Wen-ti) at first hoped to focus upon subjugating wealthy Ch'en, which largely relied upon the protection afforded by the Yangtze River, while fending off the dangerous but momentarily quiescent steppe peoples by simply strengthening China's border defenses. However, renewed belligerency compelled him to resort to a surprisingly wide array of diplomatic, coercive, subversive, and military measures to quell the Turkish threat. Consequently, he deceitfully nurtured harmonious relations with Ch'en and even acquiesced in the enactment of a peace treaty.

After deflecting the northern threat, the emperor resurrected his plans for the long postponed southern strike in 587 by soliciting strategic advice from his ministers and staff. In response, the highly principled yet immensely successful field commander Kao Chiung suggested adopting incendiary warfare as a strategic measure, apparently the first time incendiary assaults were viewed as more than just a combat multiplier or battlefield expedient even though Liu Pang had exploited them to similar advantage. In an analysis well reflecting the traditional belief that the enemy should be weakened before initiating an aggressive campaign, Kao advocated exploiting the significant distinctions in northern and southern material culture stemming from their climatic and environmental differences:

> The area north of the Yangtze is cold and our agricultural harvests comparatively late, but south of the Yangtze their wet cultivation comes to fruition earlier. If we estimate when they will undertake their harvest and summon a small number of soldiers and officers but speak conspicuously about mounting sudden strikes, they will certainly encamp their troops in defensive positions along the river. This will be sufficient to cause them to neglect their agricultural work.
>
> When they have assembled their soldiers, we will take off our armor. After we do this two or three times and they have become accustomed to it, they won't give it much credibility

when we subsequently assemble our troops. While they are hesitating, we can have our armies launch amphibious assaults across the Yangtze River. In such circumstances our armies' spirit will be more than double in intensity.

Moreover, the soil south of the Yangtze River is thin and their sheds are mostly made from reeds and bamboo. Whatever provisions they have accumulated are not stored in earthen pits, but in them. Therefore, if we secretly dispatch agents to exploit favorable winds to set fires and then wait until they rebuild their structures before burning them again, in just a few years their material strength will inevitably be exhausted.

As commentators have pointed out, when Kao Chiung surprisingly spoke about the southern soil being thin—despite its reputation for being well watered, highly fertile, and mostly situated within a semi-tropical climate—he was referring to the high water table that prevented grain being placed in earthen cellars. Since southern houses and sheds were constructed from readily available reeds and bamboo, both highly flammable once dry, any grain stored in them offered a vulnerable target.

Attritional measures normally require years to become fully effective but in the fragile context of sixth-century agricultural production and the generalized ravages of war the loss of a single harvest could prove devastating. Most likely they were not initiated until late 587, in which case a scant three rice harvests (based upon two crops annually) would have been affected before Sui invaded Ch'en in the twelfth month of 588. Nevertheless, Kao's integration of incendiary techniques based upon a comparative analysis of terrain and practices, just as advised in Sun-tzu's chapter "Initial Estimations," was strikingly innovative. Moreover, employing secret agents known as *hsing jen* fully accorded with Sun-tzu's dual emphasis on incendiary warfare and clandestine agents while reflecting the frequently seen historical practice of exploiting incendiary techniques for subversive purposes.[8]

When the invasion was finally launched, the Sui land and riverine forces, having been deployed into eight operational prongs, easily achieved Sun-tzu's fundamental tactic of spreading the enemy's defenses and keeping them ignorant of an attack's location. Secret reconnaissance determined where crossings might readily be undertaken and great energy expended to create a general façade of weakness, even disguising the navy's armada of well-prepared vessels as a limited and decrepit force. Frequent talks about border incursions, designed to wear out Ch'en's troops and interrupt their agricultural productivity, had the ancillary effect of inducing laxity and luring them into assuming no attack would be forthcoming, especially when they witnessed numerous, inconclusive training exercises, just as in the Yom Kippur War of 1973.[9] Thus, when the onslaught was actually launched at the end of 588, it still caught them by surprise and achieved its objectives in a mere two months.

Although the invasion's startling speed is traditionally attributed to Ch'en's rulership having been muddled by debauchery, corruption, and incompetence, Sui's 518,000 troops concretely realized Sun-tzu's ideal of overwhelming strategic power. Furthermore, as Ch'en's Yangtze River defenses were operationally divided, Sui launched their initial actions in the upper sector in order to draw forces away from the capital of Chien-k'ang (Nan-ching). Thus despite Ch'en's numerous, though squandered strategic advantages and occasional stalwart resistance, through surprise and the rapid execution of nighttime amphibious assaults Sui quickly wrested control of the countryside. Their forces also prevailed in the collateral naval clashes by overwhelming the enemy with massive numbers of vessels.

Beset by internal dissension, Ch'en didn't react to the threat until the invaders had crossed the Yangtze and even then fatally vacillated between mounting an attritional defense with their 100,000 troops and attempting incisive strikes against the columns moving against the city. Only after being completely surrounded did they foolishly engage in the decisive battle that saw their disorganized forces easily vanquished and the state extinguished before the end of the first month, though their many powerful clans required another year to fully subdue. Rather than heeding the lessons of history, Ch'en closely mimicked Wu's behavior three centuries earlier and therefore needlessly suffered the same fate.

The next work of theoretical importance after the *T'ung Tien* was Hsü Tung's early Sung *Hu-ch'ien Ching,* completed in A.D. 1004. Hsü's views on incendiary warfare are compressed into two brief sections, "Huo Li" ("Advantages of Fire") and "Huo Kung" ("Incendiary Attacks"), the latter encompassing just a few techniques originally found in the *T'ai-pai Yin-ching.* Unique in not quoting Sun-tzu, Hsü merely asserts that the proper days must be chosen—no doubt an indirect reference to those specified in the *Art of War,* but not necessarily so—and a favorable wind present.[10] When the latter can be counted on for assistance, projectiles ("flying fire") should be the chosen method, whether hurled from trebuchets or fired from bows. However, when caught in a stalemate, so-called licentious fire, apparently referring to subversive or special operations that can directly strike the enemy's heart, prove more advantageous. Smoke can also be generated and dust raised when deployed forces clash, but it is more advantageous to prepare "fire oxen" and await developments. However, incendiaries released upwind must be similarly countered to prevent the enemy from gaining an advantage.

"Advantages of Fire" concludes with a rather startling admonition, one no doubt reflecting long practice but nevertheless rarely voiced amidst more vocal though futile pleas for restraint and avoiding wanton destruction. Hsü advocated destroying any city vital to the enemy's cause whenever invading foreign territory so as to dash their hopes and realize the great profits incendiary techniques entail. However, all incendiary attacks should focus on their necessities rather than being indiscriminately inflicted upon their cities, trees, or grass.

The *Wu-ching Tsung-yao,* a massive military encyclopedia compiled in A.D. 1043 at imperial behest was intended to preserve and disseminate martial knowledge during an era of resurgent steppe threat. Although the chapter on "Incendiary

Attacks" begins by citing Sun-tzu's opening passage, the targets are interpreted somewhat differently:

> What is termed "incinerating men" refers to burning their encampments together with their officers and troops. By terrifying and attacking them, they will certainly crumble. "Incinerating provisions" refers to burning their provisions, foodstuffs, firewood, and fodder so that their armies lack the means to survive. "Incinerating baggage trains" refers to the soldier's[11] equipment, goods, and clothing of army's officers while on the road, before they halt. "Incinerating storehouses" refers to their storehouses in their citadels or encampments when they have halted.[12] Burning these causes them to suffer shortages and deprivation. "Incinerating formations" refers to burning their rows and files, for if you exploit the [ensuing] chaos to mount a sudden strike, you can vanquish them. These five are of great advantage for exterminating the enemy.

Thereafter, the *Wu-ching Tsung-yao* follows Sun-tzu's original passages with a minor explication of such essential materials as reeds, grass, lard, and oil from Li Ch'üan and other commentaries to the *Art of War*, finally appending the well-known *Liu-t'ao* passage on employing backfires. However, virtually every previously known incendiary device, both offensive and defensive, is discussed and illustrated, the first gunpowder formulas introduced, noxious gas bombs described, and warfare advanced to a new level of ferocity, though without radically diverting from previous practice. Numerous historical battles are cited in illustration, though they are consigned to the later half of the vast corpus rather than interspersed among the theoretical discussions.

The Southern Sung (1127–1279) was a politically ignominious period that saw the once glorious dynasty compressed into the lower half of its former domain, totally reliant upon the Huai and Yangtze as defensive barriers because cowards, sycophants, and appeasers controlled the government. While the emperor desperately clung to a highly passive posture and therefore suffered repeated invasions, first by the Jurchen who gradually eroded Sung terrain and then the Mongols who finally extinguished it, the dynasty's destruction was neither fated nor inevitable. Protected by formidable rivers, fielding massive numbers of troops, and benefiting from terrain which northern cavalrymen found unbearable in the summer months, the Southern Sung could have adopted a more aggressive stance and thereby overcome the generally dismal performance of its generals, many of whom fled at the first sign of the enemy, subverting the efforts of more courageous and capable commanders.

Three interesting works attributed to the period discuss incendiary warfare, although more briefly than might be expected given the prevalence of its employment: the *Ping-ch'ou Lei-yao*, *Ts'ui-wei Pei-cheng-lu*, and *Pai-chan Ch'i-lüeh*. The first of these, generally dated to around A.D. 1130, was written by Ch'i Ch'ung-li and originally comprised part of his encyclopedic *Pei-hai Chi*. Concerned primarily with generals and generalship, it includes two short sections on incendiary and aquatic warfare filled with historical examples framed by minimal theoretical observations. In particular, on the basis of Wang Shih's flooding of T'ai-yüan and Ts'ao Ts'ao's fiery debacle at Ch'ih Pi he concludes that both incendiary and aquatic techniques are essential: "Warfare is the Tao of deception, so if you can be victorious over the enemy, neither launching incendiaries nor breaking open rivers are discarded. One who excels at warfare takes water and fire as materials for employment."[13]

Accordingly, Ch'i not only accepted Sun-tzu's theories of incendiary attack, but also uniquely denigrated the *Kung-yang* and *Ku-liang*'s condemnation of the duke of Lu for having initiated incendiary warfare by burning Hsien-ch'iu: "Even though it was brutal and they condemn the duke, insofar as victory was seized it is the same."[14] Despite an already lengthy heritage of employment, his lack of compunction in resorting to incendiary techniques may well have been prompted by the Southern Sung's desperate need to keep the Jurchen fleets at bay. However, none of his examples target men, only supplies and fleets, though Ts'ao Ts'ao's losses at Ch'ih Pi entailed horrendous casualties. (He also notes Ts'ao Ts'ao's good fortune in not suffering a second incendiary attack while escaping through the narrow passes, as well as his success in burning Yüan Shao's supplies prior to Kuan-tu.)

"Incendiary Attacks" emphasizes the need to respond to developments, especially when great conflagrations are achieved. T'ien Tan is credited with having done so on a moderate scale, others with achieving much greater impact. Moreover, based upon a somewhat puzzling comparison of two famous historical incidents—Han Hsin's water ram and Ts'ao Ts'ao's burning of provisions—he concludes that "water is not as good as fire," thereby accounting for the absence of aquatic techniques in the *Art of War*. His brief though surprisingly comprehensive review of historical cases then ends with the fatalistic exclamation that even though incendiary attacks are powerful, one still can't go against Heaven, Wang Lin's self-incineration being cited in evidence.[15]

The *Ts'ui-wei Pei-cheng-lu* by Hua Yüeh, a central government military official who apparently never held active command, was conceived and presented to the emperor as a disquisition on the fundamental strategic measures necessary to defeat the ever threatening Jurchen and Mongols.[16] Since the preface dates to 1207, shortly before he was executed for complicity in an alleged plot, the book represents the revised theorizing prevailing in the very middle of the Southern Sung. Based upon a comparative analysis of national character and strength, his proposals emphasized logistics, finance, and such major concepts as exploiting the terrain, though few comments upon incendiary and aquatic warfare are appended.[17]

Nevertheless, key passages provide a somewhat reoriented vision for implementing effective defensive measures, including incendiary and aquatic techniques. To anchor his meditations upon terrain ("Ti") he advances an essentially new technical concept, "shun," which basically means "to accord with something," but here "according with and thereby exploiting the natural tendencies of situations." (There are precursors, including the *Hu-ch'ien Ching's* idea of warfare being a matter of harmonizing with and thereby exploiting the flux or flow, essentially its latent or potential energy, in consonance with Sun-tzu's concept of strategic power.) Hua identifies three compelling situations marked by natural forces or inherent tendencies: mountains (which naturally engender tactical imbalances due to the effect of gravity), rivers, and the wind:

> Two strategic powers cannot both be established nor two techniques fully implemented. If you establish yourself in the "conducive," the enemy will always dwell in the "contrary." If you occupy the "contrary," they will inevitably be in the "conducive." By failing to win the struggle for the mountain, Wei's army was defeated. By establishing their resistance upstream, Shu's riverine forces were victorious. According with the wind to raise dust caused rebellious armies to crumble. Such was the experience of the ancients with the "conducive."[18]

After noting that summer winds are mostly southerly, winter winds the reverse, and failing to recognize these tendencies might result in perishing amidst wind and hail, he explicates what might be considered three "concordances":

> This method of concordance must be discussed. The first is called "according with mountains." You must ensure that our armies are the first to occupy the heights and ravines, for then the brigands will naturally be confined to the lower points below. Thus, when the arrows and stones are fired in attack, we will be far off but they will be close; when men and horses race in pursuit, we will be at ease, they will be labored. We will have the heights about us and the ravines to the rear, with no direction in which we can't proceed, while they will have low ground within and high ground outside, and suffer from enemy forces on all sides.
> The second is called "according with water." We must ensure that we occupy the upper reaches first for then the brigands

will naturally be downstream. Thus, when you maneuver boats and ford troops in accord with the flow, the advantages and disadvantages of strategic power are already apportioned. By confronting the river to make camp and keeping the river at your back when deploying, difficult and easy are already settled.[19] When someone wants to move from above to below, it's as easy as snapping the dried out and breaking the rotten. But when someone wants to move up from below, they have the difficulty of climbing up high and traversing ravines.

The third is termed "according with the wind." Should the wind arise while you are engaged in combat, you must ensure that our armies are first to have the wind behind their backs, for then the brigands will be unable to avoid the wind. Thereafter, if we drag brush to raise dust, the enemy will not know our vacuity and substance. If we blow sand and then rush forward behind it, they will not be able to withstand our sudden assault. If we accord with the wind to deploy drugs, their mouths and noses can be poisoned. If we take advantage of the wind to set fires, the enemy's encampment can be thoroughly incinerated. This is what is termed "achieving concord."[20]

In elaborating upon the mysteries of evaluating men when trying to apportion talent and tasks, Hua suggested that ten generals should be deputed to command segregated troops with specialized skills, such as for night attacks. Among them, the General of Smoke and Fire leads men who are to burn the city, who excel at implementing the era's incendiary techniques, including "flying smoke," "shooting fire," "flowing brightness," and "moving explosions."[21] When the enemy fortuitously suffers from daytime disasters, such as setting their city afire or accidentally burning their provisions and their formations become chaotic, of if they are hastening about to extinguish fires at night, the opportunity should be exploited, provided only that it is genuine rather than a ruse.[22]

The third Southern Sung work, the anonymous *Pai-chan Ch'i-lüeh* or *Hundred Unorthodox Strategies*, was probably created near the end of the dynasty or shortly thereafter.[23] A systematic summation of earlier military writings supplemented by historical examples that convert an otherwise conventional manual into an astute casebook, the unknown author culled China's extensive dynastic histories for battles that would concretely yet succinctly illustrate abstract tactical principles in context. The applicability and limitations of some forty paired tactical concepts and a few fundamental principles are examined. Only one chapter, "Incendiary Strategies," focuses on incendiary warfare, but several others tangentially consider it or cite examples in which it played a major role, as will be seen in the upcoming thematic sections.

Although the Mongols were astute students of military theory and avidly absorbed Chinese martial technology and whatever battlefield lessons might be learned to dominate China's radically different environment, integrating them with their own insights and steppe cavalry practices, they also proscribed the dissemination of military knowledge. Only after the Ming wrested power through actively exploiting gunpowder and incendiary techniques did military manuals again appear, the most important being the *Ts'ao-lü Ching-lüeh, Wu Pien, Wu-pei Chih, Teng-t'an Pi-chou,* and Ch'i Chi-kuang's training manual.

Several chapters (including the first one dedicated to smoke) in the anonymous, possibly mid-dynasty *Ts'ao-lü Ching-lüeh (Essential Ruminations in a Grass Hut)* discuss interesting aspects of incendiary warfare or include historical battles in which incendiary techniques played an important role, and one focuses on incendiary attacks.[24] In accord with common practice, *Huo Kung* first enumerates Sun-tzu's five targets but then immediately comments that "incinerating men and formations is especially tense and difficult." Abandoning any hope of effectively attacking men on open terrain, the author advises: "To incinerate men, incinerate their encampments, warships, and deployments. Incendiary techniques can only be employed against deployments where there are reeds, woods, or tangled vegetation. If you set fires in accord with the wind, the enemy's deployments will certainly be affected. If you then employ your troops to strike across them, no one will remain unconquered." Perhaps because of the ghastliness of being so entrapped, he then reminds readers of fire's inherent cruelty: "Even though planned incendiary attacks produce complete victory, they are actually extremely grievous."

Explicating Sun-tzu's concept of exploiting attacks, the text advises: "When you ignite fires within an encampment and their troops respond, they should be confused and turbulent, so beware of tranquility and order. Turbulence indicates laxity in the enemy, but tranquility indicates they are prepared. Incendiary carts should be employed to burn palisades, fire boats and rafts used to burn wooden barriers across rivers. Have them approach close on but don't support them further. Burn formations by using specialized troops to lure them onto terrain with reeds, grass, or trees and inflict raging fires upon them."

Given the prevalence of these techniques, commanders are warned to always be prepared, especially during the dry season, in windy conditions, and amidst flammable materials. Defensive methods, the first specifically directed to surviving an imminent attack, are deferred to the chapter's concluding lines:

> Anyone who wants to defend against incendiary attacks must know when the enemy is about to strike so as to empty out the encampment. However, some residual troops should be left behind to put flags all about and convey internal orders with drums and horns. Soldiers and horses should go in and out in a continuous loop to show that you have not yet departed from the encampment.
>
> Have your troops assume positions in ambush on the left and right and wait for the fires to arise, at which time the soldiers remaining in camp should set up a clamor and pretend to be in chaos, for then the enemy will certainly advance to attack. Our troops lying in ambush can strike them from both wings and we can also mount a surprise attack on their rear. In this manner we will defeat everyone.[25]

T'ang Shun, an experienced Ming dynasty coastal commander, probably completed the *Wu Pien* around 1550 or slightly later. The chapter entitled "Fire" simply incorporates the initial paragraph of "Incendiary Attack" from the *Wu-ching Tsung-yao*, showing the essential continuity of tradition despite the evolution and widespread employment of cannon and muskets.[26] Even more significantly, he copies the chapters on concordance and terrain from the *Pei-cheng-lu* just discussed. The intelligent practice of incendiary warfare must accord with these parameters, employing fire and smoke only when the wind is conducive and launching fire boats downstream or when tail winds can overcome the river's current. Correspondingly, positions downstream or contrary to the flow must be sedulously avoided.[27]

The various devices employed in T'ang's historical examples contained in the later half of the work under the rubrics of "Defense" and "Boats" well illustrate these principles. While they are primarily gunpowder based in accord with the book's extensive sections on incendiary formulas and gunpowder mixtures, incendiary arrows still rely upon oil as their ignition source. However, such highly inefficient and unpredictable delivery systems as small birds and fire oxen have vanished, though other animals and large birds remain viable vehicles for transporting burning materials into enemy encampments.

The work entitled *Hsiang Yüeh* or *Prescriptions for Villages (Defense)*, also written about 1550 by Yin Keng, indicates that denial polices were still viewed as fundamental in the border region. To reduce their mobility and undermine their staying power, the mostly nomadic enemies who mount incursions from out of the steppe, including residual Mongol groups, must be prevented from gaining access to grass and feed stocks.[28] Although external buildings seem to have escaped, it was a true scorched-earth policy because anyone who failed to cut and harvest the grass in their fields upon the announcement of an approaching enemy would have them burned without exception.

Despite the increasing deployment of cannon and early muskets and the continuation of antique methods such as dropping stones and swinging boulders from ropes, eruptors retained a primary role in city defense and had to be provided in quantity. A two-stage technique was often employed, first sprinkling saltpeter, sulfur, and oil on top of the assault structures, then using eruptors as flamethrower to ignite them.[29] Moreover, while bemoaning the low height of most parapets, Yin Keng cleverly advised using dummies on top of the wall to draw enemy fire.[30]

A few decades later Ho Liang-ch'en compiled another focal text entitled the *Ch'en Chi*, whose chapter on "Incendiary Warfare" succinctly encapsulated the thinking prevailing near the end of the sixteenth century. Ho envisioned surpassing military power being derived solely from fire and water:

> Only those who excel at using fire and water have the awesomeness to shake Heaven.[31] Thus their efforts are not wasted and their results are doubled. The *Methods* states that "implementing an incendiary attack depends upon the proper conditions. Equipment for incendiary attacks[32] should be fully prepared before required."
>
> "Proper conditions" means relying upon climatic conditions such as wind and dryness and the enemy's occupation of heavy vegetation. "Equipment" means that the implements for incendiary attack are fully prepared within the army. Having gained conducive climatic conditions, directly moving against the enemy's position and then employing your previously prepared equipment is the method for mounting an incendiary attack.
>
> When examining the seasons and considering the day, you must have wind. Accord with the wind to release smoke and dust, being certain to choose a conducive method. Ignite fires from dark corners so that the enemy will not have any means of rescue. Resolutely defend their routes of retreat, don't let them flee.
>
> If you have to withstand an incendiary attack, deploy such devices such as *fu-ti-lei p'i-li* and *huo-hung shan-p'ao*, all forms of spiritual attack, what are referred to as firing once to slay a million.[33] These sustain our Heavenly troops who proceed beyond the passes and are among the secrets of border defense.

Moreover, if employed in China proper, there is nowhere they would not be appropriate. Similarly, the strategic power and great combat achievements of the famous generals and heroes of antiquity which caused the enemy to have no place to establish preparations, no place to mount resistance, fully stemmed from the advantages of fire and water.

The different implements for incendiary attack include those employed on land, on water, in combat, in defense, and in ambushes. As for the types of device, there is *fei-huo* [flying fire], *lieh-huo* [fierce fire], *fa-huo* [explosive fire], *tu-huo* [poisonous fire], and *shen-huo* [spiritual fire]. Their power lies in fire, their cleverness in the implements. Sun-tzu referred to the moon being in [the lunar lodges of] *chi, pi, yi,* or *chen* as days when the wind would arise, but surely this lacks evidence. One who can exploit Heaven's dryness and gain the subtle crux of Earth to launch an attack on the wind, whose incendiary equipment is spiritual and ingenious, can be said to excel at incendiary warfare. Those who simply adhere to Sun-tzu's five types of incendiary attack and four lunar lodges cannot be said to have fathomed the employment of fire.

The most difficult aspect of employing incendiary measures is detonation. Fuses [are employed] for land mines buried several feet deep and dispersed over several *li,* and for water mines intended for ambushes sunk ten feet deep or more in coves and streams. But when fuses are buried in the ground they become moist, when immersed in water they become rotten, so how can they not be wet after weeks or months and still ignite once the trigger is released?

Even more so, the oil and wax in bamboo [fire] tubes cannot withstand water. Only someone whose skill surpasses Li Tsai will be able to realize the essential secrets. Burning provisions, incinerating encampments, shooting arrows, and firing trebuchets is nothing more than a question of slower or faster, convenient or obstructed, appropriate or inappropriate, ingenious methods and hand skills. How are they worth speaking of? Those who excelled at fabricating incendiary [devices] had secrets they didn't pass down, those who excelled at employing incendiary measures had personally attained skills.

Whenever "fires are started within the camp, you should quickly respond from outside." If, by chance, fires are ignited outside, you should respond expeditiously, don't wait for fires to erupt internally. "If fires are ignited but the enemy doesn't stir,"[34] they must be relying upon something or perhaps the camp is empty. You should briefly wait without attacking, observing the fire's power. When it is raging both internally and externally, if they are in chaos, then follow it up; if quiet, then avoid them.

Having been written in an age when the destructiveness of gunpowder explosives and tubed weapons had become commonplace, Ho not unexpectedly offers the most power-oriented appraisal of all the military writings. However, he doesn't simply advocate the mass adoption of gunpowder weapons but instead the full exploitation of incendiary techniques and endorses the traditional techniques by extensively reprising their principles and methods of application. In addition, while emphasizing Sun-tzu's ideas, he remains firmly rooted in the reality of actual practice, rejecting the more artificial and inexplicable aspects of the puzzling wind theory while lamenting the Ming's failure to adopt incendiary measures more fully against border aggressors.

Yeh Meng-hsiung's chapter on incendiary attack, "Huo Kung," in his late Ming *Yün-ch'ou Kang-mu* represents the final exposition of the incendiary tradition. A thoughtful elucidation of various aspects within the context of increasingly formidable border threats and volatile domestic conditions, Yeh's observations are dispersed throughout the chapter, invariably followed by two or three examples drawn from the standard histories. Shifting the illustrations to our topical chapters yields a somewhat surprising exposition of strategic implications and fundamental tactical principles, much in the tradition of Sun-tzu's "Incendiary Attacks."

Sun-tzu probably regarded incendiary attacks as the lowest strategy because giving security to the state and preserving the army is valued by the Tao. Many are injured and harmed as soon as fires arise, so he considered them inferior. However, barbarians today are fierce and cruel and it is difficult to match them in strength. But if we are enlightened about incendiary attacks and launch them on a timely basis, following up with our troops, they will certainly be startled into collapsing, flee northward in defeat, and not dare reenter our borders. Accordingly, I have elucidated the crux of incendiary attacks below.

*Burn the grass to defeat the barbarians:* The barbarians rely on horses for their strength and the horses upon grass to live. When the grass out in the wilds is burnt, the horses become weak and emaciated. If we exhaust their provisions and meat, put our warriors and horses into good order, and shift and stretch so as to move them about, won't they be defeated? Alas, the ancients all employed the technique of burning grass to defeat the barbarians, why do we alone now fail to do so?

*Nighttime incendiary attacks force the enemy to withdraw:* Even when barbarians enter our borders to plunder, they are concerned about falling into traps. Nighttime actions taken to mislead them are invariably believed. Thus having everyone carry a torch at night will cause the enemy to withdraw.[35] Now "using fire to assist an attack is enlightened."[36] In present day Yün-chung, Sui-chou, and Tai-chou, won't another Lien Fan appear?

*Incinerate the grass and heavy vegetation:* Sun-tzu said that "if fires are ignited but their troops remain quiet, then wait, do not attack. If the fires flare into a conflagration, you can follow up and attack them."[37] The T'ai Kung said "when you see the fires arise, set fires in front and behind us and then broaden and extend them."[38] Thus you can set fires to preserve yourself. Accordingly, Li Ling responded to the Hsiungnu by unleashing fire and shouting loudly, Huang-fu Sung destroyed the Yellow Turbans by launching a fire attack and exploiting its power, and Chu Ch'uan-chung destroyed Chu Hsüan. Didn't their actions subconsciously cohere with Suntzu and Wu-tzu?

*Incinerate baggage trains:* The Three Armies rely upon their baggage trains for their employment. If the enemy succeeds in burning them, even though the army remains unharmed, it has been destroyed. An army conducting a punitive campaign with its baggage train at the rear must have well-disciplined troops deployed to defend it rather than being like Yüan Shao who was trapped by Hsü Yu's plan, Mu-jung P'ing falling into Wang Meng's scheme, or the Western Ch'iang being caught by Ma Yüan's devices.

*Defend against evening blows to your encampment:* When armies ensconced in opposing fortifications are about to do battle, whoever unexpectedly first bludgeons the other's encampment at night will realize what the military thinkers term the unorthodox tactic of going forth when unsuspected, striking where they are unprepared. Accordingly, knowledgeable strategists will certainly prepare, for then the enemy will fall into a trap instead. Thus both Man Ch'ung and Feng Hung were able to conceal sudden strikes and achieve success. As for Fu Yung using fire to confuse the enemy's actions, this is more unorthodox than the unorthodox! Isn't changing and transforming in accord with the enemy to seize victory spiritual![39]

*Launch incendiary attacks amidst wind:* Sun-tzu said that "incendiary attacks have their appropriate seasons, igniting fires their proper days." He also said that fires can be initiated from outside, you do not have to rely upon the inside.[40] When Liu Yi, Li Hsiao-yi, and Wang Chin-t'an engaged in combat with the enemy, they all exploited the wind to launch incendiary attacks and defeat them, thereby actualizing their schemes. Even so, armies must know the five changes of fire and calculate appropriately. We want to incinerate the enemy, so shouldn't we be prepared against the enemy incinerating us?

*Burn animals to achieve success:* Everybody in both ancient and modern times is well aware that T'ien Tan's fire oxen defeated Yen's army and restored Ch'i's cities. But when Wang Tse used them he was defeated by Ming Kuo, and when Ts'ao Ch'ing used them he was defeated by Wang Te. Why is that?

Those who excel at modeling on the ancients take their intentions as their teachers rather than getting enmired in their traces. Weren't T'ien Tan's fire oxen modeled on the king of Ch'u using fire elephants? Even so, he first spoke deceitfully about a heavenly teacher in order to cause doubt in the enemy's mind and then used painted dragons to befuddle their eyes. Externally, they mounted a sudden nighttime strike, internally they used [banged on] copper vessels to augment their awesomeness and in an instant were rescued. Lacking good plans and simply relying upon fire oxen, this is what Wang Tse and Shao Ch'ing did. As for Yang Hsüan's use of incendiary horses, he excelled at modeling on T'ien Tan and thus he was able to pacify all the brigands of Ts'ang-wu and clear the area within the district's borders.

*Burn their boats to achieve results:* Li Chien-chi leading his death defying warriors with their axes to destroy Ho Huai's bamboo rafts and break open the barrier hardly merits discussion. As for Chou Yü burning [Ts'ao Ts'ao's] warships and P'an Mei burning the water barriers, they achieved success in their own time and transmitted their names to later generations, but they did not have detailed plans to destroy them. I note that the ancients fabricated long poles and iron forks in order to fend off incendiary boats that, after a brief interval, would be completely consumed. Every one of our boats should prepare several tens of poles in advance, then we will have no worries even if the enemy mounts an incendiary attack.

*Exploit the terrain to employ fire:* Ch'ao Ts'o said that one should first learn about the configuration of terrain and Mencius said that "the seasons of heaven are not as good as advantages of earth." Whether two armies are attacking each other or employing incendiary attacks, it does not go beyond this. Thus, Han Hsin used Ch'en-ts'ang-ku, Lu Hsün utilized dark and deep woods, and Chu-ko Liang exploited P'an-she-ku. Don't our present border areas have terrain such as this? When the barbarians deeply penetrate them, we can lure them further in and incinerate them.

*Balk the enemy and burn them:* Even though those who excel at warfare use fire to assist the attack, those who excel at defense thwart plans with plans. Accordingly, they are good at implementing unorthodox tactics which the enemy is unable to fathom. Thus Chu-ko Liang and Teng Ai at one time set torches ablaze and their troops ambushed the enemy, at another they burned dummy provisions and drew the enemy in to extinguish the fires, and again desisted from pursuing Chiang Wei's retreating forces and thus prevented his incendiary tactics from being implemented. These are what are referred to as "subtle subtle, approaching the formless, spiritual, spiritual, approaching the soundless."[41]

Mao Yüan-yi, who finished compiling the vast compendia known as the *Wu-pei Chih* in 1619, introduced his lengthy section on incendiary warfare by noting that the Ming initially conquered through firepower and thereafter continued to improve and exploit it. However, within the context of his time, Mao feared that the fundamental techniques were in danger of being lost and therefore decided to cull the many military manuals still available to preserve them. The result was a section consisting of sixteen heavily illustrated chapters of just over 600 pages devoted to incendiary warfare, a veritable repository of both historical methods and contemporary practice.

Although his introduction returns to the ancient concept of the five phases of earth, metal, water, fire, and wood, it interprets their character, potential, and impact rather differently:

> Among the five phases, the basic nature of metal, water, and fire is fierceness. Accordingly, earth generates things, wood nourishes them, metal maims them, water slays them, and fire incinerates them. Weapons gain their utility from metal, but metal's ability to maim is limited. Thus, breaking open river embankments to flood cities and blocking the current's flow in order to soak fortifications are water's great employment. But where water doesn't reach, resort is to fire. However, fire exhausts the employment of the five phases and the benevolent man does not speak about it. Sun-tzu brought forth the basic principles, but when dry reeds are bundled for torches, fire need not rely on anything else.

Slightly later, he concludes with remarks about his own time and the grievous yet necessary nature of incendiary warfare: "These days, when people speak about weapons there isn't anyone who doesn't speak about fire. If we unravel these two words [weapons and fire], they are extremely worrisome. Alas, if one exhausts the employment of the five phases but they yet prove insufficient to protect our people, there's nothing more inhumane."

The idea of fire being a fierce element seems to have suddenly burgeoned in the early sixteenth century as the *Ping Ching*, which is cited and preserved in the *Wu-pei Chih*, already termed it the fiercest element: "Now the employment of fire is the fiercest among the five elements. The ancients knew its basic nature was fierce and could not be withstood."[42] However, Mao's assertion that metal, the basis for weapons, and water are both inherently powerful and destructive broadened the destructive array considerably and represents a new understanding. Furthermore, his belief that incendiary warfare is inherently brutal echoes another Ming dynasty work, the *Ts'ao-lü Ching-lüeh*, while his conclusion harks back to a sentiment found in the *Ssu-ma Fa* that to prevent even greater killing, warfare is not only unavoidable but justified.

Another section of his vast corpus observes that "incendiary methods will always result in victory, that no one can withstand their power. Assuredly they cannot be lightly employed nor can they be wantonly employed. Moreover, the essence of military science is that one accords with the times of Heaven above, gains advantages of earth below, and harmonizes with men in the middle. When these three factors are penetratingly prepared, the commander will be able to know the enemy and himself, take benevolence as his heart's model, make righteousness the army's reputation, manifest clarity in rewards and punishments, ensure credibility for the laws and orders, govern what is appropriate to the time, and establish the unorthodox in order to evaluate the enemy."[43]

Mao freely integrated materials from the earlier works, sometimes incorporating entire sections unaltered, at others integrating selected passages for effect, often with his personal commentary interspersed. Although several military manuals discuss the topic known as *ti li* or "advantages of terrain," only he subsumed its discussion under the rubric of fire. As numerous eruptors and mortars are included in the following summary, the term "huo kung" no longer refers to just incendiary warfare, but encompasses the employment of a wide variety of gunpowder-based weapons, including the incendiary devices which are described in our upcoming methods section:[44]

Incendiary attacks require being in accord with the seasons of Heaven above and responsive to the advantages of earth below.

In broad wilds and on level rivers, whoever mounts a sudden, distant strike will be victorious.

In dense forests and narrow passages, striking from two sides will produce victory.

Relying upon the heights to strike an enemy below accords with the strategic configuration of power, so employ heavy weapons and raging fire to suppress them.

Striking an enemy from below is contrary to the configuration of power, so employ tubed weapons[45] and fierce fire in order to spray them.

When two sides possessing incendiary equipment suddenly encounter each other and there isn't time to properly deploy, their configuration can easily be thrown into chaos, so striking first with long-range weapons will produce victory.

When both sides have established encampments protected by barriers and palisades, when plundering for provisions and supplies you must first examine the route for ambushes. If their configuration is changing and doubtful, employ signaling equipment and strike from all four sides to gain victory.

When striking forces outside a city from within, you should attack their solidity, but when attacking the interior from outside, you should attack their flaws.

In riverine warfare you must first achieve a position upwind and employ various equipment to create smoke screens. You should chemically treat your sails so that they won't become saturated by the wind-blown smoke.

These are the methods for responding to combat situations. If you fail to discern the terrain's advantages when employing them, you will not realize their benefits. If you abandon your equipment and in the end run off, you will only provide material resources for the invading enemy.

Finally, a minor work composed just after the fall of the Ming by a disaffected patriot, the *Ping-fa Pai-yen* expounds the essential meaning of 100 terms, perhaps in loose imitation of the *Hundred Unorthodox Strategies*. However, there are no definitions for fire or water, nor do any of the chapters discuss incendiary techniques beyond burning any tress and grass the enemy may rely upon. Thereafter, texts composed by Ming survivors and then Ch'ing writers (who, although heavily suppressed, needed populist techniques) ironically ignored incendiary warfare for the quickness and violence of explosiveness.

## TARGETING PROVISIONS

Recognizing the vital need for adequate provisions, many military writers emphasized the misery and debilitation that might be inflicted by denying them to the enemy. Although seizing foodstuffs would be doubly profitable (as Sun-tzu counseled), the problem of transport often meant that burning them remained the only feasible method. However, even as their bulk and density facilitated incineration, their storage in conspicuous depots and movement by highly visible supply trains and river convoys made them readily accessible targets. Invaders and raiders also burned immovable provisions upon departing to prevent pursuing armies from acquiring them, often to the detriment of the local population when all the available foodstuffs were included, though sometimes the fires were extinguished quickly enough to allow a major portion to be saved.[46]

A number of noteworthy incendiary attacks deliberately targeted enemy provisions long before the T'ang made it a component of strategic doctrine and many more of lesser scope certainly went unreported. For example, in addition to P'eng Yüeh's marauding attacks on Hsiang Yü's provisions and Ts'ao Ts'ao's famous raid prior to Kuan-tu, in A.D. 369 Former Ch'in mounted an incendiary attack designed to compel the Hsien-pei state of Former Yen to abandon their advantageous attritional strategy.[47] The Ch'in commander, Wang Meng, who had come forth with just 60,000 cavalry and infantry, found himself confronting some 300,000 enemy troops. However, he managed to structure the battle by aggressively manipulating the enemy rather than becoming entangled in a debilitating stalemate across a river deep in enemy territory.

In addition to the incendiary attack, a marked discrepancy in their respective spirit and commitment had a major impact. Wang Meng was able to inspire his soldiers and elicit heroic behavior from key warriors who repeatedly penetrated the enemy's formation and decimated their numbers at a crucial moment. In contrast, the Yen commander, who ironically had thought Ch'in was probably too weak to merit any defensive preparations, generally antagonized his troops and incurred the king's wrath by monopolizing the encampment's water and fodder and greedily sold them to his own soldiers.

Prior to the campaign Ch'in had aided Yen when the latter had been endangered, but Yen reneged on the territory originally offered in recompense once the crisis passed. Enraged by this perfidy, Fu Chien, king of Ch'in, immediately dispatched a punitive force that easily seized the promised territory. After ostensibly ceasing hostilities in order to visibly establish his reputation for righteousness, by the fall of 370 Fu Chien's new multi-prong campaign had conquered several cities, including Chin-yang which was breached when a tunneling effort allowed elite troops to penetrate the city and seize control.

However, the ensconced troops at Lu-chou presented a rather different situation, one which Wang Meng precipitously ended by dispatching a small force of 5,000 men in the middle of the night around the nearby mountain behind the enemy to set fire to the vital provisions being stored at their rear. The resulting blaze, being visible throughout the district, panicked the king into ordering his field commander to abandon his attritional approach and go forth to vanquish the enemy. However, Ch'in's forces easily prevailed, some 50,000 Yen casualties and prisoners resulting from the first wave of strikes and another 100,000 surrendering or being killed in follow-on attacks. Not long thereafter Yen was itself extinguished.

A dedicated chapter in the T'ang Dynasty *T'ung Tien* introduced by eliding key statements from consecutive chapters of Sun-tzu's *Art of War* succinctly analyzes the objectives and advantages of denying provisions to the enemy:[48] "In order to prevent the enemy from coming forth, show them harm. If they are well fed, you can make them hungry.[49] If you reduce the army's size to contend for advantage, your baggage and heavy equipment will suffer losses. Accordingly, if the army does not have baggage and heavy equipment it will be lost; if it does not have provisions it will be lost; if it does not have stores it will be lost."[50] After citing several historical battles attesting to the veracity of Sun-tzu's assertions, Tu Yu discusses the theory of incendiary attacks (presumably because they provide the most effective means for destroying provisions) by integrating Sun-tzu's entire chapter into his assessment.[51] Three focal attacks on the enemy's provisions already noted—Ts'ao Ts'ao's raid prior to the clash at Kuan-tu, the early Sui dynasty's systematic debilitation of Ch'en, and the case just cited—number among his limited illustrations.

Among later disquisitions on the subject, the Southern Sung's *Ts'ui-wei Pei-cheng-lu* emphasizes debilitating the enemy by causing them to suffer from hunger and thirst.[52] The *Hundred Unorthodox Strategies* ponders the powerful effect of disrupting the enemy's logistics in a chapter appropriately entitled "Provisions" which asserts that an army deprived of provisions will be forced to retreat and thus become vulnerable to attack.[53] Moreover, in a chapter pointedly entitled "Make the Enemy Hungry," the *Ts'ao-lü Ching-lüeh* bluntly states that "an army which lacks provisions will be lost. This has always been this way since antiquity. Therefore you should always cause them to have a deficiency." Somewhat surprisingly, the ensuing tactical discussion never mentions incinerating the enemy's provisions even though carts, supply wagons, and supply boats are all burned in one of the examples, causing the enemy's provisions to be exhausted and their forces to eventually succumb.[54] However, the *Teng-t'an Pi-chiu* advises that incendiary projectiles should be utilized to burn supplies stored within cities.[55]

Other *Ts'ao-lü Ching-lüeh* chapters similarly stress that preserving your own supply lines while destroying the enemy's provisions is the most effective way to achieve victory. For example, "Striking the Rear" asserts that the primary objectives of maneuvering to mount unexpected rear attacks are stealing and incinerating supplies and provisions, and occupying supply depots, thereby impoverishing their army and making their troops hungry. Furthermore, as previously suggested in the *Ts'ui-wei Pei-cheng-lu*, guerrillas ("yu ping") should also be employed to filch the enemy's foodstuffs and burn their provisions, as well as mount disruptive actions against their baggage trains and rear encampments, though without ever becoming entangled in prolonged combat.

Incendiary-based programs were also implemented to deny sustenance to the raiders and invaders in the zone of interaction between the mobile steppe peoples and sedentary Chinese towns. A reoriented form of the ancient, generalized effort to deprive aggressors of all usable materials and directly attack their provisions, it sought to diminish their mobility by eliminating potential equine supplies through burning the grass and other edible vegetation around border towns. However, not every dynasty had the ability to undertake such active border programs nor were they adopted more than locally and sporadically even when imperially mandated. For example, despite facing severe threats the Ming seems to have vacillated between vigorous implementation and complete neglect, the latter prompting Yeh Meng-hsiung near the end of the era to conclude that the discontinued policies of denial should be reinstated.[56]

The T'ang, which aggressively battled various steppe groups early in its existence but suffered unremitting incursions later in the dynasty, sporadically effected policies of denial. For example, to frustrate growing Khitan strength in the latter part of the ninth century, the T'ang burnt the grass outside the walls to starve their horses. A century and a half earlier, in the winter of A.D. 727, the Turfan under General Hsi-juo-luo invaded the border area of Kan-chou (in modern Kansu), which they burned and pillaged before moving onward.[57] Entrusted with countering the raiders, Wang Chünch'uo felt that his troops were tired and therefore merely followed to their rear. However, it happened to snow heavily and the cold caused numerous deaths among the Turfan, prompting them to withdraw back onto the steppe.

Anticipating their line of retreat, Wang dispatched a small contingent that proceeded by indirect routes to burn all the grass and any available provisions. At their intended resting point, half the horses had already died from lack of fodder. Wang and another general pursued them to the banks of the Ch'ing-hai but the enemy had already crossed over the frozen river and fled, leaving behind a weak rear guard which was easily vanquished, resulting in the capture of tens of thousands of sheep and cattle.

Nearly a century earlier, during the dynasty's early days, in A.D. 641 the leader of the Hsieh-yen-t'o clan of the T'ieh-le thought to exploit the emperor's eastward journey to offer sacrifice to Heaven[58] to attack the Eastern Turks under A-shih-na Ssu-mo now settled to the east of the Ordos, including those within the T'ang's walls.[59] Gathering some 200,000 clan troops, he had his son Ta-tu-she take command of the primarily infantry force, cross the Gobi desert, and attack. The Eastern Turks withdrew to the protection of the Great Wall, where they were reviled by the aggressors.

> Learning of the incursion, Emperor T'ai-tsung dispatched a somewhat smaller, multi-prong force that included various steppe cavalry components from among the Turks and others and proceeded by both eastern and western routes. When instructing his generals prior to their departure, the emperor stressed the importance of first debilitating the enemy:

"Relying on their great strength, the Hsieh-yen-t'o have crossed the desert and come south, traversing several thousand *li*. Their horses are tired and emaciated. The Tao for employing the army is to rapidly advance when you see profit, but quickly retreat when it is not advantageous. They were unable to intercept Ssu-mo unprepared, yet when they hastily attacked and Ssu-mo withdrew within the Great Wall, they didn't quickly retreat.

I have already commanded Ssu-mo to burn the vegetation and autumn grass. Their provisions and fodder must soon be exhausted and they will be unable to obtain anything in the wilds. A little while ago a reconnaissance agent came and reported that their horses had already eaten almost all the small branches and bark from trees. Your forces should form a triangle with Ssu-mo. You do not need to quickly engage in battle, instead just wait for them to be about to retreat. Then if you fervently attack in unison, you will certainly destroy them!"

According to the reports, when Li Shih-chi and Ssu-mo encountered Ta-tu-she with 30,000 cavalry at the wall, the latter fled and was pursued by just 6,000 T'ang cavalry. After several days the Hsieh-yen-t'o finally turned about and engaged in battle across a broad front and succeeded in driving back the Eastern Turkish component, but then made the mistake of pursuing them. This allowed Li Chih-chi to overwhelm them with a frontal assault despite having had most of their horses shot dead by the steppe bowmen. Advancing on foot with long spears against the crumbling enemy who had lost their mounts in a collateral action effected by T'ang cavalry, Li's troops killed several thousand T'ieh-le warriors and captured 50,000 more. Ta-tu-she fled back out into the desert with his remaining troops but they met with heavy snow and nearly all of them perished from the cold en route back home.

On the other hand, the steppe groups, being more accustomed to raiding and carrying off limited amounts of goods and supplies, often burned whatever they could not remove except when they viewed it as simply being stored against their future wants. Moreover, they frequently resorted to burning each other's provisions in raids and in more extensive clashes with Chinese armies. For example, the lengthy conflict between the Turfan and the T'ang saw both sides burn the other's provisions, the Turfan armies striking in Shanhsi in 765, the T'ang out in Kansu in 768 and during their sweep in 786. The Turfan also employed fire as an aggressive weapon when they rampaged through Western Shanhsi in 787, targeting all the cities and structures for destruction and setting as many as possible afire. When punitive Chinese expeditions seemed imminent, they sometimes resorted to scorched earth policies to deny grass to the armies, as the T'u-ku-hun futilely did early in T'ang T'ai-tsung's reign though Li Ching still penetrated their territory and scored a major victory.[60]

As forces increasingly relied upon water transport for logistical purposes, severing the enemy's supply lines by destroying or at least immobilizing their boats became a priority. Incendiary measures were the primary means to accomplish this end, though various river barriers and fortified obstacles might also be employed to block movement. Astonishingly large numbers of vessels were often burned in these efforts and in riverine clashes in general. Among numerous instances, when Eastern Wu was preparing to attack Chin in A.D. 278, Wang Hun of Chin mounted a preemptive strike which killed 5,000 men and burned 600 boats and the huge amount of 18,000,000 *tou* (pecks) of grain.[61] Nearly three centuries later, the Liang commander Ch'en Pa-hsien cut off Northern Ch'in's supplies to its beleaguered city of Shih-t'ou-ch'eng near Nan-ching with a nighttime incendiary attack on their boats, burning the staggering number of 1,000.[62]

# 5

# Methods, Weapons, and Techniques

Numerous means and techniques for mounting incendiary attacks evolved over the centuries ranging from simply setting the environment ablaze to incendiary arrows and animal delivery systems. While the theoretical manuals sketch their essence, they appear in the historical records in many variants. Naturally the earliest forms remain unattested apart from neolithic archaeological reports, their methods no doubt limited to the direct ignition of flammable structures. Thrown torches and probably the transport of ignition materials to deliberately set fires marked the next advance, leading thereafter to carts and wagons filled with burning debris which could be wheeled into place or even allowed to roll downhill onto the enemy. On the water, fire boats propelled by the wind or carried along by the current provided a similar sort of "release and forget" delivery system, effective but also uncontrollable once launched. Finally, missile delivery systems, whether arrow powered or hurled by trebuchets, allowed soldiers to stand off at a distance yet ignite blazes, readily reaching previously inaccessible targets in city and camp interiors.

The simplest form of incendiary attack required troops to physically approach the gates, palisades, or other exposed perimeter targets to set them afire. Extensively practiced in city assaults from the Spring and Autumn onward, it required little theorizing, just courage to execute under a hail of enemy projectiles. However, the *T'ai-pai Yin-ching* describes a spectacular variant under the name of "incendiary troops" which proved so successful that they were continuously employed on the battlefield and elucidated in the theoretical manuals right through the Ming.[1] Exploiting silence and darkness, a number of cavalry with gagged mouths, and whose horses' mouths have also been bound to minimize sound, are to race toward the encampment during the night with an ignition source and bundles of reeds and firewood. Upon reaching the palisades and stacking their kindling materials against it, they ignite them in unison for maximum effect and then exploit any ensuing confusion, though further action should be foregone if the camp remains unperturbed.

A few soldiers or even just a single man, whether in disguise or simply exploiting the cover of night, could also start a major conflagration by penetrating the camp during quiet hours and setting any readily flammable structures ablaze, though the primary targets would always be stores of firewood, oil, and eventually gunpowder.[2] However, as these would normally be well guarded or protected with fireproof materials, at least in cities or long-term camps, other targets would frequently have to be chosen, even purely symbolic ones such as palaces if the objective were more psychological than destructive. Since oil lamps and torches were the only means of providing light, ignition sources would always be ready to hand if a brief period of visibility could be braved. Of course, oil-soaked materials and glowing embers might be carried, albeit less conveniently and with far greater risk of premature detection.

Although Sun-tzu's *Art of War* speaks about internally originated blazes and employing agents, they always remain separate, the specter of agents employing incendiary techniques for sabotage purposes never being explicitly raised. Thus, despite great fear of them from Mo-tzu onward,[3] the

FIGURE 5.1 *Incendiary Thief*
*(Wu-ching Tsung-yao)*

earliest description of "incendiary agents," saboteurs specifically tasked with employing arson against enemy encampments, appears in the *T'ai-pai Yin-ching* under the rubric of "Huo Tao" or "Incendiary Thief": "Pick a man who is courageous and nimble, whose speech and clothes are the same as the enemy. After filching their password, he should be dispatched to sneak into the enemy's encampment bearing fire and burn their stores and provisions. When the fire starts, he can exploit the confusion to get out."[4] Succinct yet complete, this passage was incorporated into numerous theoretical writings over the succeeding centuries, appearing as late as 850 years later in the *Teng-t'an Pi-chiu* which merely adds that an attack should then be mounted.[5]

The *Ts'ao-lü Ching-lüeh* chapter entitled "Internal Response" is the only military writing in which subversives are introduced into a city specifically for the purpose of starting fires even though the imposition of strict controls to prevent traitors from setting them as a signal or to create confusion had long been advocated. The manual advises that rather than resorting to common, easily balked techniques, commanders should "select clever, skilled warriors who are strong enough to oppose a hundred men, have them pretend to be merchants or traders and enter the city long before any action develops. Then, when your soldiers reach the city walls, they can respond by burning the peoples' dwellings in the middle of the night. When the flames illuminate the entire area, they should falsely yell out that the enemy has penetrated the city. The people and soldiers will be totally confused and you can exploit the opportunity to achieve your objective."

Plots which relied upon setting such highly visible targets as palaces or warehouses afire to signal the initiation of an external attack were not only numerous, but also facilitated city seizures by stirring confusion or igniting blazes which grew out of control. A small contingent of men often proved adequate to overwhelm any defenders assigned to the gates or drop ropes over the side of the newly deserted walls. Many plots also proved unsuccessful, were discovered, or betrayed before they could be implemented, such as in A.D. 195 when, amidst rampant internal strife, subversives within the camp set fire to a number of huts. However, the fires failed to catch and lacking the necessary internal chaos, the conjoined external attack failed.[6]

Nevertheless, being the only means other than assassination a single man might have to affect a situation, the disaffected frequently resorted to arson. In consequence, internal fires came to be an integral part of aggressive ruses. For example, in A.D. 303 Li Hsiung, a popular rebel leader, manipulated Luo Shang into attacking the secondary city of P'i by starting a large fire inside the city as an ostensible signal and then, when Luo's army attacked the city in response, striking them with a concealed force to score a clear victory.[7]

## ASSAULT DEVICES

A variety of assault devices, several incendiary based, were also developed over the centuries to overcome the advantages

FIGURE 5.2    *Basic Incendiary Cart (Wu-ching Tsung-yao)*

enjoyed by defenders ensconced behind formidable walls and broad, deep moats.[8] Arching projectiles, primarily stones, hurled by trebuchets and arrows from a wide range of bows, crossbows, and arcuballistae (oversized crossbows) could easily overfly such obstacles, but siege engines and other equipment which required proximity to the walls had to be transported across external ditches and moats, whether by filling them in, bridging them, or utilizing rafts.

In its earliest form, the "*huo ch'e*" or "incendiary cart"— simply a cart or wagon preloaded with faggots or dry brush that might be set afire just before being wheeled into position—both simplified and expedited the quantitative delivery of ignition materials onto a target, thereby minimizing the soldiers' exposure to enemy weapons while increasing their chances of success. Somewhat more advanced forms intermixed accelerants such as oil or lard to significantly raise the temperature and ensure the target's ignition. However, as

FIGURE 5.3    *Fire Oil Cart (Wu-ching Tsung-yao)*

most could be thwarted by soaking with water, whether by simply pouring large quantities downward or dropping water sacks which broke across them, even more complex versions soon developed.

The most ingenious incendiary cart, employed from the Sung onward, combined the buoyant properties of oil, a strong incendiary source, and unknowing enemy complicity to disperse flames all about the vehicle.[9] As described in several military compendia, its core was a cauldron of bubbling oil and lard overlaid, even intermixed, with vines or rushes so that the oil would not be immediately apparent.[10] Heated to the boiling point by a fire encased in the cart's lower portion, the entire unit was disguised as a simple incendiary assault vehicle by placing faggots all around it, as shown in the illustration. Once pushed into position against the gate or tower, rather than extinguishing the blaze any water dumped upon it would cause the volatile oil to splash out of the cauldron onto the nearby walls and gate, as well as probably creep along the walls and float underneath the door leaves, swiftly spreading the fire to the enemy's surprise and consternation.

As described by T'ang Shun, another form of *huo ch'e* found in the Ming derived its lethal power from the noxious gasses it emanated rather than its incendiary potential, though the latter was not completely absent since anyone who came into contact with the burning wagon would certainly be wounded. Drawn by horses or oxen, it would be directed into the enemy's encampment just like the early fire oxen, with "everyone who inhaled the smoke losing their lives without knowing how they ended."[11]

## ANIMAL DELIVERY SYSTEMS

Animal delivery systems constitute a primitive form of automated strike falling somewhere between soldiers directly attacking the enemy and utilizing missile fire at a distance. The first employment of animals for incendiary warfare purposes has traditionally been attributed to T'ien Tan, who ingeniously exploited a large number of "fire oxen" at the epochal battle of Chi-mo.[12] Decades earlier, in 333 B.C., the eastern state of Ch'i had exploited Yen's mourning to invade and seize some ten cities. Although they were eventually returned, the affront continued to rankle. However, two decades later civil war caused such disaffection among Yen's populace that they refused to defend the state, allowing King Min of Ch'i to occupy it in 314 B.C. Persuaded not to annex it, in 312 B.C. King Min supported the ascension of King Chao, who immediately committed himself to the task of reviving his vanquished state. Assiduously cultivating his Virtue in the prescribed fashion, he nurtured the people, sought out talented men, revitalized the military, and adroitly avoided conflict with other states. Finally, prompted by King Min's arrogance and recent conquest of Sung, King Chao embarked upon a campaign intended to punish Ch'i for its predatory behavior.

Having recently defeated armies from Ch'u and the Three Chin, attacked Ch'in, destroyed Sung, and aided Chao in extinguishing Chung-shan, Ch'i's power and territory were unsurpassed. Yen therefore cobbled together an allied force consisting of the states of Han, Wei, Chao, and Ch'in and invaded Ch'i in 285 B.C. with Yüeh Yi as commander in chief. The coalition was disbanded shortly after they severely defeated Ch'i's forces west of the Chi River, though Yen's armies continued to sweep through the countryside, seize the capital, subjugate several cities, and persuade others to voluntarily submit, all within six months. However, despite King Min having been slain, two Ch'i cities resolutely resisted demands to surrender and Yüeh Yi's tempting promises of leniency.

Unwilling to needlessly incur heavy casualties, Yüeh Yi undertook a virtually interminable siege. However, detractors back in Yen assailed his failure to swiftly reduce the remaining cities and accused him of wanting to prolong his authority or even become king of Ch'i. Since King Chao perspicaciously disbelieved these slanders, the siege continued for nearly five years. However, when King Chao died in 279, T'ien Tan, who had been named commander at Chi-mo by popular acclaim, exploited the new monarch's flaws and inexperience to sow discord by employing double agents who successfully reiterated the same accusations, resulting in Yüeh's replacement by Ch'i Chieh.

T'ien Tan then embarked on a multi-stage effort to simultaneously undermine the enemy's will and rebuild the defenders' spirit. First he created an "auspicious omen" by having food left out in the courtyards whenever the people offered sacrifice, thereby attracting flocks of birds, a phenomenon which puzzled Yen's soldiers. Second, he imparted a transcendent veracity to his measures by pretending to receive spiritual instruction. Third, correctly anticipating it would make his troops resolute, he ruthlessly sacrificed the well-being of prisoners held in Yen's camp by volubly worrying that Ch'i's spirit would be adversely affected if their noses were cut off. Fourth, he had double agents bemoan the severe consternation they would suffer if the outer graves were exhumed, thereby tricking Yen into enraging the populace when they burned the corpses. Next, his family led in the fortification work, he personally feasted his officers, and he nurtured Yen's overconfidence by concealing the able-bodied, visibly displaying only the weak and wounded. Finally, T'ien Tan not only exploited the antique ruse of a false surrender to induce laxity, but further augmented its effectiveness by bribing Yen's generals.

As recorded in his *Shih Chi* biography, T'ien Tan then implemented his famous unorthodox measures:

> T'ien Tan herded the thousand cattle within the city together and had them covered with red silken cloth decorated with five-colored dragon veins. Naked blades were tied to their horns and reeds soaked in fat bound to their tails. They then chiseled dozens of holes in the walls and that night ignited the reeds, releasing the cattle through them. Five thousand stalwart soldiers followed in the rear. When their tails got hot, the cattle angrily raced into Yen's army.
>
> Being the middle of the night, Yen's troops were astonished. The brightness from the burning torches on the cattle tails was dazzling. Everywhere Yen's soldiers looked there were dragon veins, everyone the cattle collided with died or was wounded.

Accompanied by a great drumming and clamor from within the city, 5,000 men with gagged mouths exploited the confusion to suddenly attack. The old and weak all made their bronze implements resound by striking them, the tumult moved Heaven and Earth. Terrified, Yen's army fled in defeat. Thus, through psychological operations, unorthodox tactics, and a touch of fire, just 7,000 exhausted soldiers and another 10,000 inhabitants trapped in Chi-mo defied a siege force of perhaps 100,000. Thereafter, aided by uprisings in the occupied cities, Ch'i's reinvigorated armies quickly drove Yen's disorganized forces out beyond the borders, allowing Ch'i to reclaim its position, however weakened and tarnished, among the extant states.

This episode has long stirred the popular imagination and been justly considered the epitome of imaginative command,

*FIGURE 5.4    Traditional Fire Ox (Wu-ching Tsung-yao)*

accounting for its inclusion among the *Thirty-six Strategies*.[13] However, it merits far less acclaim for initiating the use of animals as delivery vehicles because it was neither their first such employment nor one with an incendiary intention. Unlike true fire oxen carrying flammables to set enemy encampments ablaze, fire served simply to enrage and panic the animals, identical in effect to pricking them with lances. The oxen merely constituted a shock element, four-footed tanks intended to forcefully penetrate Yen's siege lines and sow the confusion needed for Ch'i's forces to break out and mount an assault, any fires ignited in Yen's camp being merely ancillary. Nevertheless, their breakout was ever after remembered as an "incendiary assault" and immediately called to mind whenever besieged forces required desperate measures.

The first recorded use of fire to provoke animals into a directed rampage actually dates back to 506 B.C. when Wu successfully invaded Ch'u after decades of having survived their onslaughts through adroit battlefield measures.[14] In a rolling campaign presumably reflecting Sun-tzu's teachings and influence, Wu's forces won several successive battles and eventually occupied Ch'u's capital of Ying. Just after crossing the Sui River during his flight, the king of Ch'u resorted to stampeding several elephants into Wu's pursuing forces, whether by tying firebrands to their tails or using torches to enrage them.[15] Although no details have survived, the tactic proved sufficiently disruptive for the king to escape.

Fifteen and a half centuries after Chi-mo, the Sung commander Wang K'uei employed fire oxen in A.D. 1241 to break out of a Mongol encirclement at Han-chou.[16] Just prior to the incident, aided by the defection of a Sung lieutenant general who opened the city gates for them, Mongolian forces had subjugated Ch'eng-tu and captured the commander, Ch'en Lung-chih. They then tried to compel Ch'en to persuade his subordinate Wang K'uei to surrender Han-chou only to be balked when Ch'en instead called upon Wang to be resolute. Wang sent forth 3,000 troops in response but found himself trapped in Han-chou when they were annihilated in a pitched battle. He therefore resorted to fire oxen to effect a midnight escape, though Han-chou fell immediately after his departure and the populace was slaughtered before the Mongolian forces moved on to reduce an additional twenty cities.

Stampeding fire oxen were not invariably successful. For example, in A.D. 1047, Wang Tse, whose mother had earlier tattooed the character for good fortune on his back, led a Buddhist messianic splinter group in a revolt against the Sung. Initially successful through seizing armories, releasing prisoners, and generally attracting the disaffected, Wang eventually found himself besieged at Pei-chou by Sung troops. Although he managed to thwart Sung attempts to erect mounds capped with overlook towers by burning the latter, he also suffered a betrayal which required them to repulse a night incursion after his own towers were burnt.

Finally, 200 Sung soldiers managed to penetrate the city through a tunnel dug from the south and overwhelm a portion of the defenders, clearing the way for troops to ascend the walls. Confronting them within the city, Wang attempted to employ fire oxen to spearhead a counterattack, but the Sung troops merely stabbed the animals in the nose with long lances—hardly an easy feat—causing them to run back into the rebel army, which panicked and crumbled. Although Wang and a small band escaped, they were subsequently trapped and burned to death in village huts, ending his charismatic career.[17]

A slightly different but subsequently famous example of provoking animals with burning rags affixed to their tails unfolded in the Later Han around A.D. 180 when Yang Hsüan, Grand Protector of Ling-ling, attempted to suppress heavy rebel activity with badly inadequate forces.[18] Yang's solution was to load several tens of wagons with sacks of lime and mount automatic crossbows on others. Then, deploying them into a fighting formation, he exploited the wind to engulf the enemy with clouds of lime dust, blinding them, before setting rags on the tails of the horses pulling these driverless artillery wagons alight. Directed into the enemy's heavily obscured formation, their repeating crossbows (powered by linkage with the wheels) fired repeatedly in random directions, inflicting heavy casualties. Amidst the obviously great confusion the rebels fired back furiously in self-defense, decimating each other before Yang's forces came up and largely exterminated them.

In A.D. 1115, imaginatively employing an animal delivery system to ignite fires and stir confusion allowed Chao Yü's 30,000 Sung troops to suppress a much stronger minority people's rebel force under Pu Lou in Szechuan. After having achieved significant victories amidst several defeats, Pu's adherents—nominally 100,000 if various local subtribes are included—had been thwarted in their attempt to proceed north across the Yangtze River and were now solidly ensconced atop a several thousand foot high mountain. Extensively fortified with rock walls and ringed with wooden palisades, the rebel's defenses easily withstood repeated government attempts to break through. Moreover, the frustrated

Sung forces sustained heavy casualties on a daily basis as the rebels viciously rained arrows and stones down upon them even as their own crossbows remained largely ineffective and out of range. However, Sung reconnaissance units discovered a steep, unguarded cliff to the rear that could provide tortured access to the mountaintop.

In order to fully exploit this avenue of approach, Chao mounted a special operation that began by having local guides catch several dozen monkeys.[19] While the main force prominently engaged in a vice-like holding action to the fore, a special force of 2,000 men mounted a nighttime operation spearheaded by climbers who dropped rope ladders down the cliff once they completed the ascent. After the main body successfully negotiated the mountain, they cut openings in the defensive system and released the monkeys to whose backs (or perhaps wrapped around their bodies) had been tied hemp cloth soaked with grease and wax which was set afire. In great pain, the screeching monkeys raced wildly about the mountainside, igniting many of the bamboo and reed huts within the encampment.

Suddenly awakened in the indistinct predawn light, the equally terrified rebels attempted to extinguish the fires and catch the monkeys, augmenting the confusion. The 2,000 elite Sung troops atop the mountain then exploited the noise and chaos to breach the now undefended palisades and strike. Down at the base, Chao Yu unleashed a coordinated attack that employed flying cloud ladders to surmount the previously impenetrable walls. Converging, the two forces quickly overwhelmed the rebels, many of whom perished in the fires or fell off the cliffs, before mopping up the remnant forces.

As unlikely as it might seem, chickens were also employed to set fires amid enemy camps. In a widely cited incident, about A.D. 353 Chiang Yu was deputed by the Chin dynasty to suppress a rebellion being mounted by a previously surrendered Ch'iang chieftain, Yao Hsiang, who had been provoked by government actions into reasserting his independence.[20] Finding Yao's forces well protected by solid stockades while his own forces were badly outnumbered,

Chiang decided to defeat the enemy through artifice rather than mount the futile, direct assault that had been ordered. He therefore had several hundred chickens collected before affixing fire brands or small containers of burning embers to their feet with long cords and scaring them into flying off toward the enemy's encampment. The hot embers ignited fires wherever they alighted, allowing Chiang to attack the camp and score a minor victory.

## THEORETICAL TEXTS AND CONSIDERATIONS

Large, stampeding animals employed for their disruptive effects, including the elephants used in Szechuan, often proved problematic because their panicked behavior was uncontrollable. Except in the case of livestock kept with the army for transport or food purposes, domestic animals would have to be locally confiscated and wild ones, such as monkeys, caught before any action could be taken. They might maintain their original orientation and rush into the enemy's camp, but might erratically turn back upon the troops tormenting them if wounded or terrified by enemy weapons. Delivery methods that could take advantage of normal behavior (such as birds returning to roost) and be more predictable, even if not fully controllable, obviously held appeal and therefore began to appear.

As already noted, the T'ang dynasty *T'ai-pai Yin-ching* contains the first discussion and depictions of "animal delivery systems," though they were incorporated into many subsequent military writings.[21] For large animals, Li advised employing gourds, no doubt because of their reasonably large carrying capacity:[22] "Stuff burning moxa into gourds, make four holes, then tie them to the necks of wild pigs or deer. Singe their tails and release them toward the enemy's encampment, causing them to race into the grass there. When the gourds break, fires will start." Although Li's manual doesn't include horses or fire oxen, later manuals frequently reintroduce them, though not always without appending some derisive comment about them being "antique."

For example, the *Wu-ching Tsung-yao,* while incorporating Li's descriptions, places gourds upon the animals' heads, illustrating the method with a horse.[23] Fire oxen also reappear from time to time, such as in the comprehensive *Wu-ching Tsung-yao,* though clearly specified as a shock weapon employed for their disruptive effects despite being included in a chapter entitled "Incendiary Attack."[24] (Attaching spears to the sides and firebrands to the tails in the traditional fashion ensures the generation of exploitable confusion.) Many manuals also acknowledge that even larger animals, such as elephants, were similarly employed in antiquity.

According to the *T'ai-pai Yin-ching,* smaller tinderboxes are required for birds, even large game birds:[25] "Empty out walnuts and make two holes in them. Fill them with burning moxa and tie them to the feet of wild chickens. Prick their tails and release them so that when they fly into the grass and the walnuts split open, fires will start." For sparrows (or chickadees), the smallest delivery vehicle, even more limited tinderboxes had to be created, though their normal behavior could be exploited as part of a concerted attack on fortified cities:[26] "Hollow out apricot (cores), stuff them with burning moxa, and tie them to the feet of birds. Toward dusk, release a flock of them so that they will fly into the city to roost for the night. Fires will shortly break out in the huts wherever they congregate." In such cases numbers compensate for the limited amount of ignition material that can be conveyed.

Despite all the advances that occurred in gunpowder weaponry over the intervening centuries, even such late Ming-dynasty military compendia as the *Teng-t'an Pi-chiu* and *Wu-pei Chih,* but not the *Wu Pien,* contain illustrated discussions of animal delivery systems. The *Teng-t'an Pi-chiu's* section on "Attacking Cities" includes five incendiary-based methods, all drawn from earlier texts but with slightly different explanations, presumably the product of additional experience. "Fire birds" employ walnuts as the fire carrier by affixing them to their necks rather than feet, a method reserved for sparrows and similar small, flocking birds. Local birds (specifically chickens but presumably others would

FIGURE 5.5    *Fire Bird (Wu-ching Tsung-yao)*

suffice) have to be caught and then their tails pricked so that they race into the grass near the enemy where the walnuts will ignite fires upon breaking open. The small bird variant requires capturing hundreds of birds from the enemy's city and warehouses and attaching almonds to their feet.[27] As in the *T'ai-pai Yin-ching,* they are expected to fly back into the fortress where their incendiary packages will set roofs and provisions afire after alighting.[28] (Surprisingly, in neither case are the attackers advised to exploit the fires.)

Of the other three attack methods found in the *Teng-t'an Pi-chiu,* only one is actually an automated, incendiary delivery system. A gourd filled with burning moxa is affixed atop the head of a locally caught wild horse or other large animal which is then oriented to run into the grass near the enemy's encampment. More humane since the horse should escape unharmed once the gourd falls off, the usual negatives still apply: the animals have to be caught and their orientation maintained. Unlike fire oxen, no weapons are attached—allowing enemy soldiers to more easily snare the animal—nor is the ensuing confusion exploited. However, the fire oxen, which have spears attached to both sides, are really automated weapons' delivery systems triggered in the usual fashion by burning cloths wrapped around their tails. They are utilized solely to stir confusion as they race about enemy formations or encampments, any wounds inflicted being of secondary importance, though still a valuable contribution to the overall effort of slaying the enemy.[29]

The final compendium of import for traditional incendiary technology is the massive *Wu-pei Chih*. Although compiled within decades of the *Teng-t'an Pi-chiu* some interesting variations are noticeable in the few automated delivery systems. First, while spears and other blades are still attached to the animal's sides, the fire ox's lethality is significantly augmented by securing a three-layer, pyramid-shaped explosive to the animal's back whose fuse would be lit at the same time as the fire brands on the tail.

Two modes of attack are suggested, one premised upon concealing the explosive package with a cloth cover that maintains the animal's overall outline, thereby facilitating its stealthy nighttime introduction into enemy camps. The other simply orients the animal to rush into enemy field deployments, a more easily achieved technique.[30] Even though the incendiary and consternation effects were primary, the explosive would of course detonate and the ox perish. However, another variant mounted a large explosive bomb on the ox's back and boldly employed it as a brutal, automated bomb-delivery system though with the usual side spears affixed to prevent it being easily intercepted. Not surprisingly, it was to be employed when badly outnumbered.[31]

Fire birds also assume extremized, final form in the *Wu-pei Chih* with two artificial birds designed to float into enemy cities and encampments. Melding kite experience and explosives technology, they were produced in two dramatically different sizes. The smallest, probably about as large as a Western pigeon, were simply small spheres with wings intended to be launched into cities where they would burst, spraying a small quantity of burning material onto troops and structures, as well as blinding them with smoke.[32] However,

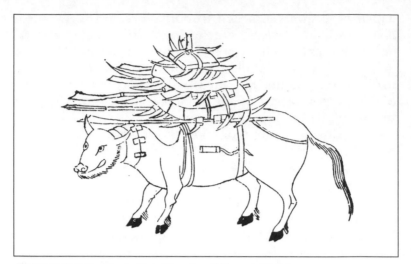

FIGURE 5.6   *Exploding Fire Ox (Wu-pei Chih)*

they might also be used against troop deployments, the range being limited only by the strength of the wind (and length of their fuses).

The second, called a "spiritual fire flying duck," was considerably larger and depended upon four rockets mounted beneath the wings, two to a side, for lift. The bird's core was an explosive sphere fashioned into an appropriately elongated shape that would detonate while over the enemy's encampment with a brilliant flash, igniting fires. Said to have a range of over 1,000 *chang* (800 Western feet), it was considered invincible in riverine conflict because it could easily set enemy boats (and no doubt bamboo sails) afire.[33] Whether it was ever fabricated and deployed requires further research, for it is an odd contraption more expressive of simplistic thinking—flight means wings, therefore imitate birds—than weapons development, especially since rockets and large rocket-powered incendiary arrows already existed.

The *Wu-pei Chih* also describes a unique weapon, one which fancifully exploits the fire animal tradition by constructing a dummy cavalry rider around a complex gunpowder arrow launcher, mounting him on a horse, and then lighting the fuse before sending him off into an enemy field deployment or encampment by igniting firebrands on the tail (as illustrated). Approximately human size, the rider imitated the envisioned appearance of a minor deity or spirit so that when the device triggered, it would terrify the soldiers. Multi-colored smoke was generated by an incendiary device suspended underneath the horse; layer by layer, down through all seventeen layers, 105 arrows were explosively fired in all directions from out of the dummy; and another three arrows were similarly ejected.

Although real horses are not so easily constrained, poles affixed to the horse's side and head supposedly kept them from turning away from their initial orientation. A non-flammable saddlecloth was used even though the animal would eventually perish and the cosmological correlates were enhanced with appropriate decorations. Apart from the core explosive which powered the arrows, a large watermelon-shaped bomb was encased at the bottom to further stun and blind the enemy. The eyes and mouth even emitted small pebbles, while the core had a mixture of "spirit fire" and pebbles in addition to the spiritual arrows. Thus, it was a self-powered offensive weapon with the character of a doomsday device, a clever precursor of twenty-first-century suicide bombers.

The animal motifs used to decorate weapons and other implements of war seen as early as the fierce visages on Shang dynasty shields, while often entailing magical aspects, were primarily intended to exploit normal emotional reaction to their fierceness and sudden appearance. Conversely, paint and color were also used to enhance otherworldly images just as in T'ien Tan's employment. These practices found particularly vivid expression on the early devices created for incendiary attack and defense, such as the individual shields which concealed hand-held incendiary weapons effective out to twenty to thirty feet,[34] the so-called "fire dragon" (which looks more like a lion with wings) mounted on a cart,[35] and various "wooden fire animals," life-size or larger animals mounted on wheels for pushing by one or more soldiers

FIGURE 5.7 *Exploding Wooden Cavalryman (Wu-pei Chih)*

whose firepower derived from eruptors and flame throwers mounted on the front and along the sides.[36] Although lions, tigers, and other predatory animals could all be used, dragons were especially popular. Within its body one "fire dragon" concealed twenty-four tubes designed to emit a variety of noxious smokes, gasses, and flames from its mouth while a number of lethal blades projected out from the front. Pushed by four men, it was intended to penetrate even the strongest enemy deployment.

## ACTION AT A DISTANCE

Incendiary arrows, normally termed "huo chien" but occasionally "huo shih," without doubt being the earliest means of setting fires at a distance, almost certainly originated from simply wrapping rags soaked in a fuel such as lard or sesame oil to ensure a hot fire on target and preclude being extinguished by the rapid rush of wind during acceleration and flight.[37] Thereafter, their sizes and shapes multiplied over the centuries with the evolution of the arrow itself, the development of powerful crossbows in the Warring States period, and then huge arcuballistae capable of firing multiple and oversized bolts several hundred paces before the Sung.[38] In addition to specialized incendiary versions, several basic arrow types were noted as capable of having incendiaries attached near or at the tip, especially once gunpowder mixtures dramatically increased the potency of even the small quantity of igniter which might be affixed, the only limitation being that they had to "accord with the bow's power."[39] However, the effects on flight characteristics and increased difficulty of the archer's already arduous task were largely ignored.

Over the centuries some basic operational principles were deduced and it was realized that the arrows had to strike something relatively flammable to ensure igniting a fire before they sputtered out. Moreover, they had to impale relatively inaccessible surfaces to prevent being immediately pulled out or extinguished with the sand or water kept ready for such purposes. Heat, low humidity, and the presence of dense, dry vegetation were regarded as requisite facilitating factors, but most important of all was the presence of a moderate wind to amplify their efforts. Finally, although single arrows might strike an opportune target, mass volleys had a far greater chance of succeeding, if only because they would require more extensive and frantic efforts to extinguish.

Prior to the T'ang their effectiveness was well realized by numerous commanders such as Tuan Shao who, in the ongoing conflict between Northern Ch'i and Northern Chou, had been dispatched with a moderate Ch'i force to the western border to repel a Chou incursion in A.D. 571.[40] The Chou forces ensconced themselves in Po-ku-ch'eng, a well-fortified city protected by stone walls located high up within a precipitous gorge.[41] The city presented such a formidable target that Ch'i's subcommanders were reluctant to attack, but Tuan Shao cajoled them into action by noting that since Ch'i already controlled the northern region, expelling their enemies from this border area was vital. Moreover, because the city it-self was quite narrow (as might be expected within the con-fines of a gorge), it was completely vulnerable to attack by incendiary arrows and therefore could quickly be destroyed.

Ch'i prevailed by implementing this tactic with crossbows, though only temporarily as major attacks resumed the next year and Ch'i itself was eventually vanquished. However, by including the clash in his T'ang dynasty *T'ung Tien* selec-tions, Tu Yu reminded commanders that however daunting the citadel, unless it is unusually broad and expansive (and well protected by appropriate preventative measures), incen-diary arrows alone would be sufficient to destroy it. There-after, it continued to be included in many military compendia, including the Ming dynasty *Wu Pien*, in various forms.[42]

According to the *T'ai-pai Yin-ching*, by the T'ang, incendi-ary arrows had advanced to using gourds affixed to near the tip filled with burning materials. According to the instructions for fire arrows,[43] the commander should "select archers capable of shooting three hundred paces and cap the ends of arrows with gourds filled with fire. Employ several hundred of them, wait-ing until the middle of the night to shoot them en masse into the enemy's encampment to burn their stores and provisions. When the fires arise and their army is in chaos, exploit the opportunity to fervently attack."[44] Just a few decades later the *T'ung Tien* would refer to them as "incendiary crossbows" and require that crossbows with strong arms capable of shooting the requisite 300 paces be employed, thereby shifting the bur-den from the simple strength of stalwart archers to mechanical advantage. Moreover, it specified that piles of fodder and straw within the encampment be targeted, though the standard admonition to exploit any ensuing chaos has dropped out.[45] By the turn of the millennium powerful crossbows capable of simultaneously firing one heavy incendiary arrow accompanied by six lighter versions, causing immense destruction, even appeared.[46]

The invention of gunpowder with comparatively low salt-peter composition (allowing it to burn hot without being explosive and thus ideally suited for incendiary devices) increased the effectiveness of incendiary arrows. However, centuries before their appearance in the Sung a hybrid delivery method had been developed employing distinct stages and discrete components to initially disperse a flammable medium onto the target and then ignite it, ensuring a high temperature and maximum duration of exposure. According to the instructions which first appeared in the *T'ai-pai Yin-ching* but continued to be copied for centuries: "Take small gourds full of oil, affix them to the tips of arrows, and shoot them onto the roofs of towers and turrets. After the gourds break and the oil disperses, use flaming arrows to hit the dispersed oil. As soon as fires are ignited, continue shooting gourds of oil. The towers and turrets will be completely incinerated."[47]

After noting that incendiary measures can be used to flush out ambushes and break enemy assault formations, in the mid-sixteenth century T'ang Shun suggested another use for incendiary arrows.[48] When the enemy is ensconced in a citadel, they can be employed during nighttime hours to determine their "vacuity and substance" (in Sun-tzu's terminology). Thereafter, other incendiary devices can be employed to wreck havoc and volleys from archers and crossbowmen firing from the concealment of darkness at the many suddenly illuminated targets exploited to cause chaos and no doubt inflict numerous casualties.

Even at the end of the Ming, when cannon were displacing trebuchet-hurled explosive and incendiary bombs, both historical accounts and theoretical writings indicate that incendiary arrows—being the easiest, most convenient, and therefore most common means of assaulting cities and camps—were still being employed in massive numbers on both land and water. As late as 1599, in essentially repeating sentiments already voiced in the *Wu-ching Tsung-yao* at the turn of the millennium, Wang Ming-ho wrote, "use incendiary catapults, incendiary arrows, and incendiary animals to burn supplies and provisions within the city."[49]

In introducing his material on incendiary arrows in the *Wu-pei Chih*, Mao Yüan-yi claimed that they were still equally advantageous for both riverine and land warfare, and that their effectiveness was no less than tubed weapons (by which he meant cannon and eruptors).[50] Nevertheless, he concluded that because his contemporaries weren't manufacturing or employing them properly, they rarely realized their unique advantages. However, the incendiary arrows depicted in the *Wu-pei Chih* are not simply antique versions with flaming tips, but two new forms instead.

The first consists of a traditional arrow to which has been added, either by affixing or integral molding, any of a number of incendiary devices ranging from ancient forms to tubes and bomblets fully exploiting all the advances in gunpowder and incendiary formulas. The second has a rocket tube attached, whether near the head or the feathers, to provide a "jet assist" through the expulsion of hot gasses. Naturally this allows longer and heavier arrows and more dramatic, often oversized heads in a variety of shapes, several even imitating traditional weapons such as cutters, axes, and halberds rather than the usual metallic arrowhead. While somewhat amusing in appearance, these hybrid arrows easily doubled the range of the strongest crossbows (as well as those employed in oversized arcuballistae), and were reportedly capable of instantly killing a horse or several men, penetrating the strongest armor, and piercing the walls of wooden superstructures, all at the surprising distance of 500 paces or more, striking terror into the enemy.[51]

Upon impaling, rockets attached near the tip would have a collateral incendiary effect through the intense heat applied in close proximity to the target. They could therefore be employed against wooden structures, provisions, and boats, though in riverine combat they would ineffectively pass right through the sails unless the latter were fabricated from thicker, interwoven bamboo strips.

What might be termed hybrid or compound incendiary arrows represent a melding of these two concepts. Rockets affixed to the bottom near the feathers provided additional propulsion, the tube attached to the upper portion of the shaft being either explosive or incendiary. Bamboo and simi-

*FIGURE 5.8    Incendiary Arrow (generic)*

lar materials were used for the shafts and multiple launchers
concocted in a variety of forms that were capable of carrying
and firing anywhere from ten to sixty such devices. (Ordinary
arrows fired out of launchers using explosive power should be
distinguished from those employing propulsive assist.) Incendiary rockets were particularly appropriate for riverine warfare, being the only method available for striking the enemy's
vessels before they could close for combat or undertake amphibious landings.[52]

A small warhead could also be attached to a crossbow arrow in essentially antique fashion so that when the arrowhead
impaled the target, the incendiary device burst and burned.[53]
Used against men, horses, and sails, the small explosive employed a powerful mixture which water could not easily extinguish. It and the "whip arrow" were still being employed
in the Ming against materials being transported to fill in
ditches and moats during siege efforts.[54]

## HURLED INCENDIARY BOMBS

Trebuchet of the type illustrated in the accompanying diagram from the Sung dynasty *Wu-ching Tsung-yao* may well
date back to Mo-tzu's era even though the only references to
"throwing devices" appear in Sun Pin's recently rediscovered
classic. Originally they hurled stones, then noxious items and
containerized substances, and finally, with the development
of incendiary warfare, also pots of burning oil, naptha, and
eventually pre-explosive incendiary devices based upon early
gunpowder mixtures. A trebuchet mentioned in the *T'ai-pai
Yin-ching*, termed a *pao ch'e*, has the so-called fire signifier

(rather than wood or stone) in the first character *(pao)* of its name, possibly implying incendiaries were being hurled, but no definitive conclusions may be drawn.[55] The *Wu-ching Tsung-yao* describes an incendiary ball which employs caltrop-type points to ensure sticking to its intended target and could be dropped over the walls in defense, but was also hurled both by attackers and defenders.[56]

As the result of indigenous development over the centuries and even input from Persia during the Mongol attacks upon the Sung, field-deployed trebuchet naturally grew larger and more unwieldy. The Ming dynasty *Teng-t'an Pi-chiu* includes an illustration for a "well sweep" type hand pulled by 100 men said to be capable of hurling 25 *chin* stones over eighty paces. More importantly, it is the only one specified for hurling "incendiary balls, incendiary chickens, incendiary lances, and loose star stones" over the reduced range of sixty paces.[57]

Similar to the *Wu-ching Tsung-yao*, the *Wu Pien* describes a "fire sphere" which incorporates poison so that despite crashing to the ground and breaking open it continues to burn and emit poisonous smoke. Surprisingly, it was felt to be particularly effective for attacking and burning ships.[58] Of course, virtually all explosives had ancillary but inescapable incendiary effects.

## SPECIAL OPERATIONS

Just as discussed in the theoretical manuals, special operation by small numbers, usually at night, often achieved dramatic effects through incendiary measures. Numerous examples from over the centuries, some reprised here, may be found in which generals obviously failed to learn the lessons of history and therefore neglected their defenses, growing even more lax as darkness descended. For example, in the Later Han, Ma Yüan surprised the Hsien-ling Ch'iang,[59] and later Mujung Hui's vast force was badly defeated.[60] Once, an attack by raiders on the enemy's provisions coupled with the sinking of their boats on the nearby river so dispirited them that they simply surrendered.[61]

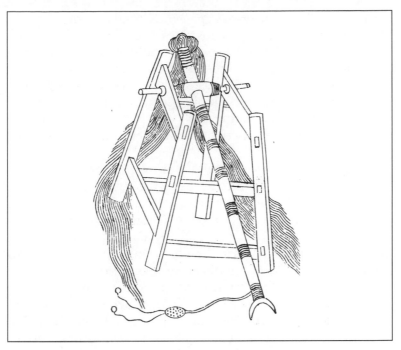

FIGURE 5.9    *Sung Trebuchet (Wu-ching Tsung-yao)*

During the revolutionary strife that saw Northern Wei oust Later Yen, forces totaling some 400,000 moved against the latter's towns and strongpoints, reducing all but three of them in quick succession.[62] However, in the second month of 397 internal strife in Wei and the defection of important commanders provided Later Yen's ruler Mu-jung Pao with an opportunity to strike the campaign force then moving back to their capital. He therefore ensconced his 120,000 infantry and 37,000 cavalry on the north bank of the Hu-t'uo River in Hopei to await them. Northern Wei's forces, although greatly reduced after having deputed several armies to collateral actions, were still more numerous when they encamped on the south bank of this minor river.

Mu-jung Pao mounted a nighttime incendiary operation employing the 10,000 brigands and villains he had recruited with the spoils of war. Despite their proximity, in the strong north wind the surprise was apparently total and the incendiaries caused widespread chaos. However, just when victory seemed assured, the attackers inexplicably commenced fighting among themselves, even killing each other, perhaps over the potential rewards. The astonished Northern Wei commander managed to regroup his disordered forces and attack the raiders, quickly clearing the camp before turning to the massive army that had crossed the river and deployed just outside.

A single thrust easily threw them into chaos and surprisingly compelled their retreat. Subsequent assaults on Mujung Pao's still numerous troops as they strove to gain the security of their distant bastion at Chung-shan equally produced victory. Not only had Later Yen's spirit been broken, the weather was also brutally cold, causing the troops to freeze to death in great numbers. Pao therefore jettisoned the infantry entangling their retreat and sped off with his remaining 20,000 cavalry, but heavy snow hampered them as well. He finally escaped alone after they dumped all their valuables, weapons, and other weighty equipment in a futile effort to improve their maneuverability. Northern Wei forces then turned back to respond to their own internal challenges, though Later Yen's power was ended.

In A.D. 525 Southern Liang besieged Northern Wei's forces at Hsiao-chien near the border to Szechuan and occupied the nearby mountain, where they erected heavy wooden barriers to protect their rear.[63] One night Northern Wei raiders secretly climbed the mountain and set fire to the wooden palisades, resulting in a huge blaze that cut off Liang's retreat. Even though they still enjoyed a superior position and had no need to withdraw, panic ensued which Northern Wei exploited in textbook fashion, inflicting tens of thousands of casualties.

In suppressing rebellious forces, Yang Su undertook the river's reconnaissance by crossing with oiled sacks, then forded at night in force and used unorthodox techniques to burn provisions stored behind the enemy's encampment. He then exploited the terror of the troops who found their retreat cut off with a frontal attack that quickly vanquished them.[64]

One of the strongest and most popular of the people's armies that arose in the chaos marking the end of the Sui was led by Lu Ming-yüeh in the northeast region just outside Peking. Originally active in Shantung, he quickly attracted 100,000 adherents and rapidly expanded his domain. In the twelfth month of A.D. 614, the emperor dispatched Chang Hsü-t'o with a mere 10,000 men to intercept him at Chu-a, where both sides, despite the discrepancy in their numbers, for some ten days assumed fortified positions well protected by wooden palisades. (The Sui armies were better trained and equipped, whereas those in the people's rebellion, depending upon what weapons they may have seized, were essentially a disorganized rabble burdened with numerous accompanying persons.)

To overcome the numerical disadvantage Chang decided to tempt the enemy into abandoning their secure fortifications by conspicuously retreating in the middle of the night, though only after having first secretly deployed two 1,000-man regiments in the nearby reeds. Learning of their apparently clandestine departure, Lu carelessly came forth in pursuit with the bulk of his forces, whereupon Chang's two generals raced to the enemy's encampments, clambered over the walls, overwhelmed the guards, and subdued the confused troops before setting some thirty encampments afire. The smoke was so thick and extensive that it "reached Heaven," and the fire was soon visible to Lu who rushed his troops back to their camps.

However, his forces became completely disorganized in the rapid pursuit and quick reversal, allowing Chang's 8,000 men to turn about and fall upon the rebels now engaged in simultaneously attempting to defeat the Sui raiders and extinguish the fires ravaging their camps. Chang scored a devastating victory as the enemy completely collapsed, though Lu managed to escape with a few hundred picked cavalry. (He even resurged the next autumn, acquiring upwards of 400,000 adherents before finally being defeated and slain by Wang Shih-ch'ung in the first month of 617.)[65] Chang's victory thus stemmed from astutely manipulating the enemy and then undertaking a special incendiary operation to create the chaos necessary for mounting a fervent attack.

In the founding days of the T'ang, the conflict between Li Tzu-t'ung and the nascent dynasty saw a recently absorbed army mount a suppressive campaign which quickly succeeded in taking Tan-yang (Nan-ching) before finally being opposed by Li's forces.[66] Although Li was at first thrown back by a dedicated regiment of resolute fighters, he finally prevailed, compelling the imperial forces to seek refuge in their fortified camps. However, an energetic subcommander named Wang Hsiung-tan disobeyed orders to remain in place by going forth in the usual classic style with gagged mouths to conduct a nighttime incendiary raid with his personal contingent of several hundred men. Just as Wang predicted, Li's overconfidence at having turned defeat into victory had resulted in them neglecting their defenses and failing to erect protective palisades. Exploiting the camp's easy access, Wang's raiders took advantage of the wind to set fires and then score a major victory.

During the chaotic years of the Five Dynasties period, the king of Min's younger brother Wang Yen-cheng frequently criticized his older brother's brutality and perversity, prompting the latter to dispatch two punitive forces totaling some 40,000 men against his bastion, the city of Chien-chou. After deploying to the east and south, they encamped across a stream from the city and soon inflicted a decisive defeat on one of Wang's small secondary forces nearby.

Badly outnumbered, Wang then mounted a desperate nighttime operation, which employed "death-defying" warriors to ford the stream and attack the western encampment. Remarkably, despite their large number—1,000 rather than just a handful—these "incendiary thieves" penetrated the outer fortifications undetected and then exploited the locally strong winds to set the camp afire. In classic fashion, troops positioned back on Chien-chou's city walls immediately set up a great clamor, augmenting the confusion. The king's troops crumbled and their commander was slain.[67] Exploiting the success achieved by his unorthodox measures, Wang proceeded to the enemy's southern encampment, but found the frightened troops had already fled.

Nighttime incendiary raiders didn't proceed just by land, but also infiltrated through amphibious routes and even swam to their targets. In A.D. 907 fifty soldiers with superior swimming ability, camouflaged with twigs, branches, and leaves upon their heads, went down the Yüan River at night to strike an enemy encampment at the confluence with the Yangtze River.[68] Upon reaching their target, they snuck into the camp and set fire to the external wooden defenses, precipitating sufficient chaos for a follow-on attack to achieve decisive victory.

Finally, special incendiary operations invariably undertaken at night by small contingents of troops from cities under siege who raced forth to burn the enemy's siege engines, palisades, and provisions were more common than might be expected. In some cases they simply dropped down over the walls or clandestinely slipped out of a concealed sally port, in others laboriously tunneled out beyond the enemy's position before emerging to wreck havoc. Even when not extensive enough to raise the siege, they could severely disrupt the enemy, weaken them from lack of supplies, and dispirit them, all while evincing their own resolute determination.[69]

## GUNPOWDER-ERA INCENDIARIES

By the late Ming, experienced commanders such as Ch'i Chikuang commonly claimed that gunpowder devices were manifestly superior to traditional weapons. The *Wu-pei Chih* thus contains a lengthy section on incendiary warfare which includes a vastly expanded enumeration of techniques and devices. Our theoretical survey therefore concludes by briefly describing many of these devices, some of which seem quite fanciful and unlikely to have ever been employed in combat. However, the state had vast resources, including martial manufacturing facilities well capable of concretely realizing the most outlandish conception, so no design, however contorted, should ever be rejected because of presumed absurdity.

The exact evolution and appearance of these devices from the Sung onward remains somewhat uncertain despite the seminal work of Joseph Needham and Robin Yates and recent, technically oriented studies based upon cataloging recovered artifacts, primarily iron and bronze cannon, which allow the history of the latter to be seen with increasing clarity.[70] However, more perishable or disposable items, such as eruptors, even though deployed by the thousands in siege defense and attack, being consumed in use lack nontextual vestiges, making it difficult to reconstruct their exact nature and function.

While incorporating numerous previous illustrations, Mao didn't simply reiterate earlier methods and conclusions, but added his own insights, even in the area of equipment. The chapter entitled "Equipment Appropriateness" outlines essential contextual principles:

> For implementing incendiary attacks there are combat devices, assault devices, defensive devices, equipment for land warfare, and equipment for riverine warfare, each and every one of them different. If you employ them appropriately, you will always be victorious.
>
> Combat devices are advantageous when they are light and responsive, for then the soldiers' strength will not wane and their sharp spirit will always be replete.
>
> Assault devices are advantageous when they are subtly skillful, for then the soldiers can flourish their courage and their actions will be extraordinary.
>
> Mines are advantageous when they strike explosively, shatter easily, their flames are fierce, and their smoke intense.
>
> Defensive equipment is advantageous when the projectiles can strike far out in unison, when the gas is expansive and poisonous.
>
> Equipment for land warfare is advantageous when it can be used for both far and near, while the long and short are inter-

mixed. Divide them by type and layer them, segment them according to the deployment's indications.

Incendiary trebuchets, incendiary arrows, fire tubes (cannon), and large bullets are long-range equipment and should be intermixed with such long implements as spears and great knives (sabers).

Fire spears (muskets), fire blades (rocket arrows with knife heads), fire shields, and fire clubs are all implements for close use and are short. They should be intermixed with strong bows and stiff crossbows. Select elite soldiers and train them in methods of deployment. For equipment, one should esteem advantage rather than value weight; for soldiers, value selectivity rather than numbers; and for generals, value plans rather than courage. One superlative general and 3,000 troops equipped with incendiary weapons are sufficient to oppose a strong force of 100,000, to be unmatched by any enemy under Heaven.

The equipment for riverine warfare is different from that for land warfare. To penetrate the enemy's front, focus upon responding to their head with a direct strike. When you're intercepting an enemy to make a sudden attack, focus on cutting through the middle, attacking from both sides. If you encounter a chaotic formation, focus on incinerating their sails. If you are behind their rear guard, focus on employing numerous cannon.

When the general obtains the necessary men and accords with the subtle to respond to change, no one will remain unconquered.

Since Joseph Needham's massive "Gunpowder Epic" describes many of them in considerable detail and gunpowder technology is not the focus of our study, we will limit ourselves to succinctly sketching some of the more interesting and widely employed devices.[71] Gunpowder having gradually evolved from incendiary to explosive formulations from the early Sung through the Mongol period, explosives were available, though not yet widespread, at the start of the Ming, but rapidly proliferated during the period.

A variety of simple smoke balls *(yen ch'iu)* were fabricated by encasing incendiary concoctions in heavy paper spheres. Variants might include any of several poisonous substances (such as arsenic) for augmented effect and have slightly different designs.[72] Up to 100 layers of paper might be used, though 20 or 30 were most commonly employed depending upon the glue and resin applied, the ultimate purpose, the ball's inner structure, and the volatility of the gunpowder mixture. The basic smoke ball or sphere encased three *chin* of incendiary gunpowder within an outer wrap of yellow artemesia, certainly a deadly combination. However, among the others likely to have been employed the most interesting include the following:[73]

The *ta-huo-ch'iu* or "great fire ball" used a special gunpowder formulation so that when slung into the enemy, the enemy's clothes become fully involved in fire which water cannot extinguish whether it lands and breaks up in grass, on boats, or in the woods. In land warfare it's especially effective for burning the enemy's stores and provisions.[74]

The *huo-chuan* or "fire brick" came in at least three forms, one of which encased three individual items: twenty each "flying swallows" *(fei yen)*, small firecracker-like explosives, and caltrops. Hurled onto enemy boats, the flying swallows would disperse in all directions, igniting fires wherever they struck. Other forms also existed which encased short rockets known as earth rats *(ti shu)* and numerous small explosives.[75]

The *t'ien-chui-p'ao* or the "bomb falling from heaven" is hurled in an extremely high arc into the enemy's encampment where it explodes, dispersing tens of incendiary clumps *(huo k'uai)* which ignite fires everywhere about the encampment. It's considered especially effective in causing great confusion at night.[76]

The *chung-lei-p'ao* or "colliding thunder bomb" is another spherical bomb made from multiple layers of heavy paper that uses half poisonous gunpowder and half incendiary gunpowder to achieve both incendiary and noxious effects. Moreover, on bursting it disperses caltrops tipped with poison and earth rats which ignite fires, "seizing their minds and blurring their vision," both startling and wounding the men. It is considered functional in both land and riverine warfare.[77]

The *fei-huo chiang-mo-ch'ui* or "flying incendiary club for subjugating demons" looks more like an inverted vase than a club and is about eight inches tall by three inches in diameter. Equipped with numerous spikes sticking out in all directions, when hurled against the superstructures of enemy boats it sticks firmly and therefore readily ignites fires. Being difficult to remove, it is said to be greatly superior to incendiary bricks and other devices lacking metal probes.[78]

The *chi-li huo-ch'iu* or "caltrops fire ball" shoots out caltrops upon exploding but is basically incendiary in nature.[79]

The *pi-li huo-ch'iu* or "thunderclapfire ball" is an elongated device which explodes like a thunderclap. Designed to fumigate and burn enemy soldiers tunneling beneath the walls, it is dropped down through a countermine or a well shaft, stunning them first with an explosion.[80]

The *shen-huo hun-yüan-ch'iu* or "spiritual fire turbid origin ball" has a bamboo structure overlaid with many layers of paper. Basically a poison gas generator, it is designed to be stealthily carried into an enemy camp where it should be set off in conjunction with muskets. When it bursts, the poisonous smoke severely affects the noses of men and horses. As with many devices, it may also be used in city defense by dropping over the walls.[81]

An extremely strange contraption, obviously the product of thought trains which envision combinations of effective measures as being surpassingly good, the *shao-t'ien meng-huo wu-lan-p'ao* or "burning Heaven fierce fire unhinderable bomb" contained some twenty-three supposedly different types of spiritual fire said to "fly, run, jump, and leap" and "to strike their eyes and burn their hair." Deployed on the wind, it was used to burn provisions and scare horses, creating the chaos necessary to achieve victory.[82]

The *chih-hu yüan-p'ao* or "paper and paste round bomb" disperses twenty to thirty small caltrops and ten to twenty fire rats and is designed for city defense, being dropped over the walls upon the attackers below. Upon exploding, the rats scatter in all directions, burning the enemy soldiers and causing great consternation, prompting them to flee, whereupon the caltrops wound their feet. Although follow-up attacks are said to be possible, since the caltrops would still litter the ground this seems problematic.[83]

The *li-chih-p'ao* or "lychee bomb" is shaped like the fruit and fashioned from clay in the size of a goose egg. Employed in the usual fashion in city defense, the encased gunpowder burns soldiers when it explodes. When employed in attacks each soldier can carry twenty or thirty of them. Upon exploding the clay fragments inflict wounds, but the core feature is the poison sand and gas which are said to cause men and horses to weep uncontrollably and lose control of their limbs.[84]

Obviously these various antipersonnel devices did not rely upon single effects or simple explosive force, but instead dispersed one or more secondary devices upon bursting. A particularly complex, trebuchet-hurled version known as the *ch'ün-feng-p'ao* or "swarming bees bomb" encased three types of different projectiles: small explosive charges, small iron caltrops, and miniature flying sparrows which clung to anything they struck, such as enemy sails, and quickly burned through them. Said to be particularly effective for riverine warfare, they were fabricated from many layers of heavy paper.[85]

The *Wu-pei Chih* includes a very strange device supposedly employed when a commander found himself outnumbered and unable to realize the ideal condition of being at ease while striking the tired, or incapable of formulating an imaginative plan that would allow the few to successfully strike the many.[86] Probably another of the impractical devices concocted by armchair militarists, its inception is unknown. Basically a fiendish trap constructed by mounting a variety of weapon heads on an open four-wheel frame pulled by iron cables and concealed for suddenly yanking into any enemy which crosses its path, it mimics the ancient method of affixing firebrands to the tails of horses or oxen to stimulate them into sudden movement. While the basis for such devices may be realistically simple, in this case the realization is too complex, especially as it was to be used across an intervening waterway, though certainly one whose width could not have exceeded a small stream.

The *Wu-pei Chih* also depicts a personal protection device carried especially by defenders for sudden use against unexpected enemies.[87] Fashioned from a large *hu-lu,* the famous gourd of China, and reinforced with a coating of clay, it was designed to spray flames and gas thirty to forty feet and was carried already primed for use, a glowing ember emplaced at the top ready for intermixing at the crucial moment. (How many exploded as they bumped and jostled about, wounding the soldiers who concealed them in the suggested manner in their sleeves, might be questioned.) This sort of device falls somewhere between a full-size flamethrower and a pistol in utility, but rather than a single shot had the advantage of longer duration, even if it only burned for twenty to thirty seconds. Gourds were also mounted at the end of staves for the same purpose, some emitting clay or lead pellets with sufficient velocity to inflict wounds, especially if they struck the face or unprotected flesh.[88]

The *huo-tan* or "fire bullet" derives its power from the poisonous concoction encased within and is an example of a small projectile on the cusp of explosives and incendiaries.[89] The *huo-yao* or "fire goblin" is another example which is effective for both riverine and land warfare, including the defense of cities, and relies upon poisonous gas and smoke for its effects[90] while the *ta-huo-ch'iu* or "great fire ball" uses a particularly virulent gunpowder.[91]

A device called the *feng-lei huo-kun* or "wind thunder fire roller" is constructed from large diameter bamboo about three feet long reinforced with forty or fifty layers of paper and stuffed with poisonous and incendiary gunpowder mixtures, as well as five small iron encased explosives.[92] Because of its open-ended design, it reportedly rolled about on the ground or even flew about, so in enemy encampments could be advantageously employed to induce terror, as well as fully incinerate provisions, grass, clothes, and even armor.

FIGURE 5.10    Hu-lu for Incinerating Men in the Darkness
(Wu-pei Chih)

Another roller, a strange device known as the *p'ing-kuang pu-chan sui-ti-kun*,[93] consists of a three-foot log some four inches in diameter which would be partly hollowed out for an explosive charge and have ten blades or spikes affixed, as well as some sixty small gunpowder tubes mounted on the outside.[94] Employed in land warfare, it was lit approximately 100 feet from the enemy's encampment and somehow hurled (or rolled, powered by the outside tubes?) towards them, causing their feet and hooves to be badly burned. It also dispersed noxious gasses and smoke to confuse the enemy, causing them to weep, their eyes to crack, and their lips to split. Unorthodox troops and *shen huo* (spiritual fire) could then exploit their extreme misery and confusion to achieve certain victory.

The *ta-feng-k'o* or "big bees nest" encased caltrops and miniature arrowheads and was employed in virtually every circumstance ranging from offense to defense, from land to water.[95] It supposedly seized the minds and befuddled the eyes, startling and wounding the men, and was sometimes considered the primary incendiary weapon for both land and riverine contingents.

A sphere filled with "spiritual fire to confuse the mouth" is another variant containing layer upon layer of different devices such as caltrops, earth rats, and poisonous smoke, though with a major incendiary effect.[96] Made from clay and weather-proofed, when hurled into enemy encampments or formations, the projectiles were blasted outward in sequence, striking them; the caltrops wounded their feet; the earth rats penetrated their clothes and armor and jumped about; and the miniature explosives struck them, causing them to be badly confused and completely susceptible to a follow-on incendiary attack.

Finally, a hurled device which looks like a sort of a helmet with an open top called the *wan-huo fei-sha shen-p'ao* or "10,000 fire flying sand spiritual bomb" was designed to spray poison gas and create an obscuring fog which attacked the eyes and made a follow-on attack by other means possible.[97]

# 6

# Wind, Smoke, and Issues of Defense

As already seen, from inception Chinese military theorists discerned an innate connection between wind and the possible effectiveness of incendiary attacks, whether mounted on land or water. The *Wu Pien* thus succinctly asserted, "If you unleash incendiaries by exploiting the wind, the enemy's encampments and citadels can be extensively burned."[1] However, while constant breezes provide the oxygen necessary to "fan the flames," swirling zephyrs cause severe problems. When too strong, volatized materials are transported away before they can combust while sudden reversals not only spare the enemy, but also incinerate the aggressor force. Furthermore, smoke deliberately deployed as a weapon, rather than obfuscating the enemy and cloaking movements, may unexpectedly blind the perpetrators.

Even seventeenth-century military manuals still considered incendiary attacks an essential part of the commander's tactical repertoire and therefore continued to comment on the close inter-relationship between wind and fire. For example, the *Ping Ching* states: "In employing incendiary attacks, wind provides the power. In strong winds, the fire will be fierce. When the fire is intense, wind will be produced. When wind and fire mutually pulse each other, you can seize victory."[2]

The *Wu-pei Chih* continued the discussion by explicating the implications of Sun-tzu's four lunar lodges:[3]

> Those who would act as generals must know the indications of wind and prepare according to the moon's progression through the lodges. When the moon transits *chi, chen, chang,* or *yi,* these four lodges, then within three days there will certainly be a great wind. Several days after it stops, if you look up and observe the lunar lodges and the light scintillates unsteadily, there will certainly be a great wind in less than three days.
>
> If the wind stops at the end of the day and black clouds obscure the mouth of the dipper that night, wind and rain will arise together. If the clouds arise from the north, the wind will be great; if black clouds fly over and block the Milky Way, there will be great wind for several days. If the moon has a halo and is surrounded by several greenish layers, there will invariably be wind but no rain. When the rays of the setting sun intersect black clouds, wind will arise the next morning.
>
> Wind with a speed of ten *li* will raise dust and move leaves; of a hundred will shift sand and blow off tiles; of a thousand will have enough strength to move stones; and of ten thousand will have the strength to uproot trees. Knowing the wind's timing and excelling at employing it is the key to ten thousand victories in ten thousand engagements.

Even though Mao Yüan-yi couldn't abandon Sun-tzu's defining views and consciously echoed his "hundred victories in a hundred engagements" (though multiplied a hundredfold), he obviously felt the wind's behavior was foreseeable and therefore exploitable. Another section, too detailed for inclusion here, in fact contains a lengthy set of predictive criteria that correlate the wind's behavior with other weather phenomena.

A lack of wind does not completely preclude incendiary attacks, but newly kindled fires may sputter and easily be extinguished. Although commanders preferred to wait for moderate breezes that might fan the burgeoning flames into a roaring conflagration, artificial means were also proposed. For example, the *Wu-pei Chih* includes a diagram showing two men turning horizontally mounted fan blades identical to that found in the *Wu-ching Tsung-yao*, though in the latter it is being employed to disperse poisonous smoke within confined tunnels.[4] However, they are standing in an open field while the accompanying description, even though expressing a concrete knowledge of the relationship between wind and combustion, seems somewhat impractical. "When you mount an incendiary attack on the enemy's provisions or grass but there isn't any wind, you can use these to propel the fire. One horse can carry two such devices. When you engage in a punitive campaign, you should prepare lots of them."[5] Presumably, even though cumbersome and effective only in quantity, they could oxygenate the flames at the outset of a well-orchestrated assault.

Fundamental, even simplistic tactical principles were accordingly formulated to ensure that the most benighted commander would remember to exploit the wind's potential. The *Hundred Unorthodox Strategies* reduced riverine warfare to achieving an advantageous position relative to the wind and current's direction: "Whenever you engage an enemy in combat along or on rivers and lakes, you should assume a position upwind or upstream. One who is upwind can, by exploiting the wind, employ an incendiary attack to set the enemy afire. One who is upstream can utilize the current's strategic power to ram the enemy with high walled war vessels. In such cases you will always be victorious in battle."[6]

Accordingly, commanders were also warned, "On the march, you must prepare against being intercepted; when halting, defend against being attacked by surprise; when encamped, prevent theft; and in the wind, be wary of incendiary attack."[7] A famous Three Kingdoms' incident is cited in illustration:

> Wei's commander-in-chief, Wu Lin, went south on a campaign of rectification. When the army reached Ching Lake,

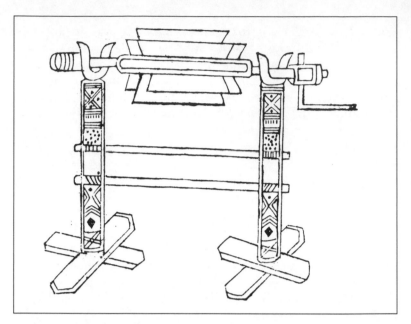

*FIGURE 6.1    Field Fan (Wu-ching Tsung-yao)*

General Man Ch'ung's forces at the front deployed directly across the river from the enemy. General Man then addressed his subordinates: "Tonight the wind is extremely fierce, so the enemy will certainly come to set fire to our encampment. We should prepare for them."

The generals were all frightened. In the middle of the night the enemy indeed dispatched ten companies to advance and ignite the encampment, but General Man mounted a surprise attack and destroyed them.

In creating expectations, commonly held beliefs immediately offer fertile possibilities for initiating unorthodox actions. Thus the *Unorthodox Strategies* advises: "Whenever engaging an enemy in battle, if you encounter a favorable wind and fully exploit its power to attack, or meet a contrary wind but unexpectedly strike, you will always be victorious. A tactical principle from the *Wu-tzu* states: 'If the wind is favorable, exploit the strategic advantage and follow it; if the wind is contrary, solidify your formation and await the enemy.'"[8] Contrary to the *Wu-tzu's* instructions, rather than assuming an ensconced stance in the face of an unfavorable wind, an aggressive course is instead advocated. The chapter's historical illustration emphasizes that approach, one that was largely accepted thereafter.[9]

At the end of the Later Chin in A.D. 410, the powerful rebel general Lu Hsün, who had been expanding his base for a decade, moved down the lower Yangtze with an armada of large boats and some 50,000 troops for a decisive battle with Liu Yü who had assumed emperorship of Later Chin and would change the dynastic name in 420 to Southern Sung. Anticipating his strike at Chien-k'ang (Nan-ching), Liu deployed a large contingent of mixed infantry and cavalry troops equipped with incendiary equipment on the northwestern bank of the Yangtze River just above where it turns upward toward the northeast. Liu also deployed a fleet of light, nimble boats to mount a harassing crossbow attack which deliberately exploited the combined effects of a strong wind and the current's flow to gradually force Lu's armada, said to clog the river, against the northwestern shore. Once they came in range of their incendiary arrows and trebuchet-hurled devices, Liu's land forces mounted a devastating incendiary attack that consumed the tightly packed boats. Having suffered a severe defeat, Lu was forced to retreat back up the Yangtze with the remnants of his force.[10]

Foreign armies also adopted incendiary techniques over the centuries, employing them equally against Chinese forces and other steppe peoples. For example, in A.D. 654 the kingdom of Kao-li situated in the northern portion of the Korean peninsula, after having endured a century of Sui and T'ang invasions and been the victim of T'ang incendiary attacks, struck Khitan forces nominally allied with the T'ang near Hsin-ch'eng in Liao-tung with the support of the Mo-ho. During their assault the wind grew so strong that arrows shot at the Khitan simply blew back harmlessly. Accordingly, the Khitan astutely exploited the wind to mount a fierce incendiary attack that decimated their enemies, ending the campaign.[11]

However, the lesson was not completely lost because Kao-li soon employed incendiary measures against another Korean kingdom.

Not every attempt to exploit the wind proved successful, open field and riverine defensive measures sometimes thwarting them despite the wind's propulsive power. For example, during the siege of Shao-hsing in 1359 the defenders managed to prevail despite being in a strategically disadvantageous position downstream. As recounted in a chronicle of the siege:[12]

> Our armies all went forth from the earthen fortifications, deployed, and engaged in combat. Arrows and stones flew about, the troops clashed several times, and victories and defeats were achieved on both sides. After noon a brutal wind suddenly rose, flinging stones and raising sand. Dust obscured our faces, neither men nor horses could stand upright. The large pennants of the enemy generals snapped, their equipment and protective siege devices were scattered in all directions. Bright day became dark and murky.
>
> Our armies exploited the strategic situation to strike them, our blades clashing in the midst of the wind blown dust. Neither side could distinguish the other. The enemy then tied four boats together and loaded them with dried firewood to take advantage of the wind to set fires, moving directly against the city gate with follow on infantry support. Chao Ch'un ordered our naval forces on the north bank to hook the boats and pull them in, supporting the effort with incendiary arrows that completely burnt them in an instant. Our armored troops following along the bank resisted the enemy's onslaught in a pitched battle.
>
> Our boats were arrayed along the northern bank and when the wind's power turned and shifted, one floated away toward the southern bank [controlled by the enemy outside the city].
>
> Regimental Commander Ch'eng and nineteen men thus penetrated the enemy [and were lost]. With two subcommanders, Chao angrily pursued the enemy's troops across the Hung bridge and burned all their assault shields and

other equipment on the southern bank. Our army captured more than ten boats loaded with grass and many of the aggressors around the other gates fled back to their encampment in terror.

Despite its remarkable power, wind alone was deemed insufficient to ensure the incineration of unconfined field forces in the absence of combustible materials and hot and dry conditions. However, reeds and brambles, tangled undergrowth, grass, and forests immediately create the possibility of a successful attack and were therefore increasingly specified as essential in the military manuals from the T'ang onward. Hsü Tung's *Hu-ch'ien Ching* succinctly reminded readers, "The *Art of War* states, 'In heavy vegetation and dense grass you can exploit wind and fire.'"[13]

Thereafter, the *Unorthodox Strategies* noted: "In warfare, whenever the enemy occupies a position near grass and brush, constructs his shelters from ramie and bamboo, or has gathered grass for fuel and piled up his provisions, if the weather has been hot and dry you can exploit the wind's direction to set fires and incinerate them. If you immediately follow up by striking with elite troops, their armies can be destroyed. A tactical principle from the *Art of War* states: "Implementing an incendiary attack depends up the proper conditions." And even the *Hsü Wu-ching Tsung-yao* (A.D. 1517) added, "when there is deep grass to the enemy's fore, we can slacken our pace in order to take advantage of it, forcing the enemy to advance into the grass before incinerating them. However, if they maintain a defensive posture without advancing, then attack them by an indirect route."[14]

Yeh Meng-hsiung then summarily stated: "If the enemy encamps near grass or vegetation or their huts are made from reeds or bamboo, or they have accumulated fodder and piled up provisions while the weather has been dry and parched, if you exploit the wind to unleash an incendiary attack to burn them and then select elite troops to suddenly strike them, their army can be destroyed. The *Art of War* says implementing an incendiary attack must have a basis."[15]

Topographical features being an inescapable element of tactical formulations, not surprisingly *Tso Chuan* battle descriptions indicate that they had already been recognized and were being exploited by astute Spring and Autumn commanders. Thereafter, Sun-tzu conceptualized this knowledge, classifying the innumerable naturally occurring variations into basic configurations with correlated tactics. Military manuals such as the *Six Secret Teachings, Hu-ch'ien Ching,* and the *Wu-ching Tsung-yao* subsequently grounded their operating principles in his terrain theory.

Historical recountings indicate that both theoreticians and battlefield commanders came to understand that all of the terrain's salient features, not just the impediments, must be integrated into any battle plan, just as Sun-tzu stated: "Configuration of terrain is an aid to the army. Analyzing the enemy, taking control of victory, estimating ravines and defiles, the distant and near, is the Tao of the superior general. One who knows these and employs them in combat will certainly be victorious, one who does not will certainly be defeated."

Incendiary attacks mounted against mobile targets, whether infantry on the march or cavalry racing to an objective, become vastly more effective when their freedom of action is constrained. Accordingly, so-called "constricted," "precipitous," and "encircled" configurations of terrain have to be identified before they can be advantageously exploited. However, theoreticians such as Hsü Tung gradually realized that slavishly following Sun-tzu's operational tactics, such as on dispersive terrain or in mountain ravines, was not always advisable or advantageous whereas deliberately contravening them might prove remarkably effective. Meanwhile, the various military writings continued to expand the repertoire of possibilities and foster a pronounced consciousness of topographical features and their import.

Because incendiary attacks mounted under conducive conditions were inevitably lethal, numerous writers stressed that heavily vegetated areas should be avoided. Not only might armies moving through them be easily bottled up and incinerated, but enemy forces might also be concealed in ambush.[16] Even more radically, the *T'ou-fu Pi-t'an* concluded that since wind and fire mutually bolster each other, armies should not only avoid heavy vegetation but also cut off the enemy's access to the wind, preventing them from assuming a position upwind.[17]

Nevertheless, over the centuries many commanders were distracted by prospects for a quick advance or became enthralled with pursuing fleeing enemies only to rush into virtual fire traps, just as the Three Kingdoms incidents already reprised have shown. A well-known incident during the last years of the Sui saw the youthful rebel commander Tu Fu-wei, who eventually grew powerful enough to control much of Chiangsu and Anhui before submitting to the incipient T'ang and eventually being assassinated, lure a Sui army onto heavily vegetated marshy terrain and incinerate them all. This was accomplished by first engaging the enemy, then pretending to be defeated and fleeing back onto fatal ground to assume a position upwind before launching an incendiary attack which inflicted massive casualties in textbook style.[18]

Unsurprisingly, strong winds often prompted commanders to consider, though not necessarily employ, incendiary-based tactics. Perhaps the most famous example of exploiting locally strong winds coupled with enemy negligence in encamping amidst vegetation occurred at the end of the Later Han:[19]

> After Chu Chün was defeated by Po Ts'ai's Yellow Turban forces, Huang-fu Sung advanced and secured Ch'ang-sheh. Po Ts'ai then led a large number of troops to besiege the city. Because Sung's troops were few, he summoned the army's officers and said: "The Tao of the military lies in unorthodox changes, not in numbers. It happens the brigands have built their encampment with straw so it will be easy to exploit the wind to launch an incendiary attack. If we set them afire at night they will certainly be thrown into chaos. By sending our soldiers forth to suddenly strike and engage them from all four sides, we can repeat T'ien Tan's achievements."

That night when a strong wind arose Sung had his soldiers ascend the city walls carrying burning torches and his elite soldiers secretly work their way out through the siege lines to set fire to the enemy's encampment from outside with a great yell. The men manning the wall responded by raising their burning torches and Sung drummed a rapid assault into the enemy's deployment. Terrified, the brigands ran off in chaos. It happened that Ts'ao Ts'ao, who had been dispatched by the emperor, arrived and united with Chu Chün and Huang-fu Sung to severely vanquish Po Ts'ai's forces, killing several tens of thousands.

For incendiary measures to be successful, a minimum amount of material must be delivered on target and the wind sufficiently strong and properly oriented. However, once the materials or the objective are ignited, should the wind shift or the fire prove unexpectedly vehement and spread back toward the attackers, escape might prove impossible. Among the numerous disasters attesting to this danger, a well-known incident cited by the *T'ung Tien* as an example of "Exploiting the Wind to Seize Victory" vividly shows that stupidly attempting to launch incendiaries in the face of a zephyr results in seizing defeat.

As recounted in the *Tzu-chih T'ung-chien*, immediately after rebelling against the state of Ch'en, General Wang Lin constructed a substantial riverine force to complement his land forces in order to exploit the Yangtze River and seize power.[20] After a standoff of several days in the vicinity of Wu-ch'ang, in the tenth month of 557 Lin benefited from his opponent's sudden lack of commitment and ongoing dissension between Ch'en's two field commanders to severely defeat their naval forces in the initial engagement.

Despite much indecisive maneuvering, over the next two years Wang's fleet gradually proceeded down the Yangtze. Having gained additional naval support from Northern Ch'i and enjoying the protective cover of a small but elite cavalry contingent following on the riverbank, Wang Lin resumed the offensive upon the demise of Ch'en's ruler. Following a significant victory, by the second month of 560 he was within 100 miles of his main target of Yang-chou while the government's forces under Hou Chen had been compelled to withdraw to the security of Wu-hu slightly down river. Here they maintained their relative positions for some 100 days before the normal rise in the Yangtze's spring water level and its tributaries allowed Lin to bring substantial reserves from Lake Ch'ao-hu to the northwest, swelling his forces. A decisive confrontation seemed inevitable, but after a few days' standoff strong nighttime winds from the northeast blew many of Lin's ships onto the western bank, requiring a major effort to refloat and reorganize them while Chen's fleet remained sheltered at Wu-hu on the eastern shore.

Because of external military developments and increasing threats upstream, Wang feared his troops would lose their resolve and therefore decided to chance a major offensive to overwhelm the forces obstructing his passage to Yang-chou. In contrast to the northeast wind prevailing just days earlier, a strong southwest wind fortuitously arose, causing Lin to remark that Heaven must be aiding them since it would swiftly propel them directly to their objective. (Because the river runs north-northeasterly at this point in Anhui, the wind pushed them off the shoals along the west bank and provided a sustained thrust up the Yangtze's course.) By exploiting it, Wang departed and raced downstream, reaching several miles past Wu-hu before Ch'en's commanders awoke and came out in pursuit, equally benefiting from the wind.

To forestall any attack from the rear and vanquish his pursuers, Wang Lin mounted an incendiary attack by throwing blazing torches at the enemy's ships rather than hurling them by trebuchets or relying upon bows and crossbows to shoot incendiary arrows, common practices in his era. This surprising reliance upon simple arm strength—no doubt because of the closeness of the enemy's vessels—proved fatally short-sighted because the wind simply blew them back upon their own ships, setting them all on fire. Ch'en's forces then exploited these unexpected developments to smash Wang's boats with the overhead battering rams mounted on their large vessels, disperse molten iron spray, and dispatch numerous small, leather-covered boats which maneuvered among the enemy's blazing ships with relative impunity to effect further direct attacks. Wang Lin suffered a severe defeat, some 20 to 30 percent of his naval forces drowning and the rest abandoning their floundering ships for the shore's security. The small cavalry contingent along the western bank also panicked and soon found themselves enmired in deep mud. Forced to abandon their horses, only 20 or 30 percent managed to escape while Wang Lin fled on a small boat.

Nearly two centuries earlier in Fu Chien's waning days as emperor of the Former Ch'in, Mu-jung Chung, emperor of Western Yen, encircled Ch'ang-an in the fifth month of A.D. 385 where a desperate but ultimately futile defense was attempted. Apart from compelling the local people to serve in the army, Western Yen's troops engaged in brutal rampages and widely plundered the area, prompting the inhabitants to secretly communicate with Fu Chien and offer to raise an internal incendiary response if he could muster the forces necessary to launch an attack. Although he believed the effort was doomed, in the end Fu Chien dispatched a small, 700-man cavalry contingent to probe the situation. Fires soon arose within the enemy's encampment, but the wind suddenly shifted and all but a few of the subversives were consumed by the fire, ending Ch'in's hope for survival.[21]

A major naval engagement near Wu-han at the confluence of the T'un-k'ou and Yangtze Rivers saw the minor powers of Later Liang and Northern Chou proceed down the Yangtze to engage a riverine force from Ch'en in a major clash. Occupying a strategically disadvantageous position downstream and downwind, Ch'en's commander deliberately sacrificed his smallest boats in a strike that depleted the enemy's prepoised overhead rams. Then, before they could raise them again, his large warships went forth and employed their own crushers to smash and sink numerous enemy vessels. The Liang-Chou coalition resorted to incendiary measures, but the wind suddenly shifted direction, igniting their own ships.

Ch'en went on to score a total victory in which only the enemy commanders managed to escape in a single boat.[22]

During the much-reviled rule of Empress Wu when the Li clan was being increasingly marginalized in both the central court and provincial posts, Li Ching-yeh—who soon reverted to his surname of Hsü—raised forces in rebellion in the Chiangsu area for the avowed purpose of rectifying the court. In A.D. 684 Li Hsiao-yi, in command of the imperial forces, was dispatched to suppress him.[23] Learning of their approach near the middle of the eleventh month, Hsü deployed on the south bank of a small river. A subcommander's initial amphibious assault not only failed, but resulted in numerous T'ang casualties, many from drowning. Li Hsiao-yi directed a series of attacks himself but when they were repulsed, he became fearful and opted to assume an ensconced defense.

Both sides clung to their respective positions without stirring. However, a T'ang strategist emphasized that as the wind was strong and favorable, the vegetation heavy and dry, it would be advantageous to launch an incendiary attack preliminary to attempting a decisive strike. (A meteorite seen passing over Hsü's encampment, a certain precursor of doom, no doubt augmented their courage.) Li therefore adopted his suggestion, launching an incendiary attack that inflicted casualties and immediately disrupted their formations. The subsequent assault saw some 7,000 slain outright and many more drown in attempting to flee across the river. Although Hsü managed to escape in a small boat, he was murdered by his subordinates shortly thereafter.

An example of alertly employing fire to cause chaos in the enemy's ranks preliminary to seizing victory occurred in A.D. 894 during the final days of the T'ang dynasty. In a thrust against two so-called rebel factions, the former rebel Chu Ch'uan-chung, now serving the T'ang as a regional military governor, led his armies north via an eastern route around Fish Mountain. Coming about the mountain they found the enemy already deployed and were therefore compelled to assume a position in opposition.

A strong southeastern wind arose which blew down their battle flags and threw their terrified troops into turmoil. However, Chu managed to stabilize them until the wind abated somewhat before suddenly shifting to swirl in from the north. Since the two armies had deployed amidst heavy vegetation, Chu took advantage of the wind to launch an incendiary attack, no doubt by setting the vegetation afire, and then exploited the ensuing turmoil to vanquish the two rebel contingents. More than 10,000 of the enemy were burned and otherwise slain. Although Chu had simply followed antique practices and fundamental tactical dictums, he still benefited enormously from the enemy failing to exploit the same opportunity before the wind shifted.[24]

In the turbulent Five Dynasties period (907–959), Wu-yüeh dispatched a force of some 30,000 to attack Ch'ang-chou in Wu but they were intercepted in Wu-hsi where a heated battle unfolded. Wu-yüeh seemed likely to prevail as Wu's commander in chief had fallen ill, but a subordinate assumed authority and rallied the troops. He then took advantage of a favorable wind to launch an incendiary attack that exploited the long drought and the vegetation's dryness, immediately creating the turmoil necessary for a decisive strike. Wu-yüeh not only suffered a severe defeat and the loss of 10,000 lives, but also another crushing loss shortly thereafter.[25]

The rising Sung destroyed the Southern Han in just five months through a series of victories achieved by manipulating their large forces and mounting a nighttime incendiary attack on the wooden palisades of their final bastion. Despite its ostensibly submissive attitude, powerful Southern T'ang was then targeted for extinction. Several thousand small boats were constructed, military and topographical intelligence gathered, and estrangement techniques employed before a five-pronged attack, which included 50,000 troops from Wu and Yüeh, set forth. Late in 974 the large Sung fleet successfully traveled down river past 100,000 bemused defenders because their commander stupidly mistook them for some sort of parade or patrol. The boats were then deployed as the base for a floating bridge, permitting the main body to invade the kingdom and score several successive victories, including over a 100,000-man riverine force, before the ruler finally mounted a counterattack. Han troops moved downstream on large bamboo rafts to incinerate the troublesome bridge, but the shallow winter water compelled them to proceed slowly. When the wind suddenly shifted, their boats became trapped in the flames and were immediately attacked to effect. Following the conflagration, Han's beleaguered forces surrendered and the Sung's founding emperor died shortly thereafter.

Sudden reversals of the wind, while primarily disastrous in riverine combat where the current impedes maneuverability, not only affected armies in the field but on occasion also thwarted direct assaults on citadels and cities. This is well illustrated by an episode from 688 when the T'ang's hereditary kings, anticipating that they had been targeted for elimination by the despotic and increasingly powerful Empress Wu, plotted to revolt. When Li Chung moved prematurely with a mere 5,000 troops, he quickly found himself opposed by government forces. However, only 1,700 soldiers could be mustered for the task so the commander ensconced himself in a nearby fortified town which Li felt compelled to reduce in order to preclude any threat to his rear.

Carts piled with straw were wheeled into position against the south gate and set ablaze, a time-honored technique with good prospects for breaching the defenses, but just as the fire caught, the wind also shifted, blowing the flames away from the gate toward the attackers, compelling them to retreat. Not only was their enthusiasm dashed, but when the assault commander muttered something about them being rebels, they grew further disheartened. His immediate execution for having undermined the army's spirit frightened all but a handful of Li Chung's personal retainers into deserting into the surrounding woods and marshes. Li fled but was ignominiously killed shortly thereafter by a T'ang contingent guarding the gate of a nearby town, ending a rebellion which lasted a mere seven days.[26]

Conversely, defensive incendiary measures could also backfire as they did at the siege of K'ai-feng at the end of the

Southern Sung when troops atop the wall dropped straw onto the enemy's five assault towers to burn them. However, as the assault towers contained a lot of wood and a large amount of straw had been employed, the fire blazed up and, being propelled by a south wind, easily overspread the wall itself, consuming three watchtowers.[27]

Temporary wooden defenses erected from reeds and locally available trees were equally susceptible to incendiary attack, whether emplaced on land or in river beds to comprise barriers. When a Szechuan rebel general ensconced himself at Han-chou, a town protected only by wooden (or bamboo) fences rather than ordinary walls or moats, Tung Cheng mounted an incendiary attack from all four sides. The intensity of the ensuing conflagration drove the rebel general out and his 50,000 troops were rapidly defeated in the turmoil.[28]

Similarly, while the incipient Sung was aggressively consolidating the southern regions with a campaign against Southern Han, P'an Mei observed that the latter's defenses were constructed from local reeds and therefore highly flammable.[29] He therefore dispatched night raiders by obscure routes, each carrying two torches (for a total of at least 10,000) to throw en masse against the barriers before exploiting the confusion with a devastating follow-on attack.

## SMOKE

Although seen as an important defensive tool, smoke's basically uncontrollable nature and susceptibility to the wind caused it to be lumped with other miscellaneous incendiary materials in the theoretical manuals. Nevertheless, because of its crucial role in countering miners in enemy tunnels, the early Mohist writings already contain focal discussions. Even though the Yellow Emperor reportedly created a miasmic fog to defeat his nemesis Ch'ih Yu in the legendary period, smoke was primarily regarded as a vehicle for dispersing poisonous substances, a medium for incapacitating and slaying aggressors rather than concealing and occluding.

Dust, closely associated with smoke by many discussants, was more often employed for the lesser purpose of temporarily disabling the enemy at the onset of open field clashes, as well as for obscuring field armies and encampments.[30] The *Wu Pien* succinctly asserts, "If you accord with the wind to raise dust, enemy armies will collapse. If you drag firewood and raise dust, no one in the enemy's army will discern our vacuity and substance. If you blow sand and follow up afterward, no enemy force will be able to withstand our thrust."[31] However, fine sand, lime, chaff, and other grainy materials were also dispersed in relatively confined situations such as wall defenses and assaults, though poisonous substances might also be deployed on the wind (just as Yang Hsüan did) and from eruptors when opportune.[32]

Because smoke invariably accompanies incendiary attacks, it constitutes an exploitable factor for aggressors but a tortuous, inescapable complication for defenders. The development of gunpowder formula and the realization that burning characteristics were mixture dependent allowed the deliberate creation and deployment of smoke bombs, permitting action at a distance rather than simply with handheld proximity devices. Early eruptors whose gasses had sufficient velocity to be reasonably controllable and could therefore be aimed at the enemy also provided a delivery method for noxious smokes as well as small particles and were soon employed in great numbers in city defense, though less so in attack.

The Sung dynasty *Wu-ching Tsung-yao* discusses two smoke weapons for use against cities, prefacing the first, "When savage smoke assaults men, there is no means to withstand it."[33] Moreover, deploying smoke was clearly envisioned as a secondary effort, to be considered only after a sustained stalemate of at least several days, an attitude that persisted into the late Ming long after cannon and other gunpowder-based weapons had been fully adopted.[34]

As described in a *Wu-ching Tsung-yao* passage which continues to appear right through such Ming military compendia as the *Teng-t'an Pi-chiu,* the basic smoke assault method consisted of "preparing raspberry, moxa, faggots, and grass for some ten thousand bundles. After gathering them together, distribute them by weight into packages that a man can carry. Use dry grass as the core and wrap wet grass outside. Wait for the wind to be very powerful, ignite them upwind, and as they begin to generate smoke, disperse them to gradually move closer to the city walls. However, you must still carry leather and bamboo leaf side shields to defend against arrows and stones." As formulated, the burning faggots and grass not only give off smoke, but the moxa (and possibly raspberry root) would also release volatile oils that cause irritation and blistering. Moreover, although designed to drive defenders off the walls, it essentially duplicates Mo-tzu's formulation for the smoke propelled into enemy tunnels.

The second device, an early smoke ball, was assembled by "putting three *chin* of gunpowder within the ball, wrapping at least one *chin* of yellow pine layer by layer on the outside, and plastering it by the usual method for making incendiary balls." Basically a resin-wrapped paper sphere with a hole bored in it, it was designed to smoke rather than burn intensely like an incendiary and could be hurled into cities by trebuchet, as well as dropped off the heights of fortifications.[35]

Finally, the text includes another formula for a poison gas variant of the basic smoke ball or *tu-yao yen-ch'iu,* which uses sulfur, arsenic, and other materials. In summarizing its employment and effects, the *Wu-ching Tsung-yao* notes that "blood will come out of the mouths and noses of anyone exposed to the gas." Naturally it can also be employed both offensively and defensively by hurling with trebuchet.

The next theoretical work to ponder the nature and role of smoke was the Ming dynasty *Ts'ao-lü Ching-lüeh,* whose dedicated chapter "Smoke Warfare" ("Yen Chan") systematically records thinking and practices not otherwise preserved:

> Generating smoke before engaging in combat will keep the enemy ignorant of your vacuities and substance and they won't dare advance. But if they should advance, they will succumb to your techniques.

You can set a trail of smoke out along an entire river, concealing your masses and keeping the enemy from perceiving your movements and deployments.

You can have elite forces strike from ambush, actualize the unorthodox technique of concealing armored troops on a vast expanse, or create the solitary silence of troops having returned to camp.

You can thunder the war drums amidst the smoke and thus turn the enemy's hearts cold with just a few men while actually proceeding by secondary routes to execute unorthodox tactics.

You can have your soldiers follow the smoke to advance, every foot seeming like a thousand miles, until the whole army suddenly arrives before the enemy realizes it.

Amidst the smoke you can empty the center and divide and conceal your troops on the two wings. If you then manipulate the enemy into rushing forward through the smoke, they will find it difficult to withstand sudden strikes from the flanks.

When your strength is exhausted and you are resting your warriors and ordering your troops, with smoke you can cause the enemy to be muddled, slow, and doubtful, and thereby be unable to calculate whether to undertake a surprise attack.

When a vanquished enemy flees through minor paths in the smoke's murkiness, you can capture and slay them as easily as taking things out of a sack.

You can employ massive smoke clouds to make the enemy doubtful, then allow them to disperse in order to manifest emptiness, prompting them to laugh and recklessly advance.

Generally speaking, smoke and violent winds are not viewed as conjoined without reason, but are used to establish the crafty and ephemeral and thereby multiply the number of unorthodox techniques. Smoke warfare will conceal the appearance of troops and horses, so you should generate these miasmic changes. Commanders shouldn't regard this as something trivial and ignore it.

Following an array of examples, the chapter concludes by noting that ancient generals employed smoke in warfare and the wind must always be analyzed: "When the wind is favorable, the smoke will blind the enemy's eyes. You can then exploit it to suddenly strike them. However, should the wind be contrary and the smoke overspread your own army, you will need to signal a partial withdrawal. You can use smoke for unorthodox purposes, to establish doubt, or conceal yourself and rest your warriors." In a similar vein, "Wind Warfare" ("Feng Chan") repeats the antique refrain that it is advantageous to attack with a favorable wind, but under contrary conditions wiser to maintain a stalwart defensive stance and await developments.[36]

The comprehensive, late Ming *Wu-pei Chih* also includes several formulas for smoke bombs ranging from the merely obscuring and irritating through decidedly caustic and poisonous.[37] While the formulaic details require specialized discussion, the main types and their intent merit briefly reprising. First, *shen yen* or "spiritual smoke," prepared as a very fine powder and deployed from a bamboo tube, creates a miasma that disperses over 100 paces and has good persistence. (In contrast, "spiritual fire" or *shen huo,* which is similarly prepared as a fine powder but ignited in a metal barrel, is employed to burn enemy troops in close proximity.) Dense smoke and a variety of single smoke colors including green, white, red, purple, and black, as well as a poisonous formula are also enumerated, though other sections itemize additional poisonous elements which might be incorporated into various incendiary and anti-personnel weapons to augment their lethality.

The chapter actually begins by outlining a method for creating and entrapping the enemy in an extensive ground fog through a short, feigned withdrawal: "Roast sawdust and *t'ung* oil and combine them together, making the mixture very fine. Fill cloth bags with it and have the troops each carry as many as possible. When you encounter a conducive wind, first pour the mixture out onto the ground and pretend to retreat more than a hundred paces. After igniting with a running fuse, it will produce a dense fog that will obscure five *li*. When the enemy's soldiers and horses smell the vapors, their tears will flow endlessly and they will wound and slay each other."

Although the brief combat accounts found in the historical records frequently mention that smoke obscured the battlefield, generally it was an ancillary effect of an incendiary attack or simply the byproduct of using smoky eruptors for defensive purposes. However, deliberate smoke attacks were sometimes employed to obfuscate the enemy and cloak aggressive actions equally with naturally occurring fog,[38] both in riverine engagements where they proved particularly dramatic and land warfare. To cite just a single well-known example of the former, Hsi K'ang-sheng of Northern Wei launched an incendiary attack with fire boats against Ch'i's vessels under the cover of a heavy smoke screen and scored a major victory.[39]

Turning to non-aquatic clashes, in A.D. 36 Later Han imperial forces engaged in suppressing independent generals in Szechuan near Ch'eng-tu came under heavy attack and were compressed into a solid defensive position. Badly outnumbered, in order to escape they resorted to the ploy of setting out multiple flags and created a heavy smoke screen to conceal their activities before silently departing during the night.[40]

During the Three Kingdoms period when T'ien Yü of Wei penetrated deep into Hsien-pei territory with few forces and found himself cut off, no doubt to conceal his actual intentions he continued to press forward toward the main enemy encampment.[41] He had his troops gather a large quantity of horse and cow manure which was set afire, providing heavy clouds of smoke that temporarily concealed their escape by an obscure route even as the enemy negligently assumed they were still encamped. They managed to proceed some ten *li* before the ruse was discovered, were pursued, and again encircled.

At the very founding of the Sui, Ho Juo-pi led a light cavalry force to attack armies from the state of Ch'en but was repulsed several times in their initial encounter. Because his troops were disordered and tired, Ho created a heavy smoke screen to obscure their movements and deployment. Ch'en's troops carelessly took advantage of this apparent hiatus to report back with evidence of their accomplishments (enemy heads) and claim their rewards, creating an opportunity for Ho to attack and be victorious.[42]

In the last days of the Ming, during Li Tzu-ch'eng's siege of K'ai-feng in 1642 the aggressors burned noxious materials to create poisonous smoke which rode the prevailing wind into the city, thereby deterring the populace from reaping the nearby reeds which the rebels wanted for their own horses. Detecting the odor and realizing the danger, the defenders withstood three days of localized gas attack by "putting *pin-lang* [areca or betel nuts] and *kan-ts'ao* [licorice] in their mouths and placing more than a hundred large pots atop the walls filled with water, licorice, and other drugs to counteract the poison." Whatever its mode of action, apparently the antidote was successful because the chronicle asserts the gas was unable to harm them.[43]

Even steppe armies adopted smoke as a viable technique for use against Chinese forces. In A.D. 917 a Khitan force reported to be a million strong but probably only a third that size surrounded Yu-chou, a Later T'ang fortified city. After the siege had dragged on for 200 days despite Lu Wen-chi, a Chinese defector, having provided detailed guidance on tunneling and assault methods (coincidentally illustrating how a single traitor might transfer numerous martial techniques to steppe enemies), a rescue contingent of 70,000 men was finally dispatched. Being composed primarily of infantry, they sought to avoid disadvantageous open field combat with highly mobile Khitan cavalry regiments and therefore opted to proceed through the mountains. However, because the Khitan controlled the heights, they had to keep to the valleys, a time-honored method.

In their first encounter with the enemy they drove the astonished Khitan back and therefore continued to make slow progress, but had to battle ferociously for every pass. Before finally breaking out of the mountains, the commander had the troops cut large branches and erect temporary palisades. Whenever encircled by Khitan cavalry they resorted to China's one advantage in combating steppe mobility, their crossbows, to decimate and thereby deter the attackers.

When they finally approached Yu-chou, they found a vastly superior Khitan force arrayed in depth blocking their advance. The Later T'ang commander held his infantry in the rear and deployed his limited cavalry contingent in front where they dragged brush and set grass fires, creating a vast, impenetrable dust and smoke cloud to conceal their maneuvers. The infantry then advanced, attacked, and eventually wrested a major victory, extricating Yu-chou.[44]

Antagonistic steppe groups also raised dust and burned grass to produce smoke and deliberately obscure the battlefield in clashes with each other. For example, Khitan resentment at having their able-bodied males impressed by the Jurchen for military campaigns against the Sung resulted in uprisings and armed opposition in the Inner Mongolian region in 1161. Enjoying sporadic success, they grew until the Chin (Jurchen) dispatched ever larger armies to suppress them.[45] In the fourth month of 1162, after suffering heavy casualties in a surprise attack, the Khitan withdrew across the Meng-sung River and burnt the bridge behind them, compelling Jurchen forces to proceed down river until they could find a sufficiently narrow portion to cross the sandy bed by laying down a track of willow branches. Catching up with the Khitan, they immediately launched a cavalry attack that was blunted from upwind by dense smoke that overspread and obscured them, reportedly mesmerizing the Jurchen warriors. Fervent but chaotic clashes continued within the smoke until it suddenly began to rain and the wind faded, allowing the previously transfixed cavalry to renew their attack in conjunction with the newly arrived infantry component, overwhelming the defenders and inflicting heavy casualties.[46]

Finally, because smoke obscures reality it can be exploited to cause doubt, as in A.D. 316 when the state of Han-chao surrounded a Chin city.[47] Chin dispatched a rescue force of 30,000 men, but Han troops set fires all around the city walls, making it appear that the city was in flames. They then ensured this perception would be accepted by employing a turned spy who raced out to misinform the rescue commander that the city, badly obscured by heavy smoke, had already fallen. Fearing an attack, the relief armies turned about, allowing Han-chao forces still battling outside the citadel to fall upon them and easily inflict a severe defeat.

## DEFENSE AGAINST INCENDIARY ATTACK

Although the first incendiary assaults undoubtedly stimulated defensive measures, the earliest descriptions appear in the *Mo-tzu*. Thereafter, Mohist methods were widely adopted and continued to form an integral part of China's military manuals from the *T'ung Tien* onward. Two always remained primary, the first being to deny resources to the enemy, whether flammable or not, either by removing or destroying everything within a radius ranging from fifty paces to three *li*. Other Warring States military writings also advocated this policy, though it assumed its most draconian form in the *Mo-tzu's* military chapters. Thereafter, depending upon the power and influence of the families in the area to be burnt, individual commanders practiced it to a greater or lesser extent despite the hardships inflicted upon the peasants.

As might be expected, these measures often triggered problems as when a T'ang commander shifted the populace of two prefectures into nearby fortifications and burned everything over their protests. Intended to deprive the rebel leader Liu Chou-wen of all useful material, his callousness merely inflamed the people, prompting many of them to join Liu as they now had no means to survive.[48] Governments indiscriminately applied the policy in areas of rebel activity as well, severely impacting the people's ability to live.[49]

At the establishment of the T'ang, zealousness and a lack of imaginative tactics even prompted Li Yüan's staff to advocate burning and abandoning Ch'ang-an to deny it to the Turks. Fortunately, T'ang T'ai-tsung's firm opposition and guarantee that he would resolve the Turkish issue dissuaded his father from carrying out this ruthless, ill-considered policy.[50] However, when they were on the verge of being subjugated two and a half centuries later, the Southern Han deliberately incinerated their capital on the fallacious assumption that the

Sung "northerners" merely wanted their jewels and other precious items and wouldn't bother to occupy a burned-out city.[51]

Policies of denial were sometimes adopted in the border regions, though consistent implementation was required if both provisions and fodder were to be denied to the highly mobile steppe raiders. Furthermore, to preclude ambushes the *T'ai-pai Yin-ching* advised annually burning any tall grass around cities, along roads and waterways, and in passes and valleys on the first of the tenth month.[52] Being highly wasteful of desperately needed natural resources, such measures were always unpopular but still implemented, especially by aggressors such as the King of Liang, who had the woods along the Yangtze River burned to preclude local brigands from operating within them.[53]

The second primary measure was to protectively coat all exposed wooden surfaces, including any external palisades, with mixtures of clay and mud to prevent their incineration, a technique that was even employed by a clever commander for bamboo sails.[54] This basic method is found in almost all the military writings, mud and clay being applied to the decks of ships and exteriors of assault engines, often intermixed with hemp or straw as a binder.[55] Smaller objects were occasionally stored under water, in pools, and in earthen caves, but they could also be overlaid with metal or even felt materials, though the latter's effectiveness was proportional to its moisture content, or cloaked in rawhide which was the most commonly employed and effective material for a wide variety of equipment and purposes. (The defensive strength of rawhide was repeatedly attested throughout history, not only against arrows and blades, but also incendiary assaults, as at the siege of Hsiang-yang in 1206–1207 where the Jurchen used it to protect their many assault engines.)[56] These measures were implemented throughout the city, but especially in areas vulnerable to attack by incendiary projectiles.[57]

Interestingly, the *Hsiang Yüeh* or *Prescriptions for Villages* written about 1550 by Yin Keng found that contemporary defensive practices, especially for city gates, were inadequate because thin iron plates were being used. This allowed incendiaries to quickly melt the iron, exposing the wood, or heat the encased wooden doors to the ignition point.[58] As the defensive structures no longer included towers mounted over the gates, traditional top-mounted extinguishing methods were not available even though the enemy could throw bundles of faggots up to ten paces, creating massive piles and very high temperatures. Yin therefore advocated returning to the ancient method of covering the gate's wooden leaves with a mud and straw mixture that probably hardened into a sort of molded firebrick.

In addition to buckets of water that might be dumped as needed over the wall or through vertical holes above the vulnerable wooden gates, "oil sacks" were also readied atop the walls. A misnomer, they were actually animal skins which had been heavily oiled to reduce leakage and evaporation before filling with water. Manipulated by several men, they were tossed over the side onto blazing assault devices, particularly those with sharp peaks, splitting open upon impact and extinguishing the fire. First described in the T'ang dynasty *T'ai-pai Yin-ching* (though without specifying the type of animal skin), by the Sung pig and cow bladders were also being dropped upon piles of faggots stacked against the gates and set afire during favorable winds.[59] However, the invention of incendiary carts with concealed oil reservoirs designed to overflow and disseminate the flames when doused with water prompted Sung and later warnings against carelessly employing them against such devices.[60]

Amidst its concise but fairly comprehensive section on extinguishing incendiaries and fighting fires, the T'ang dynasty *T'ung Tien* describes two large fire extinguishers each consisting of a water reservoir containing about three or four piculs of water which are fabricated from horse and cowhide pieces and positioned above every gate. Gravity fed, large diameter bamboo pipes some ten feet long are manipulated by three to five men to douse any fires below.[61] However, they are still supplemented with the usual array of buckets and smaller bamboo siphon pumps which allow a directional spray, though the latter's water volume was clearly inferior to simply employing buckets, assuming an arc of access.[62] Finally, hempen flails made from eight-foot-long cords weighing a total of two *chin*, dipped in a mud slurry, could be used to beat down the flames, but required direct application rather than being deployable at distance.[63]

In addition to these well-conceived, even commonplace methods and techniques, a lack of water or even sand sometimes compelled commanders to innovate dramatically. For example, in their heroic clash with overwhelming Jurchen forces just above Szechuan in the early Southern Sung, Wu Lin resorted to using casks of wine to extinguish fires set by enemy incendiaries in their towers.[64]

For protection, soldiers patrolling the wall carried large, rectangular shields with the two faces joined in a ninety-degree angle. Constructed from bamboo poles, they employed the hollows in the bamboo and small gaps between them to catch the incendiary arrows before pulling them out and extinguishing them.[65]

Whether attempting an ascent, deploying incendiaries, battering the gates, or trying to burrow through fortifications above ground, the aggressors also required protection against incendiaries, as well as the usual array of stones, arrows, and molten materials. If anything, exposed soldiers had only their individual shields, possibly covered with wet leather or felt, to fend off incendiary arrows, but they offered little protection, easily being deflected or crushed by heavier projectiles. Siege engines required overhead structures sturdy enough to withstand 100-pound stones yet still be maneuverable on difficult terrain despite being human rather than animal powered. Heavy wooden timbers, though relatively flammable, were therefore fabricated into large angular structures that could shed oncoming projectiles. Every conceivable variation was probably tried over the many centuries of China's interminable warfare but since most of them were constructed on site from readily available materials, even well-known designs differed greatly in their realization.

The most effective compromise was essentially a movable A-frame structure with a sloped roof extending all the way to the ground or with short vertical side walls. The main horizontal beam was particularly thick so as to withstand severe impact, but the side supports were generally constructed from timbers of lesser dimensions. The overall length was ten to fifteen Chinese feet, with a height specified as seven to eight feet and the addition of six stanchions for standing when not being moved forward.[66] (Heavier, more sophisticated models were mounted like wagons, almost always upon two wheels rather than four, a highly functional compromise on uneven terrain.)[67]

The thick rawhide, which was then stretched over these ribs down to the ground, already presented a basically nonflammable surface to incendiary arrows, swallow tail torches, and similar devices though it could also be wetted or smeared with mud to further retard the effects of burning oil. Originally described in the *T'ai-pai Yin-ching*, these assault devices certainly predate the T'ang and were probably employed even in Mo-tzu's era. Thereafter, they continued to be used in varying, though generally mobile, form with roofs fabricated from rawhide or from wood overlaid with mud or rawhide.[68] Even the stationary, star shaped huts used by engineers to build overlook mounds came to be similarly protected.[69]

In addition to dispersing sand onto boat decks, riverine warfare similarly relied upon rawhide stretched over ship superstructures for protection against ordinary and incendiary arrows. First specified in the *Wu-ching Tsung-yao* and frequently repeated thereafter, rawhide proved especially effective for shielding the smaller, more maneuverable warships.[70] In addition, it is recognized that mobility must also be maintained if riverine incendiary attacks are to be thwarted: "When the enemy sets fire to our boats but the water barriers and warships are all linked together, it will be very difficult to suddenly untie them. If we keep our boats dispersed while engaging in combat, we will avoid any need for defense."[71] Nearby encampments should equally be protected and boats anchored along the shore never lashed together (as at Ch'ih

Pi) or connected to the banks with wooden catwalks to preclude "inviting" an incendiary attack.[72]

Field defense against incendiary attacks presented a rather different problem, particularly when enemy cavalry could exploit relatively open terrain to effect the sort of sudden strikes advised in the later military manuals. Wooden palisades and strongpoints tended to be established close to actual structures, allowing incendiary arrows to be successfully employed against encampments. (The historical records are replete with disasters resulting from failing to deploy perimeter guards and reconnaissance scouts.) In the ensuing chaos, the defender's attention had to be equally divided between extinguishing—or at least avoiding—the fire and repelling subsequent enemy assaults. Astute commanders practiced dispersal and protective measures for their vulnerable stores and provisions, but their tents, fodder, and various wooden implements were all highly flammable.

The section on wind and vegetation has already illustrated how perspicacious commanders prepared against probable attack, but apart from the *Ts'ao-lü Ching-lüeh,* the theoretical writings rarely discuss the subject. However, armies entrapped on heavily vegetated terrain found the *Six Secret Teachings'* ancient methods eternally viable: "When the army is deployed in the wilds, should you happen to encounter fire, cut down the grass and reeds to the sides of the army and in accord with the wind's direction burn them in advance on the left or right, front or back. Then shift the army onto the burned-over terrain, assuming a strict formation in order to wait the enemy." As noted, Li Ling became famous in the Former Han for employing this method against the Hsiungnu forces which, being upwind, attempted to incinerate him by setting the marsh vegetation afire.

## INCENDIARY MEASURES IN DEFENSE

Numerous battle accounts indicate incendiary measures played an integral role in defense from the Warring States onward, if not earlier. In imitation of the *Mo-tzu* remnants, the

T'ang dynasty *T'ai-pai Yin-ching* lists four broad categories of materials as applicable in defense: metal, especially molten blobs; wood splits and logs, presumably burning as well solid; fire, ever present in stoves and cauldrons atop the walls; and stone in various sizes and shapes, though there is no indication that they were heated.[73] In many cases attackers were repelled simply by dumping stones and noxious materials upon them, showering them with burning embers, or clobbering them with logs, whether blazing or not. However, Mo-tzu's heavier mats seem to have become outdated, perhaps because they were too unwieldy even though the large iron "fire beds" certainly exceeded them in weight and size. A variety of incendiary measures and devices, some simplistically brutal, others imaginatively complex, also evolved over the centuries, often in response to larger, well-protected siege engines.

The simplest innovation, merely torches soaked in oil thrown at enemy siege engines protected by rawhide and mud, obviously had an early origin.[74] Far more awkward to deploy was the swallow's tail torch (*yen-wei-chü*) designed to sustain an attack on the protective covering of wooden framed assault engines, though its employment is well attested in the historical records as early as A.D. 548.[75] According to the *T'ai-pai Yin-ching*, rather than any sort of hook, needle, or barb to prevent the ignition source from tumbling down the sharply sloped roof (as would be found somewhat later in "caltrops incendiary balls"), this torch relied upon a construction feature: "Tie reeds and straw to make torches. Divide the ends into two forks like a swallow's tail. Infuse them with oily wax, set them afire, and drop them down from the walls, causing them to mount and burn the wooden donkeys."

Despite their ingenuity, their effectiveness necessarily depended upon the harried troops atop the wall dropping them so adroitly that they would alight with the tail perfectly split across the sharply tapered peaks and thus hold while they continued to burn. The Sung dynasty *Wu-ching Tsung-yao* thus depicts a simple emplacing device, essentially a horizon-

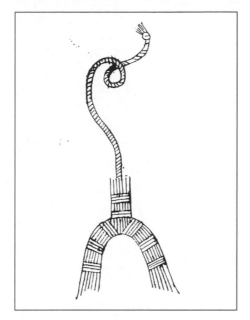

FIGURE 6.2   Swallow's Tail Torch
(Wu-ching Tsung-yao)

tal pole which extends out over the wall from which the reed
bundles can be lowered, though no release or pulley mechanism is shown.[76] However, destroying the enemy's siege
equipment with incendiaries, whatever the type, often persuaded them to abandon the effort and withdraw in frustration.[77]

Portable stoves, cauldrons, and a variety of open fire containers were deployed atop the walls as early as the Warring
States period to provide ignition and heating sources. T'ang
and subsequent theoretical writings say little about employing hot water or oil, though later accounts of actual defense
ordeals as well as secondary sources indicate that it was
poured upon the attackers, whether to make their task slippery or to ensure incinerating rather than just scalding them.

Molten iron was also maintained for "sprinkling" upon the
unsuspecting soldiers from earthen jars just when they were
absorbed in making their ascent,[78] and for attacking assault

FIGURE 6.3 *Molten Metal Dispenser (Wu-pei Chih)*

vehicles protected by wet rawhide or fabricated from relatively impervious wood. During the T'ang dynasty, in fending off an incursion by external peoples at Ch'eng-tu, the provincial capital of Szechuan, the defenders had to resort to molten metal to overcome the protective shields used by attackers undermining the walls.[79] These shields were actually makeshift arches formed from the reed pickets of local fences which had been soaked in water, bent, and over layered, allowing several soldiers to work beneath them. Being wet and hard, like the rattan personal shields often carried by southwestern peoples, they were virtually unaffected by arrows, stone, and fire.

Later on, larger and more complex stoves were maintained on the walls, often with pouring tubes or troughs to direct the drops more precisely, as shown in Figure 6.3.[80] Red hot balls of metal were also flung at besiegers trying to fill ditches in with sacks of straw or wooden splints when incendiary arrows, the most common and convenient method, could not penetrate the layers of dirt.[81] A variant technique ensured that metal sprinkled from atop the walls would achieve maximum effect by first dispersing clouds of ash or lime mixed with chaff dispersed on a favorable wind to blind the attackers.[82]

Projectiles generally similar to those employed by the attackers were also used in defense, though sometimes reduced in size to suit the space constrictions suffered by fighters atop the walls. Incendiary arrows targeting siege engines, various flammable materials being moved forward, and eventually gunpowder comprised the initial response, with the farthest, powered by oversized crossbows (arcuballistae), reportedly reaching some 500 paces out.[83] Crossbows supplemented by reflex bows still constituted the main defensive response, while arrows and bolts generally became more complex in design over the centuries, being used in ever more massive numbers right through the Ming.[84] Small trebuchets positioned on the walls supplemented by larger ones within the citadel complex also played an important role. Stones were the most commonly hurled projectiles, but poisonous smoke balls caused field forces to rapidly disperse and incendiary bombs set their siege engines and supplies alight, destroying materials being employed to fill trenches and moats, and inflicting horrendous wounds on the slow of foot.[85]

Although city defenses necessarily relied upon pine torches, oil lamps, and burning faggots to illuminate both the interior and exterior, especially the base of the walls, often by suspending them by iron chains,[86] some variants were designed to directly attack anyone lurking below. For example, bundles of reeds were set alight and dropped down[87] and iron skids and baskets containing "raging fires fueled by oil and lard" were hung down from iron chains and employed "to incinerate anyone digging (in the darkness) at the walls,"[88] even sometimes being suspended in enemy tunnels to incinerate the miners.[89]

Two other torch variants appeared in the Sung, the "iron beaked fire chicken" and "bamboo fire chicken, the two

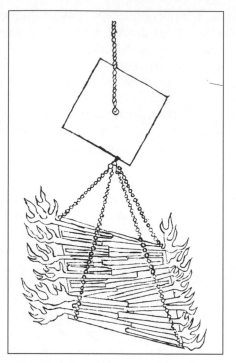

FIGURE 6.4　*Light for Wind and Rain (Fang-shou Chi-ch'eng)*

oddities shown in the illustrations which continued to be found right through the Ming.[90] The former had a weighty charge of gunpowder dispersed throughout the grass tail, the latter encapsulated it within the main body composed from bamboo strips glued together with paper, dried grass, or straw also being employed for the tail. Its overall weight was increased with small stones and both were intended to be hurled by trebuchet at approaching enemy forces to burn their supplies and provisions, startle their troops, and strike them while they tried to fill in ditches and moats.

The rectangular "iron beds" specified in the *Wu-ching Tsung-yao* were simple open lattice work frames five to six feet long and four feet wide upon which up to twenty-four bundles of reeds (termed "fire oxen") might be affixed and

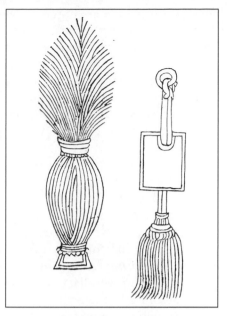

*FIGURE 6.5    Bamboo Fire Chick-
ens (Wu-ching Tsung-yao)*

ignited before being lowered outside the wall. Equipped with
four wooden wheels to allow reeling down, the iron chains
attached to one end also allowed trolling along the base of
the wall to both illuminate and incinerate any enemies
there.[91] However, extra long pine and lard torches could also
be thrust through specially designed holes in the wall to
strike attackers engaged in ascending.

Incendiaries, particularly arrows early but increasingly trebuchet-hurled bombs, were also employed for defensive purposes in both riverine and open terrain warfare. The simplest
form consisted of exploiting readily flammable vegetation,
whether by surprising the enemy upon conducive terrain or
luring them there, as separately discussed. By the Southern
Sung more complex operational tactics sought to impede the
enemy by various means, especially by augmenting natural
water barriers to make them impassable and thereby entangle
the enemy, rendering them easy targets. All sorts of hindrances

might be employed on wet or marshy terrain where progress was already tortuous, including stakes, fences, and sluices, while solid barriers and fences might be erected in active waterways. Streams and minor rivers could be further cluttered with trash and brush, decreasing the maneuverability of enemy boats and rafts prior to attacking them with incendiary arrows and other projectiles.[92] If the wind's speed and direction were conducive, moribund enemies would be unable to extricate themselves.

Flamethrowers, gas ejectors, and other tubed devices powered by early gunpowder formulations designed to emit smoke and other noxious substances were initially developed for defensive rather than offensive use. They probably appeared by the early Sung after some decades or even a century of prehistory since the first military text to discuss them is the Sung dynasty *Wu-ching Tsung-yao*. In particular, the device for "dispersing fierce incendiary oil," now known as a "flame thrower," is described at length and illustrated with a depiction which continued to appear in such subsequent military compendia as the *Wu-pei Chih* and *Wu Pien*.[93]

Apart from the pumping mechanism, which remains a matter of some speculation, the key components were the ignition chamber where a gunpowder wick provided the continuous flame essential to igniting the oil, and the reservoir of "fierce incendiary oil"—presumably naptha or benzene—that was sprayed onto the target. The flamethrower of A.D. 1050 was obviously not a portable, handheld weapon, but a cumbersome bronze contraption that required a level footing, such as a city wall, to be deployed, though ship's decks, however rocking and rolling, eventually served equally well, allowing aggressive employment against enemy vessels.

Since the nozzle was affixed to the base, enemy troops attacking a wall could probably avoid a spray of fire from single units. This perhaps accounts for one of the recommended methods of employment, one much in accord with Mo-tzu's old traps, first strewing "fire oxen" fabricated from bundles of dry straw on the ground outside the fortifications to create a highly flammable killing field. When the

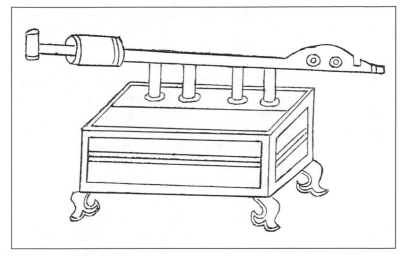

FIGURE 6.6    *Flame Thrower (Wu-ching Tsung-yao)*

flamethrowers were then employed, they would not only strike and burn any troops directly in the line of fire but also ignite the straw bundles, engulfing the soldiers crowded below in a lethal sea of fire. (Simply dropping already blazing straw oxen, although a common technique, would more likely scatter the troops, perhaps even cause them to temporarily retreat, but the straw bundles might also be avoided, pushed aside with "fire forks," and even extinguished with comparatively few casualties.)

The first historical account of "incendiary oil" apparently dates to a riverine clash in A.D. 919 in which some 400 vessels were incinerated.[94] Thereafter, it's next mentioned in A.D. 975 when Southern T'ang, one of the last obstacles to Sung consolidated rule, employed it against the latter's fleet on the Yangtze River. However, just when it appeared their incendiary attack would prove effective, the wind turned and the southern fleet was essentially destroyed.[95] Whether the flamethrower had already appeared or the oil was simply thrown in clay containers or poured down upon the enemy before igniting, practices which continued even in the Ming,[96] remains unknown.

An interesting historical incident suggests it was already available in sufficient quantity to offer to steppe peoples in A.D. 917, prompting Needham's conclusion that "fierce oil," a distilled petroleum product in contrast to the naturally occurring deposits known in China and employed for military purposes from the Han, was first imported from the West around A.D. 900.[97] A quantity of "fierce incendiary oil" was sent to the Khitan ruler with the suggestion that it could be employed to burn the wooden defensive towers on the fortifications and would flare up even more vigorously if attempts were made to extinguish it with water. (This property explains the sudden Sung emphasis upon not employing water against fire.) Although the ruler thought to employ it on an attack on Yu-chou, his consort dissuaded him by citing the possible embarrassment if it failed, whereas they could simply employ an attritional strategy and starve out the defenders.[98]

The needs of defense coupled with the increasing power of gunpowder formulations in the Sung, if not somewhat earlier, also stimulated the evolution of a variety of tubed antipersonnel devices designed to forcefully emit flames, gasses, noxious particles, and eventually small projectiles, as illustrated. Though not yet at the stage of a proto-gun insofar as the explosive force was not being utilized to fire a close-fitting projectile, the effects were still painfully dramatic, the weapons capable of blinding, choking, scalding, and burning the troops' leather armor, wooden shafted weapons, and assault devices.

Constructed from a variety of readily available materials, including large-diameter bamboo tubes wrapped with cord and affixed to the end of wooden shafts and short, bottle-shaped bronze tubes, they were increasingly employed through the Sung, being widely deployed in siege defenses in the twelfth and especially thirteenth century, often by the thousands, against steppe groups who also quickly adopted them. Over the centuries they also increased in range and power, being lethal at fifty feet or more, and thus capable of aggressive action, setting palisades, equipment, and vessels afire in more open field combat.[99] Eventually these "eruptors"

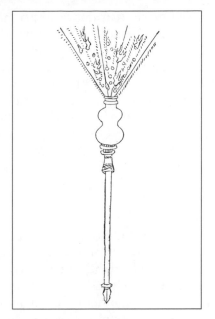

*FIGURE 6.7   Eruptor for Pene-
trating Assaults (Wu-pei Chih)*

(in Needham's terminology) also grew in size, coming to resemble primitive cannon rather than oddities such as the fire
lance which essentially combined a smoking tube with a long
shaft, before finally evolving into cannon and then musket
type hand held weapons.[100]

The development of these tubed eruptors and "coviative"
projectile emitters, including arrows, eventually saw them
combined with a bizarre array of mobile, oversized shields
studded with various bladed weapons and decorated with
fearsome creatures. Because they could be quickly wheeled
into position even in confined areas, they could be employed
as a stopgap measure anywhere, though they proved particularly effective against breaches in the walls and gates, and for
blocking and combating aggressors in tunnels.

Numerous weapons and tools, many highly localized, were
also created for various defensive tasks, including the implementation of incendiary measures and defending against

them. Few achieved more than minor importance, but some saw wider use over centuries. For example, the "fire fork" *(huo ch'a)* was a long shafted device with top blades configured like a figure eight designed to manipulate firewood within a tunnel, allowing the addition of lard and oil so as to bring down the city walls. [101] Some three days of constant burning were said to be required to achieve the intended result, during which time the fires had to be attended.

Finally, the *Fang-shou Chi-ch'eng* compiled by Chu Lu in 1853, a vast but not necessarily comprehensive monograph of more than 1,000 woodblock pages, represents the culmination of the poliorcetic tradition. A response to obvious mid-nineteenth-century Ch'ing defensive inadequacies, it simultaneously marks the end point for traditional incendiary theory and practice. Although cannon and other gunpowder weapons were by then widespread and employed in ever escalating numbers and generally given priority by the military writers,[102] much earlier equipment and many methods were still deemed functional, including caltrops, *cheaveux-de-frise,* eruptors, various smoke and incendiary bombs, and even trebuchets. Surprisingly, despite including a chronicle of K'ai-feng's demise by flood in 1641, Chu ignores the menace of aquatic attack.

Nevertheless, a variety of fire-fighting equipment and several antique devices, such as the swallow's tail torch, are reprised for repelling incendiary and other assaults. Moreover, the fundamental principle of mounting an active defense, of "going forth to harasses the enemy, burning their provisions and assault equipment" is still advocated despite advances in gunpowder weaponry and lethality.[103] Should enemy forces penetrate the outer defenses, rather than shooting them with arrows or cannon, Chu advocated creating a sea of fire between the main fortifications and the exterior moon wall with torches, wood, and bamboo.[104] Unable to withstand the smoke and fire's intensity, the aggressors would then be compelled to retreat.

In addition to the sieges found in the final section, two T'ang dynasty examples well illustrate the use of incendiaries in defense during the era of these first textual formulations. Chang Hsün, who gained prominence in battling the rebellious forces of An Lu-shan, numbered among the few resourceful and tactically astute T'ang dynasty commanders. Dedicated and resolute, he also excelled in motivating men under the harshest circumstances, twice commanding last-ditch city defenses against insurmountable odds. The first, at Yung-ch'iu in A.D. 756, saw his paltry 2,000 men repeatedly sally forth and wreck havoc among the 40,000 attackers over some sixty days and 300 encounters. Apart from resorting to the classic ploy of straw men to replenish their arrow supply, he utilized burning reeds and grass that had been soaked in oil to decisively repel attackers ascending the walls.

At the historically famous siege of Sui-yang in Anhui, Chang and a stalwart 6,800 soldiers then withstood the repeated onslaughts of an initial 130,000-man rebel force under Yin Tzu-ch'i, one of An Lu-shan's chief commanders.[105] Commencing in the first month of 757, Chang's external thrusts amidst virtually unremitting conflict over the next ten months inflicted heavy casualties while battles along the walls claimed many more. Reportedly 120,000 rebels eventually perished in the encounter, but the garrison kept dwindling until only 400 starving warriors remained for the final hand-to-hand battle that saw them exterminated.

Incendiaries were employed at least twice defensively, the first time to burn a massive, rainbow-shaped assault bridge which had been constructed and wheeled into place. Capable of conveying 200 men on top (with more engaged in the work below), they were hooked, blocked, and burnt by three poles simultaneously thrust out from three holes in the wall. Molten metal was also used to effectively attack the numerous wooden donkeys. Finally, a major clandestine nighttime operation was mounted to prepare the faggots and firewood being piled to create an assault ramp outside the city walls for incineration. Over more than ten nights pine splints and grass were inserted inside the mounds and then the entire mass, which had been covered with earth to provide a firm roadway, ignited amidst an exploitable wind. Although it burned for more than twenty days, Chang's techniques and heroism finally came to nought because the city eventually fell, though they had retarded the rebellion's southward advance for nearly a year and exacted a high toll.

In the turbulent decades following An Lu-shan's rebellion, Chu Ts'u rebelled, proclaimed himself emperor, and attacked the T'ang emperor at Feng-t'ien outside Ch'ang-an, where the ritual sacrifices to Heaven where being held in the tenth month of 783. Just when their initial assaults were about to penetrate the gates, the defenders set several large incendiary wagons filled with firewood afire, blocking their entrance. However, being unexpectedly forced to take refuge at Feng-t'ien, the defenders quickly ran short of food, clothes, and weapons even as they repulsed the besiegers' determined attacks only with the most fervent efforts.

To overwhelm the fortifications Chu had a renegade monk construct a giant wheeled assault ladder capable of carrying 500 men with wood forcibly salvaged from a nearby temple. However, it was quickly recognized that the machine was not only heavy and unwieldy, but had also been constructed from very dry wood. Calculating that the attack would be mounted in the northeast, troops tunneled out to excavate a pit about eight feet deep, which they filled with firewood saturated with accelerants and concealed with a thick layer of manure.

Early on the morning of the 15th, the eleventh month, backed by a strong northerly wind and fully confident that the exterior layers of heavy, wet hemp mats coupled with the sacks of water would protect them from incendiary attack, the rebels advanced. Men atop the ladder suppressed the defenders (whose stones, arrows, or incendiaries were not having any effect anyway) with a continuous fusillade of arrows while those within the base of the assault ladder laid down wooden splints and earth to fill any depressions and provide a firm roadbed. However, the front wheels eventually broke into the pit whereupon flames from the already burning firewood leapt up, igniting the structure from underneath. Although the developing flames flared perilously close to the wall's defenders, they further fueled the blaze with oil and torches. Fortunately, the wind suddenly changed to blow back upon the aggressors and fan a conflagration which fully consumed the assault ladder and everyone upon it. The stench reportedly carried for miles and the disheartened attackers withdrew only to suffer further casualties from aggressive sallies and eventually abandon the siege upon the appearance of a substantial rescue force.[106]

## INCENDIARIES IN MINING AND COUNTER-MINING

Mining techniques had already become highly systematized by the mid Warring States, if not a century or two earlier, and only minimal changes occurred thereafter prior to the perfection and application of gunpowder explosives in the Yüan and Ming. In reiterating the basic tunneling technique, the T'ang dynasty *T'ai-pai Yin-ching* simply advised that sustaining pillars be erected every *chang* or ten feet and firewood piled between them which, when burned, would bring down the walls.[107] Subsequent works, beginning with the T'ang *T'ung Tien* and early Sung *Hu-ch'ien Ching,* copy the passage with but slight variations in wording. Even such late Ming manuals as the *Teng-t'an Pi-chiu* provide only brief, though illustrated, summaries on the fundamentals of tunneling, including how to secure the ceiling and stabilize the walls with posts and beams and then cause the walls to collapse through the ancient technique of setting the pillars ablaze using firewood rather than any accelerant even though fierce oil had been around for a millennium.[108] Above-ground variants also existed which employed closely packed post-and-beam combinations to gradually extend a protected passageway right to the walls where soldiers could either directly attack the fortifications or commence burrowing downward.

Although defending against these techniques continued to be crucial, Mohist incendiary methods similarly underwent little alteration over the centuries. Detection being a requisite precursor, listening wells some twenty feet deep were sunk in varying number, but minimally at the four corners of the city and along the perimeter facing the enemy's encampment to facilitate determining the proximity and direction of tunneling activity. (More wells increased the system's sensitivity and precision, but as they required manning and protection, were generally limited to the so-called eight directions.)[109] For listening devices, the large, freshly made earthen jars originally described in the *Mo-tzu,* with or without leather membranes stretched over the mouth, were said to be sensitive enough to detect the sound of underground activity up to 500 paces away.[110] Though direct assaults were increasingly mounted upon the miners over the centuries, particularly upon those attacking the walls themselves, smoke bolstered with poisonous and caustic agents was the method of choice since it could invidiously pervade the tunnel system when adequately propelled without offering the invaders a tangible target. Incendiary measures might also be mounted at external entrances but not from within the city in order to avoid igniting flammable material already piled in the tunnel and thereby collapsing the walls.[111]

Accordingly, the *T'ai-pai Yin-ching* simply advised that a deep well *(t'ien ching)* be cut down close to the enemy's tunnel so that firewood might be piled at the bottom and then set ablaze in order to smoke them out.[112] Shortly thereafter, the *T'ung Tien* described a more lethal approach, using bellows to propel the noxious smoke from burning a large quantity of dry moxa (mugwort or artemesia) into the tunnel in order to fumigate and cauterize the unfortunate troops.[113] While its effectiveness might be questioned since the miners could presumably flee, the gas's severe caustic effects cannot. By the Sung smoke bombs such as the Thunder-clap Smoke Sphere (whose outer layers contained several noxious substances which produced poison smoke upon combustion) and the Prickly Incendiary Sphere were displacing the more cumbersome method of building fires, setting up bellows, and running pipes.[114]

Being expected, interdiction attempts were not without countermeasures. For example, in the Sung dynasty a roughly circular shield called a P'i Man ("leather overflowing") designed to temporarily block the tunnel and thus the noxious gasses was fabricated from rawhide. When successfully manipulated, it could deflect the poisonous gas back upon the launchers.[115] A second method cleverly used air flow generated by the horizontal vanes of a large, portable hand-cranked fan to propel lime, chaff, and noxious gasses from incendiary and poisonous smoke bombs toward enemy defenders who breached the tunnel, as well as deflect any oncoming smoke back toward the generator. Geophones were thus a necessary adjunct to mining work, allowing the detection of counter-mining efforts and preparation against interception.[116] In addition, soldiers who deployed thunderclap incendiary spheres underground, propelling the dense black smoke toward the enemy with bamboo fans, kept licorice water in their mouths as an antidote.[117]

The advent of gunpowder naturally saw hotter, more volatile gasses and variant methods. For example, at the end of the incendiary tradition during Li tzu-ch'eng's second siege of Pien-ching early in 1642, the aggressors attempted to tunnel into the walls but defenders dropped firewood intermixed with (incendiary) gunpowder blocks to burn them out when the latter could no longer strike them, the combination reportedly burning for a full day and night. Another attempt was thwarted when the defenders intercepted a tunnel and, encountering stiff opposition, first burned a combination of firewood interlaced with gunpowder, then extinguished it with water so as to execute a follow-on attack which ultimately captured some thirty-six shafts which were then employed against the enemy.[118]

# 7

# Riverine Warfare

Although somewhat outside the scope of our discussion, the employment of rivers and lakes as defensive obstacles requires a few observations be made on the nature of riverine engagements before examining the widespread use of incendiaries in fleet combat, though not the vast subject of naval warfare itself. Fighting along China's many rivers and streams was both hazardous and difficult, especially when they were as wide as the Yellow River or as powerful as some of the rushing torrents found outside the central plains. Lacking boats, two armies moving in parallel along an intervening river of any depth and velocity were reduced to taunts, glaring, and harassing archery fire. Moreover, rivers could also trap armies backed against them, drowning the panicked soldiers by the thousands.

Tactical principles for operating in riverine environments, for undertaking amphibious attacks and mounting riverside defense, gradually evolved. Armies attempting to ford rivers were exposed to archery fire, generally weighed down with heavy equipment, often cold and wet, and invariably entrapped in snail-like movement. Their line of attack would generally be confined to shallow areas with sandy deposits or expanses where the river had sufficiently widened for the depth to average only two or three feet. In either case, the enormous tactical advantage enjoyed by well-entrenched defenders on the far shore deterred most attempts and Sun Pin deemed "river crossings" to be one of five situations in which victory cannot be achieved.[1]

Pondering these problems, Sun-tzu formulated some basic guidelines that became virtually sacrosanct:

> After crossing rivers, you must distance yourself from them. If the enemy is fording a river to advance, do not confront them in the water. When half their forces have crossed, it will be advantageous to strike them.
>
> If you want to engage the enemy in battle, do not array your forces near the river to confront the invader, but look for tenable ground and occupy the heights. Do not confront the current's flow. This is the way to deploy the army where there are rivers.[2]

A reformulation in the late Sung *Unorthodox Strategies* shows how well accepted his views had become:[3]

> Whether deploying your forces along the banks or anchoring your vessels in the middle of a river to engage an enemy in battle, it is referred to as river warfare.
>
> When you approach a river, you must deploy your lines some distance from the edge to entice the enemy to cross and also show there is nothing suspicious. If you definitely want to engage in battle, do not approach too close to the river to confront the enemy because they might fear being unable to ford successfully. If you do not want to engage in battle, resist their forces right at the river to impede them, making it impossible for them to ford the river.
>
> If an enemy fords a river to engage you in battle, it will be advantageous to wait at the water's edge until half have crossed before striking them. A tactical principle from the *Wu-tzu* states: "When half their forces have forded the river, they can be attacked."

Not just rivers, but any body of water, including wide moats, can easily stymie armies which fail to carry boats or tools for fabricating transport craft. Even then, the difficulties presented by sequentially conveying the forces across, the delays incurred in loading and unloading materials and provisions, and the time actually expended in crossing wreck havoc with campaign schedules while making the army vulnerable to sudden attack. Several *Six Secret Teachings'* chapters thus describe fairly elaborate equipment for crossing rivers and streams, primarily winch-operated extendible bridges and chain-linked sectional assemblies that provide a fairly stable roadbed, although pontoon bridges were also common, having been used as early as the Western Chou dynasty.[4] Linked raft-like structures, though somewhat less effective, could also provide a means for soldiers to cross. Thus commanders were enjoined to always bring along Flying Bridges, Flying Rivers, and Heavenly Floats and ensure that the troops were experienced in their use, though the weight and size of the twenty-foot sections would deter carrying them unless difficult crossings were anticipated at the campaign's outset.

In the absence of such equipment, ingenious ways had to be devised for exploiting readily available materials to create the sort of temporary conveyances shown in Figures 7.1 and 7.2 taken from the Sung dynasty *Wu-ching Tsung-yao* and reproduced in many military manuals thereafter, but first described in the *T'ai-pai Yin-ching*.[5] In the south, bamboo's strength and buoyancy made it ideal for constructing traditionally shaped boats and hasty rafts, but many other light woods could be used for fabricating them and the frames of small, one- or two-man leather-covered boats. Large cooking vessels and clay pots were also pressed into service in extreme circumstances, whether singly or lashed together between bamboo poles or spears, and even their spears could be bundled together or laid out to form a raft.

Naturally these extemporaneous, sometimes comical vessels lacked stability and control, but by judiciously choosing the launching point and exploiting the current's flow, a small force might mount a surprise attack, secure a beachhead for utilizing more conventional methods, or effect a night crossing without noisy boats. Although little equipment could be carried, the soldiers would avoid the soaking they would

FIGURE 7.1    *Animal Skin Floats*
(*Wu-ching Tsung-yao*)

suffer when wading along heavy lines stretched across the river or attempting to swim.

During Liu Pang's years of conflict with Hsiang Yü, Han Hsin actually moved the bulk of his army across at Hsia-yang by using earthenware jars lashed together with ridgepoles after having created the erroneous impression that they were preparing to cross the river by boat at Lin-chin.[6] In vanquishing King Pao of Wei he thus utilized the sort of deceptive technique much advocated by the classic military writings and employed "unorthodox technical skills to cross deep waters and ford rivers." Such examples prompted the *Unorthodox Strategies* to advise:[7]

> Whenever you and an enemy oppose each other along opposite banks of a river, if you want to ford the river far off, you should prepare numerous boats and oars to show that you intend to cross nearby. The enemy will certainly mass

*FIGURE 7.2    Spear Raft (Wu-ching Tsung-yao)*

troops in response and you can then effect a crossing at some vacuous point.

If you lack boats and oars, you can employ such things as bamboo, reeds, large wine vessels, cooking utensils, or spears and lances lashed together to serve as rafts and thereby cross the river. A tactical principle from the *Art of War* states: "When your objective is distant, make it appear as if nearby."

## RIVERINE THEORY AND FUNDAMENTAL INCENDIARY PRACTICES

Simple watercraft were widespread by the Neolithic and three plank versions by the Shang, but significant military employment didn't begin until the Western Chou when they were used to ferry goods and construct a pontoon bridge.[8] Once they began conveying troops and supplies in the Spring and

Autumn period, river transport became essential to southern campaigns, facilitated every attack on Shu, and empowered Ch'in's ventures into the south. Late in the era Wu, Yüeh, and Ch'u exploited the interconnected rivers and lakes to launch amphibious assaults while seaborne invasions, although confined to littoral waters, commenced when Wu's flotilla ventured up the coast to mount an ill-conceived attack on Ch'i. Thereafter, riverine and lake-centered naval actions invariably comprised an integral part of invasion efforts, though overseas strikes against external enemies located in Korea and Southeast Asia didn't commence until the Ch'in and Han periods after Ch'in developed the first specialized sailors.

Apart from a few tactical discussions embedded in the historical accounts, prior to the Sung dynasty only Sun Pin's single chapter "Ten Deployments" advanced any principles for riverine combat. As the *Art of War* had already laid down the fundamental principle that the current's flow could not be contravened and most of the smaller boats employed on the rivers and inland lakes were rowed, Sun Pin stressed preparation and exploiting the current's force. With the development of usable sails in the Han, larger multi-decked vessels powered by both rowers and sail evolved.

Although capable of carrying more archers and thus increasing the volume of arrows, larger did not necessarily translate into better, particularly before gunpowder weapons significantly augmented their lethality. In the wind's absence these heavier vessels demanded far more muscle power, their higher profiles made them difficult to maneuver and control in a cross or head wind, and they were almost impossible to tow up river by crews struggling along the embankment.[9] Larger vessels also made ideal targets for incendiary and ramming attacks, setting up a classic confrontation between bulk and speed as massive, high, heavily staffed slow vessels contended with swifter, lighter, more maneuverable but less formidable craft.

Beginning with the Three Kingdoms, riverine fleets grew both in the size and number of vessels, though a few designs proliferated, such as are sketched (in somewhat distorted fashion) in the Sung military manuals. (Sung ships themselves required increased manpower and carried numerous weapons, including rockets, flamethrowers, small trebuchets, fragmentation bombs, and heavy crossbows.) Incendiary attacks, particularly those exploiting the wind, proved remarkably successful against these wooden boats laden with inflammable materials and were advocated as the fundamental means for achieving what the soldiers could not.[10]

Just as in city defense, various techniques were adopted to minimize the risk, including wetting all the exposed surfaces, covering the decks with sand, and overlaying with wet hemp or leather, but incendiary arrows still found apparently inaccessible surfaces.[11] Since the ships were often closely packed and sometimes even linked for stability or anchored next to encampments, minor fires easily turned into inescapable conflagrations accompanied by uncountable drownings. The astounding number of vessels, often 500 or more, employed in single campaigns after the Han produced pervasive congestion and thus immensely facilitated these attacks, particularly if fleet mobility could be aggressively compromised.

Despite the rapid escalation in riverine incendiary combat, these clashes were little discussed until the Sung dynasty *Ts'ui-wei Pei-cheng-lu* briefly described a two-stage method for vanquishing enemies on or in water: first they should be impeded with every imaginable device, including wooden stakes, fences, trash, and brush, and then attacked with incendiaries by exploiting the wind. Thereafter, the *Hundred Unorthodox Strategies* explicated the fundamental principles under the topic of "Amphibious Warfare":

> Whenever you engage an enemy in combat along rivers and on lakes it is necessary to have boats and oars. Moreover, you should assume a position upwind or upstream. One who is upwind can exploit the wind to mount an incendiary attack and set the enemy afire. One who is upstream can utilize the current's strategic power to ram the enemy with high-walled war vessels. In such cases you will always be victorious in bat-

tle. The *Art of War* states: "One who wants to engage in combat does not go contrary to the current's flow."[12]

This was an ancient view, as the chapter's historical illustration indicates:

> In the Spring and Autumn period Ho-lü, the future king of Wu, attacked the state of Ch'u. Ch'u ordered their prime minister to divine about the battle's outcome, which turned out to be inauspicious. The Minister of War said: "We have gained a superior position upstream, so how can it be inauspicious?"
>
> Ch'u subsequently engaged Wu in battle, employing massive, high-walled vessels to suddenly penetrate Wu's flotilla. Wu's strategic power was therefore weakened, and their army found it difficult to fend off Ch'u's land forces. Eventually Wu's army was badly defeated.

The most comprehensive analysis of riverine warfare principles is found in Ho Liang-ch'en's late Ming dynasty *Ch'en Chi* in the chapter entitled "Shui-chan":

> When engaging in riverine warfare, you must occupy the upper reaches. When mounting a riverine defense, you should erect palisades amidst the flow. You can exploit the wind to set fires, take advantage of heavy rain to inundate, or utilize sacks of sand and break dikes, whether in accord with or contrary to customary usage.
>
> Whenever you occupy an unfavorable position or confront an opposing wind, your boats should turn about in orderly fashion. In this case your equipment needs to be responsive and your incendiary and ordinary crossbows apportioned in advance.
>
> Even more appropriately, you should quickly set up palisades and barriers and set out numerous flags and pennants that should frequently be changed. Your warriors need to be light, nimble, and trained in advance.

While embracing several of Sun-tzu's principles, Ho obviously viewed the role of incendiary techniques to be fundamental: "Only those who excel at using fire and water have the awesomeness to shake Heaven. Thus their efforts are not wasted and their results are doubled."[13] Moreover, he concluded that in the aggressive practice of riverine warfare these tactical principles could only be neglected at one's peril: "This is the crux of aquatic warfare. Generals must fully penetrate this crux and examine its advantages, for if they don't realize these advantages, they will certainly be harmed by them."

By this time powerful, unwieldy behemoths had long dominated both riverine and coastal warfare, but smaller vessels could still exploit superior maneuverability to decimate them through incendiary techniques, just as at the battle of P'o-yang Lake.[14] In discussing the essential though supplementary role of these smaller vessels, several manuals such as the *Ts'ao-lü Ching-lüeh* equally emphasized the primacy of incendiary techniques in achieving victory.[15] Moreover, it was suggested that ad hoc forces might be created in the coastal regions simply by recruiting experienced sailors for their core. Even fishing boats could be co-opted simply by supplying the sailors with weapons and training them in coordinated maneuvers, thereby producing an elite fighting force within a year.[16]

The intensity of so-called Japanese pirate activity along the southeastern coast from the middle Ming onward also prompted several of the imperial commanders deputed to conduct suppressive campaigns, including the famous Ch'i Chi-kuang, to incorporate materials on ships and naval engagements in their military manuals. Thus Wang Ming-ho's *Teng-t'an Pi-chiu*, completed in 1599, discusses boats and related combat issues in its 100-page section on naval warfare, and also includes other sections on coastal and riverine defenses and their specific configurations.[17] Moreover, his riverine warfare subchapters are not confined to the daunting task of fording rivers or slaughtering enemies in the midst of crossing, but instead focus on clashes between powerful armadas comprised of disparate vessels. Thus, although he integrates the usual array of older views beginning with Sun-tzu's *Art of War*, incendiary measures are emphasized.[18]

Despite no amphibious attacks or riverine battles having resulted, Wang believed that China's naval history began with King Wu's conclave at Meng-chin and that the Spring and Autumn period witnessed the first employment of boats in warfare, primarily in the southeast. He therefore concluded "the saying that 'Wu and Ch'u use boats and oars as chariots and horses, the rivers and oceans as level thoroughfares' is not erroneous."[19] Numerous insightful observations on incendiary warfare are also interspersed among his descriptions of contemporary vessels.

Three stages generally marked most engagements. First, bows and arrows, including flaming arrows, and eventually canon and occasionally catapults would be employed at a distance, followed by long-handled (eleven-foot) dagger-axes, halberds, and spears in near proximity, and finally short swords for close combat after boarding the enemy's vessel. Several means were utilized over the centuries to set enemy vessels aflame, generally similar in design and action to those used in land warfare. Contact action by agents, whether sneaking down the shore, stealthily approaching in boats, or swimming in the darkness was the most direct but also most easily prevented. Next ranked incendiary arrows for acting at a distance, especially against densely packed or immobilized fleets. Thereafter incendiary bombs hurled by trebuchet and eventually shot from cannon, both of which relied on gunpowder mixtures for high temperature and certain ignition, followed.

The oldest and simplest device, one employed from Ch'ih Pi right through the end of the Ming was the fire boat, the aquatic version of the fire cart. Moreover, as the military manuals all point out, simply by exploiting the wind or current's propulsive effects fire boats could proceed to their targets without animal power or human intervention. Sophisticated designs were not required because an open raft would serve almost as well as an expertly constructed boat, though the mission's self-destructive nature mandated that inexpensive and derelict craft be employed. Every imaginable

*FIGURE 7.3    Early Fire Boat*
*(Wu-ching Tsung-yao)*

variety of raft was pressed into service in the exigency of the
moment, ranging from fresh reeds and bamboo to old timbers salvaged from nearby houses. Any vessel with sufficiently
high side walls to pack large quantities of flammable material
while fending off the spray and waves would suffice, even
boxes simply placed atop ad hoc rafts.

Although fire boats were doubtlessly employed long before
Ch'ih Pi, they were first described in the *T'ai-pai Yin-ching*
and then illustrated in the Sung dynasty *Wu-ching Tsung-yao*
with many more depictions, often the same ones, appearing
right through the Ming. Even the *Teng-t'an Pi-chiu's* incendiary boat is extremely primitive—simply a floating rectangular pan, something like a trough for mixing cement—and
therefore certainly not useful for any sort of surprise attack
since the blazing flames would be visible even at a distance,
especially if several were employed en masse. The accompanying caption in fact emphasizes their expendability: "Now in

[riverine] incendiary warfare use decrepit boats or wooden rafts, load them with grass and firewood, and then with a favorable wind and in accord with the current, ignite them to incinerate the enemy's multi-storied vessels and combat ships and warships."[20]

The *Wu-pei Chih* describes a vessel intended for close combat in the fire boat tradition known as a "mother son combo" whose lethality was premised upon it being set aflame after impaling an enemy craft, presumably a much larger and more valuable one. Described as a simple vessel, essentially a shell thirty-five feet long and twenty feet wide with a slotted stern which concealed a small boat, when engaged in battles it would be rammed into or hooked against the enemy vessel before being firmly lashed together with a slippery line. The marines on board would first let loose a fusillade of arrows and then, having ignited their own craft, surprise their enemies by abandoning it in the small boat concealed in the rear, rowing off rather than simply diving overboard and swimming away. The combustible pile in the otherwise vacant interior— an interlaced mixture of reeds and faggots drenched with oil and sesame (oil) which would be set alight by a coarse gunpowder fuse—would easily generate enough heat to ensure both vessels would be consumed in the ensuing fire.

The text also preserves evidence of another small, maneuverable vessel called a "red dragon boat" which similarly relied upon incendiary activity. The fanciful illustration depicts a boat with a full dragon's head and tail which the accompanying description confirms, though the reality was probably far more mundane: "The boat's shape is like a dragon and it is divided into three decks, the equipment and incendiary implements being stored within. The head is covered to look like a dragon's head, with an open mouth sufficient for a single soldier to observe the enemy's actions." Fitted out with several openings for firing weapons and incendiaries, its effectiveness relied upon large numbers—reportedly several hundred were to be used— to patrol the Yangtze. When enemy vessels approached the shore, they were to fire their cannon, incendiary arrows, and rockets en masse, accompanied by poison smoke.[21]

*FIGURE 7.4    Fire Dragon boat
(Wu-pei Chih)*

Finally, there is an illustration of a "fire dragon boat," a small, multi-deck vessel with long outward-projecting booms, essentially huge torches designed to set enemy vessels afire at a slight distance. Unfortunately the depiction lacks any explanation, but presumably its small crew would maneuver under oar until close enough to lower one of these torches onto an enemy warship.[22] In addition, long narrow boats powered by side wheels also deployed incendiary balls along with other missile weapons to destroy enemy boats.[23]

Further evidence that incendiary measures were commonplace may be seen in Wang's disparagement of the flammability of the smaller vessels that relied upon interwoven bamboo rather than wood for their structural covering. However, he felt that boats that completely lack protection against incendiaries, as well as arrows and stones, were even worse. External layers such as cowhide, fish netting, and coarse felt, together with wooden over-structures to shield against trebuchet-hurled stones, could not be neglected. Moreover, the men manning the boats should always be strong swimmers and skilled archers so that incendiary arrows might be shot at any time and holes stealthily bored, cannon being reserved for similarly equipped pirates.[24]

Two main weapons were apparently employed for attack in the coastal region: an overhead pounder and a gunpowder-based incendiary bomb carried in the prow which could be dropped onto the enemy, setting them afire. Although Wang Ming-ho believed that the brave could use gunpowder and other devices in the face of the enemy, he also felt that employing incendiaries was a complex task. Simplification and structure were therefore required:[25]

> For boats engaged in riverine warfare, an incendiary attack is the first device. This is certain. Yet, although the various types of incendiary equipment are extremely numerous, those that can be employed to respond in urgent situations are very few. Why?
>
> When two vessels are closing and victory and submission are about to become visible, some incendiary equipment will be appropriate for use, but because their deployment is enormously tricky, in the flurry of the moment they cannot be discharged as they should be. Or they may be repeatedly fired without effect; or their precision and skill levels are appropriate, but their power cannot be fully deployed throughout the boat; or they are too heavy and useless and cannot be fired.
>
> Upon reaching the brigands' boats, the most inappropriate of all is seeing incendiary devices arrayed with fuses in their mouths. If you wait until the flame enters the mouth, detonating them will be in our hands. But if you just ignite and throw them, they will be thwarted by the brigands.
>
> Moreover, the so-called ash bottles which contain lime are presumably effective in causing the deck to become slippery and keeping men from gaining a footing. It is also said that chicken and duck eggs should be throw down on the enemy, and even slippery mud is possible. But when we use ash bottles today, they just make the deck coarse and enable the brigands to stand more firmly. This is no good, no good.

Now if we repeatedly try these methods and winnow them down so that they accord with the troop's capabilities and inclinations so that there is no dissension, the number to be employed will amount to only two, one for near and one for far. These will achieve the objective and be sufficient. The more skillful and complex [incendiary methods are], the more they will lack actual use. Note it, note it!

Assuming that all the normal precautionary measures required for handling gunpowder are observed—such as ensuring its dryness and storing it properly—the key issue seems to have been timing the detonation. Fuses lit too early would allow the enemy time to dispose of the device, whether barrel or bomb, or even hurl it back, whereas waiting too long could prove deadly. Wang in fact found that a variation on the primitive method of merely dumping a couple of barrels of gunpowder on the enemy's vessel accompanied by burning embers to be an ideal solution. Although requiring close proximity, when used in quantity the dispersed gunpowder would be almost impossible to counter, especially as complete barrels, which might simply be thrown overboard or may miss their target, would not be employed.[26]

Nevertheless, apparently because of the inconvenience of trying to dump gunpowder from an open barrel—why paper sacks of gunpowder which would certainly break upon percussion were not employed is unknown—Wang did suggest a variation on the gunpowder bomb consisting of a barrel dropped down onto the enemy. A clay bowl partially filled with glowing charcoal covered over with ashes is to be placed in the top of the open barrel. When dropped down onto the enemy's deck, the tumbling, shaking, and bumping would intermix the glowing charcoal with the gunpowder, igniting it.

Although no purer incendiary method can be imagined, two decades later the *Wu-pei Chih* modified the construction, placing the bowl of glowing charcoal inside the barrel atop a layer of sand protectively overlaying the gunpowder.[27] Again, the intent was incendiary rather than explosive, though being constructed from wood the ensuing detonation would probably have had enough force to burst the barrel if the top were closed, dispersing the residual, relatively slow-burning gunpowder onto the wooden deck. The problem of fuses is thus completely avoided, though at the cost of putting a highly dangerous igniter inside and then not disturbing the contents until the barrel is launched, never forgetting it has been primed and incinerating your own ship in the confusion of battle.

For riverine incendiary warfare the *Wu-pei Chih* also advised employing a quantity of eggshells from large birds such as geese and ducks which would break on impact and disperse a slippery medium when thrown onto the decks of enemy ships.[28] The lubricant is an interesting combination of egg whites and *t'ung* oil, the yokes presumably being eaten, though certain formulations also specified them as an essential ingredient. Because *t'ung* oil is highly flammable, this technique quickly rendered the ship susceptible to a follow-on incendiary attack, just as incendiary arrows which had long dispersed oil onto their targets before igniting them.

Finally, a device called a *huo-lung ch'u-shui* or "fire dragon breaking out of the water" was basically a five-foot bamboo imaginatively, though no doubt minimally, carved to resemble a dragon's head and tail.[29] Powered by four incendiary arrows underneath the beast, it also included explosives in the main body and a number of incendiary arrows as well so that when it finally exploded at the end of its flight, it would splay smaller incendiary arrows onto the target. Fired from just above the water (rather than from within, despite its name), it supposedly had a range of two or three *li*. Whether it was ever employed is open to question because the fuses on the four incendiary rockets would have to be lit simultaneously for the dragon to fly in any sort of desired trajectory, though the text describes a device for exactly this purpose.

## INCENDIARIES IN RIVERINE CLASHES

Even after discounting the presence of numerous small boats manned by only a few men, the number of vessels destroyed through incendiary techniques, the only technology capable of inflicting severe devastation in traditional China, remains truly astounding. Following the battle of Ch'ih Pi, hundreds were often consumed in a single encounter, sometimes even 1,000 or more in an extended series of clashes, particularly if many of the vessels were tethered as the foundation for a floating bridge or providing logistical support as in A.D. 535 when the Liang general Ch'en Pa-hsien cut off Northern Ch'i's beleaguered city of Shih-t'ou near Nan-ching, launched a nighttime incendiary assault on their supply boats, and burned 1,000 of them.[30] Almost unimaginable energy and resources were required to construct these flotillas, yet they vanished in the space of a day as already seen as well as recounted below.[31]

The Sung experienced particularly painful losses in 1275 when the Mongols were sweeping down the Yangtze River valley and had already occupied Chien-k'ang. The Sung finally managed an enormous but belated response that included fielding an armada said to total 10,000 ships. Intended to block the Mongol naval component and completely sever river passage, a smaller contingent of 400 boats was also deployed up stream to preclude the enemy's escape. In order to properly assess the situation, the Mongol commander A-shu ascended a nearby mountain where this vast armada was visible along the river's sweep.[32] The number and density, coupled with the fact that every ten ships had been linked into a square formation with iron chains (supposedly to show their determination), thereby further decreasing their mobility, immediately prompted A-shu to opt for incendiary measures.

The Mongols therefore mounted a three-pronged land attack which overwhelmed all the Sung forces deployed about Mount Chiao ("scorched mountain") and divided their large boats into two wings staffed with 1,000 of their best archers. When the battle was joined, the smaller Mongolian vessels easily maneuvered among the Sung boats while the archers used incendiary arrows to set fire to the sails, turning the fleet into a blazing mass. Enormous casualties resulted from both wounds and drowning, and among the vessels which managed to escape at the rear another 700 were captured. In conjunction with the earlier defeat at Oh-chou which saw 1,300 boats lost and another 3,000 burned at the end,[33] this battle ended the Sung's ability to field any sort of naval force.

A famous conflict that unfolded nearly a millennium earlier in A.D. 410 saw the victorious Chin commander Liu Yü, who eventually founded the Southern Sung, astutely exploit the changing wind to incinerate a significantly larger riverine opposition force under Lu Hsün. As Lu had defeated Liu Yi's formidable armies earlier in the year and had assembled a large populist army based in Wu, Liu Yü was confronted with a somewhat desperate situation. Seeking a decisive battle, Lu had not only come forth in maximum force, but also deployed so many vessels that they formed a continuous procession up the Yangtze as far as the eye could see.

Intercepting them, Liu positioned troops on both sides of the river and fielded a fleet of smaller, more maneuverable boats to engage them. He also adroitly shaped the battlefield by prepositioning crossbows on the eastern bank. When the combined effect of the current and a strong cross wind blew the vessels to the Western bank, Liu's well-prepared forces launched an incendiary attack, causing a conflagration which consumed the congested, colliding mass of vessels.[34] Only Lu managed to escape the incendiary attack and follow-up strikes. However, Liu was not inexperienced in incendiary warfare, having decisively employed incendiary assaults against Huan Hsüan in A.D. 404 after he usurped the Chin throne from Emperor An, as already seen.[35]

As the T'ang disintegrated, the provincial military governors, having become de facto warlords and self-proclaimed kings, battled among themselves even as their domains were fractured by their powerful subordinates. When T'ien Chün revolted against the king of Wu, he kidnapped the wife of the powerful general Li Shen-fu to coerce him into cooperating, but Li refused, even slaying T'ien's emissary despite the promise of splitting the new kingdom.[36] T'ien therefore dispatched two generals with greatly superior riverine forces against him.

During the initial clash Li's son was also captured by the enemy, but Li had him shot with arrows to eliminate any coercive value. As dusk was falling, he then retreated by taking his ships upriver, remaining just out of reach of his pursuers. Much to his advantage, T'ien's vessels all set out large torches to combat the darkness, immediately making them easy targets for Li's archers. Once they extinguished the torches, Li turned about and mounted a fierce incendiary attack that exploited the enemy's growing confusion in the darkness and took advantage of the wind and current to score an unexpected victory.

Amidst the chaos of the Five Dynasties that immediately followed, at the behest of the Later Liang emperor the king of Wu-yüeh dispatched a large 500-boat riverine force to attack the recalcitrant state of Nan-yüeh. Their conflict unfolded in Chiangsu, the ancient site of the state of Wu and a land of rivers, lakes, and marshes. Naval forces were therefore essential, though conjoined land forces were also fielded.[37]

In the fourth month of 894 the two riverine forces met for battle somewhat above the mouth of the Yangtze. Ch'ien Ch'uan-ch'üan, Wu-yüeh's commander in chief, having encountered strong adverse winds, decided to withdraw into a nearby cove sufficiently to allow Nan-yüeh's ships to pass by, thereby gaining an advantageous position upwind from where an incendiary attack might be safely launched. Prior to the engagement he also directed that their vessels be provided with sand, beans, and lime dust.[38]

While they were still approaching the Nan-yüeh fleet he ordered impenetrable clouds of lime dust dispersed which kept their sailors from opening their eyes. Upon drawing close the beans were thrown onto their ships where they rendered the decks slippery and treacherous, an effect enhanced as they became mixed with blood from the wounded. Meanwhile, the sand that had been spread on their own vessels improved their foothold and provided additional fire protection as well. Benefiting enormously from these measures, Wu-yüeh easily prevailed in the ensuing clash even though the enemy fought viciously, Nan-yüeh's commander finally battling them with a wooden staff after his sword was severed. Ch'ien achieved a substantial victory, slaying thousands and taking many prisoners.

Nevertheless, despite incinerating an astounding 400 enemy boats, the victory did not prove decisive. Another land engagement fought in the seventh month saw Ch'ien's armies attack Nan-yüeh's forces near Wu-hsi only to surprisingly suffer a serious defeat, again due to an incendiary attack. After an initial barrage of arrows from both sides, Nan-yüeh exploited the wind to set fire to the heavy vegetation, causing enough chaos to wrest victory. Wu-yüeh sustained some 10,000 casualties before they could retreat to the mountains where they suffered additional losses. Shortly thereafter, the two sides concluded a peace pact that allowed the region to enjoy relative tranquility for two decades.

The internecine strife which erupted over the kingship of Ch'u at the end of the Five Dynasties not only saw rival armies fielded by two brothers brutally clash, but nearby powers and settled barbarian peoples also entangled in the conflict. After his initial thrust was defeated, Ma Hsi-oh's barbarian-supported riverine campaign intended to wrest the throne from his older brother proceeded fairly expeditiously despite being badly outnumbered, causing King Ma Hsi-kuang, who had to be dissuaded from stepping down, great consternation. In A.D. 950 Liu Yen-tao proceeded through Tung-t'ing Lake up the Yüan River to oppose Ma Hsi-oh with 6,000 troops and 150 warships and engaged the latter's fleet at Mei-chou.[39]

After deliberately blocking the river to his rear with interconnected bamboo and timbers, Liu sought to exploit the prevailing winds to incinerate the enemy's vessels. However, just when all the materials had been prepared and ignited, the wind suddenly turned, setting the boats to the fore on fire. Because the bamboo blockade prevented his remaining vessels from extricating themselves, nearly the entire force was quickly lost in the fire and follow-on attack. Ma Hsi-oh then continued toward Ch'ang-an, his large fleet exploiting the rivers and his troops plundering and decimating the countryside. Just two months later, aided by defections, he took the city through an incendiary attack, devastated it, and slew his brother the king.

The third Jurchen invasion of the recently established Southern Sung in early winter, 1129, sought to resolve the chronic boat shortage by constructing and seizing numerous vessels, even tearing apart houses near the river to fabricate rafts. A three-pronged campaign, it initially focused on the area between the Huai and Yangtze Rivers but entailed secondary strikes as well. Although occasionally stymied by patriots who were invariably slaughtered once their towns were reduced, it made rapid progress as Sung commanders performed abysmally and fearfully refused to attack the still exposed enemy forces. In the west, Ch'ang-an was again taken and the countryside in general suffered the combined effects of enemy plundering and destructive Sung policies intended to deny provisions and resources to the enemy. The dowager empress was pursued into the southwest and the emperor driven from Hang-chou as key cities, including the capital, were abandoned or succumbed and subsequently torched. Only a determined defense at Ming-chou allowed the emperor, whose entourage had embarked on hundreds of boats to commence a floating existence, to avoid capture.

Eventually the change of seasons, dangerous exposure of their far-ranging probes, stalwart resistance at a few points, and guerrilla actions prompted Wu Shu to retreat from the deep southeast. Despite being inexperienced with boats and unfamiliar with eastern littoral waterways, the sheer mass of their plunder compelled them to resort to water transport, immediately rendering them vulnerable to Han Shih-chung's long-prepared fleet and eventually Yüeh Fei's marauding strikes as they battled northward. (Even Han's wife actively participated in the engagement by beating the drums that controlled their advance.)

On 3/25, 1130, Wu Shu's forces were attacked and blockaded into a narrow cove where they deteriorated for forty days until a local traitor advised them of a possible outlet through an old riverbed. Through a determined dredging effort, they escaped only to be again encircled until it was realized that the Sung vessels, being large and sail dependent, became virtually immobilized on calm days. Wu immediately launched an incendiary attack and his smaller, more maneuverable vessels escaped in the confusion.[40] Meanwhile, aggressive action continued on the eastern flank, reducing Yang-chou and Ch'u-chou.

After the Jurchen administration controlling north China had conscripted every male subject between twenty-five and fifty and built up major riverine and open sea naval forces for several years, in the eighth month of 1161 the brutal Chin usurper generally known as Hai-ling Wang finally mounted a massive, four-pronged attack upon the Southern Sung entailing perhaps 300,000 infantry and cavalry, as well as 600 vessels with an additional 70,000 men. Despite having vast numbers of soldiers under arms, the complacent Sung belatedly mounted a feeble response under its aged generals which saw many important commanders simply abandon their commands, letting the Jurchen pour through. However, others such as Wu Lin mounted strong, localized defensive efforts which thwarted their advance into the passes above Szechuan and directly southward, and Liu Ch'i even conducted guerrilla operations across the river.

Near the end of the 10th month Li Pao, who had finally managed to take the puny Southern Sung fleet of 120 vessels northward after battling heavy northerly winds for a month, engaged the nascent Jurchen Navy at T'ang-tao, scoring the crucial victory that prevented an amphibious assault on Hang-chou.[41] (A collateral land effort mounted by his 3,000 marines first effected the relief of Hai-chou.) Gaining crucial intelligence from defectors among the conscripted Sung naval personnel, Li—who had initially proposed this venture to exploit the relatively enervated attitude of men still on home terrain—took advantage of the enemy's laxity and close packing of their vessels to launch a surprise attack.

Profiting from a sudden shift in the wind and deliberate efforts by the Sung sailors manning the enemy fleet to keep the Jurchen forces ignorant of his approach, Li launched an incendiary attack which exploited not only the skill of his carefully chosen bowmen to launch fire arrows, but also the newly developed fire lances, certainly one of the first times gunpowder weapons were employed in a naval engagement. Targeting the cloth sails heavily greased with oil said to have been extracted from Sung corpses, they quickly destroyed a major portion of the Jurchen fleet and then vanquished the remainder through close combat. Even though this clash occurred in littoral waters near Ch'ing-tao, Li Pao is credited with having achieved a decisive victory in China's first sea battle.

Hai-ling Wang, still determined to conquer the south before returning north to reclaim Jurchen leadership, attempted to cross the Yangtze with his main force at Ts'ai-shih. Although command of the defensive forces had crumbled, Yü Yün-wen rallied the despondent riverside troops for a determined effort that achieved a marginal victory against the initial amphibious assault through concealing their land defenses until the last moment and fighting fervently on the river with their fewer but much larger vessels. The second day then proved decisive because Yü positioned his forces during the intervening night to thwart the Jurchen fleet from proceeding out onto the river. Their heavy archery fire forced the smaller vessels into the muddy shallows where an incendiary attack destroyed some 300 boats and any possibility of invading the south, achieving a victory ever after viewed as symbolic of "civilization" prevailing over "barbarism."

The monumental clash in which Chu Yüan-chang finally destroyed his nemesis Ch'en Yu-liang known as the Battle of P'o-yang Lake well illustrates the nature of inland naval warfare and the pivotal role frequently played by incendiary strikes.[42] By 1363 Mongol rule had generally broken down throughout the realm under the pressures of popular disaffection and peasant-based revolutions, including the quasi-religious amalgam known as the Red Turbans whose leadership Chu Yüan-chang had assumed after the death of senior commanders and several years of rebellion. Exploiting his base in the middle eastern part of China, Chu mounted a westward drive along the Yangtze River through Anhui and Chianghsi, directly threatening Ch'en Yu-liang who had amassed a far more powerful army.

The contested area of northern Chianghsi lying immediately south of the Yangtze River being very wet, numerous warships of various types and extensive lift capacity were required to wage war on its rivers and lakes. From the outset Ch'en Yu-liang therefore decided to construct a massive navy which would include several hundred behemoths some three stories tall partially protected by iron plates and manned by dozens of rowers, each supposedly capable of transporting 2,000 to 3,000 marines. (Their very height made an assault on T'ai-ping possible because troops could readily cross over planking extended onto the city walls and quickly overwhelm their defenses.)

Chu, while similarly forced to construct a large fleet, benefited immensely from having scored three successive victories over Ch'en in which he not only inflicted heavy casualties and destroyed several hundred boats of various sizes, but also captured hundreds more. For example, the sudden appearance of Chu's combined land and river forces at An-ch'ing so surprised Ch'en's generals that many surrendered without a fight, 80 of his cruisers were destroyed, and more than a 100 captured, with Ch'en himself being compelled to flee for his life. These defeats prompted him to mount an assault at Nan-ch'ang, then under the overall command of Chu's nephew (Chu Wen-cheng), with a newly built fleet and total troop strength wildly pronounced as totaling 600,000 men.

The siege of Nan-ch'ang, which must be considered an integral precursor to the battle of P'o-yang Lake, commenced with land and water assaults on 4/15 that pounded the walls with catapult-launched incendiary projectiles and a few primitive cannon, accompanied by fervent attacks on the city gates. Every assault was rebuffed by a roving, elite force of 2,000 men. A major section of the walls crumbled, but a stopgap palisade was quickly constructed and emplaced under the cover of their own gunpowder weapons. Meanwhile, invaders at the water gates were repelled by using long spears which had been heated red hot so they couldn't be seized by the enemy.

In the sixth month, although Nan-ch'ang still hadn't been taken, just when provisions were lacking and the city seemed about to succumb, Chu Wen-cheng exploited the well-known ruse of promised surrender to lull Ch'en into laxity until they could be rescued. When Chu Yüan-chang finally gathered enough strength to sally forth—his main army having been deployed northward to assist the embattled, nominal king of the Ming—he shifted some 200,000 men from Ying-t'ien up the Yangtze River and into P'o-yang Lake. Arriving about 7/16, he quickly moved south to the lake's widest point and then perspicaciously acted to cut off its various access points. After an extended siege at Nan-ch'ang of eighty-five days, Ch'en found himself compelled to sail some fifty miles down the Kan River into Lake P'o-yang to confront Chu.

This historic battle unfolded on what has now become China's largest lake, although in the early Ming two presently severed southern lakes were also part of P'o-yang's waters, providing even more area for maneuver than currently. The Kan River down to Nan-ch'ang, roughly fifty miles away, actually had four usable outlets onto the lake, the major one to the north capable of accommodating large vessels and at least two others being used for the flourishing trade to the south and southwest. Fed by five rivers in all, the lake stretched roughly 120 miles from north to south, expanding from a mere two miles wide at the upper neck to nearly fifty miles across in the general area of the engagements around Mount K'ang-lang which projected up out of the water's surface.

Marked by an average depth of fifteen feet, but up to seventy at its deepest point, naval maneuvers were generally unhampered except when the fleets crowded the shore. The highest water levels usually occur in May and June, but might extend as late as September, with the lowest point being reached in December and January. (The conflict thus commenced just when the water levels had started receding.) The P'o-yang Lake area also suffers from frequent high winds, generally southerly from June through August, but northerly the rest of the year, ensuring that properly directed incendiary attacks will almost invariably produce a savage conflagration.

Seriously outnumbered, Chu divided his naval forces into eleven operational groups and had them fully provided with various incendiary devices and bows and crossbows with the intent that they should first use their incendiary weapons (catapults or cannon) and then their missile weapons before finally closing for close combat. However, since his vessels were smaller and lighter, they suffered the disadvantages of being outgunned and forced to fire upward at an enemy that overlooked them. Chu was therefore forced to rely upon quickness and maneuverability.

On the very first day, the 21st, Chu Yüan-chang resorted to incendiary warfare to destroy twenty of Ch'en's vessels in their initial encounter, after which the fighting intensified. Both sides suffered significant losses, but the battle descriptions indicate that Chu's forces must have been on the defensive despite having a more valiant spirit, and Chu himself barely escaped death. The second day, the 22nd, unfolded similarly with the Ming forces sustaining such heavy losses that Chu rashly had his group captains executed for leadership failure, hardly an act to recommend him to history but certainly symptomatic of his ruthlessness.

However, a subordinate belatedly reprimanded him with the observation that it wasn't the commanders' fault, but the size disadvantage that allowed Ch'en to generally prevail. Since Ch'en's vessels were not only large and unwieldy, but also chained together (presumably to frustrate penetrating attacks by the smaller vessels), an incendiary attack was obviously indicated. Adopting his suggestion, Chu had seven incendiary boats prepared and then positioned straw dummies in them fitted out in real armor to preclude suspicion. Taking advantage of a favorable wind, he launched them against the enemy on the third day, the 23rd, quickly incinerating several hundred boats and inflicting such horrendous casualties that Ch'en lost half the original force which had initially outnumbered Chu ten to one.

However, the fighting continued until dusk and on the fourth day, the 24th, Ch'en still came forth, deliberately targeting what he believed to be Chu's distinctive white boat. Because Chu's informants had alerted him to the danger, all the Ming boats had been painted white overnight, frustrating the assassination attempt. Ch'en's forces had by then become dispirited, accounting for the ease with which Chu's operational groups penetrated their lines to inflict substantial additional casualties without being seriously challenged.

Viewing the situation as untenable, Ch'en sought various escape routes and temporary shoreside havens only to find them and the sole exit out onto the Yangtze River all blocked. At the end of the fourth day, although still in close proximity, both sides initially stood down, but Chu moved his navy out through the lake's narrow upper channel into the Yangtze under cover of nightfall and then proceeded to deploy his troops on both banks, establish defensive barriers, and prepare additional incendiary boats to quash break-out attempts. After some thirty days of indecision marked by increasing disaffection and desertion among his generals, several insulting provocations by Chu, and severe provision shortages because the Kan River supply route from Nanch'ang had essentially been cut off, Ch'en finally burst through with his remaining 80 to 100 large ships. Suffering a savage attack at the lake's mouth and then on the Yangtze River mounted by fire boats as they tried to proceed upstream and escape, Ch'en perished and his remaining 50,000 leaderless troops surrendered, further adding to Chu's inland navy.

What might be termed the second battle of P'o-yang Lake unfolded in 1519 when a direct descendant of Chu Yüanchang, Chu Ch'en-hao, who held the title of king of Ning, attempted to displace the famously dissolute emperor Wutsung. For many years Ch'en-hao had been accumulating power by encroaching upon the people, exploiting clandestine alliances with brigands, seizing lands, appropriating offices, and fitfully nurturing his core military forces. Despite the blatancy of his intentions, Chu's minions in the court were so successful in undermining and deflecting every incriminating report that the emperor ignored his machinations until the last moment. In the end, prompted by the emperor's belated decision to dispatch a punitive force, Chu initiated his rebellion, though in part only through coercion and the slaughter of outright opponents.[43]

Fortunately for the Ming dynasty, Chu's campaign force of perhaps 100,000 proved incapable of proceeding from his bastion at Nan-ch'ang down the Yangtze to attack the capital of Nan-ching. After an initial but minor victory and the tactically unwise segmentation of collateral forces to attack two secondary objectives, Chu moved against An-ch'ing in force only to become entangled in a protracted siege when it refused to succumb. However, his initiative was blunted from the outset because Wang Shou-jen cleverly employed disinformation—false reports that a massive imperial army was already approaching him—to win a delay of more than ten days during which he conscripted some 80,000 men for a punitive campaign and assembled the fleet required to transport them and their provisions.

Rather than engage Chu at An-ch'ing where he could have crushed the rebels between the local defensive forces ensconced in the city and an outer encirclement created by his field armies but exposed to attacks from the rear, Wang adopted Sun-tzu's classic strategy. By threatening Chu's home base of Nan-ch'ang, Wang compelled him to abandon his well-organized, fortified position to hasten back in disarray. Quickly capturing Nan-ch'ang, the imperial forces then intercepted Chu's army, cut them in half, and eventually inflicted a severe defeat.

When rescue forces hastily recalled from the two collateral objectives were blocked and Chu suffered another battlefield disaster, he withdrew to P'o-yang Lake. However, despite his supposedly comprehensive military knowledge, he foolishly repeated Ts'ao Ts'ao's error of immobilizing his vessels by linking them together in squares to create more stable fighting platforms and apparently failed to deploy any blocking or security forces. Therefore, in a virtual replay of Chu Yüan-chang's famous strategy, at first light on the morning of the 26th, the seventh month, while the pretender was holding court with his ministers, Wang Shou-jen exploited the prevailing winds to send a number of fire ships laden with burning faggots against the fleet at anchor, setting many of them ablaze and inflicting heavy casualties. Chu temporarily escaped by switching boats, but was eventually captured, ending the rebellion's threat.

## RIVERINE INCENDIARY TARGETS

Although the chief employment of incendiary techniques in riverine and eventually littoral warfare was destroying opposing fleets, other significant targets, including bridges and riverside encampments, also commanded attention. In one of the earliest known clashes over a bridge, when the Later Han was still engaged in recovering the realm Ts'en P'eng was dispatched up the Yangtze into Szechuan to suppress strong opposition forces. In order to access the enemy, he first had to destroy a floating bridge across the Yangtze. Exploiting the seasonal eastern wind, his subcommander Liu Ch'i maneuvered up current and approached the bridge to set it afire. However, his boats became impaled on a protective bank of wooden poles and were forced to engage the enemy in a fierce firefight during which Liu resorted to "flying torches" to ignite the bridge. The strong wind fanned the flames into an intense conflagration that soon consumed the bridge, allowing the fleet to advance upriver.[44]

Following Liu Pei's ignominious defeat, riverside deployments also became high-priority targets. For example, when the Sung was campaigning against the Southern T'ang, the latter deployed over 100,000 men and sailors in encampments along the Huai.[45] The Sung therefore employed several large warships filled with flammable grass and faggots to mount an incendiary attack by floating them downstream. In conjunction with P'an Mei's maneuvering along the shore, they achieved a major victory.

The advent of combat fleets, marine forces, and floating supply lines further stimulated the development of methods to prevent boats from freely traversing the rivers. Iron chains were stretched from shore to shore, spikes and more solid palisades emplaced in channels, and stones, wagon wheels, chariots, and entire wagons sunk to create unsurpassable obstacles. Even the water level was sometimes manipulated, being lowered to deny passage to the enemy but raised to facilitate fleet movement.

Countermeasures naturally evolved in response, but to clear a riverine obstruction, deny an archery platform to the enemy, or preclude maneuver, the only feasible means continued to be incendiary, generally implemented with unguided fire boats launched from upstream to minimize human risk. The scope of riverine incendiary efforts to burn obstacles often reached massive proportions, one attempt early in Three Kingdoms period bundling "several million" reeds into numerous large fire rafts intended to ride the current down into Wu's floating bridge about fifty *li* away.[46]

Iron chains were eliminated through melting by positioning floating forges under them or crushing rafts piled with flaming materials against them, though they could also be cut away by marines on rafts or swimmers employing brute force without preliminary heating.[47] Booms and sweeps secured to the prow of specially reinforced, limited draft boats also exploited the current's power to sweep away palisades and flatten obstacles, though not always successfully.

Bridges, especially temporary floating structures, were attacked by both land and water to thwart their several purposes. Fire boats were utilized to destroy the bamboo and iron linkages and even sections of pontoon versions which, having been created from hundreds of small boats, equally obstructed fleet passage and permitted enemy infantry movement. Follow-on attacks exploited the smoke and confusion to overwhelm the defenders, cut away any remaining bamboo cords lashing the stone piers together, and undertake other measures to sink or destroy the remnants. Floating blockades consisting of larger warships linked with heavy chains could also effectively thwart river movement and therefore had to be destroyed to preserve campaign momentum. In A.D. 923 Hou Liang blocked the Yellow River by linking more than ten large warships across the river. However, being immobile they were easily incinerated by Hou T'ang raiders who overwhelmed the shore guards and set the boats on fire.[48]

Although bridges were primarily intended to facilitate the movement of troops and material across rivers, they could also function as fire platforms for controlling the river and nearby embankments, and might even become part of an extended fortified complex, such as at Chung-li. Defensive measures were therefore implemented to reduce their vulnerability to ramming and incendiary attack, including the stretching of chains, emplacement of obstacles such as piles of rocks, erecting of wooden barriers, affixing of horizontal poles, and anchoring rows of small boats to absorb the impact. However, even when they were augmented with dense protective fire from the bridge and nearby embankments, unmanned fire ships floating down river and dedicated bands of stealthy operatives, especially at night or moving against the current, often managed to ignite fires and cut away crucial ropes, dramatically affecting the course of battle.[49]

Near the end of the Six Dynasties period when Northern China was occupied by steppe peoples, Northern Wei sought to expand its territory by annexing the state of Liang to the south.[50] Clashes arose in several theaters as both had extensive territories across the breadth of China, though marked differences in terrain and customs engendered the usual tactical dichotomies. The north exploited the swiftness of cavalry but was handicapped by the south's comparatively warm riverine conditions and therefore tended to be active from late fall to early spring, moving quickly to mount concentrated infantry and cavalry attacks. However, the south normally adopted a persisting strategy, staffing their well-supplied border citadels with small forces and sometimes launching successful counterattacks in the spring and summer.

With considerable economic and administrative success (as well as dissension), Wei had embarked on a deliberate policy of acculturation beginning in 493, moved the capital to Luo-yang, and surprisingly shifted away from semi-nomadic Hsien-pei traditions in order to more thoroughly unify rulers and subjects. Liang succeeded Ch'i in 501, though Ch'i had itself come into being when internal strife doomed the Sung dynasty established by the great general Liu Yü. Surprisingly, even though the Northern Wei emperor benefited greatly when key generals such as Hsiao Pao-ying (who had detailed knowledge of Liang's defenses and capabilities) defected at Liang's inception, he ignored Yüan Ying's advice to exploit the south's vulnerability during these turbulent years.

By 503, having decided to conquer all China, the emperor attacked the contiguous state of Liang, thereby initiating twelve years of conflict which Wei generally dominated despite occasionally successful Liang counterattacks. Among the early targets was Chung-li, a citadel manned by only 3,000 men located on the south bank of the Huai River which might have been bypassed but had been deemed pivotal to their efforts. However, according to the prominent Wei general Hsing Luan, it presented a formidable obstacle. His analysis, formulated as part of a remonstrance against attacking it in the fall of 506, identified certain disadvantages that have traditionally been given great credibility.

First of all, the citadel was well designed and constructed, with solid walls and such deep moats (which could draw upon the Huai River for water) that they could not possibly be filled in to gain access to the walls themselves. In addition, though only defended by a small force, the troops were well supplied and rested whereas Wei's own army was suffering from long exposure in the field and, though markedly superior in strength, lacked the energy for battle. A siege would further tire them, depleting the state's reserves and reputation, whereas victory would merely result in the capture of a largely indefensible strongpoint, one difficult to supply because it abutted the river's far shore.

This sort of analysis, much in the tradition of Sun Pin's *Military Methods* and Sun-tzu's *Art of War,* especially the tomb text materials, would however be proven partly fallacious. The moat was in fact filled in, though through such massive, concerted effort that after the initial wagonloads of earth had been brought up and dumped in, the cavalry's relentless pressure at the rear resulted in some of the laborers being pushed in and buried by the crush of dirt being piled on. Hsing's supply concerns would also become moot once Wei occupied the surrounding countryside.

Wei initially besieged Chung-li in the first month of 504 but having failed to overcome it, withdrew amidst heavy rains in the fourth month even though the traitor Hsiao Pao-ying had defeated a collateral Liang strike at Shou-yang that sought to exploit their preoccupation with Chung-li. After Liang attempted a counter strike to recover lost territory in 505, Yüan Ying led a major campaign army of 100,000 southward and Wei subsequently enjoyed increasing success in 506, particularly when one of Liang's cowardly generals panicked during a thunderstorm, resulting in some 50,000 casualties in the ninth month. Exploiting their recently captured provisions, Wei then moved to attack Chung-li, prompting Liang to dispatch a large rescue force of some 200,000 men from the capital of Chien-k'ang under Ts'ao Ching-tsung early in the eleventh month.

Upon reaching the Huai in the tenth month of 506, Wei's massive force—reportedly 200,000 to 300,000 but probably 125,000 to 150,000—constructed a broad bridge that traversed a small mid-river island, thus resulting in two separate spans connected to the north and south banks of the Huai River.[51] Designed to ensure an uninterrupted flow of men and materials, the bridges, island, and immediate embankment access areas were all fortified with heavy wooden palisades. Yang Ta-yen, one of Wei's two commanders, erected a citadel on the northern bank and Yüan Ying, entrusted with the main assault efforts, an encampment on the south, responsibility for the defense of the massive bridge complex falling to the traitor Hsiao Pao-ying.

In the first month of 507 Yang Ta-yen and Yüan Ying's troops began a series of intensive attacks and filled in the moat to allow their assault engines to be brought up. However, whenever they managed to breach a portion of the walls, the defenders quickly repaired the damage and blocked the attackers from penetrating the interior. Thereafter, despite employing numerous assault measures both day and night—though surprisingly not incendiary techniques—they not only failed to take it, but suffered casualties numbered in the tens of thousands as they tried to swarm over the fortifications, the bodies of the fallen piling as high as the walls themselves. When the spring rains first came late in the second month, Wei's emperor wanted to break off the conflict but was persuaded to continue the effort to conquer the still isolated defenders for another month when drier weather would prevail.

Meanwhile, Liang's first rescue force, deployed late the previous year and ordered to assume a forward position without moving to intercept the enemy until consolidated, remained encamped on the southern bank nearly forty *li* to the east. Its somewhat headstrong commander Ts'ao Ching-tsung, hoping to magnify his personal achievements, had precipitously advanced up river only to encounter turbulent weather, witness his fleet founder, and have some 50,000 of his troops perish in a riverine disaster. Surprisingly, he was neither executed nor removed from command, but instead his armies were augmented with a major contingent from the Ho-fei area under the more experienced Wei Jui.

Wei Jui quickly came up from the southwest by "cutting trails through the mountains and building bridges where necessary" to assume a temporary position some twenty *li* from the enemy. However, that night he clandestinely advanced his forces to within a 100 paces of the southern Wei encampment and quickly threw up defensive bulwarks by exploiting the skills of a martial engineer accompanying them, thereby astonishing Yüan Ying the next morning. (Only a complete lack of reconnaissance and perimeter scouts, no doubt the result of overconfidence since Wei dominated the battlefield and probably thought a counterattack to be unthinkable, could have allowed their advance and construction work to proceed undetected.) In addition, Liang's two armies were said to be very martial in appearance, another factor further subverting Wei's now flagging spirit.

A probing assault by a contingent of 10,000 under Yang Ta-yen prompted the new Liang encampment to bolster their defenses by using wagons to create an additional barrier. Their 2,000 crossbowmen also suddenly rose up to fire en masse, decimating the attackers and even wounding Yang Ta-yen in the shoulder. That night Ts'ao Ching-tsung managed to dispatch some men along the river bed into Chung-li, immediately strengthening their resolve just when Wei's armies had suffered a double blow to their morale.

The next day Yüan Ying personally came forth to attack Wei Jui's position, but another day and night of intense fighting produced only indeterminate results. Ts'ao also employed a small but select force of 1,000 to establish a strong point below Yang Ta-yen's main encampment, effectively isolating the latter's field forces and gaining access to grass for their horses. Yang immediately attacked but was successfully repulsed.

Liang then formulated an amphibious operation designed to attack the bridges, protective palisades, and adjoining fortifications with a combined riverine infantry assault and incendiary attack. To achieve their objective they first built warships tall enough to match the bridge's roadway and a number of smaller fire boats. Then, in the third month when the seasonal surge saw the river suddenly rise by several feet and its speed greatly increase, Ts'ao Ching-tsung employed their new warships to strike the island fortifications and the north bridge while Wei Jui struck the south bridge and associated palisades, no doubt with conjoined land support.

At the same time the fire boats quickly ignited the bridges, creating chaos and cover for the troops to ascend and overwhelm the defenders before the structures were entirely destroyed and the remnants washed away by the current. Wei's armies totally collapsed in the ensuing confusion and sustained attacks, resulting in a devastating defeat in which a reported 100,000 were cut down, drowned, or perished in the fires, with another 50,000 being captured in the subsequent pursuit of Yüan Ying's forces to the southwest. The other commander, Yang Ta-yen, burnt his encampment before retreating northward back into Wei's interior.

Nearly twenty-five years later during an outbreak of internecine strife in Northern Wei a civil official with no military experience led a small band of soldiers upstream to release fire boats and incinerate the great bridge on the Yellow River in order to block the advance of a rebel force.[52] A typical nighttime special operation, once the boats collided with the bridge a great conflagration ensued, trapping and burning both the troops manning the bridge and those who foolishly attempted to flee across it to the other shore.

The most famous example of defeating massive chains arose at the end of the Three Kingdoms period when Wu Ch'an, a perceptive Wu commander whose warnings of imminent invasion had been ignored by the besotted emperor, personally attempted to thwart Chin's invasion with iron links stretched across the great Yangtze River at Chien-p'ing.[53] (Reasons given for the emperor's refusal to heed this intelligence range from simple desire to avoid perturbing himself to foolishly disbelieving that Chin would ever violate their supposed friendship to attack.)

Until Wei conquered Shu, the formidable Yangtze River had proven an effective obstacle against incursions, ensuring southern states could survive if they defended the fords and prepared adequate vessels to repel small-scale riverine operations. Even major amphibious assaults could be thwarted because they would require highly visible staging, allowing the timely dispatch of opposition forces. However, the Wei (termed Chin from 265) conquest campaign not only reduced the Yangtze to a surmountable inconvenience but also redefined it as an exploitable topographical feature. As subsequent Chinese history would repeatedly show, self-contained fleets sweeping down from Szechuan could easily vanquish enemy forces, whether on water or nearby land. Moreover, because their speed upon the current exceeded all but the fastest relay horses while the upper Yangtze's winding, often mountainous banks made signal fires unfeasible, little advance warning could be expected.

Chin's strategists recognized the strength of Wu's naval forces, but being convinced that Wu lacked the will for a sustained battle, they opted to mount the first conjoined land and river attack in Chinese history in order to draw them away from the water. Chin's preparations required some fifteen years, with the last seven being devoted to constructing several hundred large warships and training an aggressive naval force in Szechuan. Control of the riverine forces was eventually transferred to the land commander, the first time integrated command of this sort was exercised.

Some 200,000 troops embarked on the invasion in the second month of A.D. 280, though the land components made little contribution. However, the naval contingent of 70,000 swept down the Yangtze largely unopposed until they encountered the massive chains, the only real obstacle since the numerous troops deployed in camps along the river's banks stood about idly. Having assiduously gathered intelligence through their own spies and captured agents, Chin was well aware of the various obstacles placed in their path, including Wu Ch'an's chains and an array of metal spikes lurking just beneath the water's surface. They accordingly fabricated a few dozen large rafts said to be more than 100 paces on a side, set dummies of straw on them dressed like soldiers wearing armor and bearing weapons, and then deployed outstanding swimmers with the front rafts. The immense rafts easily knocked down the spikes buried in the riverbed and large torches more than ten *chang* (or eighty Western feet) long set in bundles of ten and soaked with sesame oil were set afire when they became caught in the chains. (Some accounts suggest the chains were raised up onto the rafts to facilitate melting, which would require herculean efforts in the depths and current of the river.) Eventually the intense heat melted the links and the fleet proceeded unimpeded.

Although the Yangtze's great length posed defensive problems for Wu, particularly as they chose to disperse their forces rather than concentrate them at a few choke points, and hindered their ability to communicate, they still had major contingents deployed along the river, certainly exceeding 100,000 men. However, because the troops were ill-prepared and lacked the will for battle while many of their commanders simply sought to preserve themselves, Chin's riverine assault quickly scored numerous victories, often without even engaging in combat, and the land contingent defeated the few challenges which materialized. Surging forward, the naval forces placed unremitting pressure on the defenders, eventually compelling the emperor to surrender without a fight. Thereafter, the entire campaign not only entered the historical records but also came to be frequently cited by subsequent theoretical military writings, including the *Wu-ching Tsung-yao*,[54] as exemplifying the concentrated exploitation of riverine and incendiary power.

Although the most common riverine barriers, especially on smaller streams and in marshy areas, were simply variants of wooden palisades and thus easily breached, more formidable ad hoc structures were also cobbled together, such as chain-linked boats, as at the battle of Te-sheng City. Part of the ongoing conflict between the states of Chin and Later Liang, which were essentially separated by the Yellow River, it unfolded in the fourth lunar month of A.D. 919.[55]

In 917, after defeating a Later Liang force, Chin had occupied the Yellow River area around Te-sheng (modern-day Puyang in Honan) and erected two fortified towns on the northern and southern banks of the Yellow River to exert control and serve as bastions for enlarging its domain. In an attempt to retake the immediate region, Chin launched a multi-pronged, conjoined land and riverine assault against the southern citadel whose stalwart defenders soon found themselves facing certain defeat due to a lack of arrows and provisions. (Their status was determined by a heroic swimmer who crossed from the northern bank, still controlled by Chin, clandestinely entered the city, and then returned to report.)

To prevent Chin from sending reinforcements across the river, the Later Liang commander Ho Huan had positioned some ten large warships across the Yellow River and secured them in place with tough bamboo cables and poles. Reinforced with additional knee walls and protected by rawhide coverings, they presented such a formidable obstacle that the Chin king, commanding in person, futilely offered large rewards to anyone who could suggest a plan for defeating them. Despite even resorting to magical formulae and flourishes, "spitting fire and mumbling curses," no one proved successful. In disgust, Wang Chien-chi, a resolute subcommander already known for his bravery, noted the decisive character of the situation required immediate action and therefore volunteered to go forth and resolve the problem.

Wang led 300 heavily armored warriors in launching large ceramic jars[56] filled with burning faggots that had been soaked in oil down onto the immobile fleet and quickly followed up by deploying his warriors in smaller boats so they could maneuver amidst the larger vessels and flames to hack away the cables and lashings. The newly freed, burning vessels soon began to float away with the current, ending the blockade. The attack was so successful that reputedly half of Hou Liang's forces on board perished and Chin was able to send a relief force across to the southern citadel from the northern bank, driving the enemy back. Thus decisive action which simply exploited the current's flow and incendiary techniques to assault an immobile target resolved the stalemate.

The famous Three Kingdoms conquest of Wu did not witness the only use of amphibious forges to melt chains blocking a river. For example, in A.D. 923, just prior to Later Liang's extinction by Later T'ang, when the imminence of the crisis had finally become apparent to the former's emperor, he dispatched Wang Yen-chang to the east to blunt the T'ang advances.[57] Queried as to how long he would need to achieve victory, Wang brazenly replied three days, a time so absurdly short that the court laughingly ridiculed him. After traveling the 100 *li* (nearly thirty-five miles) in just two days, he arrived at a town some twenty miles from the target of Te-sheng where he convened a large drinking feast that night.

While they were immersed in the festivities, he had boats prepared with hooks, long poles, charcoal, forges, and long axes about five miles upriver from Te-sheng. Manned by 600 men, they sailed downriver that night to attack the iron chains obstructing the river by raising and melting them before proceeding to sever the cables holding the floating bridge linking the fortified town on the southern bank with its twin on the northern side. Meanwhile, Wang had slipped out of the festivities and personally led 6,000 cavalry along the southern bank until they reached Te-sheng after a fevered race. No doubt because the defensive commander thought Wang was drinking heartily some miles upstream and T'ang forces would never attack in the rain, the defenders were completely surprised and easily vanquished when reinforcements could not be dispatched over the now severed bridge from the bastion to the north.

## DEFENSE AGAINST RIVERINE INCENDIARY ATTACK

With their freedom of movement and perch upon the water, boats would seem difficult targets for incendiary measures, yet they were easily incinerated because their wood and bamboo construction rendered them highly flammable. Moreover, while single boats, even large unwieldy ones, might maneuver freely and thus be elusive, the density marking the huge armadas prevailing from the Three Kingdoms onward made independent movement impossible, yet guaranteed that the smallest fire could quickly turn into a conflagration, especially under windy conditions. Conversely, aggressors could avail themselves of several means of attack, including launching incendiary missiles from oversized bows or trebuchets deployed on the nearby shore, but little remained to the defenders except coatings of mud, quick action to suppress fires, and water buckets to extinguish arrows upon impact.[58] Surprisingly, unlike the many sections devoted to city defense over the centuries, the numerous military manuals contain no dedicated chapters on vessel defense.

Boats at anchor or moored in a floating bridge configuration were particularly vulnerable and could only be protected by keeping enemy troops and incendiary launchers at an adequate distance. The *Ts'ao-lü Ching-lüeh* thus premised its riverine defensive measures on the need to maintain mobility: "When the enemy sets fire to our boats but the water barriers and warships are all linked together, it will be very difficult to suddenly untie them. If we keep our boats dispersed while engaging in combat, we will avoid any need for defense."[59] While the author concluded the chapter by noting that riverside anchorages and encampments should be thoroughly protected, in "Riverine Warfare" ("Shui Chan") he warned against lashing the boats together to avoid inviting an incendiary attack.

A variety of strategic obstacles were conceived and emplaced amidst rivers to thwart these incendiary attacks including chains, wooden palisades, rock piles lashed together with bamboo, and metal and wooden spikes. During a pivotal battle between Shih Ssu-ming (who had recently assumed mastery of all the rebel forces and vanquished Pien-chou and Cheng-chou in succession) and Li Kuang-pi at Ho-yang on the Yellow River in Honan in A.D. 759, Shih decided to mount an amphibious assault with several hundred boats.[60] However, the floating bridge just above the city had to be eliminated first. Shih therefore adopted the usual approach of releasing fire boats to run on the current before his fleet, but Li had prepared an unusual defensive measure. Several hundred long poles were attached to heavy wood bases before iron forks wrapped in hemp (which presumably remained wet and therefore kept the probes cool after they impaled the fire boats) were affixed to the top. While the details remain unknown, this array of multiprong pitchforks with their bristling heads easily caught the approaching fire ships and held them securely at a distance until they burned to the water line and sank.

Smaller boats were also tethered some distance out to intercept fire boats riding down the current or fix them with anchored chains, and roving preemptive strikes were mounted to thwart forces from deploying either upriver or upwind, though with lessened possibility of success. Overhead rams might smash and sink approaching fire boats and as a last resort sailors with poles could attempt to hold them off, but if they were burning intensely enough any embers carried by the wind would balk their efforts and large vessels propelled by the current would exert too much force to be withstood by mere muscle power. Large-diameter, lengthy poles affixed to the sides to fend off approaching craft provided greater solidity, but only through a limited arc.[61]

An example of employing chains and small craft arose in 543 when Kao Chung-mi rebelled against Eastern Wei and allied himself with its western counterpart, prompting the latter to dispatch an army to consolidate the territory around Luo-yang. These forces quickly scored several minor victories and seized the citadel on the south bank of the Yellow River at the great bridge located just above the mountains north of Luo-yang. Kao Huan, commander in chief of Eastern Wei's forces, mobilized 100,000 men in response and quickly advanced to the northern bank, prompting the Western Wei forces to withdraw slightly. Anticipating that Western Wei would attempt to destroy the vital bridge with fire boats, Kao Huan had more than 100 small boats with long chains essentially block the river upstream. When the fire boats indeed descended on the current, these small craft intercepted them, nailed the end of a chain to each one, then pulled them to shore, avoiding incineration by letting the chains out as far as necessary. Kao Huan was therefore able to cross the bridge and continue his advance to repel Western Wei's forces.[62]

One of the most ingenious devices, a combined river obstacle and bridge, was constructed by the Northern Wei commander Ts'ui Yen-po across the Huai River in A.D. 516 from wagon wheels whose outer rims had been removed, leaving the hub and spokes. After sharpening the ends of the spokes (presumably to provide some defense against attackers approaching on the current), the wheels were paired and then strung onto heavy plaited bamboo cords that were attached to winches on either side for raising and lowering after being extended across the river. Ten such "roads" were closely deployed, thwarting the enemy's ships from coming downriver while providing a suspension bridge for crossing. Because the entire barrier could be raised as needed or lowered well into the water, it was relatively impervious to the usual forms of incendiary attack, the fire boats simply floating over the submersed structure.[63]

Finally, a single historical reference to "earthen dogs" appears in connection with defenses mounted against fire ships coming downriver to incinerate a vital bridge. Commentators all describe them as mounds of earth with the general posture of a sitting dog constructed in the river so that the dog's front or head would face upstream and be higher than the rest of the body, with the rear downstream being both broader and lower. However, this description is somewhat problematic because simple earthen mounds, whatever their shape, would be quickly eroded and easily overridden by rafts except in the most languid stream. Dynamically, the guard dogs would have to block the way and perhaps catch the "sticks" in their mouths, something more certainly accomplished by stone piles lashed together with bamboo strips, just as employed for dams and bridge casings. Being higher in front they would protrude sufficiently to obstruct oncoming vessels while the broad, well-anchored foundation would have the strength to withstand sudden impact.[64]

# AQUATIC WARFARE

Two problems have always plagued China: a seasonal surplus of water and vast regions where the semi-arid climate makes plant cultivation difficult, if not impossible. China's mythology depicts flooding as having been a constant problem, the land so inundated that people were frequently forced to live in trees and hang their cooking pots from branches in order to survive. The earliest efforts at water control subsequently coalesced around the image of Yü, the legendary sage figure also known as the grand progenitor of the shadowy Hsia dynasty, traditionally dated from 2200 to 1600 B.C. His story reflects not only this antique struggle but also a pervasive consciousness of water's potential as an inescapably destructive element.

According to common tradition, Yü ascended to power when Emperor Shun, the very embodiment of Virtue who first brought order to civilization, voluntarily ceded the emperorship to the most worthy person in the realm. However, Yü subsequently bequeathed the throne to his son, thereby establishing a lineal heritage of clan rule. More significantly, Hsia culture has always been inseparably intertwined with the human quest to master a hostile environment of unpredictable rivers and roiling currents. Thus Yü's ultimate achievement, undertaken at Shun's behest, was taming the rampant waters that periodically inundated the Yellow River basin by planning and overseeing the construction of ditches and canals to disperse them.

Yü's methods apparently differed radically from those of his father, Kun, whom Emperor Yao had similarly saddled with the task and eventually executed for his incompetence. Kun probably failed because his dikes and dams impeded the water's flow rather than reducing the overall pressure, resulting in disaster whenever seasonal surges from rain or melting snow overflowed or burst the dikes. (Dikes also caused silt to be deposited in the river's channel rather than carrying it off to refertilize the fields, further blocking the flow and constantly raising the riverbeds.)[1] However, even though the techniques for constructing tamped-earth fortifications were already well advanced in the Lungshan period, because he employed embankments—the core of subsequent actual practice—on the positive side Kun has traditionally been credited with creating the practice of wall building.[2]

According to the classic account embedded in the *Mencius:*

> In Yao's era, when the world was not yet tranquil, the rampant waters flowed uncontrollably, inundating the terrain everywhere under Heaven. Grasses and trees grew luxuriantly, birds and beasts proliferated and prospered. The five grains did not flourish, birds and beasts encroached upon the people. Trails from hooves and tracks from birds transected the Middle States. Yao, alone being troubled by this, entrusted Shun with responsibility for administering corrective measures. Shun therefore had Yi employ incendiary techniques, so Yi ignited and burned the mountains and marshes, forcing the birds and beasts to flee for refuge.[3]
>
> Yü deepened the Nine Rivers and dredged the Chi and T'a, facilitating their flow toward the sea. He cleared out the obstacles in the Ju and Han Rivers and arrayed the Huai and Ssu, facilitating their flow into the Yangtze. Only thereafter could the Middle States feed themselves. During this time Yü spent eight years outside his home, and even though he passed by his gate three times, never entered it.[4]

Although various legends speak of three Sage Emperors, Yü may simply have been a totem or clan figure emblematic of the tribe's devotion to water management, a symbol of their effectiveness in reducing catastrophes and increasing agricultural productivity. This would be particularly appropriate considering the Hsia's close identification with Hou Chi, Lord of the Millet, and claims the Hsia emerged through its newly developed agricultural strength. (Ameliorating dramatic river fluctuations and developing irrigation systems would have generated the surpluses necessary for diverting vital manpower to military tasks.) However, whatever his actual achievements, Yü's contributions were increasingly magnified over the centuries as these and other legends evolved from the Warring States onward.[5]

In conjunction with this long struggle and the origination of cities alongside rivers and lakes, China early on developed a diverse contemplative tradition that focused on water's many aspects, active and passive.[6] The crucial insight that water, the softest and most flexible of things, can paradoxically subvert and even destroy the hardest was first embodied in a subsequently famous *Tao Te Ching* verse:

> Under Heaven there is nothing more pliant and
>     weak than water,
> But for attacking the firm and strong nothing
>     surpasses it,
> Nothing can be exchanged for it.
> The weak being victorious over the strong,
> The pliant being victorious over the firm,
> No one under Heaven is capable of knowing this,
> No one capable of implementing it.[7]

While the experiential insight is undeniable, in application it is virtually impossible, as the last two lines indicate. To exploit this potential, the principles had to be fathomed and methods and techniques arduously developed which might be implemented on the battlefield.

Even though water can be exploited as an offensive weapon, it was initially adopted in a defensive role. Early on it was recognized that the strong currents of major rivers, the expansiveness of lakes, ponds, and marshes, and the quiescent depths of artificial moats could all provide protection against aggressors. Natural configurations of terrain were preexistent and immutable, but moats appeared as early as the neolithic period in China and quickly attained considerable width and depth, being far more expansive than necessary to preclude men from simply jumping over or dropping a tree trunk across as a temporary bridge. They also naturally evolved in association with increasingly massive city walls, their excavation furnishing the bulk of the soil required for the tamped earth fortifications.

However, not every city would employ both walls and moats because surplus water supplies were necessary to turn ditches into functioning moats. Technically and organizationally challenging, massive labor forces had to be mobilized for the excavation and building work and fundamental engineering principles scrupulously observed to prevent collapse. Thereafter, regular maintenance was required to keep the ditches and moats free from debris and vegetation, as well as ensure an adequate water level from a possibly distant source.

Doubtlessly in response to external threats and escalating violence, as early as 5000 to 4500 B.C. simple protective ditches were already being excavated. The classic Yangshao village of Pan-p'o (dated between 5000 and 4000 B.C.) located on a bluff near the Ch'an River is delimited by a massive protective ditch some six to eight meters wide at the top, one to three meters wide at the bottom, and an average depth of five to six meters.[8] Pan-p'o's relatively sophisticated, though dry, defenses and minimal wall system seem to mark a transitional stage between simply employing ditches or palisades and erecting rammed-earth walls.[9]

An early, true moat protected P'ing-liang-t'ai, a typical raised Lungshan fortified town that probably functioned as a late Hsia military fortress.[10] Located in Honan along the middle reaches of the Yellow River, the fortifications outline a slightly distorted square with rounded corners. The four 185-meter-long walls retain a height of between three and 3.5 meters and a width tapering from thirteen meters at the base to between eight and ten meters at the top. More importantly, a broad, conjoined moat some thirty meters wide and an original depth of approximately three meters, whose excavated soil was incorporated into the walls, provided a formidable initial obstacle.[11]

Yin-hsiang-ch'eng in Hupei on the Chiang and Han River plains near Ching-chou consists of a significant wall system that was reconstructed and extended numerous times down through the Shang and Chou dynasties.[12] The walls vary between ten and twenty-five meters wide and probably totaled some 1,500 to 1,600 meters. Although rising only one to two meters over the interior platform, they tower five to six meters over an outer moat with an immense thirty-to-forty-meter width.

Four kilometers from the Yangtze River, the ancient city at Tso-ma-ling was protected by an irregular circle some 1,200 meters in circumference whose configuration derived from exploiting the terrain's characteristics while minimizing construction difficulties.[13] Moreover, the twenty-five-to-thirty-meter-wide moat that surrounds the site similarly exploited preexisting depressions.

Ch'eng-t'ou-shan, another well-known Yangtze plains site, is located slightly northwest of Tung-t'ing Lake, historically an extremely wet area where rice had already long been cultivated.[14] A fortified town, its double layer of defenses consisted of a circular wall some 325 meters in diameter augmented by a vast moat ranging between thirty-five and fifty meters wide. Generally four meters deep, part of its course exploited an old riverbed. In addition, it was connected to the nearby river, ensuring adequate water for defense, drinking, and transport. Dated to approximately 2800 B.C., it may be taken as representative of the early stage of compound fortifications combining substantial walls with expansive moats.

Similarly situated in the middle of the Yangtze watershed, Chi-ming-ch'eng's walls total some 1,100 meters, configured in a square with rounded corners, and are roughly thirty meters wide at the base, tapering to fifteen meters at the top, with a height of two to three meters. This fortified town was completely surrounded by a protective moat ranging between twenty and thirty meters wide and average depth of one to two meters.[15]

Coming to decidedly historic times, the early Shang bastion at Yen-shih, essentially a very irregular rectangle some 1,700 by 1,215 meters, was protected by an exterior moat roughly twenty meters across and six meters deep. In comparison, the walls were roughly eighteen meters wide at the base and a surprising fourteen meters at the top, with a remnant height even today of nearly three meters and a sharply defined, perpendicular outer face.

The key Shang citadel at P'an-lung-ch'eng, probably constructed to sustain a powerful enclave and dominate access routes just north of the Yangtze River, despite being only 290 meters by 260 meters in extent, was protected by a ten-meter-wide moat. San-hsing-tui and Ch'eng-tu, although markedly different, were both independent, powerful local cultures which interacted with, but were not submissive to, the Shang. Even today the former, a theocratic center, still retains massive walls some six meters high and a deep moat, though Ch'eng-tu apparently had no walls at all, relying instead upon a complex system of moats for whatever defenses it may have mustered.

Early Chou cities were often erected upon preexisting foundations and aggressively employed walls for protection in border areas and former Shang territory. The initial century of relative peace quickly devolved into conflict as the Chou enclaves became more powerful, independent, and warlike states. The Spring and Autumn and then the Warring States saw all aspects of warfare escalate, and cities, which were rapidly expanding in size and importance due to population and economic pressures, move toward being more impenetrable. The culmination of this trend was the frequent adoption of stone and brick-faced walls, multiple moats, and the ever increasing exploitation of nearby rivers for their natural protective value and as reliable water sources for defense.

The imperial period, frequently a time of merely nominal geopolitical unity despite appearances, was marked by almost unremitting warfare in one form or another and thus no diminishment in defensive requirements. The Han dynasty capital of Ch'ang-an had walls some 6,000 meters on the east, 7,600 on the south, 4,900 to the west, and 7,200 in the north. Twelve to sixteen meters wide at the base, they towered some twelve meters above the countryside. However, the protective moat was a mere eight meters wide and had a depth of three meters.

The major city of Luo-yang was similarly distorted in shape, being 3,900 meters on the east, 2,460 to the south, 3,400 on the west, and 2,700 in the north. However, shielded by the Luo and Yi Rivers, it didn't have a moat. In contrast, Yeh-ch'eng in the Three Kingdoms period, which would be flooded several times over the course of its history and was well protected by moats, was roughly a 3.5-by-2.5 kilometer rectangle. Cities in the Sui, Tang, and thereafter tended to rely more upon walls than moats, though those located in wet areas naturally exploited the advantages of terrain.[16]

Water's effectiveness as an obstacle was not confined to moats alone, whether filled with stagnant water or marked by constant flow that made traversing them even more challenging. Every river and stream, however slow and shallow, provided some degree of obstruction to massive armies heavily laden with equipment and therefore figured prominently in defensive thinking.[17] The idea of accumulating water for defensive purposes is expressed as early as the *Yi Chou-shu*,[18] and in 685 B.C. the state of Lu relied upon the Chu River to thwart an incursion by Ch'i to the east.[19] Jurchen invasions of the Southern Sung were frequently frustrated, even stopped, by a lack of water craft capable of transporting them across the Yangtze rather than Sung strongpoints and concentrated deployments, particularly since several Sung generals fled at the first signs of danger.

Lakes and marshes provided similar protection, prompting a few commanders to create large bodies of water between themselves and their enemies. When establishing his son Liang as heir apparent in Wu in A.D. 250, Sun Ch'üan dispatched a force of 100,000 to construct an imperial city for him called T'ang (T'ang-yi). As it was situated near their border with powerful Wei to the north, he also had a series of ponds excavated which were then filled with water diverted from the nearby Ch'u River to create an impassable obstacle against potential invaders.[20]

After failing to exploit their victory outside Wei-chou in the clash with T'ien Yüeh already recounted, Ma was assigned to T'ai-yüan, where he retrenched and prepared for enemy onslaughts primarily by employing aquatic measures. First, he created a lake to the east through exploiting a pre-existent pond area by diverting a portion of the Chin River's volume so that it augmented the Fen River, causing it to overflow. Then, when the aggressors approached, he broke open the Fen River embankment to provide water for the moats (presumably dry ditches already prepared around the city) and create numerous pools and ponds whose embankments were reinforced with branches from willow trees, thereby frustrating the enemy.

Much earlier in the third century, finding himself in a disadvantageous battlefield situation that developed while suppressing Han Sui's revolt, Tung Chuo similarly created a large body of water for defensive purposes. Alone among the six armies being fielded, Tung's forces were dispatched to the northwest border area where they found themselves confronted by a large coalition of Ch'iang and Hu warriors. After participating in an initial victory over Han Sui's forces and vigorously pursuing the remnants, Tung's 30,000 troops became isolated and nearly surrounded by a superior force of Hsien-ling Ch'iang. Being temporarily protected on one side by a minor river, Tung astutely dammed it, causing the water to back up as if he were trying to create a pool for fishing, completely inundating several square miles and effectively obstructing the enemy. Exploiting this temporary lake as a screen, Tung had his troops cross down river and then broke the dam to dramatically increase the water's flow and raise the river's level, precluding enemy pursuit. While his escape can hardly be deemed a victory, he managed to preserve his forces, unlike the five other commanders.[21]

Defensive measures based upon water, whether simply flooding nearby fields or preexistent ditches, were also resorted to in exigencies. An enigmatic entry in the *Bamboo Annals* records the first use of flooding for such purposes in 358 B.C. "when an army from Ch'u diverted water from the Yellow River outside the long wall."[22] During Hsiang Liang's campaign to vanquish the Ch'in, retreating Ch'in forces occupied P'u-yang and survived until Hsiang Yü and Liu Pang departed by encircling the town with water.[23] Early in the fourth century Chin thwarted a potential invasion by Chao by blocking the T'u River to create a large watery expanse.[24] Armies frequently broke open riverside embankments to block, as well as entangle, their opponents, [25] and even rebels and border peoples resorted to diverting rivers to temporarily augment the defense of their encampments or recently seized cities.[26]

However formidable, obstructive bodies of water were not invariably effective. Alertness and the aggressive employment of countermeasures remained essential because they could all be negotiated by boat while rivers might be blocked or diverted. Despite their impressive dimensions, moats were particularly susceptible to countermeasures, including swimming, traversing by a variety of rafts and craft, laboriously filling in, crossing by extendable and floating bridges, and even draining. For example, when the fortified city of Yün-chou came under attack in 897, the badly outnumbered commander remained ensconced in his citadel and relied upon the moat's depth for defense. However, the enemy surreptitiously broke open the dikes, releasing much of the water, and built a floating bridge which allowed them to cross and attack the walls, prompting the commander to flee.[27] Similarly, in 1368 Ming forces attacked Ching-chiang, which relied upon a deep moat as its primary line of defense. Ming raiders therefore slew the guards at the gateways, released the water, and built access ramps over which they assaulted and subjugated the city.[28]

Dramatic seasonal variation in rainfall amounts and river levels also deprived moats of essential resupplies and sometimes allowed fording normally impassable torrents. For example, in the drought of A.D. 309 the Yangtze, Yellow, Han, and Ming Rivers all dried up in their lower reaches, allowing people to cross freely almost everywhere.[29] Winter cold could also unexpectedly thwart plans to rely upon rivers or moats as vital defensive obstacles. Early in the eleventh month of A.D. 395 the Yellow River froze when the temperature suddenly plunged, allowing Northern Wei to surprise Later Yen which had confidently assumed the water would prevent any crossing even though ice patches had already appeared.[30]

More ingeniously, in the wintry tenth month of A.D. 376 the king of the small kingdom of Tai in lower Inner Mongolia attacked the Hsiung-nu Worthy King of the Left just above the Ordos where the Yellow River's loop turns downward.[31] The Hsiung-nu had felt safe because the river was far from being frozen even though ice could be seen on the river. However, during an especially cold night the king of Tai cleverly had ropes made from interlaced reeds stretched across the river to still the flow and allow ice to form. Although somewhat successful, the process was still too slow and the ice obviously too thin to be useful so he had the ropes raised to the surface and added more reeds. The water flowing over and lapping about the reeds soon coated them with a layer of ever thickening ice, creating a usable bridge overnight. Tai's troops carefully crossed over and launched a true surprise attack, forcing the astonished Hsiung-nu king to flee, though some 60 percent or more of his people were captured.

Several centuries later An Lu-shan similarly crossed the Yellow River at Ling-ch'ang on the second day of the twelfth month, A.D. 755, to unexpectedly attack the T'ang heartland. This was accomplished by creating an ice bridge from coarse ropes stretched across the river to which every variety of refuse was lashed, including decrepit boats, grass, reeds, and pieces of wood. Being the very heart of winter, the water lapping over these materials froze sufficiently solid overnight to provide a bridge for the rebellious armies to unexpectedly cross before racing forward on their brutal path of conquest.[32]

Although not directly relevant, Ts'ao Ts'ao's clever employment of freezing water to firm up his soft dirt fortifications over a single night in the face of a powerful enemy subsequently became famous and was eventually included in such late texts as the *Yün-ch'ou Kang-mu* and *Thirty-six Stratagems*. Moreover, in 443 an anticipated assault was frustrated when the defenders erected a palisade from willow branches which they soaked in water, forming an ice wall which proved too solid and slippery to overcome.[33]

However, even when a moat's effectiveness had apparently been diminished by the sudden cold, recently formed ice could also prove unreliable, even treacherous. In 794, during his campaign to overcome a rebel force ensconced in the city of Ming-chou located along the Ming River, Wang Ch'ien-hsiu had the city flooded in the seventh month and sustained the water pressure until the beleaguered forces finally abandoned the city in the first month of 796 due to a lack of provisions. In the twelfth month of 794, the static waters outside the city froze sufficiently solid that Wang's forces were able to mount an attack across the ice. Surprisingly, they were not only repelled by a rebel counterattack, but in the course of their retreat the ice cracked, reportedly due to the sun's effects. More than half of Wang's men drowned, evidence that the flood waters were at least several feet deep.[34]

Although a few cities rendered virtually impregnable by expansive, deep moats managed to hold out for months or even years, others fell due to overconfidence. For example, in 908, finding himself under attack by superior forces, the commander at Lang-chou diverted the minor Yüan River to successfully flood the area around the city, apparently thwarting further assaults. After a month of inactivity during which the defenders grew lax, the aggressors mounted a sudden, clandestine night attack through a drain into the interior, set fires both inside and outside the wall, and then penetrated the gates to overwhelm the negligent inhabitants.[35]

In pondering the nature and means of city defense military texts such as the T'ang dynasty *T'ai-pai Yin-ching* continued the basic thinking first expressed in the classic military writings: make the moats deeper and wider, solidify the fortifications, and keep them in good repair, if not augmenting them.[36] Moats were seen as equally vital for expeditionary armies[37] and some texts even suggested appropriate dimensions and proportions for both cities and temporary field encampments, generally a minimum width of twenty to thirty feet and an average depth of ten, but with an irregular profile which would include some significant pits and holes to thwart raiders.[38]

However, it was also recognized that relying on terrain features, including China's mighty rivers, had a psychological downside. In the middle of the Southern Sung, in explaining why the Sung populace and even their generals abandoned the fight so easily, Hua Yüeh pointed out that when people rely upon the mountains and rivers as protective barriers, once a single cavalryman or boat breaches them, their "collapse and scattering cannot be stopped. It shouldn't be regarded as strange that they bind their hands and are captured."[39]

Moreover, hard on the impetus of Warring States internecine strife, increasingly sophisticated, mobile assault techniques capable of surmounting the difficulties posed by moats and rivers quickly developed. Although outside the scope of our study, some have already been described in conjunction with our discussion of incendiary measures in siege defense. However, even such primitive technique as simply swimming across, linking masses of rafts or small boats, laboriously filling in the watery obstacles with dirt, stones, and brush, and draining them off, leaving only a muddy ditch, continued to be commonly employed throughout the centuries.

252    AQUATIC WARFARE

Irrigation and flooding respectively being matters of control and victimization which surpass individual human ability, the latter accounted one of the four disasters stemming from Heaven (with drought, hunger, and famine),[40] organized measures and directed response evolved early on, no doubt coincident with their emblemization in the form of Yü's tireless efforts. Since rivers and streams overflow with a certain degree of seasonal regularity and historical patterns indicate likely breaches and the flow's direction, preventive action can be undertaken to forestall catastrophe and ameliorate the damage when embankments, the chief bulwark against disaster, fail. Irrigation efforts also require engineering, excavation, and constant maintenance, perhaps suggesting that such activity may have been a key factor in the evolution of administrative structures.

As early as the Spring and Autumn period the populace seems to have been liable for labor services rendered in connection with constructing and maintaining both walls and embankments. Although the army was also sometimes drafted for these tasks, one *Ch'un Ch'iu* entry shows that the normal Spring and Autumn response to a flood included the beating of drums and various sacrificial actions (which unfortunately persisted down into the twentieth century in some areas), while the *Ku-liang* comments that the drumming was intended to rouse the troops and masses for the rescue work.[41] More important, as the *Liu-t'ao* early on noted, the skills developed in such routine situations readily translate into military contexts, whether for erecting walls, building embankments to direct flood waters away or onto targets, or destroying them.[42]

The proliferation of aquatic assaults inevitably stimulated the innovation of specific countermeasures, some ad hoc, others more systematic. The first line of defense—in fact the very reason commanders resorted to inundation—was the massive tamped earth walls which, when properly constructed, proved virtually impervious to static pressure. However, the gates and requisite openings for water channels, as well as any slots for firing or thrusting at aggressors, were all highly vulnerable and virtually impossible to impregnably seal with the metalworking and construction techniques of the time. Incendiary attacks might be thwarted with metal or coatings of mud, but neither could withstand an extended flood attack unless the gate area was completely blocked with a solid, supplementary internal wall.

As the classic military writings are remarkably silent about every aspect of aquatic assault and defense, resort must once again be had to the Mohist military chapters to discern the fundamental countermeasures developed during the Warring States period. Although succinct, the *Mo-tzu*'s few passages depict a highly systematized response, implying that aquatic assaults were employed far more often than the few recorded incidents would suggest. Two key methods, draining away any water that penetrates the walls and using a flotilla of small boats to attack the external dikes channeling the water or maintaining its pressure, are outlined:[43]

> All around the perimeter of the city, just within the walls, excavate a dry moat eight paces wide as preparation against flooding. Carefully ascertain the relative heights of the four sides and the low points throughout the city. Also have sluices dug toward the interior and drill deeply on the lowest terrain in order to cause the water to drain down to the level of the springs. Then tile the wells. When you observe the external water level exceeding one *chang* [ten feet], cut holes in the walls to draw the water into the sluices.
>
> Make ten assault craft consisting of two boats coupled together.[44] Each assault craft should be manned by thirty men, six tenths of whom should carry crossbows, while four tenths should wield pitchforks. They must fully exert themselves.
>
> When employing boats like tanks, twenty boats will comprise a company. Pick thirty strong warriors for each boat. Among them twenty will similarly carry pitchforks and swords, as well as wear armor, helmets, and boots, while ten will wield spears.
>
> You must nurture these skilled warriors beforehand, housing them in separate quarters and providing food to their

mothers and fathers. Their wives and children will serve as hostages. When you perceive that the flood waters can be released, employ your assault and tank like craft to break open the outer embankment. Archers atop the city walls should provide fire support, and [troops] urgently assist them.

The usual translation problems apart, both methods were obviously premised upon the walls, including well-sealed gates, being virtually impervious and therefore capable of withstanding heavy static pressures. (Moving river water would constitute a different challenge, one requiring a more rapid response to prevent the walls from being quickly eroded since few were encased in stone until well into the imperial period, though pebbles were sometimes embedded as a protective facing.) How this was to be accomplished is not indicated, but it appears that the Mohist engineers felt the walls could not withstand much more than ten feet of pressure. At this point they advocated chiseling holes to keep it from rising further, perhaps also fearing that the overflowing water might saturate or erode the tamped-earth construction from the top.

These deep wells may have had enormous capacity, being dug down to the level of interior springs or underground streams, but certainly not infinite. The internal sluices would transport any water simply leaking in, but more massive amounts would certainly have quickly overwhelmed them. More direct action being necessary, two types of vessel were employed, one consisting of two boats conjoined together, the other a covered vessel referred to as "tank like."

Differently manned, there is no instruction for how they might have been employed, but the assault vessel's more lethal firepower suggests it must have made the initial attack under the cover of crossbow and archery fire from the city walls, using the "pitchforks" to thrust at the onshore defenders. The tank-like vessels then probably moved forward, discharging the warriors who had to complete the amphibious assault by ascending the embankment (explaining the completeness of their armor and their bearing of swords, then emerging as a close combat weapon) to accomplish the actual work of destruction. Once a break had been made and the water began to recede, troops from the citadel would be expected to sally forth and sustain the effort, presumably conveyed on boats or rafts across the interval between the city walls and embankment.

With the addition of external walls at vulnerable points and increased emphasis upon sealing gate areas against leakage, siege records show that subsequent centuries essentially copied the methods recorded in the *Mo-tzu*, particularly the use of internal wells to drain water and amphibious assaults against the enemy's dikes.[45] Moreover, many of the theoretical writings, including the early Sung *Hu-ch'ien Ching*, include major portions from the *Mo-tzu* in their defensive discussions, almost invariably quoting (without attribution) the relevant passages on defending against inundation.[46] The *Wu-ching Tsung-yao* even warns that aquatic attacks should be expected when sieges grow prolonged and assaults have not achieved their objectives.[47] But more fundamentally, as already pointed out in our section on riverine warfare, the best defense was thought to be preventing the enemy from occupying a position upstream, precluding them from accumulating water and acquiring the power to attack.[48]

## EARLY AQUATIC WARFARE

Reportedly, during Duke Huan's reign as hegemon, after Ch'u invaded Sung and Cheng, their forces blocked two eastward-flowing rivers so that the water backed up west of the mountains for 400 *li*, destroying towns and fields alike.[49] However, just nine major floods are enumerated in the *Ch'un Ch'iu*, the sparse chronicle of the Spring and Autumn period, and a few additional ones in the *Tso Chuan*, lending credence to assertions that these are didactic concatenations rather than actual records.[50] Conversely, no "aquatic attacks" are noted until 512 B.C., just when Sun-tzu may have been serving as strategic advisor to King Ho-lü in Wu. The king had Hsü's forces flooded by apparently blocking and then diverting a mountain stream onto them before going on to extinguish the state,[51] perhaps prompting Sun-tzu's cryptic statement that "water can be used to sever but cannot be employed to seize."[52] Part of the multi-decade strife between Wu and Ch'u, Ho-lü's ready resort to flooding suggests that aquatic measures were a normal component of Wu's offensive repertoire, as might be expected for a wet state then building canals for strategic purposes.

Thereafter, just as with T'ien Tan's fire oxen, a single absorbing event—the siege of Chin-yang—dating to the very beginning of the era defines Warring States aquatic warfare and marks Chin's irreversible fragmentation. Not only does it eclipse the few other known occurrences, but it also became a classic example for future generations and provided the core of a dramatic story that would be vividly enhanced over succeeding centuries. However, while showing that an enemy might be crippled through inundation, it coincidentally taught that even extended floods could be withstood with adequate preparation. Moreover, the assault was thwarted not because of any methodological failure, but because the instigator's insatiable quest for power threatened the very men whose compliance he required. Preserved at length in the *Chan-kuo Ts'e,* the important Legalist thinker Han Fei-tzu didactically adopted the incident to illustrate the ill fate that befalls rulers who are "greedy and perverse." Many of the military writings also cite it as an example of aquatic attack, and several English translations are to be found.[53]

Shortly after mighty Chin had essentially been segmented into six enclaves, Chih Po coerced the powerful clans in Han, Wei, and Chao into destroying the Fan and Chung-hang families and annexing their territory. Then, according to Han Fei-tzu's narrative:[54]

> Several years after returning to his fief and revitalizing his troops, he had an official request that Han cede some territory to him. Earl K'ang of Han was about to refuse, but Tuan Kuei remonstrated with him: "You must grant it. Chih Po is the sort of man who loves profit and acts recklessly and

brutally. If we do not grant what he has requested, he will certainly inflict his army upon Han. By acceding, Chih Po will be inclined to continue his villainy and invariably request territory from some other state. Someone will certainly refuse, and when they do Chih Po will attack them. In this way we can avoid misfortune and wait for the situation to evolve."

Assenting, the earl of Han had an emissary transfer a district of ten thousand families to Chih Po. Pleased, Chih Po again dispatched an official to request territory from Wei. Earl Hsüan of Wei didn't want to cede any territory either, but Chao Chia remonstrated with him: "He requested land from Han and Han assented. If we do not grant what he has requested, we will remain internally strong[55] but externally anger Chih Po. For refusing his request, he will certainly inflict his army upon us." Accordingly, the earl of Wei also had an emissary transfer a district of ten thousand families to Chih Po.

Chih Po again had an official go to Chao to request the territory about the town of Kao-lang in Ts'ai.[56] However, when Earl Hsiang of Chao would not yield it, Chih Po secretly made an agreement with Han and Wei to attack Chao. [Before the attack unfolded], the earl of Chao summoned Chang Meng-t'an and informed him, "Chih Po is overtly friendly but secretly distant. He has dispatched emissaries three times to Han and Wei without including us[57] so an attack by his military forces is inescapable. Where can we ensconce ourselves?"

Chang Meng-t'an replied: "Now Tung Kuan-yü, one of your father's talented ministers, administered Chin-yang and his methods were followed in turn by his successor Yin To, so his instructions still prevail there. You should ensconce yourself in Chin-yang, nowhere else."[58]

Assenting, the earl had Yen Ling-sheng take command of the army's cavalry and chariots and proceed to Chin-yang before he followed himself. When he arrived in Chin-yang and conducted a tour of inspection of the inner and outer city walls and the treasuries attached to the five administrative bureaus, he discovered that the walls had not been well maintained, the storehouses lacked grain, the treasuries had no monetary reserves, the arsenals held neither armor nor weapons, and the city was bereft of defensive equipment.

Frightened, the earl summoned Chang Meng-t'an and said: "I inspected the inner and outer walls together with the five administrative treasuries. None of them have prepared anything. What will we use to respond to the enemy?"

Chang Meng-t'an replied: "I have heard that sagacious officials store things among the people rather than warehouses and arsenals, and focus upon improving the people's practice of their instructions rather than keeping the inner and outer walls in good repair. My lord should issue an edict requiring that after the people have set aside three years of foodstuffs, any surplus should be entered into the storehouses. After setting aside funds for three years' expenditure, any surplus should be forwarded to the treasuries. Any personnel not otherwise occupied should be employed in repairing the inner and outer walls."

The earl of Chao issued the command that evening and the next day the storehouses could not contain all the grain, the treasuries could not accumulate all the money, nor the arsenals accept all the armor and weapons. Within five days the inner and outer walls had already been repaired and the requisite defensive equipment already prepared.

The earl of Chao summoned Chang Meng-t'an and inquired: "Our inner and outer walls have already been repaired, our defensive equipment is now complete, money and grain already sufficient, and armor and weapons more than adequate. What should I do about the lack of arrows?"

Chang Meng-t'an replied: "I have heard that when Tung Kuan-yü governed Chin-yang, all the administrative buildings were walled with hedges of cane reeds. They have now attained about a *chang* [ten feet] in height. If you cut them down and use them, you will have more than enough arrows." When the earl had some cut and tested, he found their hardness unsurpassed by anything else, including *chün-yü's* sturdiness.

The earl of Chao said: "Our arrows are now more than sufficient, but what about our lack of metal [for arrowheads]?"

Chang Meng-t'an replied: "I have heard that when Tung Kuan-yü governed Chin-yang, the pillars in the halls of the administrative buildings and public hostels were all composed of refined copper. You should take them down and use them." When he did so, the metal proved more than sufficient.

Just when his orders had been promulgated and the defensive equipment all prepared, armies indeed arrived from the three states and deployed about the city's walls before attacking. However, when they were unable to reduce them after three months of fighting, Chih Po relaxed the onslaught's intensity, encircled the city, and then broke open the river embankments to flood Chin-yang.

The coalition besieged Chin-yang for three years, forcing the city's populace to live like birds in nests and suspend pots in order to cook. With their materials and provisions nearly exhausted, their officers and officials suffering from weakness and illness, the earl of Chao said to Chang Meng-t'an, "We are short of provisions and foodstuffs, our materials and strength are exhausted, and our officers and officials suffer from weakness and illness. I am afraid we cannot endure. If I want to surrender the city, to which state would it be best?"

Chang Meng-t'an said, "Your servant has heard that wisdom insufficient to preserve the lost and provide security to the endangered is not to be valued. You should forget this plan. I request permission to try and clandestinely obtain an audience with the rulers of Han and Wei."

In his interview with the rulers of Han and Wei, Chang Meng-t'an said: "I have heard that when the lips are lost, the teeth feel cold. At present Chih Po is leading you two in an attack that will shortly see Chao perish. However, when we are lost, you will be next."

They replied: "We know it. However, Chih Po's character is brutal and distant. If he discovers we are plotting against him disaster will certainly result! How can we proceed?"

Chang Meng-t'an replied: "Any plot will proceed from your mouths into my ears alone. No other man will hear of it." The two rulers agreed to turn against Chih Po, set the day, and then dispatched Chang that very night into Chin-yang to report their planned rebellion to his ruler, the earl of Chao. When the earl received Chang Meng-t'an he bowed twice before him, filled with fear and joy.

The morning after reaching an accord with Chang Meng-t'an, the two rulers went to Chih Po's court. Coming out of the headquarters gate they encountered Chih Kuo, who thought their appearance strange and therefore went in to see Chih Po: "The facial expression on these two rulers indicates they are about to change their allegiance."

Chih Po inquired: "What indicates it?"

"Their movements were bold and attitude arrogant, unlike their previous constraint. It would be best for you to act before them."

Chih Po replied: "I formed a close alliance with these two rulers to destroy Chao and equally divide its territory into three. Because of this they would never violate our alliance. Our armies have been exposed here at Chin-yang for three years. Now that we are about to seize it and enjoy the profits, how could they have any intention to betray me? It cannot be possible, so drop it and don't mention it again."[59]

The next morning, when the two rulers went to Chih Po's court, they again encountered Chih Kuo as they came out of the gate to the headquarters. Chih Kuo went in to see Chih Po and reported: "Did you inform them of what I said?"

Chih Po asked: "How did you know it?"

"This morning, when these two rulers came out from your court and saw me their complexions changed and they glared at me. Without doubt their intentions have changed, so it would be best to kill them."

Chih Po said: "Drop it, do not speak about it again."

Chih Kuo replied: "Impossible, you must kill them. If you cannot kill them you should draw them closer."

Chih Po asked: "How should I draw them closer?"

Chih Kuo said: "Wei's strategist Chao Chia and Han's strategist Tuan Kuei are both capable of altering their ruler's plans. If you agree to enfeoff each of them with a district of ten thousand households upon Chao's destruction, you will ensure their rulers' intentions remain unchanged."

Chih Po replied: "If we divide Chao into three after destroying it and I further enfeoff each of them with ten thousand households I will gain very little. It's not possible." When Chih Kuo realized his words would be ignored, he departed from the camp and even changed his clan name to Fu.

On the appointed night Chao's forces slew the troops guarding the dike's embankments and destroyed parts of them so that the water would flood Chih Po's encampment. While Chih Po's army was chaotically trying to rescue themselves from the water's onslaught, forces from Han and Wei mounted a sudden pincer attack from the two wings and the earl of Chao led his troops in a frontal assault. They severely defeated Chih Po's army and captured Chih Po himself.

According to later compilations, Chih Po was actually killed, his clan exterminated, and his head turned into a lacquered drinking vessel by the earl of Chao.[60] In concluding, Han Fei-tzu cited an opinion already common in his era: "Chih Po perished, his army was destroyed, his state was divided into three, and he became the butt of the realm's laughter. Thus I say that being greedy, perverse, and loving profit is the foundation for extinguishing your state and killing yourself."

The *Chan-kuo Ts'e* contains two other passages relating aspects of this incident, one of them an interesting expansion of Chao Chia's persuasion to the earl of Wei, slightly recast with Jen Chang as the speaker which applies Sun-tzu' principle of fostering arrogance in an enemy:[61]

Why are you not going to give the land to Chih Po?"

The earl of Chao replied: "He sought the territory for no reason, so I will not give it to him."

Chao Chia said, "When someone seeks territory for no reason, the states nearby will certainly become fearful. When he repeats these demands because his desires are insatiable, All under Heaven will certainly be frightened. If you give him the land, Chih Po will inevitably become arrogant. Being arrogant, he will slight his enemies. As his neighbors grow fearful, they will certainly come closer together. When Chih Po underestimates the armies of these now conjoined states, the Chih clan will not long endure. The *Chou Shu*[62] asserts, "If you want to defeat someone, you should temporarily sustain them; if you want to seize something, you should temporarily give it." Why don't you give the territory to Chih Po in order to make him arrogant? How can you abandon this opportunity to have All under Heaven plot against Chih Po and thereby become an isolated objective?"

The second *Chan-kuo Ts'e* passage depicts a lute player narrating an incident purportedly derived from this conflict as part of a remonstrance. Supposedly after three years, when the water was just three horizontal boards from the top of the walls, the three rulers were riding together in a chariot to inspect the dike. Somehow Chih Po was prompted to foolishly exclaim, "I did not originally know that water could destroy other people's states. Now I realize that the Fen River[63] can be advantageously employed to inundate An-yi [in Wei] and the Chiang to flood P'ing-yang [in Han]." On hearing their chief cities so threatened, the earl of Wei reportedly elbowed the earl of Han and the latter signified his understanding by stepping on the former's foot, thereby consigning Chih Po to an ignominious fate.[64]

Whether this conversation, however reasonable, actually occurred may well be doubted, but the general cognizance of water's potential and subsequent thoroughgoing belief in such events, stemming in part from writings such as these, cannot. Thereafter, generals confronted by entrenched enemies, whether in fortified cites, freestanding citadels, or amidst fields and mountains, would immediately ponder the possibility of exploiting nearby water sources to inundate them.

Two other persuasions of this type offer further confirmation that the power of flooding had become widely recognized in the Warring States period. Chang Yi, in cajoling the king of Ch'in, noted that an effective strategy would have been to flood out the Wei clan by breaking open the embankments at the mouth of Pai-ma[65] while Chu Chi, in admonishing the king of Wei, accurately predicted that Ch'in would extinguish Wei by flooding Ta-liang, though he mistakenly believed the water source would be the great Ying marsh.[66]

The actual technique employed at Chin-yang is uncertain, for without doubt the city was situated above the level of the nearby river. A countervailing wall would have had to have been constructed to encircle it and thereby maintain constant water pressure and the river dammed to raise the level adequately, or a source diverted from upriver, as well as a dike system to channel the water to the site and protective barriers around Chih Po's camp. (A catch basin may have been created upstream on the Wei River in anticipation of the rainy season to serve as the basic source or augment the river's volume.)

Reports indicate the water never overflowed the top of the wall, a height that probably exceeded all but a few buildings within. That the walls were substantial and basically impervious testifies to the rigorous employment of stamped-earth technology. However, leakage certainly occurred around the gates and coupled with seepage through weak points, accounts for the flooding which obviously attained a depth of several feet. Surviving for three years amidst the persistent dampness and accompanying sanitation problems is remarkable in itself, but the texts claim the people's will to resist never weakened.[67] Nevertheless, Chao's failure to conduct raids and other operations to disrupt the besiegers and turn the tide instead of adopting a purely passive posture, as many cities would do throughout Chinese history, remains puzzling. Even more surprising is Chih Po's negligence in not erecting protective bunkers outside his own camp to deflect any break in the dikes, whether deliberate or accidental, especially as the former might well have been expected.

Following the drama at Chin-yang only two Warring States' aquatic assaults merit note, the first arising in 332 B.C. when Ch'i and Wei were manipulated into attacking Chao by King Hui of Ch'in. Hard pressed, Chao flooded their combined forces, thereby blunting the invasion and forcing them to withdraw.[68] Thereafter, the era essentially ended when

Ch'in exterminated Wei through flooding Ta-liang in 225 B.C., as earlier foretold. Wang Pen exploited the power of the Yellow River by blocking a preexisting canal through which its waters flowed until they backed up and inundated Wei's last bastion.[69] Within three months the poorly maintained walls had collapsed, the king had surrendered and been executed, and the entity known as Wei extinguished.

## RAIN AND NATURAL INUNDATION

Water in all its forms presented ancient armies with almost insurmountable obstacles. Rain also made life miserable, soaking men, materials, and the landscape, sometimes even eroding tamped-earth bulwarks and fortifications with dire consequences.[70] Lakes and ponds required boats if circumferential marches were to be avoided while the currents on swiftly flowing rivers, especially during the rainy season, often precluded any possibility of crossing. Floating bridges were employed as early as the Spring and Autumn period and, according to the *Liu-t'ao*, rafts and temporary pontoon bridges were already being carried by campaign armies in the Warring States period, though no doubt only in limited amounts since they would be an overwhelming burden except on the smoothest terrain. Marshes and wetlands, whether standing or formed during seasonal flooding, stymied wheeled transport, prompting Sun Pin to assert: "What causes trouble for the army is the terrain. Thus it is said that three miles of wetlands will cause trouble for the army; crossing through such wetlands will result in leaving the main force behind."[71]

Thus the general principle for chariot-based armies and subsequently mixed infantry and cavalry forces was to simply avoid any terrain that might retard movement and entangle the troops, converting them into easy targets. In addition to identifying a number of highly dangerous configurations of terrain, Sun-tzu accordingly advised: "When you cross salt marshes and wetlands, concentrate on quickly getting away from them; do not remain. If you engage in battle in marshes or wetlands, you must stay in areas with marsh grass and keep groves of trees at your back."[72]

Apart from similarly admonishing commanders to quickly depart from wetlands, not long thereafter the *Wu-tzu* offered extemporaneous solutions:[73]

> Marquis Wu asked: "If we encounter the enemy in a vast, watery marsh where the chariot wheels sink down to the point that the shafts are under water; both our chariots and cavalry are floundering; and we haven't prepared any boats or oars so can't advance or retreat, what should we do?"
>
> Wu Ch'i replied: "This is referred to as water warfare. Do not employ chariots or cavalry, but have them remain on the side. Mount some nearby height and look all about. You must ascertain the water's condition, know its expanse, and fathom its depth. Then you can conceive an unorthodox stratagem for victory. If the enemy begins crossing the water, press them when half have crossed."

Heavy rains invariably rendered many of the best roads difficult and turned the land into an impassable quagmire, enmiring even the greatest commanders, including Ts'ao Ts'ao after the debacle at Ch'ih Pi. Furthermore, sudden river surges eroded embankments, collapsed walls, and even flooded negligent enemies in the field. Seasonal river surges and torrential rises also devastated walls and fortifications (as at Fan-ch'eng), swept away bridges, eroded portions of the shore, and engulfed armies camped alongside or engaged in crossing.

Halting or heedlessly encamping on low-lying terrain might therefore prove traumatic as the frequently cited, Warring States example of Ching Yang's perceptiveness, while in command of forces dispatched by the king of Ch'u to extricate Yen from a conjoined attack by Ch'i, Han, and Wei, showed. Bivouacking for the night, he ordered his subcommanders to set up the camp but after they finished he discovered they had erected the palisades in an area liable to inundation and therefore ordered their removal to safer terrain, much to the officers' anger and consternation. During the night torrents of water in fact cascaded down the mountains from the suddenly arising heavy rains and flooded the original site, startling his subordinates.[74]

Perhaps the most historically decisive incident occurred in the eighth month of A.D. 219 when a Ts'ao-Wei campaign force of some seven armies became trapped and inundated by torrential rains in a valley near the contested city of Fan-ch'eng.[75] The 40,000 troops who survived the flooding, drowning, and attacks by Kuan Yü's forces were taken prisoner, allowing the great warrior to surround Fan-ch'eng and attack the companion city of Hsiang-yang on the southern bank of the Han River. Although it has been claimed that Kuan Yü's troops blocked the rivers and outlets to raise the water level, there is no extant substantiation. Nevertheless, according to Yeh Meng-hsiung's retelling:[76]

> At the end of the Han, Ts'ao Ts'ao dispatched a massive number of troops to Fan-ch'eng under Ts'ao Jen. Ts'ao Jen in turn had Yü Chin and P'ang Te encamp in the north of Ch'u at Hua-k'ou-ch'uan. The terrain's configuration was low, the location not far from the Pai River. It had just entered the eighth month and as the heavy autumnal rains were continuously falling, Kuan Yü had his troops build dams at all the river's outlets and make numerous bamboo rafts.
>
> Ch'eng Ho, one of Wei's lieutenant generals, met with Yü Chin and said: "We have encamped where the terrain's configuration is extremely low and our distant scouts report that Kuan Yü's armies have all shifted to the high hills. I request that you move the encampment in order to prevent a disaster from flooding."
>
> Yü Chin shouted, "Such disordered words from an ordinary lout will confuse the soldiers' minds. If you speak about it again, you will be executed." Early the next day the river massively overflowed, water entered the encampment from all four sides, and the seven armies perished. When Chin and a few generals ascended higher ground to escape the flood, Kuan Yü attacked them from rafts. Hard pressed, Chin and the others then asked to surrender.

This recounting of course reveals as much about military thinkers as about historical tactics. Moreover, even though Yeh's view lacks textual support, this sort of interpretation acquired its own validity through common belief and entered the repertoire of possible techniques.[77]

However, this wasn't the only incident in which a commander's obstinacy compounded the natural disaster of flooding.[78] During the Five dynasties period Li Shih-ku, serving as campaign commander, encamped the army on low terrain. Although similarly advised to shift to higher ground, he angrily rejected the warning. Moreover, even when informed that the flood waters had already become visible (after the enemy broke open the embankment), Li not only persisted in his stupidity, but without even confirming the error of his report had the officer executed for sowing confusion among the army! Quickly inundated, they soon found themselves unable to fight and suffered heavy losses, the general numbering among those who perished.

Pondering the problems of rain, wetlands, rivers, and other enmiring terrain, the classic military writers beginning with Wu Ch'i formulated basic operational principles, the simplest being to resort to infantry forces:

> Marquis Wu asked: "When it has been continuously raining for so long that the horses sink into the mire and the chariots are stuck while we are under attack on all four sides and the Three Armies are terrified, what should we do?"
>
> Wu Ch'i replied: "In general, desist from employing chariots when the weather is rainy and the land wet, but mobilize them when it is hot and dry. Value high terrain, disdain low ground. When racing your strong chariots, whether advancing or halting, you must adhere to the road. If the enemy arises be sure to follow their tracks."

The chapter entitled "Battle Chariots" in the *Liu-t'ao* subsequently characterized ten terrain-based situations so inimical to chariot operations as to be fatal, four of them strongly affected by water and wetness:

If the land is collapsing, sinking, and marshy, with black mud sticking to everything, this is terrain that will labor the chariots.

Luxuriant grass runs through the fields, and there are deep watery channels throughout. This is terrain that thwarts the chariots.

To the rear are water-filled ravines and ditches, to the left deep water, and to the right steep hills. This is terrain upon which chariots are destroyed.

It has been raining day and night for more than ten days without stopping. The roads have collapsed, so that it's not possible to advance nor to escape to the rear. This is terrain that will sink the chariots.

Even though cavalry forces enjoy greater mobility and can traverse more irregular terrain than wide war chariots, four disadvantageous situations predispose them to defeat:[79]

Great mountain torrents, deep valleys, tall luxuriant grass, forests and trees, these are conditions that will exhaust the cavalry.

When there is water on the left and right, ahead there are large hills, to the rear high mountains, and the Three Armies are fighting between the bodies of water while the enemy occupies both the interior and exterior ground, this is terrain that means great difficulty for the cavalry.

When we are sinking into marshy ground while advancing and retreating must both be through quagmires, this is worrisome terrain for the cavalry.

When on the left there are deep water sluices, and on the right there are gullies and hillocks, but below the heights the ground appears level—good terrain for advancing, retreating, and enticing an enemy—this terrain is a pitfall for cavalry.

Despite pervasive recognition of these problems and the advancement of remedial measures, the same lesson had to be repeatedly taught over the centuries. For example, the

*Hu-ch'ien Ching* continued to cite the *Art of War's* "when traversing wetlands and marshes put your companies in order and quickly pass through"[80] and advise "stick close to the roads along the embankment for fear of sinking into marshy terrain."[81] More expansively, the late Sung dynasty *One Hundred Unorthodox Strategies* states:[82]

> Whenever you mobilize the army and send it forth on campaign, if you encounter wetlands and marshes, or terrain where the levees are ruined, you should employ a double pace and extended marches to quickly pass through. You must not remain in them.
>
> If there is no alternative, if you are unable to get out at once because the road is long, the sun setting, and you must pass the night, you should shift to terrain shaped like a turtle's back. You should always establish a circular encampment on high ground which slopes away on all four sides so as to be able to withstand enemy attacks from every direction. This will prevent being endangered by flood waters and you will also be prepared against being encircled by enemy raiders.
>
> A tactical principle from the *Ssu-ma Fa* asserts: "Pass through wetlands, cross over damaged roads, and select ground for encamping configured like a turtle's back."

In illustration, the author cited a T'ang dynasty border incident similar to Ching Yang's Warring States triumph:[83]

> In the first year [A.D. 679] of the T'iao-lu reign period of the T'ang Dynasty it was reported that the nomadic Turkish leader A-shih-te-wen had revolted. The emperor summoned the Minister of Personnel, concurrently General-in-Chief of the Right Imperial Guards, P'ei Hsing-chien to serve as commander-in-chief for the Ting-hsiang campaign army. When the army arrived at the khan's border the sun had already set, so they established their camp and dug protective moats and ditches all around. However, general P'ei ordered them to move the encampment to a high mound.

His adjutant said: "The officers and soldiers are already settled in camp, they cannot be troubled." General P'ei refused to listen and moved them. That night fierce winds, torrential rains, and thunder and lightning explosively descended, inundating their former encampment with more than six feet of water. Startled, everyone asked how the general had known it would be windy and rainy. General P'ei smiled and replied: "From now on just rely upon my constraints and measures, do not ask how I know such things."

Commanders were encouraged to attack troops enmired on wet terrain or beset by flooding because the casualties and compounded misery they were suffering rendered them relatively defenseless targets.[84] Avoidance being the simplest solution, even the Ming dynasty *Ts'ao-lü Ching-lüeh* emphasized that armies should never encamp on low or wet ground and should also set up walls and dig moats,[85] and most of the other Ming military writers concurred, showing the continuity of tradition.

More actively, enemy armies should be manipulated onto marshy terrain where they will inevitably get bogged down, worn out, miserable, sick, and dispirited, and the possibility of flooding them through breaking dams, diverting streams, or temporarily stanching a river's flow might be realized. Tactical measures were thus formulated for constraining the enemy's movements and shaping the battlefield prior to mounting an aquatic attack or exploiting enmiring terrain.[86] As early as the Warring States period the *Six Secret Teachings* succinctly asserted, "Valleys with streams and treacherous ravines are the means by which to stop chariots and defend against cavalry."[87] Slightly earlier the *Wu-tzu* had advised: "If they encamp on low wetlands, where there is no way for the water to drain off and heavy rain falls several times, they can be flooded and drowned."[88]

The most comprehensive strategic approach was formulated by Hsü Tung early in the Sung by reformulating Suntzu's deadly configurations through emphasizing water's presence and effects:[89]

The *Art of War* speaks of precipitous gorges with mountain torrents, Heaven's Well, Heaven's Jail, Heaven's Net, Heaven's Pit, and Heaven's Fissure. These six are referred to as the "six harms." When you encounter them quickly depart, do not approach them.

What is termed a precipitous gorge is mountainous land with a deep river valley. Heaven's Well is a natural depression in which excessive water can accumulate. Heaven's Net is a mountainous gorge with a stream with the sides so narrow that it becomes land where men could be caught in a net. Heaven's Jail is where the forest is dark and overgrown, land where tangled vegetation is deep and expansive. Heaven's Pit is land where the escape road is muddy and neither men nor horses can traverse it. Heaven's Fissure is where the terrain is mostly watery ditches and pits, land where one sinks into watery gravel.

Always have our army keep them at a distance but force the enemy to approach them. When we face them, the enemy will have them at their backs. [Sun-tzu said]: "When the army advances there are roads on which one does not attack, terrain for which one does not contend."[90] He was referring to these terrains.

Most writers concurred that these configurations rendered armies vulnerable to withering attack and allowed the outnumbered to not just contend with, but actually defeat greatly superior forces, though some tacticians believed (perhaps in accord with Sun-tzu's concept of fatal terrain) that they might also be exploited by desperate troops to fight fervently.[91] Conversely, the dry season meant low water levels, synonymous with ease in fording rivers but severe frustration for movement by boat, whether large transport craft or smaller vessels plying the lesser rivers. Sun-tzu's warning "when it rains upstream, foam appears. If you want to cross over, wait until it settles"[92] represents the first theoretical acknowledgment of the dangers of variability. However, wind, especially seasonally sustained ones predominately from a single direction, could also push river and lake waters over their banks, flooding low-lying terrain, cities,[93] roads, and fields.

Certain areas were also known to be periodically impassable due to seasonal rains, others following the winter melt and dramatic rise of the great rivers in the spring. Winter normally saw the lowest water levels and could be extremely dry despite the cold. An interesting, if likely fabricated, dialogue found in the *San-kuo Chih* preserves T'ien Ch'ou's advice to Ts'ao Ts'ao, then in a quandary because his efforts to attack the border tribes supporting Yüan Shao had been frustrated by heavy rains. Not only had the roads become impassable, but some of his generals believed the entire effort had to be abandoned. However, T'ien pointed out that the area around Pei-p'ing district had always suffered from seasonal flooding, the roads frequently being severed by water too deep to traverse by wagon, yet too shallow to allow passage by boat. Nevertheless, circuitous minor routes still existed which had always been, and still could be, exploited.

Enlightened by his advice, Ts'ao Ts'ao cleverly had a large standard erected at the water's edge proclaiming that they would wait for autumn or winter before advancing. When reported by enemy observers, it naturally had the desired effect of inducing such laxity that the Shan-yü was astonished when Ts'ao Ts'ao's army suddenly appeared just 200 *li* away after crossing some 500 *li* of tortuous terrain. Nevertheless, he immediately came forth with some 50,000 cavalry but Ts'ao Ts'ao preemptively attacked before they could deploy, inflicting a severe defeat. As a result some 200,000 Hu tribesmen and Han border settlers surrendered. Coincidentally, the immediately following months of winter proved extremely dry, no water was to be found for 200 *li*, and the army had to dig wells to a depth of 250 feet to survive.[94]

# 9

# Aquatic Attack

## THEORY

China's many rivers and large streams were all capable of inflicting unexpected destruction. However, monsoon rains, spring melt in the mountains, and cyclic weather events made the majestic Yangtze, Yellow, and Huai particularly volatile. Even after centuries of concerted control and the discovery of basic hydraulic engineering principles, the Yellow River still sundered its banks some 1,500 times between the Shang and the end of the Han. For example, a break in 168 B.C. required a massive labor mobilization to stem while the *T'ung Tien* refers to floods during Li Mi's revolt at the end of the Sui that killed nearly half the populace in Honan and Shantung.[1] Lengthy portions of the Yellow River's course and even its outlet to the sea suddenly shifted over the centuries, resulting in countless deaths, widespread devastation, and the inundation of millions of acres of arable land, as in 132 B.C.

Even minor rivers could wreck great havoc, as the Chih River did in A.D. 23 when it overflowed following the torrential rains of a sudden tempest that reportedly terrified the wild animals. Coming at the end of Wang Mang's dynasty, just after his pivotal reversal at K'un-yang, the drowning of more than 10,000 soldiers proved a crushing blow to Wang's crumbling field army.[2]

The most common, easily implemented control technique was constructing embankments wherever necessary, but as the rivers—especially the Yellow River, which flowed down from the plateau—were heavily laden with silt, soil deposits rapidly raised the overall bed even with good engineering practices designed to maintain flow speeds, requiring that dikes be constantly heightened and reinforced. Thus many riverside cities and contiguous areas were threatened not only by seasonal surges, but also dike failures, whether natural or the result of enemy action. With such destructive potential ready to hand, aggressors could inflict dramatic damage with little effort.

The existence of a complex network of irrigation channels also ensured that any sudden water surge would be quickly dispersed over a vast area, ruining supplies and equipment before turning the countryside into a quagmire once the water receded. Even the complex canal network that gradually evolved from the Warring States onward, especially the channels constructed for logistical purposes, might be exploited to facilitate aquatic attacks.

Accordingly, mounting an aquatic attack did not invariably require massive effort to construct channels and embankments, but merely astute exploitation of the terrain's features and natural configuration, whether by damming a river, diverting a mountain stream, or simply smashing a dike. Often accomplished in days in the absence of strong defensive forces or assaults on work parties, the infrequency of aquatic attacks is somewhat puzzling, only minimally understandable in terms of the difficulties posed by soggy ground or the futility of salvaging items of value from collapsed and waterlogged structures.

Sun-tzu early on employed water's incredible force as an analogy for his concept of *shih* or "strategic configuration of power," saying, "The strategic configuration of power is visible in the onrush of pent-up water tumbling stones along."[3] Moreover, he initiated conscious thought about employing it to mount a direct attack with a single, oft cited statement ironically preserved in "Incendiary Warfare" which asserts that "using water to assist an attack is powerful."[4] During the Warring States period Sun Pin added "the aquatic deployment is the means to inundate the solid."[5] Finally the *Wei Liao-tzu*, written amidst a milieu that saw the *Tao Te Ching* imagize water's amorphousness as the ultimate conquest weapon, subsequently observed: "Now water is the softest and weakest of things, but whatever it collides with, such as hills and mounds, will be collapsed by it for no reason other than its nature is concentrated and its attack is totally committed."[6]

A storied, if perhaps apocryphal incident in A.D. 969 metaphorically imagized the power of water. As part of T'ai-tsu's early campaigns to consolidate Sung power by vanquishing residual opposition, a campaign was mounted against the Northern Han even though the latter were nominally allied with the Khitan. At the end of the second month, under T'ai-tsu's personal direction, the Sung initiated a siege against the strategically important city of T'ai-yüan in the center of Shanhsi where the main Northern Han forces were ensconced. Being severely outnumbered, the defenders refused to be drawn into open battle, preferring to rely upon their bastion in order to win through attrition. When a Sung commander requested additional troops to mount an assault, Ch'en Ch'eng-chao inquired why the emperor didn't use the billions of soldiers at his side and then, when the T'ai-tsu seemed perplexed, pointed to the Fen River with his whip.[7] Suddenly enlightened, the emperor ordered a channel created to flood T'ai-yüan and even personally inspected the project.

However, probably because extensive preparatory work was required, the order to unleash the river was not issued until the eighth month. An attack was launched by boat immediately after the water had risen sufficiently but failed when defenders upon the walls successfully beat it back. However, the rising water eventually broke through the outer fortifications and poured into the city until determined soldiers who braved a hail of arrows blocked the breach with straw bales. Thereafter, despite their ongoing misery, the defenders remained undeterred and eventually a Khitan force, much stronger than the contingent previously defeated by the Sung, appeared and encamped to the west. As the Sung forces were suffering from misery and illness due to the ongoing heavy rains and the T'ai-tsu found he was gradually being outnumbered, the Sung opted to withdraw, adumbrating the Northern Han campaign.[8]

Historical accounts and later theoretical writings suggest that apart from exploiting the current to poison enemies encamped downstream, four basic methods of aquatic attack were disproportionately employed. Simply inundating enemy cities and encampments was the most often undertaken and proved particularly effective against temporary positions, especially if the enemy negligently encamped in a relative depression. It could be accomplished by diverting a river's flow, which would have the additional benefit of dynamically eroding any fortified walls, or simply damming the river downstream until the water accumulated sufficiently to flood the area. Even fortifications that managed to withstand the initial impulse would normally leak to some extent from the unrelieved static pressure, immersing the inhabitants in misery and consternation, not to mention inducing such widespread disease and suffering that 60 to 70 percent often perished over the course of a water-enforced siege.

Rather than destroying structures or drowning men, the objective was often simply to immobilize forces and to coerce their surrender by destroying their provisions and equipment, "turning the people into fishes, making them live in trees and cook in hanging pots."[9] Campaign forces could be similarly targeted, whether for direct assault or more indirectly by flooding their forthcoming line of march. Enmiring transport vehicles would be the chief objective, but opportunistic archery attacks would certainly be unleashed to plague them. More dramatically, water could also be used as a ram by damming the flow upstream and then suddenly releasing it, creating a surge in which any stones and debris swept up would augment the ram's power, enabling it to more rapidly destroy earthen fortifications unimproved with stone facings and sweep away the wooden palisades of temporary encampments, engulfing men and provisions.

A variant of the ram was created by temporarily damming the river with sandbags upstream but not releasing the pent-up waters until the enemy's forces had partially crossed, sweeping away those in the river, cutting off both banks, and creating panic. Naturally this sort of ploy would only prove effective against commanders who neglected reconnaissance or could be lured into hurriedly crossing, contrary to numerous admonitions in the military writings from Sun-tzu onward. Conversely, temporarily damming a river slightly upstream would allow troops to cross where the water would otherwise be too deep or the current too strong, returning it to its original level then providing a protective barrier to the rear. Damming it or diverting the flow might also be employed to frustrate the enemy's logistics, depriving them of the depth needed to transport men and provisions by boat.

As aquatic attacks were mounted over the centuries and the repertoire of techniques expanded, certain operative principles were formulated and began to appear in the military writings. However, Sun-tzu established the fundamentals: "Water's configuration avoids heights and races downward. Water configures its flow in accord with the terrain, it has no constant shape."[10] China's continuous tradition of building dikes and excavating channels to control rivers and create irrigation canals provided an experienced workforce and ensured that water's amorphous character could be exploited to the fullest extent allowed by the terrain. The fastest-flowing waters could be interrupted and diverted, the most difficult terrain and formidable distances successfully traversed.[11]

Chih Po's monologue in the well-known siege of Chin-yang, other discussions, and Su Ch'in's persuasions reveal that Warring States period theorists were well aware that many pivotal cities could be flooded if the inhabitants failed to adequately defend river embankments and dikes or allowed the necessary excavations to proceed unimpeded. Alternatively, massive military force had to overwhelm any strongpoints, control the countryside, and thwart all martial interference. Nevertheless, Sun Pin concluded "attacking state capitals and towns with water will prove effective."[12]

The first post–Warring States theoretical discussion of aquatic assault appears in Li Ch'üan's T'ang dynasty *T'ai-pai*

*Yin-ching*, where the term *shui kung* was initially employed. Much of the section entitled "Equipment for Aquatic Attack" is devoted to describing the construction and employment of a three-chamber water level not entirely unlike a theodolite. Essential to determining relative height and thereby assessing an attack's feasibility, the design and description were adopted by the Sung dynasty *Hu-ch'ien Ching* and subsequent military texts.[13]

In a crucial opening paragraph much mimicked by later works, Li Ch'üan observed:

> The *Classic* states: "Employing water to assist an attack is powerful." Water achieves its power through terrain. When the source is higher than the city or the main course is larger than the side channels, they can be blocked and then released to flow. Thus the Chin River can inundate An-yi and the Fen River immerse P'ing-yang. After first setting up a water level to determine relative height, you can engulf cities,[14] inundate armies, immerse encampments, and defeat generals.

Li's assessment obviously presumes that water, whether flowing or accumulated in stagnant pools, will be employed merely to inundate objectives. Moreover, although he begins by citing the *Art of War*, he surprisingly fails to comment upon Sun-tzu's qualification that "water can be used to sever, but cannot be employed to seize." Nor does he discuss seasonal factors even though water levels vary significantly and his chapter on incendiary assaults is replete with discussions of astrological timing. Finally, the sort of operational questions that troubled Wu Ch'i and the other classic writers who found depressions to be potentially dangerous and advised flooding them to impact enemies no longer appear.

In succinctly commencing his discussion of "Aquatic Attacks," Tu Yu's *T'ung Tien* merely cites Sun-tzu's observations on water's capabilities. However, his illustrations encompass both direct flooding, such as Ts'ao Ts'ao utilized against Lü Pu, and the infrequently employed water ram first made prominent by Han Hsin at the start of the Han. Thereafter, the *Hu-ch'ien Ching* compiled by Hsü Tung just at the turn of the millennium contains four sections on aspects of aquatic warfare, though the one entitled "Aquatic Attacks" merely incorporates the *T'ai-pai Yin-ching's* passages on the water level. However, a thoughtful elaboration called "Advantages of Water" posits four main combat possibilities, all defined in terms of the river's flow:

> The *Military Methods* states, "Using water to assist an attack is powerful." For those who excel in employing water the Tao is fourfold: the first is called "according with," the second is called "contrary to," the third is called "theft," the fourth is called "severing."
>
> The Tao for employing water in accord [with its flow] is twofold. If someone severs the water's flow and sets [wooden] barriers up amidst the river, we must maneuver above them. By exploiting a favorable wind, we can beat the drums and raise a clamor, release incendiaries, and by according with the flow, smash into them. When the barriers have been broken, we can pass beyond. However, desist if the wind turns. Moreover, if the enemy is downstream but moving upward with their warriors and horses contrary to the flow, if we can gain a position upstream, we can poison them. These two are termed "being in accord with [the current's flow]."[15]
>
> Employment contrary to the water's flow consists of erecting high dams to obstruct its downward flow until it overflows the interior and then channeling it to inundate something. This is what is referred to as "contrary employment."
>
> Theft of water is employed where the enemy is relying upon water or about to clandestinely mount an aquatic attack. Investigate the patterns of terrain and then secretly excavate sluices in order to draw the water off to some other place, depleting any water resources they would rely upon. This is termed "theft."
>
> In severing the water's flow, boats filled with faggots and logs, earth and stone can be floated out upstream and long sluices separately created to drain the water away, or sacks

filled with sand can be emplaced in the upper flow in order to block the water. When you want the water to move again, you just have to break apart the dike of bags. This is termed "severing [the water's] flow."

The section then ominously concludes by warning that "employing water requires appropriate terrain. Persistence in employing it on inappropriate terrain will, on the contrary, result in harm. If you accord with the terrain, you will excel."

The *Wu-ching Tsung-yao* completed a half century later similarly includes several brief sections on various aspects of aquatic warfare, integrating and systematizing previous observations and principles. Partially based upon the *T'ai-pai Yin-ching* and incorporating observations from Chih Po's exclamatory monologue, the chapter entitled "Shui Chan" ("Aquatic Attack") places the methodology upon a sound footing:[16]

> Now aquatic attacks are the means to sever the enemy's routes, submerge the enemy's cities, float the enemy's huts and sheds, and destroy the enemy's provisions and stores. A mass of a million can be turned into fish! Even cases of lesser harm can still cause them to clamber up trees to live and suspend pots to cook.
>
> Thus it is said that the Fen River can be employed to inundate P'ing-yang, the Chi River can be employed to inundate An-yi, the Yellow River to inundate Ta-liang, and the Wei River to inundate Ying-ch'uan. Han Hsin squeezed the Wei River before breaking open his dike of earthen sacks to slay Lung Chü. Ts'ao Ts'ao drew the Yi and Ssu Rivers onto Hsia-p'i and conquered Lü Pu. They all controlled the mountains and hills and gained the advantages provided by the terrain's configuration.
>
> If you channel water along level ground, even after laboring mightily and expending effort, the profits and harm will be about equal. Moreover, Chih Po's perishing through mounting an aquatic attack should be an admonition to anyone undertaking an aquatic attack. Today we continue to preserve these examples.

The *Art of War* states: "Employing water to assist an attack is strong. Water achieves its power through conforming to the terrain."[17] This means that when the source is higher than the city, when the foundation is higher than the branches, it can be blocked and stopped, can be broken open and flow. It can be channeled to sever roads and be banked to inundate cities. Poison can be poured into the upper reaches to flow down or temporary dams broken open when the enemy has half crossed. Their Tao is not the same. You must first establish the water level to ascertain relative height, then you can begin to employ them.

Ch'i Ch'ung-li's *Ping-ch'ou Lei-yao* written in the Southern Sung around A.D. 1130 also includes a short section on aquatic warfare filled with historical examples but only minimal theoretical comments.[18] However, based upon selected cases he believes that "warfare is the Tao of deception, so if you can be victorious over the enemy, neither launching incendiaries nor breaking open dikes along rivers should be discarded. One who excels at warfare takes water and fire as materials for employment." He subsequently concluded the section by noting Sun-tzu's basic advice about seeking life, dwelling up high, and not going against the current when deploying the army because failing to heed such wisdom results in forfeiting advantages of terrain which the enemy will exploit to flood you, just as Ts'ao Ts'ao did in vanquishing Lü Pu.

Although Hua Yüeh focused on the need for supplies and the historical use of water transport in his *Ts'ui-wei Pei-cheng-lu* (compiled in 1207), he observed that most water sources are higher than the cities they sustain.[19] Accordingly, rivers, even lakes, can be utilized to inundate them, though dams or embankments must be constructed above or below the city sites. A few of the eleven vulnerable cities were well known, but most were not previously targeted for aquatic assault, showing how the tactical thinking was being categorically extended in his era. Moreover, the forty-two secret methods he describes for attacking cities includes flooding them with water.[20]

In his *Yün-ch'ou Kang-mu,* composed about 1562, Yeh Meng-hsiung seconded Ch'i's insights, caustically condemning the shortsightedness of commanders who failed to perceive and employ water's destructive potential:[21]

> I observe that water can be used to encroach and inundate, can be used to float and flow, can be used to sink and drown, can be used to encircle and besiege, and can be used to quench thirst. Thus those in antiquity who excelled in employing the army frequently relied upon the power of water to establish unorthodox achievements. The stupid must employ boats and vessels before they term it aquatic warfare, not knowing that if they fathomed its real meaning, prepared their implements, and took advantage of opportunities, aggressive warfare and unorthodox plans would all come out from it. What reliance must there be upon boats and vessels?

In the subsection entitled "Occupying Heights and Releasing Water" Yeh accordingly expanded the practice beyond simple inundation:[22]

> The ancients spoke about the Fen River being able to inundate An-yi, the Chiang River being able to inundate P'ingyang, and West Lake being able to flood Hang-chou. Those who excelled in attacking cities thus frequently relied upon the power of water.
>
> But when two armies assume fortified positions across from each other, if we are higher and they are lower, we can similarly employ aquatic attacks to achieve our objective. Furthermore, we need not just attack cities. Kuan Yü, Yang Hsing-mi, and Huan Tsung-tsu all provide examples of employing such attacks and accruing the benefits. Future commanders who wish to ensure the security of their encampments and strongholds can take them as a mirror.

Finally, a half century later, the *Wu-pei Chih* succinctly concluded strategic aquatic thought with the comment that "breaking open river embankments to flood cities and blocking the current's flow in order to soak fortifications are water's great employment."[23]

## SUCCESSFUL PRACTICE

Even though primarily undertaken around the major river systems, the results of flooding varied from rare, quick victories to interminable stalemates and even unexpected reversals when the aggressors became entangled and lax. Moreover, throughout the long tradition of aquatic attacks there was always a sense that they were a method of last resort, too time consuming and cumbersome to be employed early on.[24] Against this, as the practice proliferated from the Three Kingdoms onward with more frequent combat south of the Yellow River, the theoreticians emphasized their potential power and great utility, even actual ease in some circumstances. Although numerous examples might be cited, the following are particularly representative of the decision making process, flooding's role in the overall assault tactics, and the difficulties encountered.[25]

During Liu Pang's long ascension to power, he returned to Fei-chou where Chang Han had ensconced himself behind high walls and reduced the city by digging canals to inundate it. Forced to surrender (in part because he lacked support among the defenders because his previous submission to Hsiang Yü, for which he had been made one of the kings of the ancient Ch'in area, had resulted in 200,000 troops being massacred), he committed suicide.[26] Moreover, in the final stage of suppressing a rebellion mounted by several Western Han feudal kings in 154 B.C., Han-tan (which was still serving as Chao's capital) was indeed flooded by destroying the river's embankments. The ensuing flood waters caused the walls to collapse and the king, faced with inevitable defeat and trial for rebellion, to commit suicide.[27]

Although the idea of exploiting the rivers and lakes for irrigation and transportation was antique, it was more easily practiced in the south where significant bodies of water lay in close proximity. Furthermore, because Ts'ao Ts'ao clearly understood the logistical advantages of water transport, he had canals dug on at least two occasions to expedite the flow of provisions prior to initiating major campaigns.[28] In addition, in 208 he had an artificial lake constructed to facilitate training his soldiers in the fundamentals of riverine warfare before mounting the ill-fated southern invasion that ended in the fiery debacle at Ch'ih Pi. Since he also resorted to aquatic assaults, he clearly felt confident that the terrain could be manipulated to exploit water's latent powers and thereby achieve military objectives.

Among Ts'ao Ts'ao's early opponents was Lü Pu with whom he once became entangled in a 100-day standoff that ended only because both sides lacked supplies. In A.D. 195 he ambushed Lü but failed to kill him, allowing his resurgence. Situated on his eastern flank, Lü represented a significant threat, particularly if he continued to gain adherents and could ally himself with Yüan Shu. Despite the risk of leaving his base relatively exposed, in the tenth month of 198 Ts'ao Ts'ao therefore moved to extinguish him. Suffering repeated open field defeats, Lü was compelled to ensconce himself in Hsia-p'i where a vice-like siege was quickly applied. However, neither his battlefield reversals nor his inability to persuade Yüan Shu or the other powers to dispatch a rescue force inclined him to submit. Meanwhile, Ts'ao Ts'ao's own army, long exposed to the elements and the intensifying cold, increasingly succumbed to illness and deprivation as the weeks passed.

Just when he was about to abandon the siege and return to Hsü-ch'ang, Ts'ao was persuaded to exploit Lü's disadvantageous position and army's dispirit rather than allow him to escape yet again. He therefore ordered his troops to divert two small rivers, the Ssu and the Yi, which flowed southward just to the west before joining further downstream, onto the city.[29] Although badly inundated, Lü managed to resolutely endure another month of misery before the situation's hopelessness coupled with the defection of several subcommanders who opened the gates compelled him to surrender.

Ts'ao Ts'ao utilized an aquatic attack on another occasion as well, though to isolate rather than directly strike. In A.D.

204, after his armies failed to take the city of Yeh where a major contingent of troops from Yüan Shang's army under Shen P'ei and Su Yu were ensconced after two months of effort, Ts'ao Ts'ao destroyed his earthen overlook mounds and tunnels in order to encircle the city with a moat which, being some forty *li* in circumference, must have been excavated some distance from the city.[30] When first excavating it, they made the ditch so shallow that Shen P'ei didn't feel threatened and therefore made no attempt to interrupt their work with assault parties. (Shen P'ei had assumed sole command after thwarting Su Yu's attempted betrayal, the first of two different subversive attempts that had to be quashed, proof that Mo-tzu's obsession with betrayal was well founded.)

However, Ts'ao Ts'ao's visibly laughable efforts were actually part of a well-conceived deceit, for the troops clandestinely deepened and widened the moat at night to roughly fifteen feet, completely cutting the city off from provisions and external aid. Within three months half their force had starved to death and the remainder were badly weakened. One night, shortly after a rescue force under Yüan Shang's personal command had been decisively repelled, dissidents within the city opened the gates, allowing enemy raiders to enter and vanquish the last defenders in fierce hand to hand combat among the lanes and alleys.

During the widely ranging clashes between Northern Wei and Southern Liang which unfolded along the Huai River, a Southern Liang force under Wei Jui attacked Ho-fei in Anhui at the beginning of the sixth century.[31] Although not physically strong, Wei Jui was courageous, decisive, daring, resolute, and inventive, well capable of overcoming adverse odds with unorthodox tactics. After analyzing the terrain, he decided that by damming and backing the Fei River, Ho-fei would not only be inundated, but the water level would also be raised sufficiently to allow naval vessels to come down and mount an amphibious assault on the walls themselves.

In response, Ho-fei threw up two external citadels that were quickly vanquished. However, Northern Wei dispatched a 50,000-man rescue force which greatly outnumbered the attackers and threatened Southern Liang's forces with a vice-like attack. Nevertheless, instead of shrinking back, the unperturbed Jui attacked and gained a dramatic victory. He then had a citadel built on the dam to protect it from Northern Wei's armies but the latter overcame it with a major force, killing the 1,000 stalwart defenders before exploiting their victory to attack the dam en masse with digging tools. Jui's frightened generals clamored for him to retreat, but he instead led an attack that summarily defeated the aggressors.

Southern Liang then built their own fortifications on the dam and along the embankment before constructing high-walled ships that matched the city walls. Ho-fei's defenders became despondent, their commander was slain, and the city quickly succumbed. More than 10,000 were killed or wounded and tens of thousands of cattle and sheep were captured, ending a siege in which aquatic measures were employed for the uncommon purpose of raising the water level to enable amphibious attacks.

Following the siege of Yü-pi previously discussed, the war between Eastern and Western Wei saw another extended clash unfold at Ying-ch'uan from the fourth month of 548 into the fifth month of 549.[32] Once again a well-commanded, stalwart force heroically repulsed the virtually continuous onslaughts of vastly superior numbers before finally succumbing to the flood waters which, though anticipated and long resisted, could no longer be deflected. Because the deciding factor proved to be this lengthy aquatic attack when other measures failed, Ying-ch'uan's subjugation is among the illustrations found in the subsection on aquatic attacks contained in the *T'ung Tien* and then the *T'ai-p'ing Yü-lan* compiled at the beginning of the Sung dynasty for the emperor's personal knowledge.

Ying-ch'uan was first occupied by Western Wei forces when Hou Ching, the powerful Eastern Wei commander who controlled thirteen provinces south of the Yellow River, rebelled following Kao Huan's death in 547 and nominally allied himself with Western Wei before eventually shifting to the southern state of Liang and then again reasserting his independence. Although he lacked imperial authority, the highly capable Wang Ssu-cheng exploited the momentary instability to move his army into the western part of Hou's territory, occupying Hsiang-ch'eng and then the forward, though isolated, position of Ying-ch'uan with 8,000 men, the bulk of his 10,000 troops. Even though this bold move immensely benefited Western Wei, it was condemned because the fortified town of Ying-ch'uan lay south of the Yellow River and north of the Huai in an area difficult to support and provision. Wang managed to avoid being compelled to withdraw only by promising not to request reinforcements should they come under attack for at least a year if flooding was employed, or three years in the event of a normal siege.

To prevent being flanked on the south, Eastern Wei responded by dispatching a massive 100,000-man combined infantry and cavalry force under Kao Yüeh, Mu-jung Shao-tsung, and Liu Feng-sheng. Outnumbered more than ten to one, Wang manifested the appearance of an unprepared city by keeping his drums silent, walls deserted, and unit and command flags furled. Although an antique ploy, it still induced laxity in Wei's troops, which were moving against all four walls in anticipation of an easy, decisive engagement. Their overconfidence and inattention allowed a small but elite force to suddenly sally forth, penetrate their ranks, and throw them into confusion. Wang then personally led a mixed contingent of 3,000 infantry and cavalry into the fray, inflicting heavy casualties on Kao Yüeh's forces before returning to the sanctuary of Ying-ch'uan's fortifications.

Eastern Wei's armies then resorted to mass assaults employing mobile ladders and incendiary wagons and, just as at Yü-pi two years earlier, erecting two earthen overlook mounds. However, the defenders adroitly employed incendiary measures in defense, burning the assault equipment with arrows and bundles of blazing reeds hurled onto the protective wooden structures atop the earthen mounds, setting them afire. Just as advised by the *Art of War*, troops then sallied forth, seized the mounds, and immediately erected parapets, giving them an archery vantage point.

Frustrated, the aggressors lost much of their fighting spirit, but the siege continued in desultory fashion for a year during which the aggressor's forces were constantly augmented and an aquatic attack, the last resort in the face of tactical failure, was undertaken. The Wei River, which flowed to the citadel's north, was dammed and levees built to constrain the water so that it would back up against the city. (The exact location of the dam is unknown and therefore also whether the water just exerted static pressure or the effect was bolstered by the scouring action of a flowing river.) Despite the Wei being an indirect tributary of the Huai, difficulties were encountered in constructing and maintaining the dam and levees, reportedly due to collisions from "fierce water creatures" trying to escape the containment. (Mythology aside, these gaps are best explained as sections suddenly collapsing because the underlying sandy soil was unstable, as was the case with much of the Huai.)

Nevertheless, the unremitting pressure caused extensive damage to the walls and the city was inundated, compelling the populace to dwell in the upper floors and hang their stoves up to cook. In the face of constant attacks by rotating strike forces, Wang personally led his troops in repairing breaches in the walls. A sudden turn of bad weather, including three feet of snow and freezing cold, coupled with their inability to penetrate the defenses, soon thwarted the attackers, resulting in heavy casualties and complete dispirit.

Perhaps because a year had passed, Western Wei's ruler finally dispatched a 100,000-man rescue force, but they were stymied by the vast lake which now extended northward and no doubt surrounded the city. (Their failure to advance by alternate routes to the south or use extemporaneous methods such as building boats and rafts in order to strike Eastern Wei's badly entangled forces remains puzzling.) Eastern Wei also astutely sought to exploit the water's considerable depth with warships manned by expert archers that could advance close upon the walls where their effectiveness might be enhanced.

However, when a strong northeast wind unexpectedly arose, the two commanders standing on the levee sought refuge within one of their warships. Somewhat surprisingly, the tempest broke the restraining lines and the ship was quickly pushed across the gap against the wall where the defenders immobilized it using grappling hooks while archers atop the fortifications decimated the occupants. Mu-jung Shao-tsung jumped into the water and drowned while Liu Feng-sheng swam to an earthen mound where he was cut down by arrows.

Having lost his associates, Kao Yüeh lacked resolution. However, in the fifth month, Kao Ch'eng, ruler of Eastern Wei, having been persuaded that the city was about to fall, personally led another 100,000-man contingent to the site. Enraged by discovering that the levees were breached in three places, he had the laborers together with their baskets of earth thrown into the gaps. By this time a lack of salt and the rigors of combat had inflicted heavy losses on the defenders, some 80 to 90 percent having perished while the remainder suffered from sickness, wounds, and swelling. When a strong western wind suddenly commenced blowing, water cascaded over the fortifications and the long battered walls were badly damaged.

Realizing they were doomed, Wang thought to commit suicide out on the earthen mound but was dissuaded because the city had been threatened with slaughter if he were not captured unharmed. Only 3,000 of the initial contingent survived to surrender, yet they had remained loyal throughout the conflict, attesting to Wang's leadership. Moreover, unlike many sieges in which aquatic attacks were employed, flooding proved the decisive factor where other measures failed, though sustained effort was required and a lengthy period of inundation necessary.

Long thereafter, in A.D. 1081 the Sung undertook a massive steppe campaign with some 300,000 men divided among five operational armies designed to exploit the violent dissension then plaguing their nemesis, the Hsi Hsia. However, typical of Sung campaigns marked by fragmented authority, despite dramatic early success the commanders not only lacked unified plans but even refused to cooperate with each other. From the seventh month onward the Hsi Hsia adopted the classic policy of deliberately yielding to draw the invaders forward, thereby stretching out their supply lines and exhausting their troops before finally pouncing.[33] (Although consciously chosen, the ensuing defeats no doubt exceeded their expectations and the unintended loss of vital supplies also negated the effectiveness of their painful efforts.) However, guerrilla strikes reduced the Sung's provisions so that by the eleventh month, when the Hsi Hsia shifted to the offensive, many Sung troops had already perished. (For example, Wang Chung-cheng's army, which set out with 60,000 soldiers and an equal number of coopted support personnel, saw their numbers reduced by 20,000 fighters or a third of their original strength.)

The turning point came in the eleventh month when Hsi Hsia troops broke open the Yellow River embankments to flood the two Sung armies encamped nearby. Between the overflowing waters and accompanying cold that caused thousands to freeze to death, extremely heavy casualties were incurred, compelling the Sung forces to withdraw. Thus despite their large numbers and initial victories, the campaign proved an expensive failure just when every available resource was needed to withstand ongoing threats from the north.

In one of the three campaigns that arose in succession during the chaotic reign of the Wan-li emperor (the others being in the southwest and a lengthy, if somewhat inconclusive effort against the Japanese who had invaded Korea), a Ming commander finally utilized flooding after being unable to penetrate the fortifications at the rebel stronghold of Ning-hsia for several months.[34] (Ning-hsia was a major city in the vital northwest border area with a reported population of 300,000 plus rebel forces of perhaps 20,000 to 30,000 and additional camp followers.) The conflict began in the second month of 1592 when the local military commander, Li Tung-yang, and his contingent of troops, dissatisfied with their lack of payment and the conditions on the border revolted. However, rather than proceeding alone, he managed to inveigle a local, though now retired, Mongolian who had held high military command responsibilities on the border and still retained personal clan forces of perhaps 1,000 known as Pübei into participating.[35]

Taking advantage of their surprising success, the rebels quickly attracted local Ordos support and segmented into three prongs, rapidly seizing some forty-seven local outposts before fording the upward bend of the Yellow River to move toward Ling-chou. However, government troops managed to blunt their burgeoning movement, retake the forty-seven outposts, and eventually compress the rebels into the city of Ning-hsia, all within a month. Thereafter, despite aggressive strikes by both sides, the situation devolved into a stalemate.

Early on the defenders employed the unusual method of deploying fire carts as an external palisade, but these were overwhelmed and more than 100 seized, suggesting the huge military resources to be found in the border area. Government attacks over the next few weeks, including a nighttime incendiary attack that incurred heavy losses, were invariably repulsed. However, the rebels successfully seized a government supply train, thereby acquiring some 200 wagons of food and temporarily exacerbating the government's already growing shortage. Nevertheless, the Ming soon poured additional troops into the area along with supplies and substantial incendiary equipment.

When attempts at subversion proved unsuccessful, Yeh Meng-hsiung (author of the *Yün-ch'ou Kang-mu*), already serving in the field, was named commander in the seventh month. No immediate resolution being in sight, Yeh opted for the ancient method of flooding since the Yellow River was ready to hand.[36] Though some accounts indicate a countervailing wall was erected around the city to ensure adequate pressure against the walls which, when completed, totaled some 1,700 *chang* (or about 13,600 feet) in circumference, Yeh's own biography states the Ming joint command had the main Yellow River dikes broken open, flooding the area around the city.

At this juncture a two-pronged Mongolian relief force of perhaps 30,000 men mounted two waves of attacks, but they were all successfully blunted and the armies vanquished, ending rebel hopes for extrication and resurgence. Wei Hsüeh-hui destroyed additional sections of the dikes, raising the water level about the city to some eight to nine feet and apparently turning the interior into a giant fish pond.[37] Major sections of the walls began to crumble under the sustained pressure and on the eighth day of the ninth month the Ming finally launched a broad amphibious assault against the city using recently constructed boats and rafts that targeted the ruined parts of the fortifications, reportedly some 100 *chang* overall, but also employed feints to manipulate the defenders to their tactical advantage. Internal dissension in the face of inevitable defeat ended the rebel efforts and Ning-hsia was recaptured.

The chaos which pervaded China in the last days of the Ming also witnessed China's most catastrophic aquatic attack when the powerful rebel Li Tzu-ch'eng flooded K'ai-feng, then known as Pien-ching, in 1642. This possibility had already been raised in Chih Po's prophetic speech at the siege of Chin-yang and following a major shift in its course during the Sung, the Yellow River now flowed less than ten miles to the north with nothing but alluvial plains intervening. Three sieges were actually undertaken, the final one not only inflicting horrendous casualties through flooding, but also such pervasive deprivation and starvation that the populace extensively resorted to murder and cannibalism. Throughout them all the imperial court remained enmired in dissension and entangled by the Manchu threat and several potent rescue armies simply collapsed without fighting, their troops often surrendering en masse to the enemy.

According to an eyewitness chronicle penned by Li Kuang-tien who apparently exercised a command role, in the second month of 1641 Li's resurgent forces besieged this important provincial capital for the first time with 3,000 elite warriors and some 30,000 troops overall.[38] However, he found it so tenaciously defended that he abandoned the effort within a week because a small rescue contingent had broken through to the city and he had suffered an arrow wound to his left eye.[39]

Nevertheless, at the end of the year he undertook another, more serious effort in bitterly cold, snowy weather that saw intense fighting along the walls, several tunneling efforts blocked with the usual incendiary techniques, and exchanges of heavy cannon fire. It too was quickly abandoned after just eighteen days, prompted in part by heavy cavalry losses sustained when a blast from explosives they had futilely embedded in the surprisingly solid outer wall not only failed to destroy it, but exploded outward.

After acquiring vital supplies and subjugating numerous towns in the surrounding area, Li Tzu-ch'eng returned with a massive force at the beginning of the fifth month. Having failed to penetrate the exterior fortifications despite fervent efforts, he initiated an aquatic attack in the middle of the sixth month designed to inundate the city. More than 1,000 men were deputed to excavate a ditch to channel water back up to K'ai-feng, but being slow and only five inches deep, the water lacked the force necessary to impact the walls. Nevertheless, it gradually filled the defensive ditch surrounding the city to a depth of more than three *chang* (twenty-five feet), converting it into an impassable lake four to five *chang* across, said to be worth 100,000 armored soldiers.

Frustrated, Li was compelled to allot some 10,000 soldiers to filling in an access route and by the nineteenth of the eighth month, committed another workforce to destroying the embankment on the Yellow River, though reluctantly as he feared destroying the city's valuables and losing their most attractive prisoners, the children. Although unstated in the chronicle, the Ming biographies indicate this was in response to learning that the defenders were attempting to flood the rebels by breaking the embankment at Chu-chia-sai-k'ou on the assumption that their own reinforced walls would be able to withstand a moderate amount of water.[40]

Even before this an effort to reprovision the city via a protected water route down from the Yellow River, exploiting the flooded countryside since the departure point at Chu-chia-sai-k'ou was said to be less than eight *li* away, had been thwarted by Li's forces. However, a Ming contingent apparently succeeded in causing at least a partial breach and in response, after shifting his forces to higher ground, Li deputed some 40,000 to sunder the embankment at nearby Ma-chia-k'ou.

Although some of the soldiers and impressed laborers may have been engaged in building embankments to appropriately constrain the water's flow, Li's huge numbers no doubt quickly created a vast gap. Meanwhile, according to the chronicle, it was feared that the seasonal water surge experienced on the river god's birthday, the seventeenth of the ninth month, would prove disastrous if it were vigorous, prompting the defensive commander to have a few boats built. The anticipated turbulence actually started on the fourteenth after several days of torrential rains, slightly earlier than prophesied, and the "roaring" waters reached the city walls on the morning of the fifteenth. Quickly smashing through the gates despite fervent efforts to block them up with earth, they so completely swirled through the city that just a few rooftops and high towers remained above water by the morning of the eighteenth.

Only some 20,000 among the remnant populace of several hundred thousand survived, their deaths being added to the myriads which had already perished from starvation, disease, and combat. Even some 10,000 rebel troops encamped to the northeast of the city drowned, though their other positions were spared. Moreover, the city was so completely devastated that it retained no value, compelling Li Tzu-ch'eng to move onward in his quest to overthrow the dynasty, an objective successfully achieved but only briefly enjoyed when he captured the capital of Peking in the fourth month of 1644.

## STALEMATES AND FAILURE

Despite well-conceived plans and unremitting military pressure, resilient cities frequently refused to succumb to inundation. The siege attempts therefore entered the historical records as examples of frustrated and wasted efforts, serving as deterrents to later commanders confronting similar situations. As early as the crucial year of A.D. 32, in which Liu Hsiu suddenly moved toward restoring the Han, commanders on either side in the ongoing conflict with Wei Ao mounted aquatic assaults only to see them both prove indecisive.[41] In the first case, in the spring a coalition force said to exceed 100,000 loyal to Wei Ao besieged an extremely small Han contingent in the city of Lüeh-yang, eventually constructing dikes and diverting a mountain stream to flood the city. However, the defenders continued to mount a stalwart defense, even tearing apart buildings and utilizing equipment as weapons. After a couple of months the siege was finally relieved when Liu Hsiu, who was moving westward, managed to persuade key generals and regional peoples said to have exceeded 100,000 to desert Wei Ao, leaving him with few forces and little alternative to abandoning the siege for the security of Hsi-ch'eng.

Despite Liu's concern that his armies were already exhausted and supplies so problematic that desertions were likely to occur at a high rate, Ts'en P'eng not only rejected Liu's orders to stand down, but flooded Hsi-ch'eng by blocking the Ku River downstream, backing it up against the city walls. Although the waters rose to within ten feet of the top, Wei Ao held out until a small rescue force appeared from over the mountains. Being unexpected and magnified by rumor as again amounting to 100,000, its appearance panicked the Han besiegers who quickly collapsed, allowing the paltry 5,000-man rescue force to battle their way into the city and then successfully fight their way back out, taking Wei Ao and his remnant forces with them. Thus well-mounted flooding efforts, despite being technically successful, not only failed to wrest victory, but in fact saw the besieged emerge substantially unscathed both times.

In the wake of Fu Chien's astounding defeat at Fei River, Mu-jung Ch'ui, commander in chief in Former Ch'in, seized the opportunity to revolt.[42] His major thrust consisted of a focused attack undertaken with some 200,000 troops against the city of Yeh located near the Chang River in the first month of A.D. 384. The initial assault successfully broke through the outer fortifications, forcing the defenders to take refuge in the inner citadel. However, when further attempts over the next three months employing the usual array of siege engines and tunneling proved incapable of overcoming the defenders, Ch'ui decided to divert the Chang River to flood the city, a fate Yeh would repeatedly suffer over the centuries.

Even as the city remained unbowed in the seventh month, one of Ch'ui's dissatisfied subcommanders attempted to link up with the hard-pressed defenders. As part of his betrayal, he dispatched troops to sunder the dikes constraining the waters onto Yeh, but the plot was discovered and thwarted. Amidst various collateral actions the siege therefore continued and in the absence of outside support the defenders soon found themselves desperately short of food. In accord with Sun-tzu's idea of always providing an opening, Mu-jung Ch'ui futilely tried to entice them into abandoning the city. However, following the temporary dispatch of forces in the fourth month of 385 to secure supplies, after having endured some twenty months without resources, Fu P'i finally abandoned Yeh. Mu-jung Ch'ui thus emerged victorious and went on to found the state of Later Yen, though sustained flooding had failed to achieve a dramatic breakthrough and the deep waters had rendered assaults impossible except by boat.

The ongoing conflict between Northern Wei and Liang that included the clash at Chung-li previously discussed also witnessed the most ambitious aquatic attack in Chinese history.[43] By the end of the sixth century China already had a long history of banking and diking troublesome rivers requiring incalculable effort. However, though often difficult, constraining major rivers and even exploiting their flow to constitute a relentless weapon remained conceivable. But damming the powerful Huai that irregularly served over the centuries as the last obstacle between the northern and southern kingdoms borders on the unimaginable, even with contemporary earthmoving equipment and hydraulic skills.

However, late in A.D. 514, Wang Tsu, an important Northern Wei general who had recently defected, persuaded the emperor of Liang that the Huai River should be blocked slightly below Chung-li (where they controlled both banks) so as to inundate Shou-yang, still resolutely held by Northern Wei despite lying just south of the Huai roughly 100 miles upstream. As might be expected for riverside cities located in contentious areas, Shou-yang frequently suffered the misfortune of aquatic attack. It was, however, a strong point which could control access both up and down river and therefore important to ensuring the security and realizing the expansionist intent of the respective contiguous powers.

Shou-yang's vulnerability had been vividly revealed the previous year when heavy rains in the fifth month caused especially high water levels.[44] The city was so completely flooded that only the top few feet of the city wall's crenellations remained above water, forcing the populace to flee by boat for a nearby mountain. After Wang suggested the project, a vast labor force was mobilized for the effort, one male in every fourth household from the immediate area being impressed and many troops diverted from other tasks for a reported total of 200,000 men.

Although hydraulic specialists from Liang advised that the riverbed was too sandy and unstable to support the proposed project, they were overruled. The first attempt was undertaken with dirt alone, two finger-like embankments being constructed from the northern and southern banks being designed to meet in midstream. As predicted, the southern projection near Mount Fou collapsed just after being completed in the fourth month, again supposedly because it had been attacked by local river creatures of mythical proportions. Since popular belief held that these water demons could be restrained with iron, thousands of pounds of iron forged into unspecified shapes were embedded. However, when they also failed the builders turned to employing close-packed dry piers to circumvent the problem of an unsecured foundation. Empty wooden wells were constructed in place and then filled with rocks to hold them, after which earth was piled on top until the desired dimensions were achieved. Reportedly all the trees for 100 *li* inland were consumed in framing these cofferdams.[45]

A full year later Liang eventually succeeded in damming the river through this new method, creating a barrier totaling nine *li* in length, including major land portions extending to the base of the two mountains (Ch'an-shih-shan and Fou-shan) slightly north and south of the river itself. The dam averaged an astonishing width of 140 *chang* at the base, tapered to 45 *chang* at the top, and achieved a maximum height of 20 *chang* (160 Western feet), explaining the need to bridge the gap between it and the nearby mountains. Troops were deployed along the entire length and willow trees planted on the top surface.

The now blocked waters soon began to accumulate, forming a lake that not only backed up but also flooded several hundred square *li* of the adjoining countryside. Although collateral actions were fought over nearby targets as well as to seize and destroy the dam, none ever affected the barrier itself. However, deeming some pressure relief to be necessary, Liang eventually cut a channel to the east and dispatched a double agent to Wei who suggested that Liang was worried Wei might dig a channel to drain the water off. Finding his statements credible, Wei immediately undertook a major canal some five *chang* deep that similarly drained water away to the north, dispersing it further inland.

Despite these diversions, the overall level continued to rise until it completely inundated Shou-yang, though the city remained visible under the water because of its clarity. Northern Wei's ruler was about to dispatch a 100,000-man assault force but was dissuaded by advisors who believed that the river could not be permanently contained and the dam would succumb by itself. Coincidentally, after a Liang command rotation the dam's maintenance began to be neglected and when the river's volume suddenly surged in the ninth month, it collapsed with a thunderclap-like sound reportedly heard for 300 *li*.

The sudden flood surge washed away numerous small downstream communities, drowning some 100,000 people, many of whom were swept into the distant sea. In addition, more than three fourths of the soldiers and laborers assigned to the project died over the nearly two years of construction from illness, unexpectedly severe cold, and other miseries, dramatically increasing the horrendous toll from this remarkable but inherently flawed military engineering project.

In 525 Shou-yang, having been annexed by Wei, was again the victim of deliberate aquatic attack, making it almost inconceivable anyone would want to live there! Southern Liang started building embankments to divert flood water onto it early in the sixth month.[46] Upon their completion slightly over a year later the water attained the usual few boards just below the top of the fortifications and the city was about to collapse. Continuing their attempt to regain territory lost to Northern Wei, Liang then mounted widespread attacks, including at Shou-yang, and in the eleventh month their field forces won a major victory, temporarily ending the conflict. In all, they reacquired fifty-two towns and 75,000 people, but it was the land campaign rather than flooding and conquering Shou-yang that produced this result. Moreover, Shou-yang was so badly devastated that a major effort was required to rebuild it, attract the widely dispersed populace, and reestablish the economy.

Two years later Southern Liang mounted an aquatic attack against the pivotal Northern Wei city of Ching-chou in Honan by blocking the river, causing the water to rise nearly to the top of the city wall in the fifth month.[47] Since the city had been under siege for more than two years, flooding obviously constituted a measure of last resort. Internal strife prevented Northern Wei from dispatching a rescue force until the eleventh month, but when it finally appeared, it defeated the aggressors from Liang and thus ended the stalemate. Although isolated and unsupported, the city had endured through the efforts of a heroic commander who cast aside his armor and deliberately exposed himself to danger on a daily basis, fighting in the forefront, to stimulate their courage and resolve.

After Hou Ching finally defected to Liang, at his suggestion the latter's emperor ordered an invasion into Eastern Wei to seize contiguous territory that had formerly been under Hou's control. In one of their initial actions they flooded

P'eng-ch'eng with the Ssu River by damming and diverting it at Han-shan (Cold Mountain) some eighteen *li* away.[48] Their massive forces constructed the embankments necessary to channel the water all this distance in the brief space of a double (ten-day) week, after which Yang K'an, who would become famous at the siege of Ying-ch'uan, undertook their defense. Yang, moreover, wanted to exploit the higher water level to mount an amphibious attack but the commander in chief refused, and in fact declined to undertake any other action throughout their deployment in Wei.

Two months later, in the eleventh month, an Eastern Wei rescue force came forth, but the Liang commander similarly refused to authorize any aggressive actions despite the pronounced opportunities. Moreover, he subsequently became too drunk to release the troops needed to extricate one of their own detached forces that had come under attack. Most of his generals concluded the situation was hopeless and therefore returned to Liang, others followed a false retreat and were badly decimated. Yang K'an was also compelled to abandon the embankments and finally retreat. Over some two months the flooding thus accomplished nothing beyond raising the level of misery for the defenders securely locked within their citadel.

In A.D. 580, forces from Northern Chou attacked a rebel faction blocking their advance into the Szechuan area, some 100,000 troops eventually besieging the small fortified town of Li-chou and its paltry but stalwart 2,000 men.[49] The aggressors not only built earthen overlook mounds and flooded the city with the Chia-ling River but also actively excavated some seventy holes in the wall to ensure the city would be inundated. However, after they failed to subdue it despite forty days of intense conflict which saw the defenders repeatedly burst forth to inflict heavy casualties, under pressure from an approaching relief force Northern Chou finally abandoned the siege and moved off.

Immediately after An Lu-shan's son, An Ch'ing-hsü, became self-proclaimed emperor, he was besieged by T'ang forces in Yeh-ch'eng beginning in the tenth month of 758.[50]

By the second month of 759, imperial forces had flooded the surrounding area so deeply that water even poured out of the wells inside the city and people were forced to live in trees and on rooftops. (Ironically, the floodwaters were so deep and extensive that none of the officers and men who thought of defecting could even attempt it.) By the time of the decisive external clash in the third month, the populace had been reduced to eating rats, each one fetching an astronomical price, and feeding their surviving horses, which remarkably had not yet been eaten, with a combination of old grain husks scraped out of the walls and recycled manure. However, the city was spared when Shih Ssu-ming's badly outnumbered relief force of 50,000 cavalry fervently engaged the 600,000 T'ang infantry and cavalry besieging the city in a savage battle that was dramatically interrupted by a violent maelstrom which temporarily drove both forces off.

When the Mongols, who also adopted the technique of aquatic assaults, attacked the Jurchen at Nan-ching in A.D. 1232, the outnumbered Jurchen released the Yellow River and flooded the area around the city.[51] However, the Mongols used prisoners, women, and children to build paths to the walls with dirt and firewood and then fervently pressed the attack day and night for sixteen days. Frustrated at being unable to overcome them and hampered by the water, they temporarily withdrew.

After commencing in 1351, Chang Shih-ch'eng's rebellion rampaged through the Huai River Valley before suffering setbacks and then resurging to dominate the six southeastern prefectures from Su-chou. Although Chu Yüan-chang made Ch'en Yu-liang his primary focus, campaigns were intermittently conducted against Chang as resources might allow. However, after vanquishing the former in the epochal battle of P'o-yang in 1363 already discussed, Chu was free to redirect his resources to subjugating Chang's outlying prefectures and finally conquered him in a technically complex siege at Su-chou in 1367.

The siege of Shao-hsing unfolded during one of the Ming's earlier eastern thrusts under Wu Kuo-kung in 1358 which eventually saw Hu Ta-hai advance by three routes against remnant armies now ensconced in Shao-hsing. Although the battle is little recorded apart from a succinct chronicle by Hsü Mien-chih, Lü Chen (who was among those suffering defeats in earlier Chiangsu battles) mounted an astute defense distinguished by his tactical leadership and valiant command of field forces which repeatedly sallied forth to engage the Ming armies arrayed outside their citadel.[52] The actual conflict lasted from the second through the fifth months of 1359, well into the spring rains and accompanying muddiness.

This siege has been considered historically important insofar as it confirms that metal "tubed" gunpowder weapons were being effectively utilized, but water issues equally played an important role. At the end of the Spring and Autumn period Shao-hsing, then known as K'uai-chi, was Kou-chien's last refuge and the core of the ancient state of Yüeh, explaining the chronicle's title, *Chronicle of the Preservation of Yüeh*. Situated about thirty-five miles southeast and somewhat inland from Hang-chou in Chechiang, Shao-hsing was located in an area which had once been a tidal flood plain and two significant rivers still flowed around to the sea to the east and west, albeit at some distance. However, over the centuries the land had been reclaimed by an extensive system of levees and locks, creating an extensive lake running east to west behind the city for many miles that provided water to irrigate the fields.

The numerous smaller rivers and streams connecting the bay to the lake were all banked and controlled but under tremendous pressure from the area's well-known tidal surge and the lake which was several meters higher than the surrounding land. (The chronicle even notes that it was easy to destroy these levees but difficult to repair them because of the tide's "fierce teeth.") Even where drained the water level was high, numerous streams and rivulets remained, and the marshy ground was generally unsuitable for heavy siege machines. The numerous waterways and moats around the city provided a vast transportation system, but also allowed amphibious attacks and in one incident Ming soldiers even hid underneath the vegetation floating on the water.

Observing that the terrain's wetness would hinder enemy maneuver but that they lacked exploitable hills and ravines, Lü Chen embarked on a policy of enlarging the moats, widening them by fifty feet and deepening them by two. Although intended primarily for defensive purposes and therefore coupled with exterior palisades, this augmentation facilitated the passage of boats. He also added external walls, erected towers and protective shelters atop the main walls, constructed drawbridges to effect quick sallies, and adopted the usual pre-siege measures of preparing the necessary materials and denying sustenance to the enemy. Although they were outnumbered and he claimed they would adhere to an attritional policy, Shao-hsing's forces actually went forth time after time, attacking the newly arrived enemy with considerable success.

Within this context there were collateral battles over the levees, Ming forces breaking them and Shao-hsing's defenders restoring them. The actual intent is somewhat problematic because generalized flooding would only compound their own operational difficulties and inundating the farmland to the north was pointless because the farmers had abandoned their fields. However, both sides found it important to struggle for their respective objectives, and early on Ming forces breached the Pao-ku dike some miles west of Shaohsing, creating an enormous gap some sixty *chang* (about 400 feet) long which might have been even more extensive if they had not been attacked.

Shortly thereafter they broke open two other dikes and subsequently smashed less important levees in twenty places. Weeks later a major effort was finally mounted to repair the main breach in the Pao-ku system, some 3,000 troops being dispatched to ensure they could withstand attacks while completing the work which required three full days. However, Ming forces opened another breach and smashed smaller dikes, but the Pao-yü embankment was again repaired and put under constant guard, ending that aspect of the overall struggle.

The *Pao Yüeh Lu* notes at least four instances of heavy rain hampering, even halting, Ming operations over the course of the siege. Moreover, as the weather turned hotter toward the end, the insufferable combination of wetness and heat spawned rampant illness among the Ming forces less accustomed to the lethal, semi-tropical climate of ancient Yüeh, increasing the pressure upon Hu Ta-hai to finally abandon the attack. Shortly after the city's release, in a subsequent action at the beginning of the sixth month Chang Shih-ch'eng reversed their roles by having Lü Chen besiege Chu-ch'uan-chou where an embankment was built to flood the city. However, Hu Ta-hai came up with reinforcements, seized the embankment, and redirected the water into Lü's camp, forcing him to request a truce and withdraw his troops.[53]

## REVERSALS AND COMPOUNDED DISASTER

During a rebellion mounted by local military forces against the Eastern Han in A.D. 165 that quickly attracted some 40,000 to 50,000 adherents, primarily disaffected barbarian peoples, the city of Hsia-p'i came under siege. Being situated on low, damp ground and protected only by wooden palisades rather than a reasonably impervious earthen wall, the city was easily flooded. However, the astute commander discovered that the terrain's configuration allowed them to direct the water out of the city back onto the besiegers. By breaking through the enemy's defensive embankments, they managed to inundate them as well, resulting in a lengthy standoff. When an imperial rescue force finally materialized, the soggy rebels were caught in a vice and a pincer attack from within and without quickly vanquished them.[54]

In A.D. 570 flooding not only failed to work but even resulted in the aggressor force being unexpectedly defeated. After failing to take the city of Chiang-ling by assault, an army from Ch'en broke open the dikes along the Lung River to flood it. The defenders immediately sallied forth, waged a decisive battle along the levees, and conquered Ch'en's superior forces.[55]

Late in A.D. 577 an aquatic attack designed to flood the Northern Chou defenders in Hsü-chou with water from the Ch'ing River entangled the attackers, giving the rescue forces an opportunity to dictate the battlefield and not only effect the city's extrication but also vanquish the besiegers.[56] The strength of Ch'en's commanding general Wu Ming-ch'e having proven too great for the local forces, they retreated and ensconced themselves in Hsü-chou. General Wu therefore had embankments built to divert water from the Ch'ing River to flood the area around the city and then deployed his boats at the walls to mount a sustained attack.

Even before he approached the beleaguered city, Wang Kuei, who had been ordered to undertake its rescue, constructed a massive barrier across the Ch'ing River just above its confluence with the Huai designed to prevent Ch'en's forces from escaping downriver. Large logs anchored with stones and boulders were erected in the river itself, and wagon wheels connected by an iron chain stretched across above the barrier.

Upon its completion Wang had intended to clandestinely break open the embankments sustaining the water level around Hsü-chou, thereby immobilizing Wu's fleet positioned close upon the walls and thus off river. When Wu's intelligence personnel somehow learned of his plan, Wu abandoned the assault, broke open the embankments, and rode the flow back into the Ch'ing River. However, the reservoir was quickly depleted and when they reached the barrier they were stymied by the wagon wheels, unable to pass. Wang then pressed an attack with unorthodox troops by both land and water, defeated the enemy, and captured Wu together with 30,000 troops and all their supplies, only the cavalry commander managing to escape with a few men.

Sometimes adroit commanders succeeded in reverting the waters upon their attackers, as at Chin-yang, at others things went awry and the besiegers found themselves badly inundated as well. One of the most famous examples arose in A.D. 1209 during one of the frequent conflicts between the Mongols and Hsi Hsia even though both came from the semi-arid steppe region. To negate threats to their rear while undertaking campaigns against the powerful Jurchen to the east, the Mongols mounted five, ultimately successful expeditions against the Hsi Hsia. The third, under Genghis Khan himself in 1209, scored a series of victories that carried them right to the Hsi Hsia capital city before their juggernaut was finally stopped by a stalwart defense. Temporarily stymied, Genghis Khan decided to exploit the sudden rise in the Yellow River caused by the heavy autumnal rains to inundate the city in the ninth month. However, despite inflicting great misery and causing numerous deaths, the populace remained defiant. Moreover, in the twelfth month when their dikes crumbled, the Mongols were also inundated, equalizing the misery and difficulties being experienced by both sides.[57] Floundering about and faced with significant, increasing casualties, Genghis Khan felt compelled to settle for a negotiated peace and withdraw.

## AQUATIC RAM

Much discussed but little practiced, the idea received its impetus from Han Hsin's defining application during the protracted struggle between Liu Pang, founder of the Han dynasty, and Hsiang Yü, who turned glory into defeat, achievement into extinction. Deputed to conquer Ch'i, Han Hsin was accompanied by a hastily assembled, motley force of just 30,000 men because Liu Pang had personally appropriated his veteran armies. Thus, he was forced to confront a massive 200,000-man, well-supported Ch'u army in the monumental conflict which followed. Personality conflicts and more than a little arrogance turned the clash into the highly dramatic episode preserved in the *Shih Chi* and retold in ever more melodramatic fashion thereafter.[58] As slightly recast in the *Hundred Unorthodox Strategies* for a martial audience, it furnished the historical illustration for the topic of "River Warfare":

> During the Han dynasty, the Han high official Li Sheng attempted to persuade the King of Ch'i to give his allegiance to the Han, but every day the king and Li Sheng debauched themselves with wine while the king neglected his defensive preparations. When K'uai T'ung advised Han Hsin of the sit-

uation, he forded the river with his army and then suddenly attacked and destroyed Ch'i's forces. Thinking that Li Sheng had sold him out, the king of Ch'i had Li boiled in oil before fleeing to Kao-mi and begging Ch'u to rescue him.

Ch'u dispatched Lung Chü to Ch'i in command of a rescue army. Someone said to him: "Since Han's troops are fighting far from their state, they are desperate invaders whose front cannot be withstood. In contrast, both Ch'i's and Ch'u's armies will be fighting in their homeland, so when they engage in battle our soldiers will easily be defeated and scatter. Accordingly, it would be best for us to both augment our fortified walls. If you have the king of Ch'i order his loyal subordinates to summon together all those from the ravished cities, they will certainly revolt against the Han upon hearing that their king has sought Ch'u's aid. When Han's forces, occupying cities in Ch'i and Ch'u some two thousand miles from their land, find everyone has turned against them and that even with their power they will be unable to obtain food, they will surrender without fighting."

Lung Chü said: "I have always felt Han Hsin to be inconsequential. He relied on a washerwoman for food, so he never made any plans to support himself. He was insulted by having to crawl between a man's legs, so he lacks the courage to confront people. He is not worth worrying about. Moreover, if Ch'i is rescued without any fighting, what will we achieve? But if we now engage them in combat and conquer them, we will gain half of Ch'i, so why should we desist?" He then proceeded to join battle with Han Hsin.

Both sides deployed along opposite banks of the Wei River. That night Han Hsin ordered a contingent of men to make more than ten thousand sacks and solidly stuff them with sand and stones in order to block the river's flow upstream. The next day he led half his troops across the river to strike Lung Chü. However, once they clashed, he feigned being unable to wrest victory, and instead turned his forces about and fled. Elated, Lung Chü exclaimed, "I knew Han Hsin was a coward!" He ordered his army to ford the river and pursue Han Hsin's forces.

Upstream, once Han Hsin had his men break the temporary sandbag dam, a torrent of water came down. More than half of Lung Chü's troops could not ford the river while Han Hsin attacked those who had, killing Lung himself. The remaining troops all scattered and fled. King Kuang of Ch'i also fled, so Han Hsin pursued him north to Ch'eng-yang and captured him. Ch'u's troops all surrendered, and Han Hsin eventually pacified Ch'i.

At the battle of Wei River, Han Hsin exploited Lung Chü's compulsion to seek a glorious, decisive battle rather than gradually enervate his enemies through an attritional standoff. Han concocted a tactical sequence that adroitly exploited the terrain and Lung's command flaws to manipulate and defeat Ch'u's superior forces. The water's onrush not only severed Ch'u's army (as Sun-tzu had advised), but no doubt also swept away any troops in the process of crossing. Thus, more than two millennia later Yeh Meng-hsiung would comment:[59]

I note that the world refers to Han Hsin's filling sacks with sand as an example of "using water to assist an attack being powerful." They don't know that he "displayed profits to entice them" and "created disorder and seized them."[60] Didn't Sun-tzu say that "If the guest is fording a river to advance, do not confront them in the water. When half their forces have crossed, it will be advantageous to strike them."[61] Han Hsin thus obstructed the flow upstream and then drew Chü's army into half crossing before he struck.

Hadn't Chü been unhappy that Han Hsin was contravening the proscriptions of military practice? How could he have known that Han created this gap in order to lure him forth? So when Han feigned defeat, he then forded the river himself in pursuit. How could he expect that the majority of the troops could not succeed in crossing?

On the whole Han's employment of military opportunities are all similar. This can be seen from his arraying his forces with their backs to the river at K'uai-kai. In later ages Chu-ko Liang and T'ang T'ai-tsung were enlightened by Han Hsin.

But one should change and transform in accord with the enemy in order to seize victory.

Because of Han Hsin's glorious achievement, the *Hu-ch'ien Ching* advised: "If your troops are about to ford a river that sometimes flows quite full and sometimes diminishes, do not cross because some sort of temporary sandbag dam has certainly been erected upstream as part of an unorthodox strategy."[62] Moreover, it suggested that to thwart such techniques, "nothing is better than gaining control of the river upstream!"

One of the three examples Yeh Meng-hsiung provided in his chapter "Occupying Heights and Releasing Water" required such extraordinary effort that it might well be questioned whether it merited the trouble:[63]

> The Later [Northern] Wei general Liu Ch'ang attacked [Nan Ch'i's] city of Shou-ch'un.[64] In response, General Huan Ch'ung-tsu constructed a dike on the Fei River to the city's northwest and erected a small city north of the embankment, assigning several thousand troops to defend it. He then advised his chief of staff Feng Yen-po, "The barbarians [Wei] will certainly exert all their strength to attack our small city. If we destroy this dam, releasing all the water at once, its rapidity will exceed that at San-hsia and they will certainly be submerged and drown."
>
> Wei's army approached the city from the west, assembled south of the dam, and split off a secondary force to mount an interior attack from the east on the small city. When Ch'ung-tsu had the dam broken open, the water's force raced downward and Wei's troops, then engaged in attacking the city, drowned by the thousands.

In addition to Han Hsin's famous strike upon Lung Chü, Yeh mentions two other incidents which seem to merit being termed examples of water rams: Chu-ko Liang's famous "empty city" ploy and T'ang T'ai-tsung's clash with Li Hei-t'a. The former, which is drawn from the early Three Kingdoms period, finds Shu's floundering forces partly encamped in the city of Hsin-yeh. Upon the approach of Ts'ao Jen's massive northern force, Chu-ko Liang abandoned the city with the objective of enticing the enemy into its confines before destroying them with an incendiary attack. Separately, he deputed the great hero Kuan Yü up the Pai River with 1,000 men to construct a temporary dam across it, thereby lowering the water level. Kuan Yü was also instructed to break open the dam when he detected the presence of men and horses downstream.

Behaving exactly as scripted, Ts'ao Jen entered the deserted city and encamped. The incendiary attack was launched in the middle of the night, trapping and killing many, but as Chu-ko Liang expected, Ts'ao Jen managed to escape through the east gate with part of his forces. They were immediately ambushed by a detached force under Chao Yün which feigned being overcome and fled across the river. When the pursuers stopped to water their horses amidst the shallow river, now only a foot deep, Kuan Yü sundered the temporary dam, releasing a torrent of water which cascaded into the cavalrymen, drowning many, though Ts'ao Jen survived.

The third example, again a rather complex effort, unfolded while the nascent T'ang was still consolidating its power and extending its authority. Late in A.D. 621 Liu Hei-t'a's "righteous army" suddenly emerged in Hopei and Honan. (Formerly a commander in Tou Chien-te's now vanquished forces, apart from any imperial ambitions, he may have been prompted to act out of fear of T'ang reprisals.) Rapidly expanding, the rebels easily defeated several provincial forces and attracted numerous enthusiastic adherents. Eventually they commenced a series of assaults on Luo-shuo that ultimately proved successful despite a defensive moat some fifty paces wide and thirty feet deep and valiant rescue efforts by T'ang T'ai-tsung himself which witnessed the spectacular insertion of a new commander into the beleaguered city.

At the beginning of 622 the T'ang mounted a two-pronged siege at Luo-shuo, then occupied by the rebels, from both the north and south. When Liu steadfastly refused to come forth to engage them, the T'ai-tsung cut off their provisions, burned their supply trains, and sank their freight boats. After they had been isolated for some two months, certain that Liu would now be compelled to attack, the T'ai-tsung had a temporary dam built across the river, essentially blocking the flow. (Why this wasn't noticed by Liu's reconnaissance remains a mystery!)

Liu soon abandoned the citadel to strike the T'ang encampment south of the city with some 20,000 cavalry and was immediately engaged by the T'ai-tsung's own cavalry. As the battle extended into the early dusk, Liu realized he was in danger of being crushed and ignominiously fled the field, leaving his unknowing troops to continue their desperate struggle alone. At this moment T'ang T'ai-tsung released the dikes, flooding the battlefield with a torrent of water that eventually reached some ten feet deep. Suddenly finding themselves immersed in deep water and floundering about, Liu's troops crumbled, resulting in some 10,000 being killed and several thousand more drowning in the chaos.[65]

However, sometimes ignorance or natural events unexpectedly produced the same result, as this anecdote found in the *Lü-shih Ch'un-ch'iu* indicates:[66]

> Ching wanted to launch a surprise attack against Sung so they had scouts first chart the depth of the Yung River. Unknown to them, the river suddenly surged higher so that when they employed their charts to ford it that night, more than a thousand men drowned and the army was so panicked that it destroyed their own encampment.

Martial thinkers also offered some fundamental observations on the practice of aquatic warfare within the evolving theory of strategic configurations of terrain and power. Thus as early as the T'ang, Hsü Tung discussed it in terms of his concept of "contrary employment": "Employment contrary to the water's flow consists of erecting high dams to obstruct its downward flow until it overflows their interior and then channeling it to inundate something."[67] Nevertheless, the extensive preparation required made concealment difficult, betraying tactical intent to the enemy, as when Wei learned that Sung was accumulating water in an artificial pond to flood their invading forces and therefore avoided the area.[68]

Even the Jurchen adopted the water ram, though in a more portable, extemporaneous form. The skillful Pi Tsai-yü, the only successful general in the series of battles which sought to blunt Jurchen advances in 1206, not only distinguished himself with his tactical acumen but also with the results which his skillful manipulations achieved.[69] Obviously an astute student of Chu-ko Liang's tactics, he implemented both the empty-city ploy and its reverse, the "still occupied fortress" (by tying a goat so that he would stamp on a drum), and also acquired desperately needed arrows by having a "commander" walk about the parapets. Frequently going forth to attack, he preserved Liu-ho against a vastly superior force of 100,000 even as the Jurchen offensive advanced on a broad front through speed and swift maneuver.

Pi also simplified and lightened the soldiers' armor, thereafter employing it to suit up several thousand straw dummies that he deployed into attack formation during a dark night opposite a major Jurchen emplacement. Just before daybreak he had the drums sounded, startling the Jurchen who immediately released their previously constructed water reservoirs, said by commentators to have frequently been a decisive weapon, to flood the attackers. In the confusion and anger which followed the realization that they had been tricked, Pi attacked and defeated them. (These large temporary reservoirs apparently were intended to locally enmire and immobilize, even possibly exert a ram-like effect. However, apart from this incident, they are unknown.)

## THEFT OF WATER

Manipulating the water level to adversely impact the enemy, despite having a prominent place in the theoretical corpus, was practiced far less often and even then more likely seen in measures taken to completely deny water supplies rather than prevent exploitation for logistical or transport purposes. In order to block a likely Chin invasion, in A.D. 272 Eastern Wu flooded the relatively level plains about Chiang-ling located just north of the Yangtze River by damming up nearby tributaries. Chin then decided to turn this apparent obstacle to their advantage by conveying provisions destined for their expeditionary army by boat rather than laboriously transporting them overland. To ensure an adequate water level they spread disinformation indicating they wanted to destroy the dams. However, this merely prompted Wu's commander, who had fathomed their true intent, to have them broken open despite the vehement objections of his generals. Chin therefore had to shift to utilizing wagons, a task rendered even more difficult by the muddy terrain.[70]

When Wang Ching-tse revolted against Southern Ch'i, he rapidly gained a vast number of adherents from the area he had formerly commanded. Although said to have attained 100,000, they were mostly farmers equipped with agricultural implements rather than weapons, just as the *Six Secret Teachings* discussed back in the Warring States period. Therefore, a local administrative chief who believed that simply frustrating them for a few days, until the government's forces could arrive, would precipitate a fatal breakdown in their organization and discipline, had the canal locks opened and water drained off so that they could no longer advance on the water. The measure worked since the key forces were moving by boat and Wang failed to take alternative action, allowing the imperial army to attack and decimate them even as their cohesion disintegrated.[71]

# 10

# Negating Water Sources

Without water, men and animals quickly become incapable of fighting, collapse, and perish. However, long before that, in a matter of hours amid desert heat or a few days in temperate climes, dehydration makes men desperate, impedes rational analysis, and compels risk taking. Moreover, even where accessible, water's great weight makes it difficult to transport over any but the shortest distances. Thus, the *Hu-ch'ien Ching* counseled, "When you want to seize the enemy's strength, first seize their water supply"[1] and the *Ts'ui-wei Pei-cheng-lu* stressed denying water and provisions to the enemy.[2] Even Sun-tzu provided indications of thirst among his selected observations, noting "when those who are drawing water drink first, they are thirsty."[3]

In accord with their general emphasis upon denying aggressors any materials of possible utility, the Mohists consciously targeted water supplies for elimination. Water sources could easily be disabled through several means, though a complicating factor was the need to recover them once the invaders had departed or been vanquished. Radical methods such as poisoning wells or contaminating them with animal carcasses or other putrefied material, though undeniably effective, entailed drastic, long-term consequences. In comparison, relatively benign measures such as simply filling in wells, damming flowing streams, and concealing springs were temporary but readily negated.

From the inception of warfare it has been axiomatic that gaining high ground is tantamount to victory. Thus near the end of the Warring States period the *Six Secret Teachings* asserted that "occupying high ground is the means by which to be alert and assume a defensive posture." Sun-tzu had earlier proclaimed "the army likes height and abhors low areas, esteems the sunny *[yang]* and disdains the shady *[yin]*. It nourishes life and occupies the substantial. An army that avoids the hundred illnesses is said to be certain of victory."[4]

Contemplating Sun-tzu's comments and earlier history, Hsü Tung concluded: "Whenever employing the army Han Kao-tsu valued heights and detested lowlands, esteemed the sunny *[yang]* and disdained the shady *[yin]*. He nurtured life and dwelled in the substantial. Life is *yang*, so when one nurtures oneself in *yang* his *ch'i* [vital spirit] will be victorious. The heights are substantial, so by occupying the heights the low wetlands were kept distant and the hundred illnesses did not arise. Men were settled in their employment. This was to the advantage of the army, and the assistance of the terrain."[5]

The Ming dynasty *Wu Pien* considered heights so important as to list their occupation among the three crucial concordances, echoing a conclusion reached somewhat earlier in the *Hundred Unorthodox Strategies:* "Whenever engaging an enemy in battle, whether in mountain forests or on level terrain, you must occupy high ground and rely upon strategic configurations of terrain that are conducive to attacks and probes and will facilitate racing forward to assault the enemy. Then you will be victorious in combat."[6]

Despite such assertions and the many advantages that accrue from a superior field of vision, the effects of gravity, and the difficulty of wielding weapons upward, the issue was never so simple. Mountain forces could easily become isolated, cut off from supplies, and deprived of water, and thereby forced into submission. Thus the *Six Secret Teachings* conceded "whenever the Three Armies occupy the heights of a mountain, they are trapped on high by the enemy."[7] The

*Hu-ch'ien Ching* similarly pointed out that forces encamped on high, dry terrain without the advantages of springs and water could be waited out until their troops and horses became weak from thirst.[8]

To mitigate this difficulty, under the topic of valley warfare the *Unorthodox Strategies* advised: "Whenever moving an army over mountains and through ravines, if you want to deploy, it should certainly be done by relying upon the valleys. This will allow taking advantage of grass and water, and you will also have solid defensive positions available in the nearby ravines. If you then engage in battle you will be victorious. A tactical principle from the *Art of War* states: 'To cross mountains, follow the valleys.'" In illustration, the authors cited Ma Yüan's campaign to suppress the Ch'iang and other steppe raiders in the Later Han dynasty. Since their enemies occupied the mountain heights, Ma deployed his army on the tenable terrain below and seized the water and grass, though without engaging in combat. Badly parched, several hundred thousand Ch'iang troops fled out beyond the pass, and all their generals, with more than 10,000 men, surrendered.[9]

Although Chinese theorists also believed that valleys should be exploited for their ability to constrict larger enemies, stagnantly occupying the heights without being able to control the surrounding terrain, particularly when water and fodder had to be sourced below, could easily prove self-defeating. Barren outcroppings invariably mandated extensive supply lines while lengthy bucket brigades constituted prime targets. Severing them might produce victory without any further effort, thereby achieving Sun-tzu's ideal of conquest without combat.[10] Accordingly, Yeh Meng-hsiung's *Yün-ch'ou Kang-mu* observed: "The *Art of War* states, 'Keep water and marshes to your front left' and 'rely on trees and grass and keep groves of trees at your back.' Not knowing the advantages of terrain will allow the enemy to cut you off. How will the soldiers and horses then survive?"

Yeh also cited three historical clashes: "Chang Ko cut and obstructed Ma Su's path for drawing water and thoroughly destroyed him. Tzu-kan encamped close upon the river and caused the thirsty Turks to perish. Ho-lien Po-po built embankments, cut off the water's flow, and forced Wang Hsi's seizure." Moreover, he found it puzzling that such ploys were still being effectively employed against Chinese troops: "Recently I learned that our border generals have fallen into similar barbarian plots. Haven't they heard the story of Chang Ko obstructing the path to water?"

Yeh's first example arose during the Three Kingdoms period when Chu-ko Liang, exercising virtually despotic powers in Shu following Liu Pei's death, launched the first of five northern expeditions against Wei in A.D. 228. Ostensibly intended to restore Han rule, these aggressive campaigns actually functioned as a preemptive defense against Ts'ao's vastly greater army. In order to ensure their success, the normally innovative Chu-ko Liang opted to mount a cautious invasion from their bastion of Szechuan by a more distant but easier route rather than have an elite force strike directly at Ch'ang-an across difficult terrain. Moreover, contrary to Liu Pei's deathbed warning that Ma Su, an apparently talented official who had intrigued Chu-ko Liang with his encyclopedic military knowledge, should never be given significant responsibility because his words exceeded his abilities, he appointed him overall commander and entrusted him with spearheading the advance.

Unfortunately for the nascent state of Shu, Liu Pei's premonition proved correct. Once in the field Ma Su not only acted brutally and imperiously but also contravened fundamental tactical principles by deploying his troops upon isolated high ground rather than along the river as directed. Moreover, he failed to establish strong points or construct the palisades needed to control the road and guarantee access to the water below. Chang Ko immediately seized the opportunity to cut off their path and then overwhelm the parched troops after a suitable interval. Finding their advance thwarted and position untenable, Chu-ko Liang terminated the campaign and withdrew their forces, though not without further challenges. Because of the defeat's severity, he was also compelled to have Ma executed for dereliction of duty and have himself demoted three ranks.[11]

Roughly two decades later, in the autumn of A.D. 249 as part of ongoing attempts to gain the allegiance of local peoples and project power in the region of Yung-chou (roughly encompassing mid- to western Shanhsi and eastern Kansu) located to their north, Shu forces under the highly capable general Chiang Wei established two fortified towns at the base of Mount Ch'ü.[12] To prevent them from exploiting local support and succeed in their intended, ever broadening strikes, Wei quickly deputed two experienced commanders (Ch'en Ch'in and Kuo Huai) to undertake a response.

Although this northern thrust hardly constituted an overly bold strategy, Ch'en T'ai recognized that the isolation of the outposts and the difficult terrain intervening between them and their supply base made them highly vulnerable to an attritional strategy, one that could wrest victory without combat losses if potential rescue forces could be thwarted. Adopting this view, the northern armies surrounded the citadels, severing both their supply lines and external water sources, quickly compelling them to rely upon melted snow for their liquids. They also stymied Chiang Wei's rescue attempts by blocking the narrow corridor of approach while persistently refusing to be drawn into combat by troops manning the outposts. Beset by hunger and thirst in a very arid region, lacking any hope of rescue, the two citadel commanders opted to surrender, ignominiously ending Shu's efforts to convert the area into an external bastion.

In the turbulent fourth century, amidst Chin's increasingly fractured and complex internal strife, conflict erupted between Wen Chiao and Su Chün, a powerful commander whose brutality and perversity had caused him to be much hated.[13] (Some of the rebels were in fact former subordinates who deserted Su because they feared his power was eroding and might be suppressed.) In a clash near the Yangtze in Chiangsu, under Yang K'an's nominal leadership Wen Chiao's forces succeeded in burning significant quantities of Su's supplies, creating shortages, but their own detached forces dispersed among three camps at Ta-yeh came under sustained attack and suffered from a lack of water to the point where they were compelled to suck manure for moisture. Terrified by their imminent doom, the local commander abandoned his troops and fled in secrecy. However, Yang managed to extricate the camps by manipulating the besiegers with Sun Pin's tactic of "attacking what they must rescue" and eventually vanquished Su Chün, whose hated corpse even suffered dismemberment and burning.

Fu Teng, emperor of Former Ch'in, personally led an attack in Shaanhsi against Later Ch'in whose forces strongly resisted, preventing their troops and horses from reaching the Yellow River.[14] Without water, some 20 to 30 percent of Fu's forces soon perished and the rest became desperate. Later Ch'in, having decided to exploit their debilitation with a decisive battle, then counterattacked. Former Ch'in was so badly defeated that only the emperor managed to escape, but upon reaching his two closest citadels found that his sons, who had been entrusted with their command, had abandoned them upon rumors of his death. After collecting some remnant forces, the emperor was forced to fade into the hills.

Severing water supplies often proved highly effective in a relatively short time, particularly in semi-arid areas or during the dry seasons experienced during the winds of winter and heat of summer. For example, in A.D. 418 when the Hu Hsia general Ho-lien Ch'ang attacked the Chin general Wang Ching-hsien in Ts'ao Ts'ao's old fortress in the semi-arid area of Shaanhsi, he cut off their water source, thereby making them so thirsty that they couldn't sustain the fight and were all captured.[15] In A.D. 430 Northern Wei similarly cut off the Hu Hsia king's access to water, quickly causing such severe thirst among the men and horses that they were compelled to attempt a breakout and thus suffered a major defeat, sustaining over 10,000 casualties.[16]

As part of a sweep which eventually seized territory in Honan and Shan-tung upon Li Yu's death, the Hsien-pei state of Northern Wei attacked several Southern Sung cities and fortified towns across a broad front. Even though the Yellow

River failed to thwart their aggression, a few towns managed to resist. However, most succumbed because the Southern Sung's response lacked coordination and many commanders feared defeat and therefore remained inactive. The fortified town of Hu-lao, which came under attack in 423, might have fared better if several thousand troops hadn't twice been dispatched from its garrison to participate in collateral actions, thereby augmenting the enemy's already overwhelming numerical superiority.[17]

This siege and the defenders' response were marked by several interesting aspects. Early on, the commander Mao Te-tsu had six tunnels dug some seven *chang* deep extending out beyond Northern Wei's forces. Four hundred elite troops then utilized them to strike fear, wreck havoc, and incinerate the enemy's siege engines, prompting them to regroup. However, the besiegers enjoyed an insurmountable tactical advantage in controlling the vital, external water sources. Although Wei's armies had initially approached in the eleventh month of the previous year, they didn't take steps to block them from drawing water with long ropes from the nearby river until the fourth month. After waiting three days, presumably on the assumption this interval would sufficiently debilitate them, they attacked in force but failed to prevail.

Thereafter, ongoing assaults of increasing intensity compressed the defenders into the most interior of three extemporaneous walled areas, the external walls having been breached and the first two of the temporary inner ones falling as well. As external aid, despite having been deputed and deployed, was still not forthcoming, the Northern Wei commander had several counter-wells dug to draw off the groundwater, drying up the citadel's few interior wells. An immense effort undertaken in the protective cover of the nearby hills, the counter-wells attained a reported depth of forty-seven *chang* or nearly 300 modern feet. After days of such unremitting fighting that the defenders' eyes were crusted over and they were so dehydrated that they supposedly didn't bleed when wounded, a last fervent assault overran the walls, capturing and slaying all but 200 valiant warriors who managed to puncture a hole through the on-coming waves and escape.

Although this was a major defeat for Southern Sung, in blunting and entangling the Northern Wei onslaught, it has traditionally been seen as proof that town-centered riverine defenses could withstand external invasion and as exemplifying the heroic battle with barbarism. Northern Wei's emperor had even commanded in person for a time, while the losses attributed to illness and casualties amounted to a sizable 30 percent.

Returning to Yeh's examples, Ho-lou Tzu-kan was one of the early Sui commanders sent out to blunt a massive Turkish invasion force of some 400,000 mounted under five temporarily allied quaghans. Ho-lou encountered Tarda's segmented but still vastly superior forces in the K'o-luo-hai mountains where he astutely encamped along the rivers, denying the Turks access to the only water sources. Once the enemy had weakened from lack of water, Ho-lou launched a fervent attack, forcing Tarda to temporarily retreat.[18]

The *Yün-ch'ou Kang-mu's* third illustration was a victory achieved nearly two centuries earlier by the founder of the Hu Hsia dynasty just mentioned, Liu (He-lien) Po-po, amidst the turmoil of the early fifth century as multiple external peoples contended for control of China. A descendant of Hsiung-nu kings who excelled in cavalry warfare in China's semi-arid northwest border region, he adroitly employed forces of 10,000 to 20,000 to plunder and subjugate other tribal peoples and thus gradually expanded his empire until finally conquering Ch'ang-an.

During one of his initial clashes with the Later Ch'in state ruled by Yao Hsing, Ch'in forces occupied a fortified border town but then found their water supply had been severed. Rather than endure continued deprivation, the local inhabitants seized the Ch'in commander, Wang Hsi, who had fought valiantly but futilely, even wounding Po-po, and turned him over to the Hu Hsia king when they surrendered. Ironically, Yao Hsing had been counseled to employ a similar strategy against Liu Po-po by deputing a campaign army to sever his access to the crucial rivers, but had felt it would be too negative and cowardly. Moreover, another city had been lost slightly earlier when some 20 to 30 percent of the population perished from lack of water after the source was blocked.[19]

A punitive campaign mounted by T'ang forces under P'ei Chi in A.D. 619 against the powerful rebel leader and self-proclaimed emperor Liu Wu-chou in northern Shanhsi also turned upon severing the water supply. At this time, merely the second year of the T'ang, the dynasty had barely been established and controlled but a minimal core area, whereas the rebels threatened the founding emperor's first bastion of T'ai-yüan. Attempting to suppress Liu who was nominally supported by the powerful Turkish Quaghan, P'ei led a campaign army into Northern Shanhsi which eventually encamped at Chieh-hsiu. Unfortunately, the site's water was supplied by a single mountain stream that Liu's military commander, the skilled barbarian general Sung Chin-kang, easily cut off. Desperate for water, P'ei carelessly commenced shifting his encampment but was attacked en route and thoroughly decimated. In consequence, much of the T'ang's porous border was left undefended and Liu went on to occupy T'ai-yüan, remaining dangerous until finally being murdered by the Turks in 622.[20]

In their quest to dominate all of China, the Mongols similarly resorted to severing water supplies and occasionally suffered the same plight themselves. In 1219 a Chinese general serving in Mongol command, Chang Jou, undertook a generally victorious campaign that progressed southward until encountering resistance mounted by Sung forces ensconced in the mountains at Kung-shan-t'ai. Unable to overcome them, Chang cut off their access to the river below, thereby preventing them from drawing water and forcing them to surrender.[21]

Perhaps the most ignominious example of being vanquished solely through lack of water is furnished by the T'u-mu incident that unfolded in 1449 during the Ming dynasty's attempts to repress troublesome Mongolian forces in the steppe region.[22] Not only did the Ming incur devastating losses, but the battle also radically altered the political situation, resulting in two emperors, strident factionalism, and increased reliance upon static defenses. Chu Yüan-chang, the first Ming emperor, had initially sought to conquer the plateau and integrate its peoples within a traditional hierarchy of manifest relationships. However, despite some early success, when his massive campaigns failed to quash the mobile, highly motivated Mongols who generally avoided fatal confrontations, this aggressive steppe posture deteriorated into a highly enervated defensive stance over the next century. (Severely harassed Ming expeditionary armies achieved victory only when unexpectedly arriving on target, exploiting confined quarters, profiting from inclement weather, or striking groups encumbered with baggage or herds.)

The Yung-lo emperor subsequently adopted the inconsistent policy of abandoning external strongpoints to mount deep expeditionary campaigns while relying upon static defenses augmented by the forward presence of unreliable Mongolian allies. The five massive efforts mounted under his personal leadership occasionally scored impressive victories, but overall the results were barely indeterminate, yet severely depleted China's fiscal and military resources. Moreover, the last two campaigns, undertaken with vastly reduced, more mobile forces in 1423 and 1424, not only proved ineffectual but saw the emperor perish as well.

Reports of Oirat advances under the charismatic Esen in 1449 prompted an ill-conceived, blundering response under the nominal command of the inexperienced Emperor Ying-tsung upon the powerful Wang Chen's urging. One of Esen's four columns, which targeted the bastion at Ta-t'ung, sought to lure a Ming response while collateral strikes into Liao-tung and Kansu accompanied the main thrust toward the citadel at Hsüan-fu. Within a few days the weak frontier defenses were penetrated and a major victory achieved north of Hsüan-fu on 7/15 that drove the local defenders westward to Ta-t'ung. The ill-prepared Ming troops, nominally 500,000, coincidentally went forth the same day for Ta-t'ung via

Hsüan-fu. Caught by several days of rain, they ran short of supplies and quickly became dispirited after encountering vestiges of the battle's carnage on the twenty-eighth. Learning of the Oirat's power when they arrived at Ta-t'ung on 8/1, despite their vastly superior numbers the now terrified Wang Chen decided to abandon the effort.

Unfortunately, Wang's vacillation crippled the army's confidence, prompting Esen to shift to the offensive. Moreover, reportedly to avoid imperiling his own estates, Wang shortsightedly insisted they retrace their outward trek even though its northerly arc increased their exposure. The first blow, which decimated a detached Ming unit, was followed by the successful ambush of a strong relief contingent. Astoundingly, rather than ensconcing the emperor in a nearby fortified town, Wang encamped the army on an exposed, waterless height at T'u-mu where they were then fatally surrounded since they lacked the determination to break out. Esen then feigned peace overtures and a minor withdrawal, unleashing a Ming stampede toward the nearby river by the parched troops. Some 20,000 Mongolian cavalry quickly exploited their disorder to wreck havoc, inflict 70,000 casualties, slay untold senior commanders, and capture the emperor.

Although securing water thus often proved problematic for forces in the hills and mountains, operational contingents also sometimes encountered severe difficulties in valleys and ravines and even entire cities, whether or not lying aside rivers, might suffer deprivation if wells proved unfruitful. For example, in 27 B.C. a Han commander was sent out to repress rebel forces that had commenced fighting among themselves and naturally disdained imperial authority.[23] Eventually their remnants sought refuge in an inaccessible gorge where they couldn't readily be attacked or dislodged. Rather than mount headlong assaults that would entail horrendous losses, the Han commander first cut off their supplies, then severed the stream supplying their water. Boxed in, isolated, and under extreme duress, the clan heads eventually slew their leader and surrendered.

The nearly four-year punitive campaign (104–101 B.C.) mounted by the famous Han commander Li Kuang-li, often referred to as the Sutrishna General, to conquer Ferghana (Ta-yüan) set out with perhaps 100,000 men and far more oxen and pack animals. In addition, some 180,000 collateral forces were also dispatched to the border region. This massive number of troops and a nearly continuous relay of supplies were deemed necessary because a previous, highly overconfident attempt with just 30,000 troops had seen the army arrive on site too exhausted and few in number to even attempt an assault.

Since it was well known that Ta-yüan relied upon rivers and external springs for their water, from the outset Han strategists intended to cut the water supplies to speed the enemy's submission. Hydraulic engineers were therefore deliberately included in the entourage to divert the flow, exploit the water gates, and tunnel into the city. When the army approached the capital, the 30,000 troops serving in the vanguard repelled an initial counterattack. Thereafter, they besieged the city and deliberately severed its access to water. After some forty days, Li's forces finally broke through the outer wall, forcing the inhabitants to cower within the inner quarters.

The hopelessness of their situation prompted the tribal leaders to assassinate their king, whose insult of the Han, murder of the imperial envoys, and refusal to provide the famous blood-sweating horses had prompted the punitive expedition. In contrast to their massacring of another city en route that had initially resisted, Li accepted their proposals for ending the conflict without inflicting any further punishment. No doubt he feared the possible materialization of external rescue forces, as threatened, but in addition had learned that the city still had adequate food supplies and, more importantly, was now being assisted by Chinese prisoners with expertise in digging wells. Ta-yüan's ability to endure forty days without any apparent water source can only be explained by their success in somehow having early on ameliorated the shortage, allowing the city to hold out in an arid climate.[24]

## EXTRAORDINARY MEASURES

Hard-pressed but resolute forces, as well as cities and fortified towns under siege, often survived through various unpleasant and gruesome means, including cannibalism. In comparison with the humid, watery south where wells were more likely to be successful, commanders in the drier north and arid northwestern border areas quickly resorted to unusual measures. However, the first impulse was to dig wells, as at T'u-mu, and when successful their travails no doubt went unrecorded. Nevertheless, a few incidents show that even successful efforts often came perilously close to failing and were always exceedingly difficult.

While conducting a campaign of suppression against the Hsiung-nu about A.D. 75 in the arid province of Hsinchiang, the Later Han commander Keng Kung ensconced his troops in a town considered defensible because it was watered by a stream. However, the Hsiung-nu cut off the flow, forcing the troops to dig wells, one of which reached down 150 feet without obtaining water. In consequence, they were compelled to suck moisture from horse manure until the commander personally led a staff effort that struck water with the removal of several more baskets of earth. The Han forces then confounded their attackers by brazenly displaying their newly acquired wealth, causing the warriors massed outside the walls to depart because they felt Keng had benefited from some sort of spiritual intercession.[25]

During the ongoing conflict between the Hsi Hsia and the Sung, Hsü Hsi suggested that certain strong points in the heavily contested Ordos region in modern northwestern Shaanhsi, approximately at the border of contemporary Inner Mongolia, be fortified to prevent incursions and control the development of crucial economic resources such as horses.[26] However, others anticipated fatal difficulties resulting in this semi-arid area should access to the exterior springs or rivers be severed. Nevertheless, the emperor approved the plan and some 200,000 workers supplemented by 40,000 cavalry and infantry troops were dispatched to construct the fortified city of Yung-lo in the seventh month of 1082.

Construction was hastily completed in the ninth month and a 10,000-man residual force assigned to permanently defend the bastion. Hsi Hsia reconnaissance forces had long been observing its progress from the far bank of the Wu-ting River, yet Hsü Hsi remained untroubled and calmly withdrew to the interior. Shortly thereafter an exploratory enemy contingent came up, but they departed as soon as Sung reserves appeared, thereby confirming Hsü's belief that they feared engaging the Sung in combat.

Unfortunately for the ill-fated outpost, their mobile steppe enemies soon assembled some 300,000 men on their side of the river, yet it took more than a dozen urgent requests to persuade Hsü Hsi to come forth with a rescue force which seems never to have exceeded 30,000 to 40,000 men. (Hsü naively believed that withstanding an onslaught by vastly superior numbers would yield an even greater victory for the Sung.) A civil official bereft of military knowledge and experience, amidst a sea of barbarian troops he merely ordered his subcommander Ch'ü Chen to deploy outside the city near the river to await the orders which he would personally convey by signaling from atop the city walls with flags.

In an astounding repeat of the ignominious Spring and Autumn debacle, Hsü refused to attack the enemy before they had properly assembled on the far bank or while they were crossing the river—tactics espoused in all the military manuals—because such behavior would be inappropriate for an imperial army. Once the Hsi Hsia's armored troops finished fording the river Ch'ü Chen realized that his troops had lost any spirit for battle and therefore wanted to withdraw, but was instead ordered to engage them. The clash was brief and futile as the 10,000 Sung fighters were quickly overwhelmed and forced back into the city. En route they had to abandon 8,000 horses because the intervening terrain was narrow and tortuous, while their disorganized headlong rush into the city caused chaos among the defenders ensconced within.

Nevertheless, even as the troops mounted a stalwart defense Hsü Hsi adamantly refused to employ the desperate measures appropriate to "fatal terrain" or break out and abandon the outpost while their spirit was still strong. The Hsi Hsia easily blocked two columns bringing reinforcements and supplies and then severed the water supplies at the nearby river. Consternation and debilitation soon beset those trapped within the fortress and more than half died from dehydration when numerous attempts to dig deep wells failed to strike water.

The defenders battled on, sustaining themselves by consuming horse manure and urine until the sudden onset of heavy rains which slaked their thirst but ironically eroded portions of the newly built, parched walls. The enemy poured in, the city was lost, and Hsü Hsi was slain along with 230 other generals and some 12,300 officers and troops. As Hsü's inability had been foretold, the emperor suffered slight pangs of guilt and concluded that further attempts to subjugate the Hsi Hsia, which had already resulted in some 600,000 casualties overall, would be counterproductive. In fact, this was a serious understatement because troops and other essential resources had been diverted from the north and the task of repelling the Khitan, badly depleting the Sung's already irresolute martial energies.

Similarly repulsive measures are recorded for a siege that arose in 1264 when the fortress erected by the Mongols on Mount Hu-hsiao as part of their effort to finally subjugate all of Szechuan came under assault. The Sung commander, Hsia Kuei, attacked the 5,000 Mongol forces ensconced upon the hill with some 50,000 troops, but the Mongol leader, Chang T'ing-tuan, realizing the impossibility of the odds, steadfastly refused battle even though their defensive walls and wooden palisades had been pounded into non-existence and now consisted solely of animal skins stretched across poles that might be deployed where needed. The Mongol forces were further debilitated when Hsia initiated a siege that severed their access to water below, the barren mountain being incapable of supporting wells.

As an emergency measure Chang determinedly resorted to Keng Kung's methods but expanded them somewhat by having all the animal and human urine continuously collected, boiled, and then filtered through sand "to remove any odor" before being provided to the men. Even though they all suffered blistering of the mouth after drinking a few small cups, the besieged troops continued to hold out for more than a month. Finally, despite the hesitation of an external rescue force, Chang exploited Sung laxity to launch a counterattack in coordination with external support that employed the ancient ruse of each soldier carrying three torches during their night approach. Frightened, Hsia's forces fled in chaos, precipitating the severe defeat that would be thereafter cited as a prime example of a badly outnumbered force resolutely defying and then defeating a vastly greater enemy. Of course, in more fortuitous though colder circumstances, rain might have been accumulated and snow melted.[27]

Although often quickly inducing discomfort and even collapse, the technique of severing water supplies might also require weeks to prove effective, during which time unexpected events might subvert the strategy. For example, in 384 King Fu Chien of Ch'in personally led some 20,000 cavalry and infantry in a campaign against a Later Ch'in rebel army. After scoring several victories, the enemy's remnants had been unexpectedly backed onto inhospitable terrain that lacked wells. Fu Chien's army then blocked the enemy's passage and cut off their water source, the T'ung-kuan River. However, heavy rains suddenly fell just when the rebels were beginning to perish from lack of water and panic in fear, inundating the besieged encampment to a depth of three feet! Fortunately, just 100 paces away the water barely exceeded an inch. Therefore, despite their misery, the revitalized Later Ch'in army seized the opportunity to regroup, causing Fu Chien to bemoan the fact that Heaven seemed to be aiding his enemies.[28]

However, cutting off the defenders' water supplies even in comparatively dry regions did not invariably produce victory. For example, in the summer of A.D. 428, when Kansu was beset by seasonal drought, Northern Liang attacked Western Ch'in's city of Yüeh-tu shortly after their ruler's demise. Although over half the defenders died from lack of water and the city was almost subverted, they managed to hold out until a peace accord was concluded.[29]

The prospect of having water restored could also be employed to manipulate armies suffering from deprivation. In one of the conflicts between the Northern Wei and other steppe peoples that unfolded in the Kansu region in A.D. 530, the defeated clan leader Man-ai-ti Tao-luo fled through the mountains until taking refuge with Wang Ch'ing-yün at Shui-luo.[30] Man-ai-ti's courage and tactical acumen bolstered Wang's aspiration of emperorship, prompting him to establish a rudimentary administrative bureaucracy. However, Northern Wei forces soon overwhelmed the eastern of Shui-luo's twin cites, forcing the people to seek refuge in the western which lacked water, causing them to quickly weaken and have little hope for survival.

Because defectors advised the Northern Wei commander that the two leaders were probably planning to escape, he offered a specious peace accord intended to subvert popular support for immediate action. Moreover, he offered to withdraw somewhat while they were contemplating the treaty so that the populace could access the stream outside. However, as soon as night fell, the aggressors erected wooden palisades all about the camp and ringed it with chevaux-de-frise where troops were stationed in ambush. When the two leaders actually attempted to flee, they were easily blocked and captured. Thereafter, an assault undertaken in the north overran the city walls, driving the remaining 17,000 defenders out the south gate where they found themselves similarly trapped and therefore surrendered only to be slaughtered and have their wealth confiscated. Despite the probable consequences of defeat, they allowed themselves to be lured into complacency by their unexpected access to water and perished as a result.

## POISON

Programs of denial included the more direct approach of poisoning the water supply rather than laboring to sever it. Under the rubric "Use Poison to Defeat the Enemy" in the *Yün-ch'ou Kang-mu,* Yeh Meng-hsiung somewhat contrarily commented that "the case of Ch'in poisoning the Ching

River, which is an example of warfare among Chinese states, cannot be taken as a model. However, can't Ch'ang-sun Sheng and Liu Ch'i's actions be taken as models of China combating the barbarians? How much more so where the mountains lack water, where there isn't any water to poison? How can I then consider employing poison?" However, he still cited three illustrative cases: the classic Battle of Yü-lin, Ch'ang-sun Sheng's relatively unknown action against the Turks, and Liu Ch'i's employment of poison as part of his famous defense of Shun-ch'ang.

The Battle of Yü-lin, which ostensibly arose in reprisal for a negligent Chin commander having been severely defeated by a two-pronged Ch'in army in 562 B.C., witnessed the first recorded military employment of poison in Chinese history.[31] Although Chin managed to coerce some twelve major and minor states into undertaking an expeditionary campaign in 559 B.C., disaffection plagued the coalition's feudal lords. Only with great reluctance did they finally cross the Ching River and encamp their armies along the banks. Thereupon, "Ch'in's forces poisoned the river upstream, killing many of the soldiers." In addition to inflicting numerous casualties and instilling fear among the men, their unexpected action significantly augmented the friction besetting the coalition commanders. Disdaining further action, they simply withdrew, earning the campaign a lasting reputation for having been hesitant and tarrying.

By the fourth century encountering contaminated water on a projected line of march must not have been unusual. Huan Wen, Chin's commander in chief, launched a foray into Former Yen in the spring of A.D. 369 that was blocked and defeated, forcing the army to retreat. Although short of provisions, Huan surprisingly burned his boats and proceeded some 700 *li* overland, digging new wells at every resting point out of fear that the water supply had been poisoned.[32]

Yeh's second incident unfolded in A.D. 600 when the first Sui Emperor dispatched Ch'ang-sun Sheng with several thousand surrendered Turkish troops as part of an attempt to repress the chief of the Western Turks, Tarda, who had continued to mount incursions and foment trouble. For some years dissension and even armed conflict had persisted between the Western and Eastern Turks, much to the benefit of the Sui which actively fostered it, but the northern border region remained an area in flux. Any of the several tribal peoples could suddenly surge forth to threaten or overturn the immature dynasty, just as the Sui and subsequently T'ang's progenitors, both of whom originated among the area's "semi-barbarian" military aristocracy.

Very familiar with Turkish customs, Sheng proposed they poison the springs where the cavalry watered their horses. Swiftly adopted, his plan succeeded in slaying numerous horses and warriors as well as shocking the Turks who failed to recognize it as a biochemical attack and blamed Heaven for having produced noxious rain. Sheng quickly exploited their nighttime withdrawal to mount the decimating attack that scored a significant victory, greatly enhanced his reputation, and earned the emperor's acclaim.[33]

The Battle of Shun-ch'ang well illustrates how strongly motivated, ensconced defenders under expert command could defeat vastly superior numbers by employing classical tactical concepts combined with innovative techniques.[34] Even though pusillanimous imperial action would eventually negate their achievements, this astonishing victory inspired the populace and subsequently became a much studied, classic engagement. An important aspect was the use of poison to incapacitate the enemy's horses, as well as deny them water supplies and fodder, while natural water barriers were exploited to the fullest extent possible.

The conflict arose amidst a century of battlefield developments and mutually contradictory Southern Sung court policies. In the 1130s, resolute and innovative commanders such as the Wu brothers, Yüeh Fei, and Han Shih-chung retook Hsiang-yang, repulsed northern invasions, and recaptured all the prefectures south of the Huai River through maneuver warfare and entangling the enemy. However, more aggressive forays had to be abandoned because the emperor ordered successful generals such as Yüeh Fei not to "antagonize the Jurchen."

The actual battle was precipitated when the new Jurchen ruler Wu Shu, who had usurped power in 1139, launched a four-pronged invasion in 1140 to retake the prefectures recently repatriated under a new, expensive peace accord before attempting to subjugate the Sung itself. The invasion's very success was in fact premised upon the security pact being too new for the Sung to have established a military presence in those prefectures, whether out of negligence or disinclination. Since most of them had remained under their former administrators, men who readily submitted to the slightest Jurchen threat, they quickly fell.

Liu Ch'i, one of the commanders belatedly deputed to block the Jurchen advance, decided to make a stand some 300 *li* away from the enemy at the fortified town of Shunch'ang because it had adequate supplies for a sustained siege, the Huai River ran somewhat to the south, and any attacking force would have to cross the Ying River, which passed close by the town on the north before abruptly turning southeast toward the Huai.

Realizing that nothing short of total warfare would prevail, Liu immediately exploited every available resource to repel the anticipated onslaught. All the inhabitants dwelling outside the city walls, some 5,000, were moved into the town and their buildings burnt. The walls were fortified with wooden reinforcements, including shafts from disassembled wagons, and knee walls erected on top to protect the archers whose withering fire would repeatedly decimate the attackers. External ramparts were constructed and manned on a rotating basis; reconnaissance patrols employed local guides; and ambush forces were deployed.

Since Wu Shu had proclaimed that the men would be slaughtered, the women taken prisoner, and all their riches seized, the entire populace was both motivated and mobilized. Moreover, in order to forestall any suspicion that he might abandon the populace, Liu had all their boats sunk and even housed his immediate family in a temple destined to be burnt if the city fell. Because of these actions and the origin of his 18,000 troops among the so-called righteous popular forces, they remained resolute even in the face of a vastly superior enemy.

When the first Jurchen cavalry contingent reached the walls, Liu Ch'i not only had them ambushed but also exploited information gained from captives to undertake a sudden night attack with only 1,000 men, striking the main army as they labored to establish their encampment. Although this opening blow was more effective in causing chaos than inflicting casualties, it should have awakened the invaders to Shun-ch'ang's aggressive posture, yet on 5/29 the Jurchen commanders still expected their initial assault to overwhelm the city. However, their 30,000 troops were driven back by a hail of archery fire and then viciously counterattacked by several thousand valiant Sung troops who unexpectedly sallied forth. The Jurchen assault was thus broken and many of their soldiers drowned in their haste to escape the onslaught.

An assault-punctuated siege was then maintained for some six days. However, Sung archers successfully repelled every thrust and Liu Ch'i had marauding strikes mounted on the Jurchen encampment under the concealment of heavy nighttime rains. Badly decimated and thoroughly exhausted, the besiegers were compelled to withdraw. Enraged, Wu Shu hastily mobilized his main 100,000-man force and raced some 1,200 *li* to Shun-ch'ang in less than a week, abandoning much of his siege equipment en route because Liu's expendable spies advised he was dissolute and unprepared.

Arriving late on 6/8, Shun-ch'ang's quiet appearance and comparatively low walls confirmed Wu's expectation of an easy conquest, prompting him to order a full assault for the next day even though his troops were exhausted. Both the east and west gates were attacked in the morning, but the defenders again launched a devastating surprise attack that targeted the elite Jurchen warriors rather than the weaker components. Clad in heavy metal armor and helmets during the worst heat of midsummer, they quickly withered under the noontime attack.

Liu's success was not simply due to Sung resolve, but to the implementation of imaginative techniques. When sallying forth, every soldier carried bamboo tubes filled with cooked beans which served a dual purpose: when thrown onto the ground, the beans quickly distracted the famished horses which stopped to eat them and the round bamboo sections littering the ground undercut their footing. Once the Sung troops used the newly perfected method of cutting the riders down with long shafted axes and hacking the horse's legs with short ones, mounds of bodies quickly piled up. Even when the invaders enveloped them, the Sung warriors managed to break free.

Liu also resorted to chemical warfare, poisoning the river and grassy fields, felling a large number of enemy soldiers and horses. Because his troops were rapidly deteriorating, Wu decided to shift his encampment west of the city. A crack force of 500 Sung infantry then utilized the darkness of night and heavy rains to penetrate its still porous defenses and wreck havoc, rising up to slay the Jurchen whenever lightning flashed across the sky, then dissolving in darkness until the next illuminating shaft. Unable to discriminate friend and foe, the Jurchen slew each other. Ravaged by these highly resourceful measures, inundated by heavy rain and the swollen river, and threatened by Yüeh Fei on his flank, Wu Shu finally abandoned the siege and returned east.

Some 20,000 defenders thus managed to defeat two consecutive extended assaults, first by a 30,000-man contingent, then by a 100,000-man expeditionary force. Symbolic of how he anticipated and manipulated the enemy through unorthodox techniques as advocated in the *Art of War* and practiced by Chu-ko Liang, at one point Liu Ch'i even opened a gate and tempted them to enter, but fearing a trap none had the courage to do so. He thus fully exploited his limited means and never squandered the strength of his troops while unifying them and the inhabitants. This stalemate, coupled with subsequent victories in the west, so completely blunted the Jurchen invasion that they reverted to the coercive threats and peace talks which ironically succeeded in achieving most of their initial objectives, including the consolidation of the territory so recently yielded.

Appended to a *Wu-ching Tsung-yao* section entitled "Don't Eat Armies Acting as Bait" is a single example intended to be a cautionary illustration.[35] During the Later Wei, government forces confronted by a large band of brigands abandoned their camp upon learning of the enemy's approach, but not before first poisoning a large quantity of wine that was left behind. After the brigands entered the deserted camp and joyfully drank it, the Wei commander mounted a sudden strike and captured more than 10,000 sickened troops.

Subsequently, the Ming dynasty *Yün-ch'ou Kang-mu* incorporated a brief section on the advantages of poison with three illustrations, including the interesting case of P'eng Yüeh who reportedly introduced poison into Ch'u's encampment during the battle to establish the Han by infusing it into provisions presumably destined for their own use at Ying-yang. After the ten supply wagons were seized, some 70 to 80 percent of the enemy who consumed the grain fell seriously ill and died. Meanwhile, P'eng transported tons of untainted supplies to the original destination.[36]

Finally, Yeh asserts that Chu-ko Liang also resorted to drugging enemy troops who had ostensibly surrendered but were actually plotting to mount an internal response in conjunction with an external night attack. Concealed in the wine, the drugs threw them into a stupor, thwarting their plot and allowing the raiders, who were anticipated, to be easily caught.[37]

## DETECTING POISON AND LOCATING SOURCES

Aquatic warfare often being directed to cutting off water supplies and poisoning sources,[38] from the T'ang dynasty onward it was emphasized that reconnaissance should be undertaken to find water and areas of trees and grass when about to encamp.[39] (Similar criteria of course also applied to cities under attack, with troops in all circumstances always needing additional water for protection and fire-fighting purposes.)[40] Lacking streams, ponds, and other immediately visible sources, more subtle indications had to be zealously pursued to discover concealed springs or where wells might be sunk, especially on arid terrain and salty ground. These include trails frequented by local animals such as cows, horses, and sheep, and noting places where birds congregate.[41] Wells should be dug in areas heavily covered by reeds and marsh grass, where ants swarm,[42] and even where camels paw the ground[43] on the assumption they can sense the presence of water. Finally, as the historical illustrations have shown, troops can carry pieces of ice in the winter to slake their thirst[44] and water can be piped in from mountainous areas by connecting large-diameter bamboo poles whose interior sections have been properly cleared, the end then being heated to induce suction.[45]

More fundamentally, in the Warring States period Wu-tzu stressed measure and constraint in movement and advocated carefully investigating the terrain, much in accord with Sun-tzu's emphasis upon configurations of terrain and their potential dangers and advantages. Thereafter, in summarizing the essential rules for choosing a camp site, the *T'ung Tien* and then the *Wu-ching Tsung-yao* not only advise thoroughly scouting the terrain so as to avoid entrapping configurations,[46] but also several issues related to water. Areas that might be flooded,[47] were already soaked with stagnant water, were located where the enemy might employ poison, and even salt marshes should all be shunned.

On a much vaster scale, China's many lakes, rivers, and streams naturally provided the most visible and readily available water sources. Furthermore, in pondering the vital quest for potable water, Sun Pin concluded, "If an army drinks from flowing water, it is water that will sustain life and they cannot be attacked. If an army drinks stagnant water, it is water that will result in death and they can be attacked."[48] However, contrary to Sun Pin's observation, the Battle of Yü-lin had already shown that flowing water could be poisoned. Therefore, more reliable criteria must have quickly evolved, but the earliest set is found in the Sung dynasty *Hu-ch'ien Ching*.[49]

> Whenever encamping the army, if the river's flow is clear, this is the best drinking water. When its flow is yellow and turbid with sand, this is the next best. When it flows black, this is the least acceptable drinking water. However, if the river's flow should cease, do not drink it.
>
> If the river flows past the enemy's position upstream, do not drink it. If the river's flow occasionally has black streams in the midst, marking poison, do not drink it or death will result. If the river is filled with manure and refuse, do not drink it or illness will result. When there are human corpses or the bodies of dogs and swine in the river, do not drink it.
>
> If there is no potable water, you should dig a well at the side of the river because the army must have water whenever it encamps, even if only temporarily.

Shortly thereafter, the *Wu-ching Tsung-yao* provided a final, somewhat expanded set of measures in a brief section entitled "Methods for Defending against Poison":

> Whenever an expeditionary army nears enemy territory, the commander in chief should issue orders in advance to the officers on how to prevent poisoning. Whenever you acquire food or drink the enemy has left behind, you must not recklessly consume it. The liquor, meat, dried foodstuffs, pickled items, grain, and beans sold by the ordinary stalls must also be carefully examined before consumption.
>
> Now there are five means for preventing poisoning:
>
> First, when you initially occupy enemy territory, do not drink from their wells and springs for fear that they may have placed poison in them.
>
> Second, be very fearful that they have clandestinely put poison upstream in spring water that flows out from within the enemy's perimeter.
>
> Third, [avoid] water that doesn't flow.

Fourth, during the summer flood season when the even the small streams and ponds overflow from incessant rain, if the color is black and there is foam floating upon the water, or red and tastes salty, or muddy and tastes bitter, [don't drink it].

Fifth, the area has always had fierce and poisonous things such as poisonous grass, poisonous trees, fierce bugs, fierce snakes, or reptiles and water creatures such as the fabled, sand spitting tortoises: you must carefully investigate them and announce their presence in order to assiduously prevent misfortune.

In the context of ever intensifying warfare and interminable sieges that saw noxious and fetid substances routinely employed, such knowledge could prove crucial to the army's survival.[50] Nevertheless, apart from the *Wu Pien*, subsequent texts surprisingly fail to reiterate most of these concerns and measures, though they sometimes mention the importance of securing water supplies with protective walls and strong points.[51]

# 11

# Illustrative Sieges

D ue to their location, critical cities such as T'ai-yüan, Hsiang-yang, Chung-li, and K'ai-feng were repeatedly attacked over the centuries, generally by fire, often by water, sometimes by both since most of them evolved along rivers and lakes. Although the official dynastic histories barely mention these clashes despite the horrific toll in life and property, some were historically so momentous or dramatic as to demand extended coverage before becoming the core for stories and legends. A few can even be glimpsed through chronicles penned by the participants, writings which further illuminate and sometimes contradict the depictions preserved in historical works and theoretical manuals. The very few selections that follow, although focusing upon incendiary and aquatic measures, concretely illustrate the nature of these titanic clashes as well as many of the tactics, techniques, and types of equipment utilized, often in painfully compelling fashion.[1]

The history of siegecraft in China assuredly dates back to the neolithic period. Although the Shang constructed opulent capitals and a few miniature border copies, and contemporary cultures at San-hsing-tui and Ch'eng-tu also developed urban centers with populations of 80,000 or more, most Shang and then Chou towns were inhabited by only a few thousand residents. However, as populations grew, agriculture expanded, and crafts production increased, towns burgeoned in size and complexity, resulting in class differentiation, occupational distinctions, permanent military forces, and increasingly common and more massive walls.

Nevertheless, it wasn't until the individual Chou states began to disdain central authority and develop into self-assertive power centers toward the end of the Western Chou that major cities with populations exceeding 100,000 appeared and secondary cities became common. Increasing prosperity and the gradual accumulation of wealth concurrently transformed them from political and sometime military centers into economic hubs.

This slow process did not significantly accelerate until well into the Spring and Autumn period (722–481) when the individual states, suddenly finding themselves enveloped by predatory warfare, were forced to stress economic development just to fund the military forces necessary to survive. In consequence, the nature of warfare radically changed because the sparsely populated terrain of earlier eras, which could easily be traversed without encountering any cites, towns, or military obstacles, was rapidly being transformed. In the Shang and early Chou, localized conflicts and wars with peripheral peoples rarely had to confront the issue of urban assault except when absolutely necessary to destroy an enemy's military forces or administrative center.

Once cities and towns became the focus of economic activity, repositories of material wealth, military garrisons, and the locus for warehouses containing provisions and military goods, their status altered dramatically. Because the technology of rammed earth wall and conjoined moat construction far outpaced that of assault techniques until the mid-Warring States, and the wide walls allowed multiple ranks of soldiers to rain archery fire and stones down upon the attackers, the defenders enjoyed an almost insurmountable advantage and could, barring the outbreak of rampant disease, withstand a lengthy siege with impunity if they were well provisioned and had access to water supplies.

Not surprisingly, given the cost in men and materials, sieges and citadel assaults often debilitated the aggressor as much as the defender, tempting third parties to exploit the ensuing weakness. Sun-tzu accordingly disparaged them as the lowest form of warfare:

> The tactic of attacking fortified cities is adopted only when unavoidable. Preparing large movable protective shields, armored assault wagons, and other equipment and devices will require three months. Building earthworks will require another three months to complete. If the general cannot overcome his impatience, but instead launches an assault wherein his men swarm over the walls like ants, he will kill one-third of his officers and troops and the city will still not be taken. This is the disaster that results from attacking fortified cities.

Based upon this passage, Sun-tzu's admonition has frequently been incorrectly simplified to the dictum "do not attack cities" or "avoid urban warfare." However, it should be read in conjunction with his pronouncement that "The highest realization of warfare is to attack the enemy's plans; next is to attack their alliances; and the lowest is to attack their fortified cities." Recently recovered textual fragments confirm he intended to stress that the cost should be weighed against the gains. Therefore, even cities that might be subjugated, unless they can be held or will constitute a threat after being bypassed, can and should be ignored.

As concerted efforts were made to open lands for cultivation, the Warring States witnessed accelerated economic and administrative developments and a surge in population. Steps to improve the people's welfare, the foundation of any effective state or army, were increasingly implemented. Warfare escalated dramatically, towns and cities expanded greatly, and the techniques of siegecraft evolved rapidly. Fortified towns, strongpoints, border defenses, and eventually substantial state walls multiplied, quickly coming to frustrate and obstruct military movements. Even though Sun-tzu's admonition would be cited ever afterward, any reluctance to mounting sieges and massive assaults quickly diminished. Sun Pin accordingly categorized cities for assault purposes as "male" and "female," the latter being strategically weaker and therefore more susceptible to attack, but counseled that assaults on the former should be avoided.

As seen from tactical discussions in the *Wei Liao-tzu*, determining a particular city's fate became a question of feasibility and tactical value:

> When the troops have assembled at the enemy's border and the general has arrived, the army should penetrate deeply into their territory, sever their roads, and occupy their large cities and large towns. If you occupy the terrain around a city or town and sever the various roads about it, follow up by attacking the city itself.
>
> If the territory is vast but the cities small, you must first occupy their land. If the cities are large but the land narrow, you must first attack their cities. If the country is vast and the populace few, isolate their strategic points. If the land is confined but the people numerous, construct high mounds in order to overlook them.

In consonance with the criteria embodied in the *Mo-tzu*, many of the military writings from the late Warring States onward analyze the various factors that render cities vulnerable to attack and promulgate guidelines such as these from the *Wei Liao-tzu*:

> When the general is light, the fortifications low, and the people's minds unstable, they can be attacked. If the general is weighty and the fortifications are high but the masses are afraid, they can be encircled. In general, whenever you encircle someone, you must provide them with a prospect for some minor advantage, causing them to become weaker day by day. Then the defenders will be forced to reduce their rations until they have nothing to eat.
>
> When their masses fight with each other at night they are terrified. If the masses avoid their work they have become disaffected. If they just wait for others to come and rescue them, and when the time for battle arrives they are tense, they have

all lost their will and are dispirited. Dispirit defeats an army, distorted plans defeat a state.

If the enemy's generals and armies are unable to believe in each other, the officers and troops unable to be in harmony, and there are those unaffected by punishments, we will defeat them. Before the rescue party has arrived, the city will have already surrendered.

If fords and bridges have not yet been constructed, strategic barriers not yet repaired, dangerous points in the city walls not yet fortified, and the iron caltrops not yet set out, then even though they have a fortified city, they do not have any defense!

If the troops from distant forts have not yet entered the city nor the border guards and forces in other states yet returned, then even though they have men, they do not have any men! If the six domesticated animals have not yet been herded in, the five grains not yet harvested, the wealth and materials for use not yet collected, then even though they have resources, they do not have any resources! Now when a city is empty and void and its resources are exhausted, we should take advantage of this vacuity to attack them.

Many later texts include extensive passages on sieges and fortified defenses, the defender's psychology, and criteria for calculating whether a defense can realistically be mounted or a city assaulted, examined from the perspective of aggressors and defenders. Essentially, if preparations have been made, the defenders are in good spirit, provisions ample, and prospects for rescue good, the city should be defended or should not be attacked. Cities that offer a defensible stronghold should be particularly targeted, but when defeat is inevitable, surrender may be the only course.

The tactics, techniques, and siege equipment developed during the Warring States period and thereafter, coupled with subversive methods and pressure tactics, made it possible to frequently, but not invariably, subjugate cities in weeks or less. After the establishment of the Ch'in dynasty, whether in conflicts with invading steppe powers or in the interminable wars of dynastic succession and the millenarian revolts that plagued the land, despite occasional reluctance to risk becoming entangled in prolonged sieges, the main questions were when and how to attack, not whether. Discussions of siegecraft and defense therefore received extensive coverage in the great military compendiums, and a specialized work, *Records of City Defense,* based upon actual defensive experiences early in the Southern Sung, in which the authors advocate going out to attack the besiegers when opportunities arise rather than remaining statically ensconced, was well studied thereafter.

## THE SIEGE OF YÜ-PI (JADE CLIFF)

Internal discord within mighty Northern Wei sundered it into two still potent segments essentially east and west of the Yellow River's downward course in Shanhsi in A.D. 534, creating a heritage of strife that lasted until their successors were finally reunified as the Sui. Almost immediately Eastern Wei dominated by Kao Huan, the powerful general whose political machinations had forced the split, penetrated the T'ung-kuan Pass and briefly smashed into Western Wei's rugged territory before they were repulsed and even lost their capital of Luoyang. However, finality never defined their conflicts for Kao soon led a resurgence which regained their earlier boundaries before embarking on a generally aggressive course marked by periods of inactivity.

The brief but intense siege of Yü-pi in 546, a cliff-side citadel constructed in the lower portion of the Fen River basin around 538 to prevent comparatively richer Eastern Wei from exploiting the river corridor to transport troops and supplies from the northeast into the west's heartland, ranks as one of the more famous in Chinese history.[2] (An earlier attempt to take it in the tenth month of 542 had to be abandoned after an unexpected heavy snowfall isolated Eastern Wei's troops and many perished from hunger and the cold.)[3] According to the *Tzu-chih T'ung-chien's* well-known account, Kao Huan mobilized his forces at T'ai-yüan (Chin-yang) in the eighth month of 546 and succeeded in surrounding Yü-pi in the ninth, his encampments stretching back for several tens of *li*.[4] Although he initially hoped to provoke the defenders into waging battle on open terrain, Yü-pi's experienced commander Wei Hsiao-kuan well realized the tactical advantages offered by their bastion's impregnability and therefore steadfastly refused to needlessly sacrifice his troops.

Even while undertaking continuous, fervent assaults upon the citadel, Kao severed its water source by diverting the supply channel originating in the nearby Fen River. (This frequently decisive measure apparently proved no more than an inconvenience since no reports of extreme thirst or troops dying from dehydration have been preserved.) Next, when repeated attacks failed to penetrate Yü-pi's defenses, Kao commenced the construction of an earthen mound high enough to overlook the walls and provide a direct line of fire into the citadel. However, the determined defenders easily increased the height of their own fortifications because the earthen mound had been shortsightedly undertaken opposite two nearly contiguous gate towers, allowing timbers to be lashed between them and an ever higher superstructure to be erected above. Thwarted and frustrated, Kao disgustedly exclaimed that if they were going to build towers that reached to heaven, he would dig into the earth to seize them.

In accord with his brusque pronouncement, Kao then had ten tunnels started, either on the south or north side. (The terrain to the south was more conducive, but that on the north where the cliffs were supposedly the steepest apparently cohered with martial prognostications derived from the calendrical cycle of days.)[5] In response, Wei Hsiao-kuan had a long trench cut parallel to and within the city wall to intercept their projected path so that when Kao's miners unintentionally broke into the trench, the defenders immediately vanquished them. Faggots and other flammables that were maintained in readiness were also piled at the mouth of their tunnels and an incendiary-based gas attack mounted upon any troops remaining in them or attempting to penetrate the citadel. Large bellows, an ancient technique, propelled the smoke and noxious gasses into the tunnels, quickly choking and burning the enemy.

Kao Huan next brought up assault wagons that proved highly effective against the relatively new earthen walls and could not be thwarted by portable shields or other defensive measures. However, Wei Hsiao-kuan ingeniously had large cloth shields sewn together and deployed under tension between poles outside the wall to absorb the impulse of the battering rams. Once again temporarily stymied, Kao resorted to pine and hempen torches soaked in oil and mounted on long poles to try to set the cloth shields and still resilient towers afire. His countermeasure in turn prompted Wei to fabricate especially long-handled blades which were employed to slice off the burning torches, dropping them harmlessly to the ground.

Kao finally turned to persuasion, dispatching an emissary who proffered munificent rewards while stressing the hopelessness of their situation, but he was rebuffed by Wei Hsiao-kuan, who noted it was still early and they had ample supplies. An announcement was then shot into the camp offering great rewards to anyone who assassinated Wei, but he calmly returned it with his own annotation that a similar reward would be paid to anyone who would murder Kao Huan. (Some texts assert that coercion was also employed, Wei Hsiao-kuan's captured younger brother being threatened with execution if they refused to surrender.)[6]

Kao then resorted to the classic technique of undermining the walls once his assault carts and extemporaneous efforts to incinerate the cloth shields had been thwarted. Twenty-one tunnels, an odd number hardly divisible by four, were supposedly undertaken from all four sides and apparently succeeded in causing portions of the wall to collapse when the wooden pillars were set ablaze.[7] However, the defenders quickly erected stopgap wooden palisades in the openings, preventing any incursions. Completely frustrated and suffering from recurrent illness, Kao Huan abandoned the siege in the eleventh month after just fifty days. Not only was their failure a major blow to Eastern Wei's power and Kao Huan's personal prestige as its de facto ruler, some 70,000 troops or about 40 to 50 percent of their campaign force fell from wounds and illness.[8]

Incendiary measures were thus employed by both the aggressors and defenders at this famous siege in classic and innovative ways. Surprisingly, incendiary arrows were apparently not used against the citadel's interior or the cloth screens, nor are trebuchets even mentioned though they might have been conveniently ferried downstream. The potential exploitation of the Fen River's current for such purposes clearly necessitated the erection of a formidable citadel at Yü-pi or some other strategically advantageous position.

## HOU CHING AND THE SIEGE OF CHIEN-K'ANG

Hou Ching's remarkable saga lasted just over five years, from the first month of 547 through his death in the fourth month of 552, making it one of the longest accounts in the *Tzu-chih T'ung-chien*.[9] Moreover, the detail provided about the siege's effects on the populace, the maneuvering involved, and the behavior and motivations of the principal actors rank it among the work's most intriguing and illuminating episodes. In addition to nearly continuous human-wave attacks, a wide array of assault techniques were utilized over the course of the siege, including earthen mounds, tunneling, incendiary measures, wooden donkeys, and even flooding near the end. Hou Ching also employed psychological warfare, duplicity, and spying to considerable advantage while Liang's forces were plagued by disarray, cowardice, and subversion.

Prompted by his long-standing conflict with Kao Huan's son who acceded to the pinnacle of military power in Eastern Wei at the start of 547, Hou Ching exploited his expansive base south of the Yellow River to effect a temporary allegiance with Wei's western counterpart. However, under pressure from the former's forces he was compelled to withdraw, escaping only when Western Wei's armies prompted Eastern Wei's retreat, leaving Ying-ch'uan to Wang Ssu-cheng where a lengthy siege would soon unfold. Hou then nominally submitted to Liang, tempting the emperor with the immediate possession of thirteen contiguous provinces and prospects for inducing two others to revolt. As the emperor had recently dreamt that this territory would be offered to him, he dismissed numerous warnings and accepted Hou's proposal, incorporating him into the administrative hierarchy while dispatching substantial military forces to effect the area's consolidation. (Hou was widely noted as being "little experienced in handling troops, but licentious, sneaky, and difficult to fathom"[10] as well as crafty and perverse, though he confounded his critics with his clever memorializing and by skillfully employing spies.)

Liang's efforts not only proved ineffectual because of their trepidation and lack of supplies but also resulted in significant casualties and Hou himself was forced to flee back south of the Huai River. Accompanied by just a small personal contingent he ventured to Shou-yang where he managed to persuade the local administrator to admit him before seizing control of the city. As Easter Wei had now, early in 548, recovered the territory Hou had previously controlled, much to his dismay its ruler proposed the resumption of long-standing harmonious relations with Liang. The proposal was accepted despite Hou vehemently advocating further aggressive actions and widespread concern in the court that Wei's peace overtures were simply a ploy to drive Hou to revolt. Moreover, despite Hou's virtually destitute status, perhaps because of his prophetic dream the emperor continued to treat him generously in the face of criticism and numerous warnings. The emperor not only satisfied most of his requests but even provided skilled metal smiths to facilitate local weapons production, truly sowing the seeds of his own destruction.

Long before the peace covenant was finalized in the fifth month, Hou began preparing his organization for a revolt, even grouping the women and children into functional companies. In contrast, having enjoyed nearly five decades of peace, Liang was militarily disorganized and logistically unprepared. Moreover, the emperor's refusal to recognize Hou

Ching's potential threat prevented his officials from undertaking the most basic preparations. (Before Hou revolted, Chu Yi dismissed all such reports as implausible, even one from a potential co-conspirator whom Hou had futilely tried to recruit.)

When they became encircled the populace had to be sustained by the foodstuffs on hand, 400,000 pecks of grain for 100,00 people, including 20,000 mailed warriors. Some 80 to 90 percent eventually perished from hunger, illness, and wounds, only 4,000 soldiers remaining to face the final onslaught just six months later.[11] The *Tzu-chih T'ung-chien* provides a remarkable description of the people's misery, emphasizing that no salt, fish, or fodder had been stockpiled, unburied bodies were piled everywhere, and they were reduced to eating horses, cats, rats, lichen, and even each other.[12]

At the inception of his uprising Hou's ostensible justification was purging the court of corruption and perversity, his slogan being "cast out the three worms" (high officials who were monopolizing power), but as the siege of Yang-chien progressed he expanded his proclaimed objectives to rooting out the heinous inequities of imperial government, thereby at least nominally embracing a populist viewpoint.[13] To bolster his forces he generously rewarded slaves and bondservants who defected, and even though he treated much of the populace brutally, his adherents still increased.

Having decided to revolt, Hou sought out internal allies to improve his chances for success, choosing the emperor's debauched nephew Hsiao Cheng-te who, though somewhat disgraced, still enjoyed reasonable prestige and had been nurturing a private army. When Hou commenced his drive to seize the throne in the tenth month with two minor victories, the emperor heedlessly exclaimed that "he would defeat him as easily as striking him with a whip" though he did depute significant imperial forces to effect the task. Compelled to prematurely thrust toward the capital, Hou exploited two ruses to facilitate his field movements, first pretending to be going on a hunting expedition and then verbally feinting toward Ho-fei while actually moving toward the Yangtze River.

Although his army easily took Ch'iao-chou and then Li-yang, Hou's paltry forces were highly vulnerable to attack, the theoretically impassable Yangtze remained to be crossed, and the key defensive strongpoint of Ts'ai-shih had to be subjugated. As advisors in both his own and the imperial camps pointed out, a mere 2,000 men dispatched to Ts'ai-shih and Shou-yang could obstruct and cut him off. However, the court's chief miscreant, Chu Yi, who had come to monopolize power as the emperor withdrew to study Buddhism, adamantly protested that it was unimaginable that Hou Ching would cross the Yangtze, thereby thwarting the implementation of the minimal, prudent measures that could have prevented the catastrophe.[14]

The Yangtze crossing was accomplished when Cheng-te, who had ironically been put in charge of the area's defensive efforts, provided dozens of boats that had purportedly been transporting firewood. At that moment Hou's army still amounted to a minuscule 8,000 men and just 400 horses, still easily crushed with but the slightest coordinated effort. The next major obstacle was a pontoon bridge across the Ch'in-huai River, a smaller river that blocked access to Chien-k'ang itself. Cheng-te persuaded the heir apparent not to disable the bridge well in advance by claiming it would upset the people. Then, at the last moment when the local commander succeeded in temporarily severing the bridge by removing one of the large boats, Cheng-te's own men replaced it after the iron masks of the onrushing attackers scared all the defenders away, virtually ensuring Hou's subsequent victory.

Panic ensued in the city, and the garrisons at the gates and detached fortresses, except for the Eastern Warehouse, abandoned their posts and fled, giving Hou unfettered access to the outer quarters where Cheng-te opened the gates to them. To penetrate the defenses of the inner citadel incendiary measures were first employed against three of the gates, setting them afire. However, Yang K'an (who essentially commanded the defenses) had holes drilled from above the gates and poured water down, damping the fires, but they weren't extinguished until long after the heir apparent used his personal valuables to motivate men to go over the walls and finish the task. More direct attacks were also repulsed with long spears thrust through holes in the gates. Meanwhile, Hou's bowmen exploited the palace buildings outside the citadel as vantage points.

In revenge, the heir apparent set the eastern palace afire where Hou was holding festivities that night, destroying its library and piquing him into setting other important structures afire in turn. Determined to conquer the isolated citadel, Hou then had several hundred wooden donkeys built but they were easily destroyed by stones hurtling down through their roofs. Hou immediately resorted to employing more sharply peaked versions which easily shed the rocks dropped upon them, prompting the defenders to employ "pheasant tail" torches soaked with lard and wax to incinerate them all.[15] When these efforts failed, Hou had a mobile tower some 100 feet high constructed, but it proved too heavy for the soft ground and tilted over at the edge of the moat, just as Yang K'an had predicted.

Finding himself unexpectedly entangled in a protracted siege because repeated assaults had produced only numerous casualties, Hou had a countervailing wall constructed. Meanwhile, in defiance of Yang K'an's analysis that their numbers were insufficient to accomplish anything yet too great for an orderly withdrawal across the narrow bridge, a force of 1,000 sallied forth only to collapse upon encountering the enemy and perish in the ensuing chaos. (In hindsight Yang's analysis seems prophetic but such sallies, by throwing men onto Suntzu's "fatal terrain," succeeded in similar circumstances many times. However, Yang may have had a better sense of the men's spirit and commitment.)

Facilitated by subversives, in the eleventh month a small force attacked and took the Eastern Warehouse with three days of effort. Even though it contained ample food supplies, as the siege had grown prolonged Hou had relaxed the strict restraints previously keeping his troops in check so as to stem dissension and ameliorate food shortages within his camp. This resulted in widespread plundering which left the people naked and so bereft of food that half of them perished. He then had two earthen hills undertaken to the east and west, coercing the inhabitants into laboring on the mounds. Any of the weak and old who performed inadequately were simply slain and their bodies added to the mounds, yet too afraid to hide, the people continued to come forth.

All the defenders within the citadel, including the heir apparent, fervently worked at constructing counter-mounds capped by forty-foot superstructures which they protected with cloth shields and staffed with 2,000 specially armored troops who battled Hou's forces day and night. Heavy rain collapsed at least one of the inner citadel mounds, allowing the enemy to exploit their vantage point and penetrate the city. However, Yang K'an thwarted their advance by setting the nearby city on fire and hastily erecting an inner wall.

By this time armies were being mobilized in the hinterland to rescue Yang-chien but they proved too incompetent, cowardly, and disorganized to achieve more than precipitous disasters even though most of these same troops would eventually oust Hou Ching after Yang-chien's conquest. However, one contingent did eventually manage to cut off Hou's access to the Eastern Warehouse and thus his vital grain supply.

Numerous, unusually massive assault engines were again constructed including mobile versions some forty feet high which rolled across the filled-in moats on up to twenty wheels. Eventually they managed to set the southeastern tower afire with incendiary wagons, but the defenders created a barricade of earth within the city that finally stopped the fire from spreading before it could be extinguished. Hou exploited the consequent confusion to initiate tunneling efforts that almost succeeded in collapsing the walls before being discovered. Further troop penetration was then blocked by a hastily constructed semi-circular interior wall and incendiary measures were employed to burn the assault equipment and to gas anyone in the remnant tunnels.

Although defections continued in Liang, the defenders managed to undermine Hou's earthen mounds so that the outer portions collapsed, inflicting heavy casualties, and then run flying bridges out to the remnants, scaring off the enemy. Finally they used pheasant-tail torches to set the eastern mound's wooden superstructure afire, killing all those trapped within. Hou soon abandoned the mounds, but not before burning the remaining assault equipment to prevent it from being used against them.

To break their stalemate, Hou then implemented a defector's suggestion that water from the Hsüan-wu (Mysterious Martial) Lake to the north be redirected to inundate the citadel, resulting in several feet of water in front of the main entrance and presumably some leaking into the inner city. However, since aquatic attacks require time to be effective while his supplies had been cut off, Hou resorted to proposing peace, a ploy first warned against in the *Art of War*. He then exploited Liang's anxiety to have the blocking army and another external threatening force shifted away before procrastinating with excuses about having no place to go, or the weather having become too hot, before breaking the accord and simply recommencing the attack.

Shortly thereafter a valiant rescue attempt failed due to lack of coordination, resulting in 5,000 corpses being displayed in front of the citadel as a warning.[16] Hou soon broke through the walls about the main entrance, allowing the water to pour into the city before mounting multiple follow-on attacks. However, the crushing blow was a midnight betrayal that let the enemy over the walls, ending the siege and Emperor Wu's lengthy reign. Momentarily successful and apparently poised to establish his own dynasty, Hou was in turn soon driven out by Liang's previously ineffective armies and eventually perished in the east in 552, ending another saga which merely saw warfare, including incendiary measures, pointlessly decimate the countryside and immerse the ill-fated populace in unimaginable misery.

## THE CLASH AT CH'ENG-TU

The remote southwestern area of Yün-nan, an area of high mountains with interspersed plains, was populated by six independent tribal peoples who were constantly stimulated by, and frequently in conflict with, the kingdoms of both China and Tibet for centuries. Just before the middle of the eighth century they were essentially welded into a single confederation centered around the strong fortified city of Ta-li which, situated on a plain at 7,000 feet, was virtually impregnable to Chinese attack, though not Tibetan campaigns. From 859 through 866, just as the T'ang was disintegrating, Nan-chao abandoned its subservient attitude to dramatically challenge China's dominance of Annam (Northern Vietnam). Its campaigns penetrated the incredibly rough terrain as far as Hanoi which they seized and briefly held despite strong T'ang fortification measures. However, that phase of the conflict finally concluded with a Chinese victory in 866.

Because of its strategic position to the southwest, Nan-chao inherently posed a threat to loosely integrated Szechuan, making the administrative and command staffing there critical, particularly if attacks upon the T'ang capital of Ch'ang-an were to be averted. Although many experienced commanders served in Szechuan over the decades, their achievements varied and other administrators often proved corrupt or incompetent. Renewed conflict broke out between Nan-chao and imperial China in 869–870 when a local commander deliberately provoked a clash which he believed would yield an easy victory and gain him increased recognition. However, once provoked, Nan-chao's enraged forces continuously advanced upon the capital of Ch'eng-tu where tens of thousands of terrified people had already taken refuge.[17] Just the lack of preparation would have made Ch'eng-tu untenable, but this same commander discouraged rescue forces from approaching in order to comparatively mitigate his responsibility in the now certain defeat.

Shortly after a subcommander's planned betrayal of the city—to be initiated by setting the armory afire—was thwarted, Nan-chao's troops mounted their first serious assault upon the city by attacking on all four sides with cloud ladders. However, the attackers were repulsed by hooking and holding the ladders close to the walls with long staffs while burning oil was poured down, incinerating them all. An elite defensive force that sallied forth also managed to slay 2,000 enemy soldiers and burn some 3,000 assault devices, an astounding number. Their success stimulated the army's morale and the generous reward they received incited others to volunteer for similarly hazardous forays.

Several days later Nan-chao's troops commenced another assault under the protective cover of shields fabricated with reeds torn from the local residences which were then soaked in water and bent into a curved protective shape. Thereafter, neither arrows, stones, or incendiaries could prevent them from excavating the wall's foundation. Since the walls were not very formidable, the commander resorted to dripping molten iron that had been heated in portable stoves atop the walls, a method well recorded in the T'ang military compendia.

A few weeks later approaching T'ang forces finally frightened Nan-chao's armies into withdrawing, though they burned their assault equipment before departing. Thereafter, the local populace was instructed in the art of building fortifications, erecting external walls to protect the vital gates, flooding the area contained within these exterior walls, and exploiting projective strong points. Because Szechuan always remained the last refuge of T'ang emperors and could no longer be neglected because of its strategic value, the intent was to strengthen Ch'eng-tu in the same way as Hanoi which had been fortified a few years earlier and was finally proving an effective bastion in withstanding Nan-chao incursions.

## THE SIEGE OF T'AI-YÜAN, A.D. 1126

An unusual instance of employing incendiaries in siege defense arose at the relatively isolated prefectural capital of T'ai-yüan in 1126 over the course of its 260-day ordeal.[18] Having extinguished the Liao dynasty, at the end of A.D. 1125 the Jurchen launched a two-pronged offensive into Sung China by fielding approximately 60,000 men in each thrust. The western component achieved early victories over disaffected Sung troops until unexpectedly becoming entangled at T'ai-yüan when fervent assaults in the twelfth month failed to conquer it, compelling them to undertake a full-scale siege effort. While the Western Jurchen component beat back Sung rescue forces, the eastern thrust vanquished several defensive contingents, prompting the terrified emperor to flee southward as the conflict continued into 1126.

Having encountered surprisingly determined local opposition deep in enemy territory and running short of supplies, the Jurchen disdainfully granted the eager Sung a new peace treaty. However, the siege of T'ai-yüan continued unabated even though the emperor had included it among the three prefectural towns sacrificed to cement the accord because T'ai-yüan's defenders contemptuously rejected imperial edicts to submit. Their stubbornness compelled the emperor to dispatch rescue forces in the third month of 1126 which, being disunified and deliberately misled by false information, were severely defeated, allowing the Jurchen to continue their accretional expansion in T'ai-yüan's vicinity.

Another massive, 150,000-man rescue effort precipitously dispatched in the sixth month suffered devastating defeats and enormous casualties, because command authority had been segmented among four generals. Meanwhile, the Jurchen employed a variety of assault methods at T'ai-yüan, including the usual one of attempting to fill in the moat so that their siege engines could approach the walls. To thwart their attempt, one of the two defensive commanders, Wang Ping (who is otherwise unknown) had holes drilled in the wall in the area of the enemy's efforts so as to deploy incendiary countermeasures.

The only description of their respective methodologies is somewhat puzzling, but still worth recounting. The Jurchen proceeded by dropping large pieces of firewood into the moat, covering them with grass mats, and finally layering them with dirt to create the necessary roadbed. Presumably the water level of the moat would be somewhat below the embankment, so part of the wooden base would be exposed and therefore susceptible to incendiaries, though the portion below the water line would be impervious to fire. However, the text asserts that when the defenders put floating oil lamps onto the water through the holes drilled in the walls and propelled them to the bridgeway, the "lamps sought out the wood," setting it afire. The defenders then pumped the bellows inserted in the holes, raising the temperature until a great blaze resulted.

In all probability, it was the wood and grass matting above the water line that was ignited, but it is also possible that the Jurchen engineers were erecting some sort of coffer dam with the heavy firewood so that a relatively dry channel resulted in the middle in which the straw would burn. (A coffer dam or relatively solid sides would be necessary to prevent the wood from simply spreading to the side as more weight was added, even floating up and away.) Whatever the crux, these counterattacks clearly stopped the assault, though eventually the city succumbed in fierce alley fighting in the ninth month of 1126 after having been constantly pounded by large trebuchets and the starving populace had been reduced to eating each other after having exhausted every edible piece of material.

## THE SIEGE OF TE-AN, A.D. 1127–1132

The extant work known as the *Shou-ch'eng Lu* integrates three separate pieces, the first two being Ch'en Kuei's ruminations (written 1140) on the Sung's recent city collapses and his conclusions from the defense he conducted at Te-an in 1127 which successfully withstood a five-year Jurchen attack, and the third T'ang Shou's retrospective, semi-chronological account of important aspects and factors in that famous siege. Assuming the *Mo-tzu* poliorcetic chapters never comprised a separate work, Ch'en's two chapters constitute the first defensive monograph in Chinese history. Moreover, despite the effete negativity of the Southern Sung, these works (and possibly another as well) were combined under the present title and designated as a text for military defense in 1172, thereby establishing their value and ensuring their influence.

Several aspects of the siege of Te-an illustrate the incendiary practices early in the twelfth century when the Jurchen overwhelmed the Sung in 1127, forcing the remnants southward to establish the Southern Sung which even then remained threatened and had to battle, however reluctantly, to survive. In his observations on the Sung failure at K'ai-feng and other cities, Ch'en already advocated new ways of fortification, defense in depth, and the adoption of an active stance incorporating appropriately timed sallies to inflict casualties, destroy provisions and equipment, and generally keep the enemy off balance rather than passively await either rescue or extinction.[19] From his experience at Te-an he concluded that erecting wooden "deer horn" palisades outside the main fortifications was useless because they provided inadequate protection against crossbows and were easily burnt in a conducive wind.[20]

However, it is T'ang Shou's recounting of their respective incendiary practices in his *Te-an Shou-yü Lu* which is particularly valuable.[21] Numerous attempts were made to set the gates afire by piling firewood and straw against them, requiring a prompt response to extinguish them. More proactively, such flammable materials as firewood and straw were also ignited with incendiary arrows at a distance of at least ten paces while they were still being openly transported. Incendiary arrows were also successfully employed to ignite the dry materials being piled in the defensive ditches, resulting in a fire so intense it couldn't be extinguished despite enemy efforts for two days, though many of the local women and children enslaved for the work also perished. However, the unremitting battle between offense and defense was far more complex because the Jurchen assault engines were so well protected with leather and hemp that neither ordinary arrows nor smoke or fire could penetrate their covering. The defenders therefore had to use poles and probes to tear the covering apart preliminary to employing incendiaries.

In one sequence the Jurchen utilized several incendiary techniques during the day to attack multiple gates with simple torches from under the cover of their assault wagons (wooden donkeys) but were repelled by a combination of poles, arrows, bolts, and stones. In the middle of the night they exploited the darkness to remount the attack with cloud ladders on all four sides but upon being repulsed again attempted to burn the gates with large numbers of torches. In addition, they used long poles to hook men on the wall and attached reeds to twenty-foot-long bamboo and wood poles, collecting some 200 or 300 of them into a volcano-like configuration to incinerate the gates and their wooden superstructures. However, they were again thwarted in heavy fighting that lasted throughout the night, and several other nighttime incendiary attacks over the course of the siege were similarly frustrated.

The aggressors also attempted to move towers close in whose height exceeded the walls, but they were attacked with a variety of weapons, including from under the cover of wooden donkeys. Nevertheless, ultimately it was the blazing firewood and straw dropped over the sides into the gap (rather than intended to set them afire) which prevented them from approaching the walls. To counter the Jurchen's Heavenly Bridges the defenders fabricated some 300 oxen out of dry bamboo, firewood, and grass; employed long poles; and adopted the gunpowder used in the fire catapults to power twenty "fire spears" or "lances" *(huo ch'iang)*, all weapons handled by two men each. (This is apparently the first mention of the *huo ch'iang*, a sort of long-shafted, handheld gunpowder weapon or eruptor.)[22] Although such measures succeeded in preserving Te-an, Jurchen forces continued to rove about the countryside, pillaging, plundering, and burning.

## THE SIEGE OF TE-AN, A.D. 1206–1207

Te-an being among the Jurchen's objectives during their late autumn campaign, it was besieged (again!) from the seventeenth of the eleventh month of 1206 through the fourth of the third month, 1207 almost simultaneously with Hsiang-yang. Reportedly upwards of a 100,000 enemy infantry and cavalry were in place well before the end of the eleventh month, completely cutting off this city located southeast of Hsiang-yang. Fortunately, the essential events during the 108 days of the siege's duration were sequentially recorded in some ninety-eight entries plus preliminary and final observations in a personal chronicle.[23] Traditional incendiary techniques were employed, often on a massive scale, on thirty of the ninety-eight days, contrary to expectations that cannon, or at least gunpowder, would already have assumed a major role.

From the very beginning when the Jurchen piled bamboo and straw outside the gates to set them afire—a technique repeatedly utilized throughout the siege—the commander exercised strong leadership, personally directing troops atop the wall in extinguishing the first flames with pots of water. To thwart these attacks the defenders frequently shot the enemy's soldiers down with arrows before they could reach the walls, and also employed incendiary arrows to ignite the materials at a distance even when they were merely slated for filling in the moats and dry ditches.

Small numbers of defenders were sometimes pre-positioned in ambush outside the walls to await enemy assaults, and contingents of 100 to 200 men conducted raids to set the enemy's equipment and occasionally camps afire at night, generally with straw or firewood carried for the purpose in the usual "incendiary thief" fashion. Raiders also repeatedly attacked and burned the enemy's wooden donkeys in quantities of 200 to 300 at a time, their other assault engines, various protective shelters, and such incendiary materials as firewood, grass, and straw, exploiting the wind whenever possible.

A new assault device, a straw tower in the shape of a pagoda that wouldn't sustain the weight of a man but was designed to set the kiosks atop the wall afire, was easily thwarted with incendiary arrows in quantity. However, only comparatively low-tech weaponry was apparently employed. Rarely are oil, other accelerants, or gunpowder even mentioned apart from the latter being interlaced with straw to burn the Heavenly bridges and other heavy towers, no doubt because they were far more massive than the wooden donkeys, goose wagons, portable shields, and similar equipment.

The most intense incendiary activity was witnessed from the twenty-fourth through thirtieth of the twelfth month. A strong incendiary offensive was mounted on the twenty-fourth but successfully repelled with incendiary arrows launched in a favorable wind. Fervent strikes by some 30,000 troops on the twenty-seventh were withstood only by employing massive numbers of incendiary arrows, torches, fire boxes, straw fire oxen, and other bamboo implements to set their mobile towers and bridges aflame. However, a temporary withdrawal was still required when the water resources atop the wall were exhausted, though the enemy was also forced to retreat after suffering heavy losses and many drowned in the nearby river.

On the twenty-ninth it was realized that the aggressor's major assault equipment, such as mobile approach towers, was limited in number and couldn't be quickly replicated; therefore, fully destroying it through a carefully preplanned incendiary attack would be highly advantageous. First, the Jurchen's pre-positioned and other water supplies had to be depleted with disposable straw fire oxen, then more powerful methods employed, ranging from *lu-pu* through *mang-pao,* the latter a simple gunpowder-based incendiary, as well as various unspecified bamboo devices (probably including eruptors). The attack's severity would prevent the enemy from reversing direction, ensuring that all their equipment would be burned. On the twenty-ninth, just as anticipated, the Jurchen assault engines became entrapped and they quickly sustained major equipment and personnel losses.

The last flurry of activity began on 3/1 with a night assault designed to incinerate the wooden structures perched on the enemy's earthen mounds. Aided by a favorable wind, it inflicted heavy casualties. On the third, since the earthen mounds were still being extended toward the city wall, ten small contingents launched a series of highly successful nighttime incendiary attacks on the flammable equipment and protective sheds atop them, as well as several hundred wooden donkeys around the city gates, two trebuchets, and all the straw oxen and other equipment deployed about the flying bridges. Since whatever they had built over the last two months was thus largely destroyed yet the Jurchen hadn't succeeded in reaching the city wall with towers or by filling in the moats, they abandoned their camps. However, before departing they carefully burned any remaining bridges, towers, and heavy equipment, including the wooden palisades themselves.

Psychological warfare was also much in evidence, the defenders even sacrificing dogs and flinging their heads against the enemy's palisades to defile them. On three separate occasions they poisoned several large bodies of water, targeting the horses' water supply more than the men's.[24] They deliberately captured prisoners for interrogation purposes and sent out spies who gathered important information. Conversely, one captured Sung officer voluntarily assumed the role of a double agent by persuading the Jurchen that he would betray the city by lighting fires atop the wall if they released him. However, he merely lured their troops into traps for several nights in succession before they finally realized his duplicity. They were also provided with false topographical information, thereby thwarting their tunneling efforts, though more traditional incendiary counter-methods were not neglected either.

## THE SIEGE OF HSIANG-YANG, A.D. 1206–1207

Any scrutiny of the several siege records passed down through the centuries leads to the inevitable conclusion that Chinese warfare was far more complex and extensive than can possibly be imagined from the materials preserved in the *Twenty-five Dynastic Histories* and theoretical military writings. For example, the siege of Hsiang-yang, which lasted from the twelfth month of 1206 through the second month of 1207 or some ninety days, is portrayed in telling detail by Chao Wan-nien in his chronicle, *Hsiang-yang Shou-ch'eng-lu*.[25] However, the era's histories, which barely mention the clash, merely note that Chao Ch'un burned Fan-ch'eng, Hsiang-yang was subsequently surrounded on the twenty-eighth of the eleventh month, attacked right at the start of the new year, and finally released when the Jurchen troops withdrew on the twenty-fifth of the second month primarily because of illness.[26]

Situated at a pivotal location on the Han River, Hsiang-yang frequently came under extended attack including during the Three Kingdoms period and the subsequent Mongol conquest. This siege unfolded almost simultaneously with one at Te-an, Hsiang-yang being among the Jurchen's objectives during a southern campaign launched in reprisal for botched Southern Sung attempts to exploit Mongol predations upon the Jurchens to retake contiguous northern territory. Approximately 200,000 well-supported Jurchen forces, a mixture of infantry and cavalry, crossed the Han River after overcoming efforts to block them and quickly surrounded Hsiang-yang.

A moderate-sized city reportedly 9 *li* and 341 paces in circumference, well-protected by the river to the north and northeast, Hsiang-yang also had outer knee walls, protective moats and ditches on the non-river sides, and exterior strongpoints, including palisades along the river bank to prevent amphibious assaults. However, the defenders numbered a mere 10,000 troops, though additional scattered army remnants and locally recruited auxiliary members apparently augmented their numbers by several thousand, still not enough to reduce the odds to ten to one. Furthermore, despite desperate requests, the court never provided a single relief soldier to support the beleaguered defenders.

Strict discipline was immediately imposed within the city, the people being grouped by families of five and apportioned among the four quarters to ensure social order. Provisions were given to everyone, including recent refugees, to maintain valiant spirit and resolute commitment, and medical care was provided. Wells were also dug and a variety of large water containers pre-positioned throughout the city to extinguish any fires that might arise, whether from carelessness, subversion, or incendiary arrows. Moreover, as the moats were evaporating and losing their defensive value in the winter's dryness, water wheels were erected at each end to revitalize them by continuously pumping water in from the river.

Chao Ch'un, Hsiang-yang's chief commander, decided to exploit the protection offered by their walls and avoid open field battles, but still mounted numerous sallies into the enemy's extended positions. These took two forms: night raids by thirty to sixty special operations personnel designed to incinerate the enemy's equipment, and larger but less frequent strikes involving several thousand, the majority being crossbowmen who provided cover fire for core forces entrusted with such tasks as tearing down earthen mounds and digging new ditches. These raiders repeatedly burned hundreds of ladders and shields; lesser numbers of much larger devices such as trebuchets, flying bridges, and boats; and large quantities of basic materials, including heavy bamboo poles. Infrequent but more sweeping incendiary operations also targeted supplies, at least one of them north of the river reportedly destroying an almost unimaginable quantity of provisions and materials.

Boats were used to raid the opposite shore, targeting enemy vessels and stores along the embankment, with some supplies and vessels being seized and brought back. By the start of the siege the Southern Sung had reportedly burned some 1,000 of the various enemy vessels being employed to convey troops and provisions. Chao also deployed impromptu fire boats, utilizing old vessels packed with flammable straw soaked in oil manned by experienced swimmers and sent downstream towards the enemy's floating bridge before being ignited, the sailors abandoning the ships at the last moment to swim to shore.

Although incendiary techniques were thus repeatedly employed during the siege, neither the methods nor materials are specified beyond noting that the troops were carrying faggots to ignite fires. Gunpowder-tipped incendiary arrows and trebuchet-hurled (incendiary) thunderclap bombs are mentioned a few times and noted as having wrought great destruction. However, no eruptors, cannon, or similar devices seem to have been utilized, nor any of the other incendiary techniques described in the theoretical manuals, resort being primarily to shock weapons in close combat and crossbows at a distance.[27] In fact, the secret to their defensive success being the latter, Chao multiplied their numbers by positioning two additional layers behind those normally stationed on the walls.

Their nighttime strikes proved astoundingly successful because the Jurchen apparently neglected their perimeter defenses and rarely deployed the reconnaissance personnel necessary for acquiring critical information about Sung activities and intentions. In contrast, one of the Sung's strengths proved to be military intelligence because they interrogated prisoners, employed spies and reconnaissance effectively, and acted upon the knowledge thus acquired. Hsiang-yang troops also went forth to dig ditches during the night, generally 1,000 to 1,500 men protected by two to three times that many soldiers and bowmen. These suddenly appearing ditches, which were designed to prevent the aggressors from maneuvering close to the walls and setting fires, astonished the Jurchen who must have been totally incompetent not to have heard or detected the excavation.

The Jurchen failed to secure their forward positions, leaving equipment positioned at the cost of great effort outside Hsiang-yang's walls in jeopardy. Moreover, their own camps remained highly vulnerable as the outer palisades were burnt several times and the interior repeatedly penetrated. (At one point the Jurchen attempted to deter night raids by maintaining blazing fires along their growing embankment, but Sung troops carrying buckets of water extinguished them all, allowing their activities to continue undetected.) Woven basket-like entanglements of bamboo and miniature *chevaux-de-frise* were also deployed in quantity to reduce the mobility of enemy cavalry and stifle their response, and even the enemy's bridges were undermined.

Jurchen subversive efforts included an assassination attempt and plots to start fires within the city, but they were detected and thwarted before they could be implemented. Psychological operations such as calls for surrender and blatant attempts to overawe the enemy were also mounted by both sides but to little avail. However, Chao Ch'un's spies and observers performed far better than their counterparts, almost always providing the Sung with superior intelligence.

The moats had to be filled in to employ ladders and similar assault equipment and bring the various siege engines close enough to be effective, whereupon they were targeted for incendiary attacks, still the only means of destroying them. At times the straw oxen, wooden donkeys, mobile shields, and other wooden equipment set afire from atop the wall blazed for days, filling the area with smoke. Follow-on attacks that further exploited these efforts routinely inflicted hundreds of casualties each time with practically no losses. In contrast, when the Jurchen attempted to burn a forward defensive position outside one of the moats, they were successfully ambushed by well-concealed crossbowmen.

Just as in Mo-tzu's era, upon the enemy's approach a wide-ranging policy of denial had immediately been effected and all standing crops, domesticated animals, provisions, wood, and other materials collected and brought into the city. Any remaining houses were burned by the Jurchen who then discovered that the still extant mud walls of the warehouses provided ideal cover for bowmen firing at defenders on the city's walls. Chao therefore dispatched a small raiding party entrusted with destroying them that even managed to repel a counterstrike by several hundred cavalry and return largely unscathed.

The Jurchen also undertook massive embankments or ramps, at least one over a 100 paces long, which initially paralleled the walls with the intention of turning toward them at the last moment. Even though they were called "earthen mountains" not all of them were constructed simply by piling earth up to a desired height, but rather through interlacing bundles of firewood braced with timbers and covered with earth. The defenders sallied forth and successfully set the interior superstructure on fire on several occasions, finally ending days of battling back and forth over the mound with an enormous conflagration created by adding fuel and accelerants which reduced the hill to ashes, deflating the enemy's spirit.

When their last mound was destroyed, the Jurchen abandoned their quest and withdrew across the river, burning some equipment but leaving most of it and their provisions behind. Not totally confident they had departed, Chao closely followed their retreating armies, mounting occasional attacks with thunderclap bombs and gunpowder incendiary arrows. Later, he blocked the return of a 2,000-man contingent which apparently sought to incinerate the materials left behind.

Overall, the enemy lost half their forces, a few thousand at a time in many larger engagements, hundreds in the smaller clashes and the multiple assaults against the fortifications even though they were protected by various devices. Several clever techniques were also conceived and employed against them. For example, instead of hurling stones which could be reused, the Sung fabricated mud balls, either sun dried or baked, out of clay and various noxious substances which would kill anyone they hit but break apart upon striking the ground. They also reused the enemy's arrows for their crossbows by cutting down the feathered end while prohibiting regular bows and arrows from being used on their own walls for similar reasons, and fired "caltrop" arrows which would impale men's feet and horses' hooves after they fell onto the ground. They even disabled the enemy's warning system, catching and eating the hundreds of dogs that had been left behind by the farmers when the local inhabitants fled into the city.

# Notes

CHAPTER 1

1. The Chinese theory of five "elements"—more properly phases because they describe the dynamic relationship of characteristics rather than substances—includes a number of production and conquest relationships. For example, wood produces fire while water conquers it, but the effects of quantity immediately balk absolute assertions. (For a general discussion, see Joseph Needham, *Science and Civilisation in China*, Vol. 2: *History of Scientific Thought* [Cambridge: Cambridge University Press, 1962], pp. 232ff.)

2. According to the *Shou-ch'eng Lu* ("Shou-ch'eng Chi-yao"), two of the five assault methods that cause fear in the people are incendiary in nature: fire carts and incendiary arrows.

3. *Tso Chuan,* Hsi Kung 21.

4. *Tso Chuan,* Yin Kung 4.

5. *Tzu-chih T'ung-chien, T'ang Chi* 12, Chen-kuan 17, A.D. 643.

6. Another, concocted incident in the *Han Fei-tzu* ("Nei-ch'u-shuo, Shang") employs Confucius as a foil:

After a man of Lu had set fire to some accumulated marsh vegetation, a north wind spread the fire southward, threatening the area of the outer wall. Terrified, Duke Ai personally led the masses to race out and extinguish the fire. However, no one accompanied him as everyone was out hunting and the fire went unextinguished.

The duke then summoned Confucius (in his capacity as Minister of Justice), who said, "Hunting is pleasurable and without penalty, whereas fighting fires is miserable and without reward. This is why no one is extinguishing the fire."

When the king concurred, Confucius added, "Rewards are inadequate in a crisis. Even if you want to reward everyone who fights the fire, the state's wealth won't be enough. I suggest you just employ punishments."

The king agreed, so Confucius issued an order that stated: "Those who fail to extinguish the fire will be punished as if they had surrendered or fled from the enemy. Those who continue hunting will be punished as if they had entered prohibited grounds." Even before the order had fully circulated, the fire was extinguished.

7. "Nei-ch'u-shuo, Shang," "Ch'i Shu" subsection. The *Hsin Hsü* ("Tsa Shih") notes that a person of courage can be sent into a blazing fire, stomp on naked blades, and endure ten thousand deaths without having the least concern for his life.

8. That is, his family would benefit.

9. Another passage in the same chapter notes the king tested the motivational power of his rewards by setting a tower afire before dispatching his troops across a river into battle.

10. This incident is preserved in Li Cheng's biography in the *Sung Shih, chüan* 453.

11. *Han Fei-tzu,* "Yü Lao." The original *Tao Te Ching* verse, from chapter 63, as translated in our *Tao of War,* runs:

> Plan against the difficult while it remains easy;
> Act against the great while it is still minute.
> The realm's difficult affairs invariably commence with the easy;
> The realm's great affairs inevitably arise from the minute,
> For this reason the Sage never acts against the great,
> So can achieve greatness.

Similar thoughts are expressed in the subsequent chapter as well, imagized in terms of a sapling.

12. Examples may be found in the *Tso Chuan,* a chronicle of the Spring and Autumn period when China's states and economy grew dramatically, for Duke Huan's 2nd and 14th years, Hsüan's 16th, Chuang's 20th, Hsi's 20th, Ch'eng's 3rd, Hsiang's 9th and 30th, Chao's 9th, Ai's 3rd and 4th, and Ting's 2nd. In the fourth century A.D., when the palace complex at Yeh-ch'eng caught fire, it burned uncontrollably for thirty days before being extinguished. (*Tzu-chih T'ung-chien, Chin Chi* 20, Yung-ho 5, A.D. 349).

13. Duke Chao, 18th year. Of particular importance, Tzu Ch'an ensured the city's fortifications were well manned to make certain that external forces could not exploit the catastrophe.

14. Coincidental evidence that the state always attempted, however futilely, to control them. (*Tzu-chih T'ung-chien, Chin Chi* 4, Yüan-k'ang 5, A.D. 295) The royal armory contained many historic weapons as well as ordinary field-grade implements because Chin, or in this case Hsi Chin, was the successor state from Han to Ts'ao, then Wei, and finally Chin. (Emergency efforts to remedy the loss were immediately initiated, weapons being gathered from among the people less than two months after the fire.)

15. *Tzu-chih T'ung-chien, Chin Chi* 14, T'ai-ning 1, A.D. 323.

16. *Tzu-chih T'ung-chien, Chin Chi* 6, Yung-ning 1. (No doubt the follow-on effort also played a role in the slaughter.)

17. *Tzu-chih T'ung-chien, Liang Chi* 14, Ta-t'ung 4, A.D. 538.

18. For example, despite the popularity of speculation on the nature of Greek fire in such works as Partington's *Greek Fire,* Pritchett's classic overview of Greek warfare contains only one reference to setting enemy ships afire. (See W. Kendrick Pritchett, *The Greek State at War* [Berkeley: University of California Press, 1974], Vol. 2, p. 140.) Not surprisingly, Needham's examination of Western incendiary practices (found in the introductory portion of his section entitled "The Gunpowder Epic") succinctly characterizes their evolution and most important historical applications. (Our discussion necessarily focuses upon incendiary warfare itself rather than all of fire's combat aspects and applications, such as multiplying cookfires and torches to create the impression of a vast force or occupied positions, or Yü Wen-ts'e's clever burning of grass piles to deter Turkish raiders [cited in the *T'ung Tien, chüan* 153].)

19. A number of informative texts may be consulted about the basic principles, though discussions of the thermodynamics tend to become highly mathematical. Particularly useful and accessible references include John W. Lyons, *Fire;* Warren C. Strahle, *An Introduction to Combustion;* and Irvin Glassman's highly theoretical *Combustion.* For gunpowder, incendiaries, and other explosives, Tenney Davis's classic dis-

quisition *The Chemistry of Powder and Explosives* still provides the most extensive and detailed discussion, though Michael Russell's *The Chemistry of Fireworks,* Jacqueline Akhavan's *The Chemistry of Explosives,* and John Conkling's *The Chemistry of Pyrotechnics* all succinctly cover the most important aspects. Joseph Needham's monumental "The Gunpowder Epic" provides an overview of basic issues, and includes a succinct but comprehensive history of incendiaries in the West; and Partington's somewhat outdated (and much challenged) *A History of Greek Fire and Gunpowder* (with Bert Hall's introduction) retains fundamental value, though it should be supplemented by the recent journal articles and especially Bert S. Hall, *Weapons and Warfare in Renaissance Europe: Gunpowder, Technology, and Tactics.*

20. Michael Faraday's classic lectures on the dynamics of a candle flame actually initiated the scientific study of combustion. (For a lucid contemporary reconstruction and analysis, see John W. Lyons, *Fire* [New York: Scientific American Library, 1985].)

21. For a discussion, see Tenny Davis, *The Chemistry of Powder and Explosives,* or Wayne Cocroft's more recent *Dangerous Energy: The Archaeology of Gunpowder and Military Explosives Manufacture* (Swindon: English Heritage, 2000).

22. The class of true explosives, which detonate upon percussion or the application of sufficient heat, occur rarely in nature and were never part of the incendiary tradition. Of course all explosive devices, in evolving large amounts of heat and gas, have secondary incendiary effects, and have been widely utilized for them over the past century. However, they represent a radically different approach, well outside the focus of our study of traditional incendiary techniques, but are extensively discussed in Needham's "Gunpowder Epic."

23. Although this is the most commonly seen account, other early writings assert that King Wu symbolically slew him with a sacred sword.

24. In another similar incident, in A.D. 307 the palaces at Ch'eng-tu burnt for more than ten days after the rebel leader Chi Sang set them afire. (*Tzu-chih T'ung-chien, Chin Chi* 8, Yung-chia 1.)

25. The synthetic account presented here is conflated from those preserved in the *Bamboo Annals,* under King Huan's initial year, the "Chin-shih-chia" section of the *Shih Chi,* and background provided by the first few years of Duke Yin's reign in the *Tso Chuan.* (Only the *Bamboo Annals* record the incendiary attack while the *Shih Chi* asserts that King P'ing of the Chou deputed Duke Kuo to mount the attack that forced Chuang Po back to Ch'ü-wo.)

26. Duke Huan, 7th year. While the *Ch'un Ch'iu* is generally viewed as the most, if not only, reliable chronicle of the era's events, it suffers from incompleteness, being the records of Lu rather than Chou or the realm at large.

27. See the *Kung-yang* and *Ku-liang* for Duke Huan, 7th year. (The *Tso Chuan* omits any reference to this event.) Whether it constitutes the term's first use is another, albeit minor, question, contingent upon the relative composition dates of the *Tso Chuan* and the *Art of War*'s "Incendiary Warfare" chapter.

28. Duke Huan, 14th year.

29. For example, in 649 B.C. (Duke Hsi, 11th year) attackers burnt the east gate; in 589 B.C. (Duke Ch'eng, 2nd year), a thatched gate roof.

30. They burned the palace in 636 (Duke Hsi, 24th year) and attacked and burnt an enemy's mansion in 543 B.C. (Duke Hsiang, 30th year). The saga of Chin Wen-kung in the *Kuo Yü* depicts the ruler's henchmen burning his palace in an unsuccessful attempt to drive him out, while in 636 B.C. an assault force similarly resorted to burning a palace to flush out their enemy (*Tso Chuan,* Duke Hsi, 24th year).

31. For example, see Duke Ch'eng, 13th year (a case of internal strife), and Duke Chao, 22nd year.

32. Duke Hsi, 11th year.

33. Duke Ch'eng, 13th year. (Despite the porosity of ill-defined frontiers, border towns were already beginning to perform defensive functions.)

34. Duke Hsiang, 8th year (565 B.C.). The attack had been mounted at powerful Chi's behest. (During the Spring and Autumn period the relatively minor but still strong states of Cheng and Sung were caught between the powerful entities of Ch'u, Chin, Ch'i, and even Ch'in.)

35. Duke Chao, 26th year.

36. In 517 B.C. a force had set fire to a city after crossing the nearby river, but it failed to produce victory (*Tso Chuan*, Duke Chao, 25th year).

37. "Wu Yü."

38. "Wu Yü."

39. *Tso Chuan*, Duke Ting, 8th year.

40. Duke Ting, 9th year.

41. Duke Ai, 16th year. (He also refused to kill the king, making the task of usurpation rather more difficult.)

42. *Huai-nan-tzu*, "Tao-ying Hsün."

43. Duke Hsiang, 18th year.

44. The records for Duke Ling's reign in "Ch'i T'ai Kung Shih-chia" and Duke P'ing's in the "Chin Shih-chia" (both in the *Shih Chi*) emphasize that the populace was slain and area thoroughly burned.

45. Which is taken here as a reasonably accurate record of events even though largely composed of creatively written dialogues.

46. "Pa Hsing." A purported dialogue between the fabled Kuan Chung and Duke Huan asserts that Ch'u had invaded Sung and Cheng and so extensively burned the latter that the walls and dwellings had been destroyed, the people scattered and separated. (For a translation, see W. Allyn Rickett, *Guanzi* [Princeton: Princeton University Press, 1985], Vol. 1, pp. 352–354.)

47. Slightly emended, this translation is taken from our single-volume *Art of War* (Westview Press, 1994), which may be consulted for translation notes, historical introduction, and thematic issues. (Throughout *Fire and Water*, English names are given for works we have previously translated, romanized versions for all other book and chapter titles.)

48. The fifth objective is variously interpreted as shooting flaming arrows into an encampment, burning their weapons, or attacking their formations, as translated. The repeated use of five—five types of attack, five changes of fire—probably reflects the original verbal (and therefore mnemonic) nature of the teachings, as well as the constraints imposed by writing on bamboo strips.

49. Even though relative force size and organization in the Spring and Autumn and Warring States periods are a matter of debate, with estimates for Ch'eng-p'u in 632 B.C. running from 50,000 to 110,000 per side, the trend is clear and irrefutable. Operational forces in Sun-tzu's time certainly attained 40,000 to 50,000, and perhaps for some campaigns, such as the famous invasion of Ch'u, even the 100,000 mentioned in his text, though this number is also cited as evidence of the *Art of War*'s late composition date (or at least that particular passage's). The famous Battle of Li-che River in 478 B.C. at which Yüeh decimated Wu saw at least 50,000 troops deployed on either side of the river. These large forces not only comprised dense targets in them-

selves, but were invariably accompanied by massive amounts of provisions and supplies.

50. Perhaps this remark about the wind was originally a line of commentary that has accidentally become interspersed as text, Sun-tzu never having envisioned any such relationship; perhaps it is simply a remnant belief.

51. For example, see Yüan Cheng-ling, "*Sun-tzu Ping-fa* 'Huo-kung' Hsin-t'an," *Chün-shih Li-shih* 2000:2, pp. 42–45. Yüan believes that the line about not using warfare unless endangered would be strategically absurd unless "warfare" is here synonymous with "incendiary warfare."

52. This conclusion is somewhat problematic since flooding often brought a city to its knees, forcing it to surrender, but once subjugated and dried out, much of its value remained and could be confiscated. (It has been suggested, without real justification, that the character translated as "seize" actually entails the extended, specialized meaning of "seize and destroy" rather than simply capture or confiscate.)

53. As Sun-tzu pointed out ("Waging War"), troops fight for rewards.

54. The "unorthodox" and its role in Chinese military history is extensively discussed in our *Art of War*.

55. For further discussion of this critical concept, see our *Art of War*, pp. 140–142.

## CHAPTER 2

1. "Ping Shou."

2. "Ching Nei," a section presumed to number among the oldest.

3. After being ignored for two millennia, the *Mo-tzu* has once again become accessible through Sun Yi-jang's extensive commentaries in his *Mo-tzu Hsien-ku* and Arthur Graham's insightful studies. More recently (1980), the seminal work of Robin D. S. Yates has provided valuable reconstructions and explications fundamental to any study of Mohist defensive techniques, many of which have been incorporated into Joseph Needham's *Science and Civilisation in China*. (See "Early Poliorcetics" by Robin Yates in Part VI, *Military Technology: Missiles and Sieges*, of Volume 5 on *Chemistry and Chemical Technology*, 1994, pages 241–485.) The remnant military writings, which comprise *chüan* fourteen and fifteen—the last two in the book's present form, suggesting they were appended quite late—encompass sections 52 through 71. However, only eleven of twenty possible chapters remain, evidence that despite frequent repetition throughout the extant text, significant material and perhaps a few critical techniques have been lost over the centuries. Nevertheless, several incendiary measures can still be discerned, indicating their overall importance within the Mohist schema.

4. For example, in "Shou Ch'eng" in the *Wu-ching Tsung-yao* and "Shou" in the *Wu Pien*.

5. "Hsiang-t'ung, Shang."

6. "Hao-ling."

7. "Ying-ti," "Ch'i-chih," "Hao-ling," and "Tsa-shou."

8. "Tsa-shou." (The suburbs would have been outside the walls.) The *Wei Liao-tzu* chapters entitled "Tactical Balance of Power in Attacks" and "Tactical Balance of Power in Defense" make similar observations.

9. Implying that the populace allowed to dwell or remain within the city was somehow prescreened or selected.

10. "Pei-ch'eng-men." These criteria are frequently repeated thereafter, mostly without citing their origination in the *Mo-tzu*, in such military manuals as the *Wu Pien* ("Shou").

11. More generally, people and the city itself were expected to maintain food reserves, ideally of three years ("Tsa-shou").

12. Techniques such as embedding bamboo spikes in marshy areas were employed to control movement across more accessible spaces and deny passage to the enemy. ("Tsa-shou." This appears to be the first historical reference to this much feared technique.)

13. "Tsa-shou."

14. "Hao ling."

15. "Hao-ling." Many of the regulations governing internal security are similar to those preserved in the second half of the *Wei Liao-tzu*.

16. These were increasingly augmented over the centuries. For example, apart from the special regulations applying to fire, there were prohibitions designed to prevent signaling and otherwise conveying information to the enemy, including against the raising of poles or performing music when enemy troops were already deployed outside the walls ("Shou," *Wu Pien*). Many texts, such as the *Shou-ch'eng Chiu-ming-shu*, would echo warnings of fire.

17. "Ying-ti." The classic military writings reiterate that vigorous action should be taken to suppress the much feared, debilitating effects of omens and rumors. (See, for example, "Nine Terrains" in the *Art of War*, "Determining Rank" in the *Ssu-ma Fa*, and "Shou Ch'eng" in the *Wu-ching Tsung-yao*.)

18. This was a common approach, for example advocated in the *Wei Liao-tzu's* "Tactical Balance of Power in Defense," as well as numerous later writings.

19. Or, in one case, 30 *li*, an impossibility except for livestock on the hoof. (However, apart from breaking down physical structures, the 100 paces in "Pei-ch'eng-men" is obviously too limited.)

20. "Hao-ling," "Tsa-shou," though not "Ying-ti."

21. See, for example, those specified in "Pei-yi."

22. "Pei-ch'eng-men." Although 100,000 is merely a convenient rubric for a massive enemy force, one found in several texts including *Art of War*, minimal operational forces at this time routinely attained, if not exceeded, this number. Thus, in discussing the conditions for defending against a siege, the *Wei Liao-tzu* assumes an aggressor force of at least 100,000, but also a strength ratio of approximately one to ten. ("Tactical Balance of Power in Defense." For a translation, see Sawyer, *Seven Military Classics*, Westview Press, p. 253.)

23. These regulations continued to be implemented throughout subsequent centuries. For example, according to the T'ang dynasty *Hu-ch'ien Ching* ("Shou-ch'eng Chü"), the penalty for accidentally starting a fire should be death, an imposition that continued through the Ming, being advocated in such works as the *Wu-ching Tsung-yao* ("Shou Ch'eng" and "Fa-t'iao") and *Ch'en Chi*. The *Wu-ching Tsung-yao*, in "Hsing-chün Yüeh-shu," applies similar regulations to army encampments.

24. Another practice continued thereafter as in "Shou-ch'eng Chü," the *Hu-ch'ien Ching*. (The *Shou-ch'eng Chi-ch'eng* ["Yin Cheng"] includes an example of subversive activities being thwarted by just such means since the rebels were relying upon the chaos resulting from fighting a nighttime fire of faggots and lard to initiate their plot.)

25. Wood was also stored in pools of water, but strangely there is no mention of underground bunkers or mud storehouses despite expertise in compressed earth tech-

niques. The mud employed must have had a high clay component and the so-called yellow earth found in northern areas was sufficiently sticky that it would tend to adhere after drying out. Although sheet metal existed, it apparently was little employed except on door leaves which were more likely to be studded with metal and then coated with mud. (Also found in "Shou-chü Fa," the *T'ung Tien*).

26. Yates, "Early Poliorcetics," p. 345. There are no specifications that oil or lard should be prepared or kept atop the walls, though Yates (p. 445) suggests that the former may have been stored in large jars there.

27. "Pei-ch'eng-men."

28. "Pei-yi." The term "lei" perhaps refers to the layered effect resulting from interweaving coarse cords.

29. Yates suggests two rather different reconstructions, both essentially stiff framed, wooden shields ("Early Poliorcetics," pages 407–409).

30. The passage seems to say the entire hopper was cut away and dropped down, but the complex construction employing wheels at the end would be completely unnecessary unless they were to provide a pivot. Cutting away the sustaining rope must therefore mean the rope holding it in upright position, preventing it from turning downward to eject the contents. Yates ("Early Poliorcetics," p. 482) interprets it as a disposable device that is simply dropped down in toto, though this raises the question as to why it had to be fireproof if it was not to be reused. (Some retardation, to hold the burning kindling until the right moment, would be advantageous even if the entire unit were to be jettisoned, but since smaller pieces of wood were to be lit whose burning time would be quite fast, it required ignition just prior to actual use.)

31. "Pei-ch'eng-men."

32. Yates ("Early Poliorcetics," p. 445) believes one fragment refers to a flamethrower. To this device might be added the simple method of thrusting extra long, burning torches through holes in the parapets and gates, as well as the thinner portions of the wall where torches would normally be positioned on the exterior at night to illuminate any nearby nighttime enemy activity.

33. "Pei-t'i." Robin Yates detects a third, interior trap in a fragment of "Pei-ch'eng-men," a deep ditch filled with firewood that might be set ablaze should the enemy breach the walls. ("Early Poliorcetics," p. 342) However, his reading is based upon the characters *fu-hao*, rather than *fu-jang* which appear in some *Hsien-ku* editions. (*Jang*, meaning rich soil, is obviously incorrect, prompting commentators to emend it to *tieh*, parapets or battlements, which could equally be set ablaze.)

34. Just as specified in the *Liu-t'ao* chapter "Explosive Warfare."

35. "Pei-t'i." While the intent of the passage, despite some difficulties, is clear, the *t'u-men's* limited effectiveness due to the passageway's necessarily small size prompts questions about its value as a trap rather than simply an emergency measure designed to quash enemy penetrations. The psychological value, though not discussed, must have loomed disproportionately large.

36. "Pei-hsüeh" and "Pei-yi." Named the "sha," a term which means to "kill" or "slay," it is extensively discussed by Yates, who terms it "the death," in "Early Poliorcetics," page 481.

37. The "Pei-t'i" version stipulates a width of five feet, but the "Pei-yi" text has five paces, which the commentators claim would be much too wide. However, to be at all effective the trap must be large enough to contain some tens of men, not just the four or five that a five-foot width would accommodate. A five-pace or thirty-foot-wide opening would certainly achieve this purpose while allowing chariots, wagons, and

provisions to pass through during the pre-siege stage, but would require multiple posting to hang functioning door leaves. (If the partition were not ten feet thick, it might be understood as being part of the interior structure.)

38. Generally understood as a partition of unknown function, its width of ten feet suggests an exterior wall, either conjoined or facing the gates, though it may equally refer to some sort of raised platform extending ten feet on either side of the trap to facilitate attack.

39. "Pei-hsüeh." The actual technique employed ropes coated in mud to lower bundles of burning wood onto the target, the ropes allowing more maneuverability than simply dropping them down. Whether this technique was ever used might, however, be questioned since only the stupidest commander would initiate a mine within drop range of the wall even though it was highly desirable to limit the distance to be excavated, though directly carving a hole in the wall could be initiated in this manner.

40. See "Pei-hsüeh."

41. No doubt some of the lumber stored under water was used for this purpose, though the extant writings lack any such recommendation.

42. For an ingenious reconstruction of this pipe work and a general explication of the method see Yates, "Early Poliorcetics," pp. 466–467.

43. Apart from the incidents mentioned herein, neither the era's primary sources—the *Chan-kuo Ts'e*, *Bamboo Annals*, and *Shih Chi*—nor the numerous secondary collations and philosophical writings which preserve vestiges of Warring States events, including the *Lü-shih Ch'un-ch'iu*, *Shuo Yüan*, *Hsin Hsü*, *Han-shih Wai-chuan*, *Han Fei-tzu*, and *Hsün-tzu*, contain even the briefest account of incendiary warfare.

44. "Yen Chao-kung Shih-chia."

45. Pai Ch'i's successful thrust into Ch'u, during which he burned the buildings and probably trees about the royal graves, is mentioned in several texts, though the primary account is found in the *Chan-kuo Ts'e*, "Ch'u Ts'e," 4. (The victorious campaign is also described in the *Tzu-chih T'ung-chien*, "Chou Chi," 5, Nan Wang 57 [258 B.C.] and included in Pai Ch'i's biography, *chüan* 73, and the "Ch'u Shih-chia" in the *Shih Chi*.) In addition, Ch'in attacked Wei in the middle of the third century, pulling down towers and burning Ch'ui-tu, a royal park rather than a town (*Chan-kuo Ts'e*, "Wei Ts'e," 3).

46. For the complete chapter see "Tao of the General" in our translation of the *Seven Military Classics*. Of course, this is but one of several circumstances in which the enemy has made himself vulnerable to attack. (Eight others, in which one might strike without even performing divination, are characterized in "Evaluating the Enemy.") The *Yi Chou-shu*, in "Ta-ming Wu," observes that implementing an incendiary attack relies upon the wind.

47. Sun Pin flourished just about the middle of the fourth century, but major remnants of his book were recovered just three decades ago after having been lost for two millennia. (For a full translation with notes and historical introduction, see Sawyer, *Sun Pin Military Methods*, Westview Press.) Several relationships have been posited for Sun-tzu (Sun Wu) and Sun Pin, including that the former never existed and that the latter actually wrote his putative ancestor's famous *Art of War*. Nevertheless, the *Military Methods* clearly falls into the same school of military thought in not only elucidating many of the *Art of War*'s principles and concepts, but also extrapolating them into the realm of concrete application.

48. "Ten Deployments," *Sun Pin Military Methods*. (As this chapter falls in the second half of the reconstructed text and is somewhat different in tenor, it may well be a later compilation reflecting an even more codified approach.)

49. "Employing Cavalry."

50. "Ten Deployments."

51. Chapter 41, "Incendiary Warfare." (For a complete translation and historical introduction, see Sawyer, *The Six Secret Teachings* in our *Seven Military Classics,* Westview Press.)

52. In the "Few and the Many." Although the *Liu-t'ao* warns that enemies will use tall grass for ambush, it never advocates employing incendiaries to eliminate the danger. Moreover, surprisingly none of the various chapters addressing questions of general staff and equipment ever indicate the need for any specialized officers or devices.

53. Chapter 27, "Male and Female Cities." "Thoroughly incinerated ground" would be unable to sustain life, offer no cover against missile fire, and probably lack potable water.

54. "Huo Chan" or "Incendiary Attacks." (For a Ming example, see *Ch'e-ying Pai-pa Shuo*, entry 17.) However, near the end of the Sung the *Ts'ui-wei Pei-cheng-lu* noted this fear of being entrapped in dry vegetation might be exploited for defensive purposes. (See "Chi Chü" or "Urgent Occupation.")

55. *Ch'en Chi,* "Huo Chan." The *Teng-t'an Pi-chiu,* "Kung Ch'eng," preserves another adaptation.

56. The basic source for this episode is Li Ling's biography in the *Han Shu, chüan* 54, "Li Kuang Su Chien Chuan" though it is also extensively reprised in the *Tzu-chih T'ung-chien, Han Chi* 13, T'ien-han 2, 99 B.C., and also included among the illustrative cases of setting fires in heavy vegetation in several later military writings, usually under the rubric of "Huo Kung," including the *T'ung Tien, Wu-ching Tsung-yao, Yün-ch'ou Kang-mu,* and *Wu Pien.* (For a translation of Li's short biography, see Burton Watson, *Courtiers and Commoners in Ancient China* [New York: Columbia University Press, 1974], pp. 24ff.) The episode became famous partly because of the consequences suffered by the great historian Ssu-ma Ch'ien, author of China's first synthetic history—the *Shih Chi*—who become entangled in court wrangling over Li's condemnation for having surrendered rather than die fighting.

57. *Hu-ch'ien Ching,* "Huo Li." (Further discussion will be found in "Targeting Provisions.")

58. *Wu-ching Tsung-yao,* "Huo Li."

59. *Hu-ch'ien Ching,* "Huo li."

60. In this context, Sun Pin's chapter "Five Names, Five Respects" might be contemplated. (For a translation, see our *Sun Pin Military Methods,* pp. 187–190.)

61. "Planning Offensives." (In this context Wang Chen's meditations on the causes and elimination of war, translated as our *Tao of War,* merit note.)

62. In a passage often cited by court critics of military endeavors, Sun-tzu concluded: "Preserving the enemy's state capital is best, destroying their state capital second-best. Preserving their army is best, destroying their army second-best. Preserving their battalions is best, destroying their battalions second-best. Preserving their companies is best, destroying their companies second-best. Preserving their squads is best, destroying their squads second-best. For this reason attaining one hundred victories in one hundred battles is not the pinnacle of excellence. Subjugating the enemy's army without fighting is the true pinnacle of excellence." ("Planning Offensives," *Art of War.*)

63. *Tzu-chih T'ung-chien, Sung Chi* 7, Yüan-chia 27.

64. "Benevolence the Foundation." (The translation is taken from our *Seven Military Classics of Ancient China,* p. 128.) An incident in the *Tso Chuan* (Chao Kung, 6th year) suggests that not just invaders and raiders behaved brutally, but even the state's own armies and diplomatic missions from other states, not to mention the entourages of powerful nobles.

65. "Responding to Change," *Seven Military Classics,* p. 223.

66. "Occupying Enemy Territory," *Seven Military Classics,* p. 87. Although the context has King Wu presumably asking about how they are to occupy Shang territory after overcoming various tactical problems, the formulation is clearly general, not restricted to the Chou usurpation of Shang authority.

The Han dynasty *Huai-nan Tzu,* in "Ping-lüeh," similarly enjoined such behavior because it contravened the idealized practices of antiquity: "When the army reached the suburbs, the general in command of rescripts would proclaim: 'Do not cut down their trees, do not disturb their graves, do not burn their five grains (in the fields), do not incinerate their stores and provisions, do not take prisoners from among the people, do not collect the six domesticated animals.'"

67. *Ping Ching.* Compiled in the early seventeenth century, this and other later Ming and early Ch'ing manuals such as the *Wu-pei Chih* have lengthy sections with gunpowder formulations which often correlate the constituent components with the phases of fire, earth, and wood. Unfortunately, the symbolic nature of the discussion places them beyond the immediate scope of our work.

68. *Ts'ao-lü Ching-lüeh,* "Huo Kung."

69. "Chin Pao." Also see the *Teng-t'an Pi-chiu,* "Kung Ch'eng," and *Ch'en Chi.*

70. For example, the Ming dynasty *Teng-t'an Pi-chiu* ("Kung Ch'eng") includes an injunction not to burn their huts or contaminate their water supplies our of fear of angering the populace.

71. "Huo, 3."

## CHAPTER 3

1. The *Yün-ch'ou Kang-mu* ("Huo Kung") uses it to illustrate "setting fires in accord with the enemy," but it doesn't appear in Han Hsin's biography or the *Tzu-chih T'ung-chien.* (It represents the sort of stories that grew over the centuries, assuming a life and veracity of their own.) The *Yün-ch'ou Kang-mu* also reprises the first extended clash between Ts'ao Ts'ao and Lü Pu in A.D. 194, which ended after a hundred days because both sides were handicapped by lack of provisions. Through the efforts of a double agent, Ts'ao Ts'ao reportedly penetrated P'u-yang at night where fires were then set all about. Since accounts vary, it's unclear whether he set the fires himself to manifest their resolve or they were sprung upon him as part of a well-engineered trap. In either case, he barely managed to escape with his life, suffering burns to his hand or perhaps having his hair singed. (The *Yün-ch'ou Kang-mu* adduces the incident in its "Huo Kung" section to illustrate how plots can lure victims in, noting he escaped with singed hair. The *Tzu-chih T'ung-chien* account for A.D. 194 envisions the fires as a symbolic expression of resolve. The incident is also cited in "Yin Cheng," *Fang-shou Chi-ch'eng.*)

2. *Tzu-chih T'ung-chien, Han-chi* 37, Yung-p'ing 16, A.D. 73, and cited in "Huo Kung" in the *Wu-ching Tsung-yao* and "Huo" in the *Wu Pien.*

3. *Tzu-chih T'ung-chien, Han Chi* 21, Chien-chao 3, 36 B.C.

4. In recent centuries this nighttime clash has been the subject of numerous paintings and even large, ornate standing screens onlaid with jade and mother of pearl. Discussed in all the secondary military histories, the basic source material is found in Ts'ao

Ts'ao's biography ("Wu-ti Chi") in the *San-kuo Chih*, and a summary account appears in the *Tzu-chih T'ung-chien, Han Chi* 55, Chien-an 5. The clash is also included among the illustrative cases for "Huo Kung" in the *T'ung Tien, Wu-ching Tsung-yao, Ping-ch'ou Lei-yao, Yün-ch'ou Kang-mu,* and *Ts'ao-lü Ching-lüeh,* and also the chapter on "Provisions" in the *Hundred Unorthodox Strategies* and *Chüeh-sheng Kang-mu.*

5. Apart from being discussed in virtually every Chinese work of military history and summarized in the *Tzu-chih T'ung-chien* (*Han Chi* 57, Chien-an 13, A.D. 208), the Battle of Ch'ih Pi is also employed as an illustration in the subsection on "Incendiary Attack" in the *T'ung Tien* and numerous subsequent works, including the *Wu-ching Tsung-yao, Ping-ch'ou Lei-yao, Yün-ch'ou Kang-mu,* and *Teng-t'an Pi-chiu,* where it appears in "Shui Chan." It is also cited in the *T'ou-pi Fu-t'an,* "Ta Ch'üan," as an example of failing to take adequate precautions against surrenders and "T'ien Ching," illustrating the effects of wind on fire; "Huo" in the *Wu Pien;* and the *Huo-lung Shen-ch'i Ch'en-fa.* Basic accounts are also found in the *San-kuo Chih* biographies of the various participants, including Ts'ao Ts'ao, Kuan Yü, and Chou Yü.

6. Stories and even contemporary television episodes based upon the battle often credit Chu-ko Liang with not only masterminding the attack but evoking the wind through magical ceremonies.

7. In actuality, even though advised by some of the classic military writings, his strategy is somewhat surprising because they could have easily exploited the advantages conveyed by constricted terrain, normally considered ideal for fighting superior forces.

8. *Yün-ch'ou Kang-mu,* "Huo Kung." Yeh asserts that this was Lu's plan from inception though his claim is not supported by the *San-kuo Chih* and his understanding of the evolution of incendiary warfare is clearly faulty because alchemists were only on the verge of discovering the combustion properties of saltpeter and sulfur. The *Wu-ching Tsung-yao,* "Huo Kung," includes purported dialogue showing that Lu deliberately chose an incendiary attack as a means of breaking the stalemate, overcoming objections that any sort of attack would be tactically unwise.

9. Basic accounts are found in the relevant biographies in the *San-kuo Chih* and a summary in the *Tzu-chih T'ung-chien, Han Chi* 60, Chien-an 24. The debacle is also discussed in virtually every secondary Chinese military history, and found as an illustration in such works as the *Ping-ch'ou Lei-yao,* "Huo Kung," and *Wu Pien,* "Huo." Liu Pei had himself used an incendiary attack after a year long stalemate at Yang-p'ing-kuan this same year to destroy the enemy's outer defenses.

10. Yeh Meng-hsiung cites this conflict in his late Ming *Yün-ch'ou Kang-mu,* under the section on city defense ("Ch'eng Shou"), to illustrate that clever tactics will not prevail when the enemy commander is both knowledgeable and a man of character. It is also cited in the *Fang-shou Chi-ch'eng* and mentioned in Chu-ko Liang's biography in the *San-kuo Chih,* but the most extensive account is found in commentary taken from the *Wei Lüeh* appended to the *Wei Shu's* annals for T'ai-ho, 2nd year, obviously the source for Yeh's version, as well as the *Tzu-chih T'ung-chien, Wei Chi* 3, T'ai-ho 2, A.D. 228.

11. Later commentary suggests that complex incendiary arrows with oil containers at the front were employed, but this is unreliable. However, this is one of the first textual references to "huo chien" or incendiary arrows.

12. For a discussion of this tradition and a translation of the preface to the *Huo-lung Ch'uan-chi* attributing the invention of incendiary attacks to Chu-ko Liang, see Joseph Needham, "The Gunpowder Epic," pp. 25–31.

13. No record of employing incendiaries in this clash appears in the *San-kuo Chih*, though this version is found in the *San-kuo Yen-yi*, a fictionalized account of the period, and in some versions of the *Thirty-six Stratagems*.

14. *Yün-ch'ou Kang-mu*, "Huo Kung," but not otherwise found.

15. *Yün-ch'ou Kang-mu*, "Huo Kung," but not otherwise found.

16. Another *Yün-ch'ou Kang-mu* illustration of "setting fires in accord with the enemy" found in the "Huo Kung" section but not in Teng's or Chiang's biographies in the *San-kuo Chih*.

17. *Tzu-chih T'ung-chien, Chin Chi* 38, Yi-hsi 7, A.D. 411.

18. *Tzu-chih T'ung-chien, Chin Chi* 34, Yüan-hsing 1.

19. *Tzu-chih T'ung-chien, Chin-chi* 34, Yüan-hsing 3. This battle is also cited in the *Yün-ch'ou Kang-mu* as an example of exploiting the wind to set effective fires, but under Liu Yi's name (following the *T'ung Tien, chüan* 153). The text also has a northeast wind and describes them dispersing tree branches saturated with oil all about the valley before igniting them.

20. *Tzu-chih T'ung-chien, Chin-chi* 34, Yüan-hsing 3.

21. *Tzu-chih T'ung-chien, Chin-chi* 38, Yi-hsi 8.

22. Primary sources are Ma Sui's lengthy biography, which preserves the most details, in the *Chiu T'ang-shu, chüan* 134, and T'ien Yüeh's, *chüan* 141. Also extensively reprised in the *Tzu-chih T'ung-chien* under the years for Te-tsung's reign and cited as an illustration for "Huo Kung" in the *Ts'ao-lü Ching-lüeh*, "Shui Chan" in the *Yün-ch'ou Kang-mu*, "Ta Shui" in the *Wu Pien*, and entry 9 in the *Ch'e-ying Pai-pa K'ou-shuo*. (A political overview may also be found in *The Cambridge History of China: Sui and T'ang China*, pp. 487–510.)

23. T'ien Ch'eng-ssu, originally a sub-general with An Lu-shan, had surrendered to the T'ang and been recognized as military governor of the Wei-po region.

24. The central government's "failure" to adequately reward long effort, battlefield achievement, and betrayals—which provoked a number of desertions and rebellions—was not simply the product of negligence, but also a deliberate effort to reduce the power and independence of the regional military governors now that the main crisis had apparently ended.

25. The smoke's impact on the course of combat caused the battle to be cited as an illustration of smoke warfare ("Yen Chan") in the *Ts'ao-lü Ching-lüeh*.

26. In addition to analyses in all the standard military histories, the battle is described in Fang's biography in *chüan* 139 of the *T'ang Shu* and briefly recorded in the *Tzu-chih T'ung-chien, T'ang Chi* 35, Chih-te 1.

CHAPTER 4

1. For further discussion of the contradictory tendencies embraced by the classic military writings see "Prognostication, Divination, and Non-human Factors" in our *Tao of Spycraft*, and for a brief overview of concepts traditionally identified with Taoism, a now somewhat discredited but still functional term, and their relationship with Chinese military thought, see Sawyer, *The Six Secret Teachings on the Way of Strategy* (Boston: Shambhala, 1997) and the *Tao of War*.

2. "Huo-kung-chü" or "Equipment for Incendiary Attacks."

3. The text also includes chapters on the seasonal phenomena correlated with the twenty-four atmospheric periods, material for orienting oneself based upon the sky at various times in the year, and a long discussion of methods for calculating seasonal indices. (For further information on the *T'ai-pai Yin-ching* and most of the other texts

discussed in this context see Sawyer, "Military Writings," in David A. Graff and Robin Higham, ed., *A Military History of China* [Boulder: Westview Press, 2002]).

4. A contextual discussion and annotated translation of the *Questions and Replies* may be found in our *Seven Military Classics of Ancient China*.

5. Passages appearing in the *T'ung Tien* are often used to correct errors in received classic military texts and supply variant readings.

6. *Mou*, also read *wu*. He also further qualified *pi* as *tung* or east *pi*.

7. *Chüan* 160, "Huo Kung" or "Incendiary Attack." (Also cited as an example of "Huo Kung" by the *Wu-ching Tsung-yao*.) This pivotal campaign merits far more extensive treatment than can be given here or is normally accorded in historical writings. As usual, Ssu-ma Kuang's insightful condensation provides a basic account (*Tzu-chih T'ung-chien, Ch'en Chi* 10, Chen Ming 1 and 2, A.D. 587–588), while Kao Chiung's advice is embedded in his biography, *Sui Shu, chüan* 41. (Ironically, "chiung" means the "blazing light of a fire" and he in fact had a bridge burnt in an earlier tactical operation.) For further discussion of the campaign, see *Chung-kuo Li-tai Chan-cheng-shih*, Vol. 7, pp. 77–104.

8. A discussion of the history and role of *hsing jen* may be found in our *Tao of Spycraft*.

9. For a general discussion of the nature of "surprise attack," see Ephraim Kam, *Surprise Attack* (Cambridge: Harvard University Press, 1988), particularly the chapter on "Information and Indicators" which cites the Israeli experience.

10. Once again there is a slight variation in the lunar lodges—*tung pi* or east *pi* and southern *ch'i*, the southern being an addition, but all qualified as nighttime.

11. Oddly, literally just officers.

12. Rather than "armories" as translated in our *Art of War* (per numerous commentaries).

13. "Chüeh Shui" or "Breaking Open Rivers."

14. "Huo Kung."

15. In Ch'i's somewhat puzzling view, despite Wang's loyalty, the wind blew the incendiary torches back upon him, ensuring Ch'en's victory. (Wang's misfortune is recounted in our section entitled "Wind, Smoke, and Issues of Defense.")

16. Hua's bio in the *Sung Shih, chüan* 455, consists of less than two pages, almost all of which is his memorial on countering the Jurchen threat.

17. He felt that China needed to exploit its chief advantage, its crossbows, rather than try to compete with mounted enemy riders. However, chariots, which offer some mobility, are essential to prevent being completely overrun and provide far more effective platforms for crossbows than having the infantry carry and fire them. Hua also believed in attrition, in manipulating and wearing out the enemy ("Hsien Ch'i").

18. "Chiu Shun."

19. The former accords with traditional dispositions, the latter throws the men onto "fatal terrain," a serious error unless the hopelessness of the situation is being deliberately exploited. (Both concepts are from the *Art of War*.)

20. "Chiu Shun" ("Achieving Concord"). Also partially repeated in "Yi," the *Wu Pien*.

21. *Ts'ui-wei Pei-cheng-lu*, "Chao Chün." However, among those selected from the forty-two secret methods for attacking a city (in "Te Ti"), only one relevant technique appears, "flowing fire" (*liu huo*).

22. "Kuan Hsin" or "Observing Rifts."

23. For further discussion of the possible author, historical context, nature of the work, and a complete translation, see our *One Hundred Unorthodox Strategies: Battle and Tactics of Chinese Warfare.*

24. Moreover, unlike other texts preceding it, there is no comparable section on aquatic attacks, just a discussion of naval combat under the topic of "Riverine Warfare." Otherwise, its 152 brief thematic chapters essentially follow the style of the *Hundred Unorthodox Strategies,* each consisting of a tactical introduction followed by two to seven historical examples.

25. Defensive measures—essentially those formulated in the *Liu-t'ao*—based upon these realizations are also advanced and the need to be prepared, as well as maintain mobility on the water, emphasized.

26. *Ch'ien-chi,* "Huo."

27. "Ti Shih."

28. "Pao Hou." The *Ch'e-ying Pai-pa Shuo,* entry 108, expresses similar views.

29. "Pao Ch'i."

30. "Pao Chih."

31. The *Huo-lung Shen-ch'i Ch'en-fa* expresses a similar sentiment—that those who employ incendiary and aquatic attacks are unmatchable. However, the *T'ou-pi Fu-t'an* (in "Wu Lüeh"), written about the same time, although envisioning fire being able to strike like water and also being capable of blazing up, would still restrict it to an ancillary, though powerful, role. Moreover, being powerful, it must be guarded against and precautions taken against the wind suddenly shifting.

32. Literally "smoke and fire," but the same wording as the *Art of War* text.

33. Literally "releasing one trigger," presumably harking back to the concept of unlashing strategic power in Sun-tzu's *Art of War* by releasing the trigger.

34. Differs slightly from the original *Art of War* text which has "remains quiet" (*ching*) rather than "doesn't move."

35. As his deleted examples show, he is speaking about multiplying fires at night to create the impression of large numbers. This may be accomplished through each soldier carrying more than one torch, increasing the number of camp or cook fires, or even starting a limited but apparently uncontrolled fire to divert the enemy away from an area. (Further discussion and examples may be found in our *Tao of Spycraft.*)

36. Originally found in the *Art of War,* "Huo Kung."

37. Sun-tzu's original sentence consists of a paired conditional, which has been dropped: "When the fire flares into a conflagration, if you can follow up then do so; if you cannot, then desist."

38. From "Incendiary Warfare," the *Liu-t'ao (Six Secret Teachings).*

39. Essentially a quote from Sun-tzu's "Vacuity and Substance:" "One who is able to change and transform in accord with the enemy and wrest victory is termed spiritual."

40. Yeh's interpretation rather than what Sun-tzu said.

41. A quotation from the *Art of War's* "Vacuity and Substance," concluding the thought that "when someone excels at attacking, the enemy does not know where to mount his defense; when someone excels at defense, the enemy does not know where to mount his attack."

42. *Ping Ching,* as preserved in the *Wu Pei-chih.* The *T'ou-pi Fu-t'an,* "Wu Lüeh," observes that fire can be employed to strike and will blaze up, but it cannot be employed as the sole means of attack. Moreover, since it is a widely available tactic,

precautions have to be taken against becoming a victim as well as against the wind suddenly changing.

43. "Ping Chieh," in "Huo, 3."

44. *Wu-pei Chih*, "Huo, 3." Somewhat in imitation of the *Wu-tzu* and *Liu-t'ao*, the chapter discusses both appropriate and inappropriate circumstances for action.

45. Cannons and muskets.

46. For an example see the *Tzu-chih T'ung-chien, Chin Chi* 20, Yung-ho 6, A.D. 350.

47. *Tzu-chih T'ung-chien, Chin Chi* 24, T'ai-ho 5; *Chin Shu, chüan* 11, "Mu-jung Wei Tsai-chi," and *chüan* 113, "Fu Chien Tsai-chi, Shang." Another *T'ung Tien* case study, it appears under "Chüeh Liang-tao chi Tsu-chung" ("Sever Supply Lines and Baggage Trains") in *chüan* 160, "Ping" 13, immediately before the section on incendiary attack, the *Wu-ching Tsung-yao* and *Yün-ch'ou Kang-mu* sections on "Huo Kung," and "Liang Tao" in the *Wu Pien*.

48. "Chüeh Liang-tao chi Tsu-chung," *chüan* 160.

49. These first two sentences, from "Vacuity and Substance," differ from the *Art of War* text only in missing an introductory "can."

50. The second two sentences are drawn from "Military Combat." (In all cases the translation follows the reading in our *Art of War*; however, Tu Yu may have understood the last item, "stores," as grass and fodder.)

51. The only changes being the addition of two lunar lodges (even though he continues to state "four" thereafter) and the deletion of any reference to water's role, the relevant sentences having been shifted to his section on aquatic attacks.

52. This key theme is expressed throughout Hua's proposed program, and in such focal chapters as "Yü Ch'i," which describes the role of roving forces, and "Kuan Hsin."

53. The historical illustration for the chapter is Ts'ao Ts'ao's raid prior to Kuan-tu. Other chapters also raise the same theme, including "The Hungry," "Advantages of Terrain," and "Defense."

54. This example will be found in our case studies.

55. "Kung Ch'eng."

56. "Huo Kung," *Yün-ch'ou Kang-mu.* (Further discussion will be found under the topic of denial in the upcoming section on incendiaries in defense.)

57. *Tzu-chih T'ung-chien, T'ang Chi* 29, K'ai-yüan 15th year, also one of Yeh Meng-hsiung's illustrations for "burn the grass to defeat the barbarians" in "Huo Kung," *Yün-ch'ou Kang-mu.*

58. Evidence in itself of the efficiency of their intelligence system.

59. *Tzu-chih T'ung-chien, T'ang Chi* 12, Chen-kuan 15, also cited in the *Yün-ch'ou Kang-mu*, "Huo Kung," as an example of "burn the grass to defeat the barbarians." (The claim of a large infantry component should be noted since they functioned in a somewhat unusual manner, apparently being grouped in squads of five, four of whom fought while the fifth held their horses until the time for pursuit arrived. Perhaps dismounted cavalry would be a better term, though it leaves unresolved the question as to why they willingly abandoned the advantages of speed and mobility.)

60. A *T'ung Tien* illustration (*chüan* 155), the campaign is recorded in the *Tzu-chih T'ung-chien, T'ang Chi* 10, Chen-kuan 9.

61. *Tzu-chih T'ung-chien, Chin Chi* 2, Hsien-ning 4.

62. *Tzu-chih T'ung-chien, Liang Chi* 22, Shou-t'ai 1, A.D. 555. Even though many were probably smaller, supplementary craft, the number is still astonishing. Rov-

ing incendiary strikes mounted by Northern Wei on Southern Sung's provisions in their ongoing river conflict similarly compromised their mobility and ability to maneuver. (*Tzu-chih T'ung-chien, Sung Chi* 4, Yüan-chia 8, A.D. 431.)

### CHAPTER 5

1. *T'ai-pai Yin-ching,* "Huo-kung Chü." The passage appears in such works as the *T'ung Tien* (*chüan* 160, "*Ping*" 13), *Hu-ch'ien Ching* (chapter 54, "Huo Kung"), and *Wu Pien, Ch'ien-chi* 5, "Huo." It also numbers among the Ming *Teng-t'an Pi-chiu's* five incendiary-based methods for attacking cities in "Kung Ch'eng," though surprisingly the "nighttime" specification has dropped out, just as it has in the *Wu-ching Tsung-yao's* "Huo Kung," and is mentioned as a basic method in the *Ch'en Chi,* "Chi Yung," and seen as a threat in the *Ch'eng-shou Ch'ou-lüeh.*

2. Nighttime would seem best for undertaking surprise attacks and mounting special operations. However, in a chapter entitled "Nighttime Engagements" ("Yeh Chan"), the *Ts'ao-lü Ching-lüeh* points out that when your troops are more numerous, it's more advantageous to fight in the daytime, but when your troops are few, it's appropriate to engage in combat at night. Moreover, this should be considered an invariant tactical principle. (Although the author cites T'ien Tan's experience as an example of nighttime activity, he never suggests that incendiary measures be used just because night has fallen.)

3. Many of the later military writings thus warn against subversives igniting fires within encampments or citadels and advise the implementation of strict controls over the populace, especially foreigners, both at normal times and during fire-fighting efforts, as already discussed. (For example, see the *Hu-ch'ien Ching,* "Shou-ch'eng Chü." The *Wei Liao-tzu* also contains several chapters of rules and restrictions clearly showing that from the Warring States onward military camps were heavily compartmentalized and regulated.)

4. "Huo-kung Chü," *T'ai-pai Yin Ching.* Repeated verbatim under the rubric of "Huo Tao" in the *T'ung Tien, chüan* 160, "*Ping*" 13; "Huo Tao" in the *Wu-ching Tsung-yao;* and *Wu Pien,* "Huo." (The *Ch'e-ying Pai-pa Ta,* entry 9, even envisioned fire carts being similarly employed for nighttime raids.)

5. See the subsection on incendiary attack appended to "Aquatic Attack" in the *Teng-t'an Pi-chiu.*

6. *Tzu-chih T'ung-chien, Han Chi* 53, Hsing-p'ing, 2.

7. *Tzu-chih T'ung-chien, Chin Chi* 7, T'ai-an 2, A.D. 303.

8. Virtually all the common ones are described in Joseph Needham, *Science and Civilisation in China:* Vol. V:6, *Military Technology* in the subsection by Robin D. S. Yates entitled "Early Poliorcetics: The Mohists to the Sung" which may be consulted for extensive details and further information.

9. Although not illustrated in the *Wu-ching Tsung-yao,* defenders are already being instructed to beware of it ("Shou Ch'eng").

10. *Teng-t'an Pi-chiu,* "Kung Ch'eng." Also found in the *Wu-pei Chih,* "Huo, 14." It is likely that so-called fierce incendiary oil augmented, if not fundamentally provided, its lethality.

11. *Wu Pien, Ch'ien-chi* 5, "Huo Ch'i." Note that T'ang speaks about using poison several times, suggesting restraints were nonexistent and poison gas was readily exploited.

12. The fundamental events of Chi-mo are scattered throughout the *Chan-kuo Ts'e* and condensed in T'ien Tan's biography in the *Shih Chi*. The entire episode is also reprised in the *Tzu-chih T'ung-chien, Chou Chi* 4, 279 B.C.

13. It also numbers among the few examples included in the *T'ung Tien* (*chüan* 141, "Ping 14") under the rubric "yin-chi she-ch'üan." (References to "huo niu" ["fire oxen"] in the histories are not invariably to actual animals because straw versions—actually simply large bundles—were also fabricated for incendiary purposes. For an example of their use, see *Tzu-chih T'ung-chien, T'ang Chi* 67, Hsien-t'ung 10, A.D. 869.)

14. *Tso Chuan*, Duke Ting, 4th year. (As this incident is generally overlooked and it appears in the context of much greater issues, T'ien Tan was probably unaware of it. The Ch'u campaign is extensively discussed in the historical introduction to our *Art of War*.) The elephant incident is also found in several military manuals, including the *Ping-ch'ou Lei-yao*, "Huo Kung."

15. Recent archaeological reports have confirmed the existence of elephants south of the Yangtze, especially in Ch'u, during the Spring and Autumn. (Also see Yang Po-chün, *Ch'un-Ch'iu Tso-chuan Chu*, p. 1545.)

16. Fragmentary accounts are found in the *Sung Shih, chüan* 449, the *Yüan Shih, chüan* 155, and *Hsü Tzu-chih T'ung-chien, chüan* 170, for the year 1241.

17. The rebellion's primary account is found in *chüan* 292 of the *Sung Shih*. (Also see *Hsü Tzu-chih T'ung-chien*, under the years 1047 and 1048.) Incendiary measures played a significant role in the rebel's early attacks and throughout the siege.

18. *Hou-Han Shu, chüan* 38 and *Tzu-chih T'ung-chien, Han Chi* 49, Kuang-ho 3, A.D. 80. This incident is widely employed as an illustration for incendiary warfare and smoke in the military writings, including the *T'ung Tien, chüan* 160; *Wu-ching Tsung-yao*, "Ch'eng-feng Ch'ü-heng"; *Ping-ch'ou Lei-yao*, "Huo Kung"; and *Yün-ch'ou Kang-mu*.

19. Some accounts, including the *Hsü Tzu-chih T'ung-chien*, claim that several thousand monkeys were caught, but this is obviously a copying error resulting from the nearly identical appearance of ten and thousand. Chao Yü's biography in the *Sung Shih* (*chüan* 348), where an account of this incident is preserved, reports several tens were caught.

20. The incident is preserved in *chüan* 83 of the *Chin Shu Chiao-chu* and cited as an illustration of *huo kung* (incendiary attack) rather than incendiary birds in the *T'ung Tien, chüan* 160, "Ping 13" and *Wu-ching Tsung-yao*.

21. For example, in the Ming dynasty *Wu Pien's* chapter entitled "Huo," but without any reference to traditional fire oxen, horses, or sparrows, and even referred to in the *Ch'en Chi's* "Chi Yung."

22. "Huo Shou" or "Incendiary Animals." The description also appears in the *T'ung Tien* (*chüan* 160, "*Ping*" 13) under the same name, as well as the *Hu-ch'ien Ching* ("Huo Kung") and *Wu Pien* ("Huo").

23. "Huo Kung." Also found in the *Wu-pei Chih*, "Huo, 13."

24. The disruptive emphasis was particularly pronounced in the Ming. For example, see *Ch'e-ying Pai-pa K'ou* and *Ch'e-ying Pai-pa Ta*, entry 97.

25. "Huo Ch'in," *T'ai-pai Yin-ching*. With but slight variations, the description also appears in the *T'ung Tien* (*chüan* 160, "*Ping*" 13), *Hu-ch'ien Ching* ("Huo Kung"), *Wu-ching Tsung-yao* ("Huo Kung"), *Wu Pien* ("Huo"), *Teng-t'an Pi-chou* (Kung Ch'eng"), and *Wu-pei Chih* ("Huo, 13").

26. "Kung-ch'eng Chü," *T'ai-pai Yin-ching*. Less commonly found, suggesting it was not deemed practical, but still occasionally included in such compendia as the *Hu-*

*ch'ien Ching,* "Kung-ch'eng Chü"; *Wu-ching Tsung-yao,* "Huo Kung"; *Teng-t'an Pi-chou* (Kung Ch'eng"), and *Wu-pei Chih,* "Huo, 13."

27. How this might be achieved is not specified, while it virtually presumes control of these cites, in which case an incendiary attack would be either unnecessary or could be directly mounted.

28. "Kung Ch'eng."

29. "Kung Ch'eng." Repeated in "Huo, 13," *Wu-pei Chih.* (The last one is actually a cavalryman engaged in incendiary attack, discussed in our section on incendiary attacks.) The text notes that the "ancients" also employed elephants and horses for this purpose.

30. *Wu-pei Chih,* "Huo-ch'i T'u-shuo, 10" ("Huo, 13").

31. *Wu-pei Chih,* "Huo-ch'i T'u-shuo, 10" ("Huo, 13").

32. This "Fei-k'ung Chi-tsei Chen-t'ien Lei-pao" ("flying into the void, striking the brigands shaking Heaven thunder explosive") is described and illustrated in "Huo, 5."

33. The "Shen-huo Fei-ya" is described and illustrated in "Huo, 13," the *Wu-pei Chih.*

34. Such as the "Shen-hsing P'o-ch'en Meng-huo Tao-p'ai" and "Hu-t'ou Huo-p'ai." ( *Wu-pei Chih,* "Huo, 11")

35. *Wu-pei Chih,* "Huo, 14," termed "Huo-lung Chüan-ti Fei-ch'e."

36. *Wu-pei Chih,* "Huo, 13."

37. These "huo chien" should be distinguished from the similarly named rocket assisted arrows which appear late in the imperial period, as will be discussed.

38. The *Hu-ch'ien Ching* preserves the first illustrations of the multiple bow and oversized arcuballista in "Kung-ch'eng Chü." (For further examples such as the *shuang-kung ch'ung-nü,* see "Ch'i-t'u," *chüan* 13, *Wu-ching Tsung-yao.*)

39. For example, the *ming-ling fei-hao-chien* could be equipped with a small incendiary container. ( *Wu-ching Tsung-yao,* "Ch'i-t'u," *Ch'ien-chi, chüan* 13.)

40. *Pei Ch'i Shu, chüan* 16. Also cited in the *T'ung Tien, chüan* 160, "Ping" 13, under the category of "Huo Kung."

41. The *Pei Ch'i Shu* (*chüan* 16, "Tuan Jung") states that the walls were made of stone, but the *Tzu-chih T'ung-chien* simply terms it an ancient city. In all cases it is said to be 1,000 *jen,* the usual term for a high cliff—literally 8,000 feet—though such heights simply don't exist in Honan. (Although there is a mountain by the same name—Po-ku—in Shanhsi, near the T'ai-hang range, according to commentators the city was located in Honan near Yi-yang.)

42. *Wu Pien, Hou-chi, chüan* 2, "Kung."

43. *Huo shih* rather than *huo chien, chien* coincidentally being a term which would gradually come to refer to rocket boosted arrows, though no particular prescience should be attributed to Tu Yu!

44. *T'ai-pai-yin Ching,* "Huo-kung Chü."

45. *T'ung Tien, chüan* 160, "*Ping*" 13. Also found a late as the *Wu Pien,* "Huo."

46. "Kung-ch'eng Chü," *Hu-ch'ien Ching.*

47. "Kung-ch'eng-chü," *T'ai-pai Yin Ching.* (Signal towers are also specified as being equipped with *huo-chien* for defense in "Feng-sui-t'ai," although they were probably simpler versions.) The description also appears in the *T'ung Tien,* "Kung-ch'eng Chan-chü," *Hu-ch'ien Ching,* "Kung-ch'eng Chü," and the *Wu Pien,* "Huo."

48. *Wu Pien,* "Huo."

49. *Teng-t'an Pi-chiu*, "Kung Ch'eng." The original passage appears in the *Wu-ching Tsung-yao*, *Ch'ien-chi*, *chüan* 11. (The *Ch'eng-shou Shou-lüeh* even contains a focal substitute on incendiary arrows.)

50. Primarily discussed in "Huo, 8." However, Chi Ch'i-kuang came to the opposite conclusion in *Lien-ping Shih-chi*.

51. *Ch'eng-shou Shou-lüeh*, "Huo Ch'i." They are also found in Ch'i Chi-kuang's *Lien-ping Shih-chi*, "Chün-ch'i Chieh."

52. The main discussion is found in "Huo, 8," but additional illustrations also appear in "Huo, 9." (An example of simply firing arrows by explosive power is found in "Huo, 11.")

53. "Huo, 8."

54. *Ch'eng-shou Shou-lüeh*, "Chou-fang, 5" and *Wu Pien*, "Shou."

55. "Kung-ch'eng Chü."

56. *Ch'ien-chi* 12, "Shou Ch'eng."

57. "Shou Ch'eng."

58. *Wu Pien*, "Huo Ch'i."

59. *Hou-Han Shu*, *chüan* 24 (Ma's biography), and also cited in the *T'ung Tien*, *chüan* 153, and *Yün-ch'ou Kang-mu*, "Huo Kung."

60. *Fang-shu Chi-ch'eng*, "Yin Cheng."

61. *Tzu-chih T'ung-chien*, *T'ang Chi* 71, Chung-ho 3, A.D. 883. (An earlier example is found for the year A.D. 319: *Tzu-chih T'ung-chien*, *Chin Chi* 13, T'ai-hsing 2.)

62. *Tzu-chih T'ung-chien*, *Chin Chi* 31, Lung-an 1 or 397, though the conflict commenced in 396.

63. *Tzu-chih T'ung-chien*, *Liang Chi* 6, P'u-t'ung 6, A.D. 525.

64. *Tzu-chih T'ung-chien*, *Sui Chi* 1, K'ai-huang 10, A.D. 590.

65. *Tzu-chih T'ung-chien*, *Sui Chi* 6, Ta-yeh 10, A.D. 614.

66. *Tzu-chih T'ung-chien*, *T'ang Chi* 4, Wu-te 3rd year, A.D. 620 and also found in Wang Hsiung-tan's biography, *chüan* 56, *Chiu T'ang Shu*, as well as cited in illustration in "Huo Kung," *Yün-ch'ou Kang-mu*. A somewhat similar incident occurred at the end of the T'ang during Li Mi's revolt. (*Tzu-chih T'ung-chien*, *T'ang Chi 1*, Wu-te 1, A.D. 618 and cited in the *T'ung Tien chüan* 155.)

67. *Tzu-chih T'ung-chien*, *Hou Chin-chi* 3, T'ien-fu 5, A.D. 940.

68. *Tzu-chih T'ung-chien*, *Hou Liang Chi* 1, K'ai-p'ing 1.

69. For four remarkable examples of tunneling out behind enemy lines and mounting incendiary strikes, see the *Tzu-chih T'ung-chien*, *Sung Chi* 1, Yung-ch'u 3 (A.D. 422), the battle of Hu-lao; *Sung Chi* 4, Yüan-chia 9 (A.D. 432), in fighting off Chao Kuang's "righteous" army; *Sung Chi* 8, Yüan-chia 29 (A.D. 452), where Wei was defending Ch'iao-ao against Sung; and the *Hsü Tzu-chih T'ung-chien*, A.D. 1130, during the Jurchen siege of Shan-fu. In A.D. 864, 300 raiders dropped down from the city walls to burn the enemy's defenses and tents, ending a siege. (*Tzu-chih T'ung-chien*, *T'ang Chi* 66, Hsien-t'ung 5.)

70. For example, Wang Chao-ch'un's *Chung-kuo Huo-ch'i Shih* (Pei-ching: Chün-shih K'o-hsüeh Ch'u-pan-she, 1991). Further technical information in English, particularly for explosive devices, may be found in the extensive studies of Joseph Needham and Robin Yates embedded in the general section entitled "Military Technology" in *Science and Civilisation in China*.

71. The *Wu-pei Chih*'s material on incendiary arrows has already been discussed in the earlier subsection.

72. See "Huo 12" for examples of both. The device known as "drawing fire ball," previously mentioned for establishing target range, is included among them.

73. For further specifications and general discussion, see Needham, "The Gunpowder Epic."

74. "Huo, 12."

75. "Huo, 12."

76. "Huo, 5."

77. "Huo, 5."

78. "Huo, 10."

79. "Huo, 12."

80. "Huo, 12."

81. "Huo, 12."

82. "Huo, 4."

83. "Huo, 5."

84. "Huo, 4."

85. "Huo, 5."

86. "Huo, 15."

87. "Huo, 12." Called a *tui-hei shao-jen huo-hu-li* or "confronting the blackness incinerating men fire gourd."

88. Examples may be found in "Huo, 12."

89. "Huo, 12."

90. "Huo, 12."

91. "Huo, 12."

92. "Huo, 12."

93. "Level, broad infantry warfare following ground roller."

94. "Huo, 12."

95. "Huo, 12."

96. "Huo, 12."

97. "Huo, 4."

## CHAPTER 6

1. "Ti."

2. Also found as the initial sentences of the *Wu-pei Chih's* "Huo 3." (Also see the *Huo-lung Shen-ch'i Ch'en-fa*.)

3. "Yung-huo Ch'i-fa" in "Huo, 3."

4. "Shou Ch'eng," *Wu-ching Tsung-yao*.

5. "Huo-ch'i T'u-shuo, 11" in "Huo, 14."

6. "Chou." As an example, imperial troops dispatched by the much reviled Empress Wu to suppress Li Ching in A.D. 684, being hard pressed, resorted to an incendiary attack amidst dry vegetation and high winds to achieve victory (*Tzu-chih T'ung-chien, T'ang Chi* 19, Kuang-chai 1).

7. Number 27, "Preparation." Also cited in the *T'ung Tien, chüan* 155 and 160, and the *Yün-ch'ou Kang-mu*, "Huo Kung," whose author similarly warns that one should always fear incendiary attacks in windy conditions. An interesting example is found in the *Tzu-chih T'ung-chien* (*Wei Chi* 1, Huang-ch'u 2) when forces campaigning against the Hu found themselves in a heavy wind and feared, perspicaciously, that the enemy was planning a nighttime incendiary attack. They therefore prepared an ambush that surprised the raiders, turning the confrontation to their favor.

8. "Wind."

9. For a translation of the illustrative incident, see chapter 93, "Wind." (As might be expected because it is the same text as the *Unorthodox Strategies* but under a different name, it is also found in Yeh Meng-hsiung's sixteenth-century *Chüeh-sheng Kang-mu.*)

10. *Tzu-chih T'ung-chien, Chin Chi* 37, An-hsi 6. Also found as an example in "Shui Chan," the *Wu-ching Tsung-yao.*

11. The incident is briefly mentioned in the *T'ang Shih, chüan* 220, "Tung Yi."

12. Hsü Mien-chih, *Pao Yüeh Lü, Pai-pu Ts'ung-shu Chi-ch'eng,* Yen Yi-p'in, general editor, Taipei, Yi-wen Yin-shu-kuan.

13. "Ni-yung Ti-hsing." This sentence does not appear in the extant *Art of War.*

14. The *Teng-t'an Pi-chou,* compiled in 1599, includes this statement. Similar assertions may be found in "Incendiary Attacks," *Ts'ao-lü Ching-lüeh,* and "Ti" in the *Wu Pien.*

15. *Chüeh-sheng Kang-mu,* "Huo Chan."

16. This idea is seen as late as the *Wu Pien,* "Ti."

17. "Wu Lüeh."

18. *Tzu-chih T'ung-chien, Sui-chi* 6, Yang-ti Ta-yeh 9 (A.D. 613), which simply indicates an area with reeds; Tu's biographies in the *Chiu T'ang-shu, chüan* 56, and *T'ang-shu, chüan* 92, indicate it was a marshy terrain, as would be expected for this area. (This incident is also cited as a historical example for "Huo Kung" in the *Ts'ao-lü Ching-lüeh.*)

19. "Huang-fu Sung, Chu Chün Lieh-chuan." Also cited in "Huo Kung" in the *T'ung Tien, chüan* 161, "Ping" 13, and employed as the historical illustration for "Huo Chan" in the *Wu-ching Tsung-yao, Hundred Unorthodox Strategies, Yün-ch'ou Kang-mu,* and *Chüeh-sheng Kang-mu,* and "Huo" in the *Wu Pien.*

20. The *T'ung Tien* account, found in *chüan* 160, commences by summarizing the situation just before Wang Lin exploited the southwesterly wind to strike downriver (but basically northeast, as the Yangtze River turns upward here) toward Yang-chou. The expanded *Tzu-chih T'ung-chien* materials, which essentially cohere, are scattered through the years corresponding to A.D. 557 to 560 in *Ch'en-chi* 1 and 2, the fire sequence appearing in *Ch'en-chi* 2, T'ien-chia 1st year. However, there are some important discrepancies between the two chief accounts of the individual commanders, *Pei Ch'i Shu, chüan* 32 (Wang Lin's biography) and *Ch'en Shu, chüan* 9 (Hou Chen's biography) which would merit further exploration were the *T'ung Tien* and *Tzu-chih T'ung-chien* accounts not the most widely read among military students. (The episode also appears as an illustration in the *Wu-ching Tsung-yao,* "Shui Chan," and *Wu Pien,* "Chou.")

21. *Tzu-chih T'ung-chien, Chin Chi* 28, T'ai-yüan 10, A.D. 385. The tendency of subversives to resort to fire first—even view it as their only possibility—should be noted.

22. *Tzu-chih T'ung-chien, Ch'en Chi* 4, Kuang-ta 1.

23. *Tzu-chih T'ung-chien, T'ang Chi* 19, Kuang-chai 1, briefly mentioned in the *Chiu T'ang Shu, chüan* 92. The episode also serves as one of the *Yün-ch'ou Kang-mu's* illustrations for "Huo Kung."

24. Another of the *Yün-ch'ou Kang-mu's* illustrations of setting fires amidst heavy grass ("Huo Kung"), the episode is originally found in the *Chiu Wu-tai Shih, chüan* 1, "Pen-chi," and cited as an example of "Huo Kung" in the *Wu-ching Tsung-yao,* but merely mentioned in the *Tzu-chih T'ung-chien.*

25. *Tzu-chih T'ung-chien, Hou-Liang Chi* 5, Chen-ming 5, A.D. 919.

26. *Tzu-chih T'ung-chien, T'ang-chi* 20, Ch'ui-kung 4, A.D. 688. Additional examples of the wind shifting and thwarting incendiary plans will be found in the section on riverine warfare.

27. Ch'en Kuei, "Ching-k'ang Ch'ao-yeh Chien-yen Hou-hsü," *Shou-ch'eng Lü*. Space unfortunately precludes a recounting of the historically important siege at K'aifeng which had been left isolated and unsupported by the emperor. However, Sung commandos successfully launched a surprise incendiary attack on the Jurchen camp early on, though another raid against lethal Jurchen trebuchet failed. The enemy maintained an active siege, inflicting almost daily punishment upon the city with assaults and incendiary attacks, but continued to be repelled in fierce fighting. Despite heavy casualties among the 70,000 quickly gathered defenders and the bitter cold, they resolutely sustained the effort under Tsung Tse, employing incendiary warfare, early gunpowder devices, and powerful crossbows which delivered withering fire. However, instead of attempting to rally the troops for a fatal last effort, the terrified emperor capitulated and dispersed the armies, ending the Northern Sung.

28. *Tzu-chih T'ung-chien, Hou T'ang Chi* 3, T'ien-ch'eng 1st year, A.D. 926. Also found as an illustration for "Huo Kung" in the *Wu-ching Tsung-yao*, "Huo" in the *Wu Pien Hou-chi*, and mentioned in K'ang Yen-hsiao's biography, *chüan* 44, *Wu-tai Shih*. (Accounts differ as to the fence's material, but moderate-diameter bamboo would have been especially likely in the semi-tropical Szechuan valley.)

29. The incident is cited in the *Yün-ch'ou Kang-mu*, "Huo Kung," found in P'an Mei's biography (*Sung Shih, chüan* 258), and summarized in the *Hsü Tzu-chih T'ung-chien* for A.D. 971.

30. Practices such as dragging brush behind chariots in order to thwart observers date back to antiquity. Thus, commencing with Sun-tzu's *Art of War*, China also has a long tradition of deriving military intelligence from clouds of dust and smoke—as distinguished from *ch'i* emanations, which have their own interpretive criteria—rising in consequence of enemy activity. For example, in his *Ts'ui-wei Pei-cheng-lu* ("Ma Cheng") written in 1207, Hua Yüeh claimed to discriminate seven configurations of dust and ten of smoke that betray enemy conditions and activities. (For further discussion of dust and *ch'i* signification, as well as their employment on the battlefield, see our *Tao of Spycraft*. For another Ming example, see *Ch'e-ying Pai-pa Shuo*, entry 26.)

31. *Wu Pien*, "Ti."

32. For example, see "Shou-ch'eng Chü" in the *Hu-ch'ien Ching*, "Ti" in the *Wu Pien*, and "Shou Ch'eng" in the *Teng-t'an Pi-chiu*. Hua Yüeh included sprinkling poison and employing windblown drugs among the forty-two secret methods for attacking cities in his *Ts'ui-wei Pei-cheng-lu* ("Te Ti") compiled in 1207. The *Wu-ching Tsung-yao* ("Shou Ch'eng") specifies that sacks of lime dust are among the key defensive materials to be kept atop the walls. Although lime dust was used to repel attackers coming over the walls in a favorable wind, they also employed chaff mixed with lime to blind their eyes. (Discussions in the late sixteenth-century *Shou-ch'eng Chiu-ming-shu* and *Ch'en Chi* indicate the technique was still being employed in the late Ming.) Poisonous smoke emitted by eruptors was also widely employed in the Ming, always in accord with the wind (*Wu Pien*, "Huo Ch'i").

33. "Hsing Yen."

34. Also found verbatim as late as Wang Ming-ho's 1599 *Teng-t'an Pi-chiu*, "Kung Ch'eng."

35. The *Wu-ching Tsung-yao* ("Shou-ch'eng") also describes a smoke bomb intended solely for the purpose of marking target range.

36. See the discussion on wind and action in the section on wind and vegetation.

37. All in the subsection entitled "Chih Huo-ch'i-fa, 2" found in "Huo, 2."

38. For example, Southern Ch'i moved a major force by boat into the Ch'ing-shui area under the cover of fog in A.D. 488. (*Tzu-chih T'ung-chien, Ch'i Chi* 2, Yung-ming 6.) Some of the military manuals also contain brief subsections on exploiting inclement weather, including rain, fog, and wind.

39. Cited in the "Huo Kung" section of the *Ts'ao-lü Ching-lüeh*, and also found in Hsi's biography in the *Wei Shu, chüan* 73.

40. *Tzu-Chih T'ung-chien, Han Chi* 35, Chien-wu 12.

41. *San-kuo Chih*, "Man, T'ien, Ch'ien, Kuo Ch'uan."

42. *Tzu-chih T'ung-chien, Sui Chi* 1, K'ai-huang 9, A.D. 589, and also found as an illustration for "Yen Chan" in the *Ts'ai-lü Ching-lüeh* which erroneously has Ch'en's forces being repulsed.

43. Li Kuang-tien, *Chieh-lü Shou-Pien Erh-chih*, entry for 7/24. (The "Shou Ch'eng" section of the *Wu-ching Tsung-yao* also advises holding one's face over a bath of vinegar and soy water, the *Wu Pien* ["Shou"] a pan of five parts each vinegar, soy sauce, and water. [Similar methods are suggested in "Li-ti Ku-shou" in the *Ch'eng-shou Ch'ou-lüeh*.] Soldiers intercepting miners in underground tunnels sometimes deployed thunderclap incendiary spheres whose outer layers contained several noxious substances, producing poisonous smoke upon combustion. Expected to propel this dense black smoke toward the enemy with bamboo fans, they similarly kept licorice water in their mouths as an antidote. ["Ts'uo Ying," *Fang-shou Chi-ch'eng*.])

44. *Tzu-chih T'ung-chien, Hou Liang Chi* 5, Chen-ming 3, A.D. 917.

45. *Hsü Tzu-chih T'ung-chien, Shao-kuang* 32nd year, A.D. 1162.

46. A much earlier clash between the Khitan and Jurchen also saw obfuscation techniques employed. (*Tzu-chih T'ung-chien, Hou Liang Chi* 5, Chen-ming 3, A.D. 917.)

47. *Tzu-chih T'ung-chien*, A.D. 316, 7th month.

48. *Tzu-chih T'ung-chien, T'ang Chi* 3, Wu-te 2 or A.D. 619. Hatred and animosity were frequently the byproduct of scorched-earth policies, whether locally or nationally imposed.

49. For an example see *Tzu-chih T'ung-chien, Ch'i Chi* 10, Chung-hsin 1, A.D. 501.

50. *Tzu-chih T'ung chien, Sui Chi* 6, Ta-yeh 10 or A.D. 614.

51. *Hsü Tzu-chih T'ung-chien*, A.D. 971.

52. "Sou-shan Shao-ts'ao." Similar advice can be found through the ages, including the late Ming *T'ou-pi Fu-t'an*, "Wu Lüeh."

53. *Tzu-chih T'ung-chien, Liang Chi* 3, T'ien-chien 7, A.D. 508.

54. A Sung dynasty example of coating sails is cited in "Shui Chan," *Ts'ao-lü Ching-lüeh*.

55. For example, in "Shou Ch'eng" in the *Teng-t'an Pi-chou* where the use of limestone coatings is also suggested.

56. Chao Wan-nien, *Hsiang-yang Shou-ch'eng-lü*, Yen Yi-p'ing, general editor, Ao-yang-t'ang Ts'ung-shu, Taipei, Yi-wen Yin-shu-kuan. Even largely lost military writings such as the reconstructed *Li Wei-kung Ping-fa* ("Kung-shou Chan-chü") emphasize the value and importance of rawhide for defense against missile fire and especially incendiaries.

57. "Shou-ch'eng Chü," *T'ai-pai Yin-ching*. Most of these techniques are found in sections on city defense, but many surprisingly appear in thematic chapters focused upon attacking cities and riverine objectives. See, for example, "Shou-chü Fa" in the *T'ung Tien*; "Shou-ch'eng Chü in the *Hu-ch'ien Ching*; "Shou Ch'eng," in the *Wu-*

*ching Tsung-yao* (*Ch'ien-chi, chüan* 12); "Shou Ch'eng" in the *Teng-t'an Pi-chiu;* "Shou" in the *Wu Pien;* and finally the *Shou-ch'eng Chiu-ming Shu.* Flammable materials such as firewood and stores should be completely removed, as the *Mo-tzu* and subsequent texts advise. (See, for example, the *Ch'eng-shou Ch'ou-lüeh.*)

58. "Pao Chih." However, his analysis focuses on the border areas where practices apparently differed somewhat from the more stable core domain. (It would seem that every technique would have been used because of the frequency of attacks, yet towers were apparently lacking.)

59. *T'ai-pai Yin-ching,* "Shou-ch'eng Chü"; *T'ung Tien,* "Shou-chü Fa"; *Hu-ch'ien Ching,* "Shou-ch'eng Chü"; *Wu-ching Tsung-yao,* "Shou Ch'en"; *Teng-t'an Pi-chiu,* "Shou Ch'eng" in which Wang notes that people formerly used oiled sacks for this purpose; *Ch'eng-shou Ch'ou-lüeh,* "Chou Fang, 5"; and *Wu Pien,* "Shou," which suits the response to the attack's intensity, flails and forks being used for light assaults.

60. *Wu-ching Tsung-yao, Ch'ien-chi, chüan* 12, "Shou Ch'eng." (Wet sand was the method of choice, though other mixtures were also employed over the centuries.) These warnings are found as late as the "Lin-ti Ku-shou" in the *Ch'eng-shou Ch'ou-lüeh* and may have been prompted by a shift to the "fierce incendiary oil" already being used in flamethrowers.

61. "Shou-chü Fa." The text notes that if bamboo isn't available, the defenders will have to improvise the necessary pipes from appropriately sized lacquered buckets and supplement their efforts with twenty additional shallow buckets. (These extinguishers continue to be described right through the Ming. For example, see *Hu-ch'ien Ching,* "Shou-ch'eng Chü"; *Wu-ching Tsung-yao,* "Shou Ch'eng"; and *Teng-t'an Pi-chiu,* "Shou Ch'eng.")

62. *T'ung Tien,* "Shou-chü Fa"; *Wu-ching Tsung-yao,* "Shou Ch'eng"; *Teng-t'an Pi-chiu,* "Shou Ch'eng."

63. *Wu-ching Tsung-yao,* "Shou Ch'eng" and *Teng-t'an Pi-chiu,* "Shou Ch'eng."

64. Cited in illustration in "Shou," the *Wu Pien.*

65. From inception, they are said to provide defense against catapult launched firebombs as well, though this seems less probable. (They first appear in the *Wu-ching Tsung-yao, Ch'ien-chi, chüan* 12, "Shou Ch'eng," but are also found as late as the *Teng-t'an Pi-chiu,* "Shou Ch'eng.")

66. The *T'ai-pai Yin-ching* specifies a length of one *chang* or ten feet, with the timber having a massive diameter of one foot five inches ("Kung-ch'eng Chü"). The *Wu-pei Chih* indicates a length of one *chang* five feet, also for a tent-shaped vehicle of this type mounted with six wheels, and illustrates another one with four, both of which use rawhide for protection and can contain ten men each. ("Chün-tsu-ch'eng, Kung 2, Ch'i-chü T'u-shuo 2." The *Wu-pei Chih's* selected passages from the *T'ai-pai Yin-ching* leave out many devices from the "Kung-ch'eng Chü" and "Shou-ch'eng Chü" sections.)

67. See, for example, *Wu-pei Chih,* "Chün-tsu-ch'eng, Kung 2, Ch'i-chü T'u-shuo 2."

68. For example, the T'ang dynasty *T'ung Tien* terms them "small-headed wooden donkeys." (hsiao-t'ou mu-lu). (*T'ung Tien, chüan* 160, "Ping" 13, "Kung-ch'eng Chan-chü") Also found in the *Hu-ch'ien Ching,* "Kung-ch'eng Chü" and the *Wu-ching Tsung-yao* ("Kung-ch'eng Chan-chü") in a variant that used cords for ribs.

69. *T'ung Tien, chüan* 160, "Ping" 13, "Kung-ch'eng Chan-chü."

70. *Wu-ching Tsung-yao*, "Shui Chan." Even the late *Wu-pei Chih* still describes vessels employing protective rawhide in one of its sections on boats, "Chou Ch'uan, 2."

71. "Huo Chan," *Ts'ao-lü Ching-lüeh*.

72. "Shui Chan," *Ts'ao-lü Ching-lüeh*.

73. *T'ai-pai Yin-ching*, "Kung-ch'eng-chü." Similar enumerations are found right through the Ming, including in the *T'ung Tien*, "Shou-chü Fa"; *Hu-ch'ien Ching*, "Shou-ch'eng-chü"; and *Teng-t'an Pi-chou*, "Shou Ch'eng."

74. Not noted until the T'ang dynasty *Hu-ch'ien Ching*, "Ch'i Chih," their use must have commenced centuries earlier and continued unabated right through the Ming. For example, the *Teng-t'an Pi-chou*, "Shou Ch'eng," still describes the use of burning faggots and grass in city defense. Conversely, the *Ping-ch'ou Lei-yao*, "Huo Kung," attributes the victory at Ho-fei (whose badly outnumbered defenders repulsed Sun Ch'üan's force of a 100,000) to torches infused with sesame oil, and they were obviously employed at Ch'en-ts'ang. Another good example is Chang Hsün's use against rebel forces in A.D. 756 at Yung-ch'iu (*Tzu-chih T'ung-chien*, *T'ang Chi* 33, Chih-te 1). Torches well soaked in oil and piled atop walls were also employed in emergencies to stop troops from overrunning the walls, setting up a "mountain of fire." For example, see Meng Tsang-cheng's actions as recorded in the *Hsü Tzu-chih T'ung-chien* for A.D. 1219 or his biography in the *Sung Shih*, *chüan* 403. (Also cited in illustration in the *Fang-shou Chi-ch'eng*.) Torches were also used in attack, as many historical incidents and such texts as the *Li Wei-kung Ping-fa* indicate.

75. *T'ai-pai Yin-ching*, "Shou-ch'eng-chü." Also incorporated into the *T'ung Tien*, "Shou-chü Fa"; *Hu-ch'ien Ching*, "Shou-ch'eng-chü"; *Wu-ching Tsung-yao*, "Shou-ch'eng"; and *Wu-pei Chih*, "Huo-ch'i T'u-shuo, 9"; *Wu Pien*, "Shou"; *Ch'eng-shou Ch'ou-lüeh*, "Chou Fang, 5"; and mentioned as still functional in the *Ch'en Ch'i*, "Chi Yung." It was employed at the siege of Chien-k'ang already described, and the siege of Ying-ch'uan.

76. *Wu-ching Tsung-yao*, "Shou-ch'eng." The text simply refers to it as a "flying torch." It is still found in the *Wu-pei Chih*, "Huo-ch'i T'u-shuo, 9."

77. For example, in A.D. 347 Later Chao's forces outnumbered the Former Liang defenders, but despite suffering heavy losses they battled on until their assault equipment was burned (*Tzu-chih T'ung-chien*, *Chin Chi* 19, Yung-ho 3).

78. *T'ai-pai Yin-ching*, "Shou-ch'eng Chü." Replicated thereafter in the *T'ung Tien*, "Shou-chü Fa"; *Hu-ch'ien Ching*, "Shou-ch'eng Chü"; *Wu-ching Tsung-yao*, "Shou-ch'eng"; *Wu Pien*, "Shou"; and *Wu-pei Chih*, "Huo, 14," where two types are shown. Even the Jurchen adopted this defensive measure, having acquired the skills through defectors such as Lu Wen-chin. For example, in battling a Khitan siege effort in 917 they not only cut counter tunnels to intercept and burn out the enemy, but also used molten metal to defeat attempts to close and ascend the walls. (*Tzu-chih T'ung-chien*, *Hou Liang Chi* 5, Chen-ming 3.)

79. *Fang-shou Chi-ch'eng*, "Yin Cheng." It's also possible that they were steam-bent into shape.

80. Two are illustrated in the *Wu-pei Chih*, one apparently pushed around, the other—called a *t'ieh-chih shen-ch'e* or "iron liquid spirit cart"—mounted on a normal four wheeled wagon ("Huo, 14").

81. The *Feng-shou Chi-ch'eng* ("Yin Cheng") cites a Five Dynasties period example in which the arrows were simply being extinguished in the dirt, but the red hot balls penetrated sufficiently to set the huge mass of hemp encasing the straw ablaze

and completely consume the mound of materials. (Their effectiveness also saw them used in attacks, such as by the Mongols in 1274 when, as part of their overall incendiary attack on a Sung citadel, they hurled red-hot metal balls by trebuchet. [*Hsü Tzu-Chih T'ung-chien*, A.D. 1274])

82. *T'ai-pai Yin-ching*, "Shou-ch'eng Chü," and *T'ung Tien*, "Shou-chü Fa." The *Hu-ch'ien Ching*, "Shou-ch'eng Chü," employs lime.

83. For example, see the *Wu-ching Tsung-yao*, "Shou Ch'eng." (As these weapons were also employed by the attacking forces, they are discussed in the section entitled "Incendiary Methods.") Their use to attack siege devices over the ages are too frequent and common to need documentation. Variants, by name and size, were also many, both shot from bows and arcuballistae. (For an example, see *Tzu-chih T'ung-chien, Wei Chi* 9, Kan-lu 3, A.D. 258.)

84. For example, Esen's attack on Pei-ching in 1449 was repulsed in large measure by incendiary arrows.

85. The composition and employment of smoke and incendiary balls are discussed in the sections on smoke and weapons for incendiary attack. The *Wu-ching Tsung-yao*, "Shou-ch'eng," describes a smoke bomb designed solely for the purpose of marking target range, with incendiary bombs with caltrop style barbs thereafter being employed against the enemy's siege devices. (Also found in the *Wu Pien*, "Shou.")

86. *Wu-ching Tsung-yao*, "Shou Ch'eng." The *T'ai-pai Yin-ching* ("Shou-ch'eng Chü") specifies pieces of pine for their brightness. (Also see the *Hu-ch'ien Ching*, "Shou-ch'eng Chü," which adds oil and lard to the torches to ensure no one can hide in the dark; *T'ou-pi Fu-t'an*, "Wu Lüeh"; *Wu Pien*, "Shou"; and *Chiu-ming Shu*, "Shou Ch'eng.")

87. *Wu-ching Tsung-yao*, "Shou Ch'eng."

88. Termed "mobile fire" (*yu huo*), they are described in the "Shou-ch'eng Chü" section of the *T'ai-pai Yin-ching* and subsequently found in the *T'ung Tien*, "Shou-chü Fa"; *Hu-ch'ien Ching*, "Shou-ch'eng Chü"; *Wu-pei Chih*, "Huo, 12"; and even the *Ch'eng-shou Ch'ou-lüeh*, "Chou Fang, 5." Later, strong explosive charges, such as the Wei-yüan Shih-p'ao found in the *Wu-pei Chih* ("Huo, 4") were also deployed in this fashion.

89. *Wu-ching Tsung-yao, Ch'ien-chi chüan* 12, "Shou-ch'eng." When used inside the walls, a well would first have to be cut down into the enemy's tunnel, but it was also possible to swing them into "holes" which the enemy might be excavating into the city walls from outside.

90. *Wu-ching Tsung-yao*, "Shou Ch'eng. For the Ming, see the *Wu Pien*, "Shou," and *Wu-pei Chih*, "Huo, 12" whose description of use has become minimal. (The circular eyelets used for the head allow them to be hooked to the trebuchet for flinging.)

91. *Wu-ching Tsung-yao*, "Shou Ch'eng." It doesn't reappear until the *Wu Pien*, "Shou," and *Wu-pei Chih*, "Huo, 13," which probably preserves it just for completeness.

92. See, for example, *Ts'ui-wei Pei-cheng-lu*, "Shou Ti."

93. For a full, insightful reconstruction of the history of the flame thrower and associated fierce oil see Joseph Needham's *Science and Civilisation in China*, Vol. Five, Part 7: "Military Technology, The Gunpowder Epic," pp. 73–94 ("Naptha, Greek Fire and Petrol Flame-Throwers").

94. See Needham, "Naptha, Greek Fire and Petrol Flame-Throwers," pp. 81–82, citing the *Wu Yüeh Pei-shih*. (Needham emphasizes the commentator' views that it was imported from Arabia.)

95. *Hsü Tzu-chih T'ung-chien*, A.D. 975 (Sung T'ai-tsu K'ai-pao 8).

96. For example the *Ch'eng-shou Ch'ou-lüeh*, "Chou Fang, 5," advises using "fierce oil" against assault engines and similar devices. The *Teng-t'an Pi-chou*, "Kung Ch'eng," similarly indicates it was used in incendiary arrows for attacking the materials being used to fill in ditches and moats. The *Ch'en Chi*, in "Chi Yung," mentions two other oils, green oil, and salamander oil.

97. "Naptha, Greek Fire and Petrol Flame-Throwers," pp. 80–81.

98. *Tzu-chih T'ung-chien, Hou Liang Chi* 4, Chen-ming 3, A.D. 917.

99. The *Huo-kung Chi-yao* compiled about 1643 in conjunction with a German advisor describes spray tubes with a range of forty to fifty paces that emit small stones but can also be employed in flamethrower fashion against flammable targets.

100. Despite being gunpowder-based, these devices were readily integrated into contemporary practice. Nevertheless, as they define the limit of our inquiry into traditional, non-gunpowder techniques and practices, their history must be left to Joseph Needham's detailed, masterful recounting in "The Gunpowder Epic," an immense work of erudition and illustration.

101. *Teng-t'an Pi-chiu*, "Kung Ch'eng," and *Wu Pien*, "Shou," among others. It was also used in defensive situations on both land and water.

102. For example, the Ming dynasty *Ch'eng-shou Ch'ou-lüeh*, in "Lin-ti Ku-shou," asserts that muskets are the primary defensive weapons, incendiary arrows secondary.

103. "Ch'eng Shou." (Also found earlier in the *Ch'eng-shou Ch'ou-lüeh*, "Lin-ti Ku-shou.")

104. "Shen Fang," *Fang-shou Chi-ch'eng*, and also found in the *Ch'eng-shou Ch'ou-lüeh* in "Lin-ti Ku-shou."

105. *Tzu-chih T'ung-chien, T'ang Chi* 34, 35. The battles are also recounted in Chang Hsün's lengthy biography in the *T'ang Shu, chüan* 192, and included in the *Fang-shou Chi-ch'eng*'s illustrative material, "Yin Cheng."

106. *Tzu-chih T'ung-chien, T'ang Chi* 45, Chien-chung 4th year, also cited as an example in *Fang-shou Chi-ch'eng*, "Yin Cheng." Chu Ts'u was slain and the rebellion ended. (Also found in the *Ping-ch'ou Lei-yao*, "Huo Kung," and Wu Pien, "Shou.")

107. "Kung-ch'eng Chü." Kao Huan (of Yü-pi fame) successfully employed this technique to overcome Yeh-ch'eng in A.D. 532. (*Tzu-chih T'ung-chien, Liang Chi* 11, Ta-t'ung 4.)

108. *Teng-t'an Pi-chiu*, "Kung Ch'eng."

109. *T'ai-pai Yin-ching*, "Shou-ch'eng Chü"; *Tung Tien*, "Shou-chü Fa"; *Hu-ch'ien Ching*, "Kung-ch'eng Chü"; and the *Wu-ching Tsung-yao*, "Shou Ch'eng."

110. *T'ai-pai Yin-ching*, "Shou-ch'eng Chü"; *Tung Tien*, "Shou-chü Fa"; *Hu-ch'ien Ching*, "Kung-ch'eng Chü."

111. *T'ung Tien*, "Shou-chü Fa."

112. "Shou-ch'eng Chü" and incorporated in the *T'ung Tien*, "Shou-chü Fa."

113. Also found in the *Hu-ch'ien Ching*, "Shou-ch'eng Chü"; *T'ung Tien*, "Shou-chü Fa"; and *Teng-'an Pi-chiu*, "Kung Ch'eng."

114. *Wu-ching Tsung-yao*, "Shou Ch'eng" and "Kung-ch'eng Fa"; *Ch'eng-shou Ch'ou-lüeh*, Chou Fang, 5"; *Wu Pien*, "Shou."

115. *Wu-ching Tsung-yao*, "Kung-ch'eng Fa." Also incorporated into the *Teng-t'an Pi-chiu*, "Kung Ch'eng," with a reduced illustration.

116. *Wu-ching Tsung-yao*, "Shou Ch'eng."

117. "Tsuo Ying," *Fang-shou Chi-ch'eng*.

118. See Li Kuang-tien, *Chieh-lü Shou-pien Erh-chih* in Chu Lu, "Ch'eng Shou," *Fang-shou Chi-ch'eng.*

## CHAPTER 7

1. Along with confronting hills, going contrary to the current's flow, occupying killing ground, and confronting masses of trees ("Treasures of Terrain," *Military Methods*).

2. "Maneuvering the Army," the *Art of War.* (Even though he reportedly served in Wu, a wet southeastern area, Sun-tzu rarely discussed the problems posed by water, presumably because his teachings resulted from pondering the nature of plains warfare.) A century and a half later Sun Pin would note, "Unusual movements and perverse actions are the means by which to crush the enemy at fords." Thereafter, military thinkers frequently advised exploiting rivers, especially in constricted valleys, to thwart enemy advances, always attacking when half had crossed. (For example, see Hua Yüeh's *Ts'ui-wei Pei-cheng-lu*, "Chi Chü" and "Te Ti.") Various means were also employed to retard the enemy's progress, such as caltrops and sharpened bamboo sticks concealed beneath the water's surface. (See, for example, "Chi Shui," *Wu-pei Chih, chüan* 118.)

3. "Rivers."

4. Especially "The Army's Equipment" and "Planning for the Army." (Pontoon bridges had the additional advantage of not requiring equipment and provisions to be repeatedly off and on loaded for transport to the opposite shore.)

5. After noting the *Liu-t'ao's* admonition to carry appropriate equipment, the *T'ai-pai Yin-ching* ("Chi-shui Chü") describes three devices for extemporaneous crossings: rafts made from spears—a bundle of ten can float one man—and two more complex forms, a mat type made from rushes and one utilizing sheep skins. It is chronologically followed by a section entitled "Kuo Shui" ("Crossing Rivers") in the *Hu-ch'ien Ching*, then the *Wu-ching Tsung-yao* material, though variants and expansions continue right through the *Wu-pei Chih*, "Chi Shui." Dwellings and other structures in the river's immediate vicinity were also torn apart for salvageable wood, especially by the large Khitan, Jurchen, and Mongol armies that attempted to cross the Huai and Yangtze Rivers.

6. *Tzu-chih T'ung-chien, Han Chi* 1, Kao-ti 2, 205 B.C.

7. "The Distant."

8. For a basic overview of China's murky early naval history, see Yang Hung, "Shui-chün ho Chan-ch'uan" in *Chung-kuo Ku Ping-ch'i Lun-tsung* (Taipei: Ming-wen, 1983 reprint), pp. 113–122; Hsi Lung-fei, *Chung-kuo Tsao-ch'uan-shih* (Hu-pei: Chiao-yü Ch'u-pan-she, 1999); Chang T'ieh-niu and Kao Hsiao-hsing, *Chung-kuo Ku-tai Hai-chün-shih* (Pei-ching: Pa-yi Ch'u-pan-she, 1993); and Joseph Needham's "Nautical Technology" in Vol. IV, part III of *Science and Civilisation in China* (Cambridge: University Press, 1971).

9. As the rowers' strength was often insufficient to make any headway against the current without the wind's assistance and poling was generally not possible, to go up-river ropes frequently had to be used to pull from the shore (though only a few ships could be moved in this fashion at the time due to problems of congestion and lack of riverside space for the necessary tractive power, whether men or animals). If the current or wind were strong, the boats might still fall into enemy hands, as in the spring of A.D. 417 when Chin lost several warships because even the heavy 100 *chang* ropes

were unable to keep the boats from blowing to the north shore where Northern Wei's forces slaughtered the sailors. (*Tzu-chih T'ung-chien, Chin Chi* 40, Yi-hsi 13.)

10. For example, see "Ta Shu" in the *T'ou-pi Fu-t'an* and "Chan Ch'uan, 1" in the *Wu-pei Chih*.

11. For example, see "Shui Kung" in the *T'ung Tien* and "Chan Ch'uan" in the *Wu-pei Chih*.

12. This passage is also found verbatim in the *Wu Pien*, "Ti."

13. "Huo Chan."

14. Another example is found under "Huo Kung" in the *Wu-ching Tsung-yao*.

15. *Ts'ao-lü Ching-lüeh*, "Shui Chan," asserts that bows, crossbows, and incendiary implements are all necessary and that when gunpowder devices are "deployed to assist riverine warfare, victory will certainly result."

16. *Ts'ao-lü Ching-lüeh*, "Shui Chan." In the coastal and riverine areas every sort of vessel was of course utilized over the centuries and sailors both recruited and coerced into serving by defensive and aggressor forces, especially those from out of the steppe.

17. Although Wang doesn't discuss the role of powerful families and officials in nurturing and exploiting the crisis, he uncharacteristically but correctly notes that the Japanese pirate issue was not simply a question of external marauders, but the participation of numerous, long-oppressed local people.

18. Even some of Sun-tzu's observations of enemy behavior are translated to riverine form.

19. "Chi Shui-chan Shuo." Wang cites several significant historical naval engagements beginning with the king of Ch'u building boats to attack Wu (*Tso Chuan*, Duke Hsiang 24) and Wu suffering a defeat in a naval engagement with Ch'u (*Tso Chuan*, Duke Chao 27) before noting that since the Han and Chin dynasties a variety of boats had been employed, all of them adequate to forcefully transforming the four barbarians, and that the topography in the southeast is particularly conducive to aquatic warfare. With respect to northern soldiers being inexperienced in water skills, he twice notes that Han Wu-ti opened K'un-ming Lake to practice riverine warfare to overcome their shortcomings.

20. Preserved in the section on *huo-kung* appended to "Kung Ch'eng." (Some editions of the *Wu-ching Tsung-yao*, such as the *Ssu-k'u Ch'uan-shu*, depict more complex vessels, such as rectangular log boxes atop rafts.) The *Ping-ch'ou Lei-yao*, "Huo Kung," asserts that small boats loaded with grass infused with animal fat were used at the Battle of Fei-shui, while the *Wu-pei Chih*, "Huo, 15," repeats the earlier material.

21. "Shui Ch'uan, 2."

22. "Shui Ch'uan, 2."

23. These were called "ch'e lun k'o." See "Shui Ch'uan, 2."

24. "Shui Chan."

25. "Chan-ch'uan Ch'i-yung Sheh." He concludes that the key problems are not hitting the target and the range being too great.

26. Surprisingly, simply dumping gunpowder over the walls, although apparently used and certainly a much easier task than heaving it onto rolling ships, was never recommended for city defense.

27. "Chan-ch'uan, 2." In the preceding section the text suggests cannon are not reliable so in addition to poison smoke, incendiary arrows, and other traditional devices, incendiary spheres should be employed, throwing them down onto the enemy's vessels from above. A number of unorthodox methods, concealed forces, traps, and

similar techniques are also discussed, all with the intent of luring the enemy in close before launching a decimating attack.

28. "Huo, 15." Actual historical incidents, including two described herein, also used beans for the same purpose.

29. "Huo, 15."

30. *Tzu-chih T'ung-chien, Liang Chi* 22, Shao-t'ai 1.

31. Among the dozens of other incidents that might be noted, a clash with the Japanese contingents that had invaded southern Korea saw T'ang forces incinerate 400 enemy boats. While suppressing a local rebellion in 1419, Ming troops burned 160 rebel boats in one battle and 250 in another before finally prevailing ("Yung Ping Nan-chiang," *Ming Shih-lu Lei-tsuan*) while several hundred more were incinerated in a different suppression campaign undertaken in 1444 ("Chen-ya yü K'ang-cheng," *Ming Shih-lu Lei-tsuan*). The Mongolians reportedly destroyed 2,000 craft with "huo-ling-chien" in 1352; as late as 1511 a millenarian rebellion saw 1,218 boats carrying provisions for the Ming imperial armies burnt even though they also were in dire need of supplies. (*Ming Shih-lu Lei-tsuan*, "Chen-ya yü K'ang-cheng." Also mentioned in the *Ming Shih, chüan 175 and 187.)*

32. The primary account is found in A-shu's biography, *chüan* 128, *Yüan Shih*, but it is also reprised in the *Hsü Tzu-chih T'ung-chien* for A.D. 1275 and found as an illustration for "Chou" in the *Wu Pien*.

33. The battle of Oh-chou late in 1274 in similarly found in A-shu's biography, the *Hsü Tzu-chih T'ung-chien*, and *Wu Pien*. Two targets were involved, Oh-chou and Han-yang, and the battle turned on a sudden thrust across the river.

34. *Tzu-chih T'ung-chien, Han Chi* 37, Yi-hsi 6. (Also found in the *Nan Shih, chüan* 1, and cited in the *T'ung Tien, chüan* 162.)

35. Huan had actually ignored a prognostication that Liu Yü, one of his chief commanders, was exceptional and therefore dangerous.

36. *Tzu-chih T'ung-chien, T'ang Chi* 80, T'ien-fu 3, A.D. 903.

37. *Tzu-chih T'ung-chien, Hou Liang Chi* 5, Chen-ming 5, A.D. 919. Also cited as an illustration in the *Wu-ching Tsung-yao*, "Shui Chan" and *Wu Pien*, "Chou."

38. Beans were employed on land as well, such as at the siege of Shun-ch'ang, to make the ground slippery and unstable, as well as to distract hungry horses.

39. *Tzu-chih T'ung-chien, Hou-Han Chi* 4, Ch'ien-yu 3, A.D. 950.

40. This well-known incident is summarized in the *Hsü Tzu-chih T'ung-chien* for A.D. 1130 and recounted in several military texts, including "Shui Chan" in the *Ts'ao-lü Ching-lüeh* and *Teng-t'an Pi-chiu*, and "Chou" in the *Wu Pien*.

41. Although this epoch-making battle is discussed in all the standard military histories, mentioned in several military writings, and reprised in the *Hsü Tzu-chih T'ung-chien* for A.D. 1161, the prime source is Li Pao's biography, *chüan* 370 in the *Sung Shih*.

42. The clash is well discussed in the *Chung-kuo Li-tai Chan-cheng-shih*, Vol. 14, pp. 57–79; found in skeleton form in the *Hsü Tzu-chih T'ung-chien, chüan* 219; abstracted in the *Ming Shih-lu Lei-tsuan*, "Hsüeh-p'ing Ch'ün-hsiang"; and also recorded in "T'ai-tsu Shih-lu" in the *Ming Shih* and Ch'en Yu-liang's biography, albeit briefly, chüan 123. (For an extensive analysis in English, see Edward L. Dreyer, "The Poyang Campaign, 1363: Inland Naval Warfare in the Founding of the Ming Dynasty" in *Chinese Ways in Warfare*, pp. 202–240.)

43. The background and political events leading up to the insurrection are thoroughly discussed in *The Ming Dynasty* volume of *The Cambridge History of China*

(1988), pp. 423–438. The actual military clashes are recounted in Wang Shou-jen's biography in the *Ming Shih, chüan* 295.

44. *Tzu-chih T'ung-chien, Han Chi* 34, Chien-wu 11. (For Ts'en, victory was brief for he was soon assassinated by rebel forces.)

45. *Hsü Tzu-chih T'ung-chien*, A.D. 975, and also included as an illustration of "Huo Kung" in the *Wu-ching Tsung-yao* and *Yün-ch'ou Kang-mu*.

46. See P'an Chang's biography, *chüan* 55, in the *San-kuo Chih*. (Their labors were entirely wasted when Wu's forces precipitously moved off.)

47. For an example of simply cutting away heavy chains see the *Tzu-chih T'ung-chien, Sung Chi* 7, Yüan-chia 27, A.D. 450. In contrast, courageous troops ferried down on boats tried to cut the chains blocking the Yangtze in Szechuan but the wind caught them and blew them onto the chains. As they couldn't maneuver, they were compressed into a dense mass by the additional boats coming down behind them, easily attacked, and defeated. (*Tzu-chih T'ung-chien, Hou T'ang Chi* 2, T'ung-kuang 3, A.D. 925.) Additional examples are also found in "Shui Chan," *Wu-ching Tsung-yao*.

48. *Tzu-chih T'ung-chien, Hou T'ang Chi* 1, T'ung-kuang 1.

49. See the *Tzu-chih T'ung-chien, Hou Chou Chi* 4, Hsien-te 3, A.D. 956 for an interesting clash between Later Chou and Southern T'ang forces which employed these techniques.

50. Their conflict, which resulted in the Siege of Chung-li from 506 to 507, is preserved in several Wei and Liang biographies and an extensive synthetic account appears in the *Tzu-chih T'ung-chien* for the years 503 through 507, the key events falling at the end of 506 and early in 507. (*Liang-chi* 2, Emperor Wu's reign.) Their clashes are also analyzed in the section entitled "Nan-pei-ch'ao chih Cheng Ssu — Wei Liang chih Chan" in the *Chung-kuo Li-tai Chan-cheng-shih*, Vol. 6, pp. 277–320, and the battle is cited as an example of incendiary warfare in the *Wu-ching Tsung yao*, "Shui Chan"; *Ping-ch'ou Lei-yao*, "Huo Kung"; *Ts'ao-lü Ching-lüeh*, "Huo Kung"; *Wu Pien*, "Chou"; and *Fang-shou Chi-ch'eng*, "Yin Cheng." (Critical biographies include Ts'ao Ching-tsung and Wei Jui's in the *Liang Shu*, and Chung-shan Wang Yüan Ying's in the *Wei Shu*.)

51. These were probably, but not necessarily, floating bridges.

52. *Tzu-chih T'ung-chien, Liang Chi* 10, Ta-t'ung 2.

53. In addition to the various biographies found in the *San kuo Chih* and a lengthy summation in the *Tzu-chih T'ung-chien*, virtually every secondary text on Chinese warfare includes extensive coverage of his debacle, and many of the military manuals, such as the *Wu-ching Tsung-yao* ("Shui Chan"), *Teng-t'an Pi-chiu* ("Shui Chan"), and *Wu Pien* ("Chou"), include it in illustration. Wu Ch'an correctly interpreted the large amounts of scrap wood and wood shavings floating downstream as evidence of enormous naval preparations

54. "Shui Chan."

55. The primary account for the clash at Te-sheng is Wang Chien-chi's biography (later named Li) in *Wu-tai Shih-chi, chüan* 25, "T'ang Ch'en Ch'uan." Including the dramatic, probably fabricated dialogue, it is included in the *Wu-ching Tsung-yao* ("Shui Chan"), *Ping-ch'ou Lei-yao* ("Huo Kung P'ien"), and *Yün-ch'ou Kang-mu* ("Huo Kung"). However, the *Tzu-chih T'ung-chien* (*Hou-Liang Chi* 5, Chün Wang Chen-ming, 5th year or 919) account, without the dramatic dialogue, is incorporated into the Ming dynasty *Wu Pien* chapter "Chou."

56. The jars apparently had large capacity but relatively small mouths so as not to take on water and sink. Wang's biography simply states they were "large," but some-

how—due to the close appearance of the characters for "large" and "wood"—they become "wooden" jars in the *Tzu-chih T'ung-chien*, even though highly unlikely.

57. *Tzu-chih T'ung-chien, Hou T'ang Chi* 1, T'ung-kuang 1. The incident is also recorded in Wang Yen-chang's biography among those in "Ssu-chieh Ch'uan," *Wu-tai Shih-chi, chüan* 32, and cited in illustration of the principle of "establishing doubt to secretly ford" in the "Shui Chan" section of the *Yün-ch'ou Kang-mu*, as well as "Chou" in the *Wu Pien*.

58. Even in the Ming, apart from stretching rawhide or wet felt, coatings of lime, clay, or mud were the first line of defense against incendiary attack. For example, see *Ts'ao-lü Ching-lüeh*, "Shui Chan."

59. "Incendiary Warfare."

60. *Tzu-chih T'ung-chien, T'ang Chi* 36, Kan-yüan 2 and also found as an illustration in the *Fang-shou Chi-ch'eng*, "Yin Cheng." (Surprisingly, the incident is not mentioned in Li Kuang-pi's biography in either the *T'ang Shu* or *Chiu T'ang Shu*.) The Sung commander Chang Shih-lieh employed similar defensive measures—poles affixed to the boats and layers of mud on the decks—to defend against a Mongolian fire boat attack which used "fire oil" in 1279. (*Hsü Tzu-chih T'ung-chien*, A.D. 1279.)

61. An example of their use is cited in "Shui Chan," *Ts'ao-lü Ching-lüeh*.

62. *Tzu-chih T'ung-chien, Liang Chi* 14, Ta-t'ung 9. Also cited in the *T'ung Tien*, "Ping 14."

63. *Tzu-chih T'ung-chien, Liang Chi* 4, T'ien-chien 15, based upon Ts'ui's biography in the *Wei Shu, chüan* 73. Ts'ui's inventiveness is also appraised in Needham's chapter "Bridges" in the section on civil engineering in Volume 4, Part 3, *Physics and Physical Technology: Civil Engineering and Nautics* (Cambridge: University Press, 1971), pp. 190–191 where it is oddly dated to A.D. 494. (Despite the written records and commentaries, including Needham's, the exact method of construction remains unclear.)

64. *Tzu-chih T'ung-chien, Sui Chi* 8, T'ai-chien 12, A.D. 580. (Ironically, after effectively deploying the dogs and crossing his troops over the river, the commander still had the bridge burnt to ensure their fighting spirit.)

## CHAPTER 8

1. For further discussion, see "Engineering and its Social Aspects in the Corpus of Legend" found in Vol. 4, part III, entitled *Physics and Physical Technology: Civil Engineering and Nautics* of Joseph Needham's *Science and Civilisation in China* (Cambridge: Cambridge University Press, 1971), pp. 247–254. Mencius, in two different passages (IIIB9 and VIB11) clearly asserts that Yü accorded with water's natural patterns and removed obstacles to the water's flow. Interestingly, the *Chou Yü* contains a remonstrance against banking the rivers as going against the will of Heaven, though the *Kuan-tzu* emphasizes properly constraining the water ("Li Cheng") and implementing policies of active control ("Tu Ti").

2. And therefore also condemned for antagonizing the people, as in the *Huai-nan Tzu* ("Yüan Tao").

3. Reflecting the common practice of burning as a tool for clearing the wilds.

4. *Mencius*, IIIA4, "T'eng-wen Kung, Hsia."

5. Another well-known account is preserved in the *Shih Chi's* "Hsia Pen-chi." (Further discussion may also be found in our *History of Warfare in China: The Ancient Period*.)

6. Texts such as the *Kuan-tzu* and *Huai-nan Tzu* extensively contemplate the virtue, metaphysics, and necessity of water in life even though no comparable tradition existed for fire despite both numbering among the five phases. Water's unrelenting force was often emphasized in military and political contexts. For example, the *Liu-t'ao* ("Civil Instructions") states, "The people of the world are like flowing water. If you obstruct it, it will stop. If you open a way, it will flow. If you keep it quiet, it will be clear." However, likening the people to water implied that they could not be suppressed, could not be opposed.

7. Chapter 78 of the traditionally received text, translation per Wang Chen's understanding. (See our *Tao of War*, Westview Press, 2002.)

8. For a general discussion of Pan-p'o, see Chang Kwang-chih, *Archaeology of Ancient China*, pp. 112–123, and for more technical aspects, including dimensions, Ch'ien Yao-p'eng, "Kuan-yü Pan-p'o Yi-chih te Huan-hao yü Hsiao-suo," *K'ao-ku* 1998:2, pp. 45–52.

9. A second, much smaller semi-circular interior ditch whose width varies between 1.4 and 2.9 meters at the top and 0.45 to 0.84 meters at the base segregates a third of the settlement. Displaying an average depth of 1.5 meters or about a man's height, it must have protected the ruling clan. Finally, vestiges of still a third ditch lie some ten meters outside the main one and may have furnished the dirt for erecting the inner wall. (See Chang Hsüeh-hai, "Ch'eng Ch'i-yüan te Chang-yao T'u-po," *K'ao-ku yü Wen-wu* 1999:1, pp. 36–43, especially pp. 41–43.)

10. See Honan-sheng Wen-wu Yen-chiu-suo, Chou-k'ou Ti-ch'ü Wen-hua-chü Wen-wu-k'o, "Honan Huai-yang P'ing-liang-t'ai Lungshan Wen-hua Ch'eng-chih Shih-chuo Chien-pao," *Wen-wu* 1983:3, pp. 21–36; Jen Shih-nan, "Chung-kuo Shih-ch'ien Ch'eng-chih K'ao-ch'a," *K'ao-ku* 1998:1, p. 2. According to radiocarbon dating, it was probably constructed somewhere between 2370 and 1975 B.C.

11. See Jen Shih-nan, "Chung-kuo Shih-ch'ien Ch'eng-chih K'ao-ch'a," *K'ao-ku* 1998:1, p. 2.

12. Ching-chou Po-wu-kuan, Fu-kang chiao-yü Wei-yüan-hui, "Hupei Ching-chou-shih Yin-hsiang-ch'eng Yi-chih Tung-ch'iang Fa-chüeh Chien-pao," *K'ao-ku* 1997:5, pp. 1–24.

13. See Ching-chou-shih Po-wu-kuan, Shih-shou-shih Po-wu-kuan, Wu-Han Ta-hsüeh Li-shih-hsi K'ao-ku Chuan-yeh, "Hupei Shih-shou-shih Tso-ma-ling Hsin-shih-ch'i Shih-tai Yi-chih Fa-chüeh Chien-pao," *Kao-ku* 1998:4, pp. 16–38 and Chang Hsü-ch'iu, "Ch'ü-chia-ling Wen-hua te Fa-hsien ho Ch'u-pu yen-chiu," *Kao-ku* 1994:7, pp. 630ff. Standing roughly four to five meters high over the interior platform and a formidable seven to eight meters above the surrounding countryside, the walls run between twenty and twenty-seven meters wide.

14. Hunan-sheng Wen-wu K'ao-ku Yen-chiu-suo and Hunan Sheng Li-hsien Wen-wu Kuan-li-suo, "Li-hsien Ch'eng-t'ou-shan Ch'ü-chia-ling Wen-hua Ch'eng-chih Tiao-ch'a yü Shih-chuo," *Wen-wu* 1993:12, pp. 19–30. Also, Chang Hsü-ch'iu, "Ch'ü-chia-ling Wen-hua te Fa-hsien ho Ch'u-pu Yen-chiu," *Kao-ku* 1994:7, pp. 630–631.

15. Being a Ch'ü-chia-ling cultural site, it should date somewhere between 3000 and 2600 B.C. (The best site report to date is Ching-chou Po-wu-kuan and Mai Han-ch'ing, "Hupei Kung-an Chi-ming-ch'eng Yi-chih te Tiao-ch'a," *Wen-wu* 1998:6, pp. 25–29.)

16. Extensive discussion of city fortifications may be found in the subsection entitled "Early Poliorcetics" by Robin D. S. Yates in Needham's *Science and Civilisation in China,* Vol. 5, Part 6, *Military Technology: Missiles and Sieges.*

17. In his *Ts'ui-wei Pei-cheng-lu,* Hua Yüeh bemoaned the Sung's failure to fully employ the rivers, the natural obstacles provided by Heaven, as barriers as they had in the past. (See "Chin She" or "Preventing Crossings.")

18. In "K'ai-chieh."

19. *Tso Chuan,* Chuang Kung, 9th year.

20. "Sun Ch'üan Chuan," *Wu Shu* (*San-kuo Chih*). (Note that the *Chung-wen Ta-ts'u-tien,* entry number 17956, defines *"t'u-t'ang"* as a place name and arbitrarily conjoins it with T'ang-yi, thereby concluding that a strongpoint was created whose troops were to intercept the enemy, rather than any idea of flooding the road to the north. However, despite the subsequent passage of the term into the language as a place name, reading *t'u-t'ang* as "muddy pools" is both more appropriate and commonly accepted.) The impact of such thinking is coincidentally revealed by Shih Pao's plight in A.D. 268 for his loyalty came into question when he diverted the river to augment his defenses at Huai-nan and reinforced his fortifications. (*Tzu-chih T'ung-chien, Chin Chi* 1, T'ai-shih 4.)

21. "Tung Chuo Lieh-chuan," *Wei Shu* (*San-kuo Chih*). (Our interpretation follows Fan Mei's commentary which points out that the text errs in asserting Tung was opposing Han Sui north of Wang-huan-hsia since the location was actually in Kansu where he confronted the Hsien-ling Ch'iang.) The incident is also cited in the *T'ung Tien,* "Shui Kung," *Wu-ching Tsung-yao,* "Yung-shui Wu-ti," and *Wu Pien,* "Tu Shui."

22. King Hsien, 10th year. Interpretations of the event vary, but the entry concludes by noting that Wei built a long wall on its Western border the same year, further evidence of extensive defensive activity focusing on walls and embankments in this era.

23. "Kao-tsu Pen-chi," *Shih Chi.*

24. *Tzu-chih T'ung-chien, Chin Chi* 15, Hsien-ho 1, A.D. 326. (Conversely, enemies could also encircle and thereby cut off cities through flooding the surrounding terrain without intending to inundate the objective itself.)

25. For example, T'ang forces in A.D. 923. (*Tzu-chih T'ung-chien, Hou T'ang Chi* 1, T'ung-kuang 1.)

26. Such as Yung-p'ing in 1362. (*Hsü Tzu-Chih T'ung-chien,* A.D. 1362.)

27. *Tzu-chih T'ung-chien, T'ang Chi* 77, Ch'ien-ning 4, A.D. 897. (Employing both measures seems a little odd because lowering the water level would have dropped the floating bridge too low.)

28. *Hsü Tzu-Chih T'ung-chien,* A.D. 1368. In contrast, a battle at Ssu-chou (cited in the *Wu-ching Tsung-yao,* "Shui Chan") at the very start of the sixth century saw attempts to drain the highly effective moat thwarted with earthen repairs and additional embankments. (In this context an interesting case of subversion occurred at T'ai-chou in A.D. 1161. [See the *Hsü Tzu-chih T'ung-chien* for 1161.])

29. *Tzu-chih T'ung-chien, Chin Chi* 9, Yung-chia 3.

30. *Tzu-chih T'ung-chien, Chin Chi* 30, T'ai-yüan 20, A.D. 395.

31. *Tzu-chih T'ung-chien, Chin Chi* 23, T'ai-ho 2, A.D. 367.

32. *Tzu-chih T'ung-chien, T'ang Chi* 33, T'ien-pao 14.

33. *Tzu-chih T'ung-chien, Sung Chi* 6, Yüan-chia 20, A.D. 443. (Also cited in the *Yün-ch'ou Kang-mu* among the examples of employing frozen water.) Pouring water on the top surface and even down the face of city walls to create coating of ice and

thereby thwart attackers trying to clamber over was also a much admired tactic, one found in some versions of the *Thirty-six Stratagems* and even the *Yün-ch'ou Kang-mu* which cites the example of a Khitan attack on Sui-ch'eng during the Sung.

34. The defenders at Ming-chou also exploited the antique ruse of a feigned surrender to entice 2,000 of Wang's troops into the city and slay them. Overall, the number of troops involved was small, the initial attack being mounted with 5,000 troops, and Wang resorting to flooding when it failed. (*Tzu-chih T'ung-chien, T'ang Chi* 50–51, Chen-yüan 10–12.) Ultimately it was the city's isolation rather than the destructive effects of the flood waters which finally precipitated their departure.

35. *Tzu-chih T'ung-chien, Hou Liang Chi*, 1, K'ai-p'ing, 2nd year (A.D. 908).

36. "Shou-ch'eng Chü." In "The Unorthodox Army" the *Liu-t'ao* simply stated "deep moats, high ramparts, and large reserves of supplies are the means by which to sustain your position for a long time." (Also see the *Liu-t'ao*'s "The Army's Indications" as well as our concluding section on sieges.)

37. The *T'ou-pi Fu-t'an*, "Ta Shu," advised that accumulating water in moats was the way to rescue the army's impoverishment.

38. See, for example, *Shou-ch'eng Chiu-ming Shu*. This sentiment was expressed in the classic military writings and even in the *Yi Chou-shu*, "Ta-ming Wu."

39. *Ts'ui-wei Pei-cheng-lü*, "Te Ti." Early on Sun Pin had similarly concluded that an enemy relying upon ravines lacks the spirit for battle.

40. *Yi Chou-shu*, "Wen-ch'uan Chieh."

41. Duke Chuang, 25th year.

42. "Agricultural Implements."

43. "Pei Shui" or "Preparations against Water."

44. The term *lin*, which means to approach and may indicate a platform like a catamaran with some sort of tower structure, more likely means "assault," as translated.

45. For example, the passage is substantially repeated in the *T'ung Tien*, "Shou-chü Fa," while Hua Yüeh lists providing holes for the water to leak out among the thirty-six measures for preserving a city in his *Ts'ui-wei Pei-cheng-lu.*

46. See, for example, "Fan Chin" (which also advises the construction of external walls) in the *Hu-ch'ien Ching*, "Shou Ch'eng" in the *Wu-ching Tsung-yao*, and "Shou" and "Shui" in the *Wu Pien.*

47. *Wu-ching Tsung-yao*, "Shou Ch'eng." Also found in "Shou," *Wu Pien.*

48. *T'ou-pi Fu-t'an*, "Wu Lüeh."

49. "Pa Hsing." (For a translation, see W. Allyn Rickett, *Guanzi* [Princeton: Princeton University Press, 1985], Vol. 1, pp. 352–354.) Ch'i apparently forced Ch'u to remove the blockages and withdraw their forces, restoring the rivers' flow.

50. Duke Huan, 1st and 13th years; Duke Chuang, 11th, 24th, and 25th; Duke Hsüan, 10th; Duke Ch'eng, 5th; and Duke Hsiang, 24th year.

51. *Tso Chuan*, Duke Chao, 30th year. (The commentators also note that this constitutes the first recorded employment of such methods.) The *Kuan-tzu* apparently preserves another episode dating to Duke Huan's reign in the mid seventh century B.C. in which an attack by Yüeh on Lin-tzu by damming the Chi River was anticipated and a core of swimmers trained to thwart them, as reportedly happened. (The incident's reliability is, however, open to question. See "Ch'ing Chung, Chia.")

52. "Incendiary Warfare."

53. The episode is found in the records for both Chao and Wei in the *Chan-kuo Ts'e*, as well as in various forms in the *Shih Chi* (Han, Chao, and Wei "Shih-chia"), the

*Huai-nan Tzu* ("Chien Hsün"), *Shuo Yüan* ("Ch'üan Mou"), and other parts of the *Han Fei-tzu* ("Shuo Lin, Shang," and "Nan San"). However, the two main versions appear in the *Chan-kuo Ts'e*, right at the beginning of the "Ch'ao Ts'e," and the *Han Fei-tzu* as part of his "Shih Kuo" or "Ten Excesses" chapter. It ranks among the most famous Warring States stories, well known throughout the centuries, and has been translated by Burton Watson (*Han Fei-tzu Basic Writings*, "The Ten Faults," pp. 56–62) and J. I. Crump (*Chan-kuo Ts'e*, #229 and #230, pp. 278–283.) The famous betrayal scene is actually preserved as a separate incident in the *Kuo Yü* and also appears in the *Shuo Yüan*, "Ch'üan Mou." However, it has obviously been romanticized and the dialogue fabricated. (Aspects are also discussed in our *Tao of Spycraft*.)

54. "Shih Kuo."

55. Rather than the usual understanding of taking itself to be strong and thereby provoking Chih Po.

56. This place name is variously interpreted as one or two towns. (For example, see *Tzu-chih T'ung-chien*, Chou Chi 1, Wei-lieh Wang 23, 403 B.C. [even though the event occurred in 453].)

57. The *Chan-kuo Ts'e* version has the three embassies referring to the three requests for land rather than any additional exchange of emissaries (for plotting an attack).

58. The *Chan-kuo Ts'e* version is far more sparse, lacking any such explanation of Tung Kuan-yü's measures other than the reeds and copper. It is somewhat odd that Han Fei-tzu, with whose avowed methods such measures would be discordant, provides such an elaboration.

59. The late Ming *T'ou-pi Fu-t'an* ("Ch'ien Chi") cites Chih Po's failure to take precautions against his allies as an example of failing to know the enemy.

60. *Shuo Yüan*, "Chien Pen." This particularly graphic form of gloating was probably prompted by Chih Po having previously poured wine over his head when they were earlier drinking together. (At that time the earl's retainers wanted to kill Chih Po, but the earl of Chao exercised restraint, as he felt was appropriate for the guardian of the altars of state to do.) See "Chien Pen" for the incident.

61. And Earl Huan rather than Hsüan. "Wei Ts'e," 1. (Crump #292, p. 370; also found with slight variations in the "Ching Shen" section of the *Shuo Yüan*.) Among Sun-tzu's techniques for manipulating the enemy prior to exploiting the resulting weakness in "Initial Estimations" is "be deferential to foster arrogance."

62. Generally taken to be the *Yi Chou-shu* or even the *Liu-t'ao*, but much more similar to the contents of late Warring States classic military manual known as *Huang Shih-kung San-lüeh*. However, the traditionally received text of the *Tao Te Ching* contains the same thought in chapter 36:

> If you want to reduce something, you must certainly stretch it.
> If you want to weaken something, you must certainly strengthen it.
> If you want to abolish something, you must certainly make it flourish.
> If you want to grasp something, you must certainly give it away.
> (Sawyer, *The Tao of War*, "Wanting to Reduce Something.")

63. Commentators have long indicated that these river names are incorrect, but the concept remains unaffected.

64. *Chan-kuo Ts'e*, "Ch'in Ts'e," 4. (Also found in Crump, #97, pp. 110–111.) Also integrated into the *Tzu-chih T'ung-chien* account and found in the "Ching Shen" portion of the *Shuo Yüan*.

65. "Ch'in Ts'e," 1.

66. "Wei Ts'e," 3. (Also found in Crump # 363, p. 438.)

67. *Tzu-chih T'ung-chien, Chou Chi* 1. Some depictions indicate the city had been reduced to truly dire straits, as might well be imagined after three years. But the duration clearly shows a will to resist, evidence that cities could not easily be subjugated. (Also cited in the *Wu-ching Tsung-yao*.)

68. *Tzu-chih T'ung-chien, Chou Chi* 2, Hsien Wang. The *Tzu-chih T'ung-chien* account is cobbled together from a brief report in the "Chao Shih-chia" and elements from Su Ch'in's biography, both in the *Shih Chi*.

69. *Tzu-chih T'ung-chien, Ch'in Chi* 2, Shih Huang-ti 20, 225 B.C.

70. For example, Wang T'eng was captured and executed in A.D. 356 when rain severely damaged his fortified walls. (*Tzu-chih T'ung-chien, Chin Chi* 22, Yung-ho 12.) In A.D. 618, at the start of the T'ang, the recently defeated rebel Chu Ts'an regrouped and went on to vanquish the overconfident T'ang commander Ma Yüan-kuei at Nan-yang when their walls collapsed from the heavy rains. (*Tzu-chih T'ung-chien, T'ang Chi* 1, Wu-te 1.)

71. "The Questions of King Wei."

72. "Maneuvering the Army."

73. "Tao of the General."

74. "Yen Ts'e," 3. (For a translation, see Crump, *Chan-kuo Ts'e,* #220, pp. 266–267.)

75. The rains reportedly fell for ten days in succession. (P'ang Te's biography, *chüan* 18, *San-kuo Chih*.) In addition, the nearby city of Fan-ch'eng, which Kuan Yü immediately surrounded and locked up in a tight siege, was badly inundated and its fortifications incurred heavy damage. Nevertheless, the frightened defenders remained resolute and thus survived because Kuan Yü suffered the surprise attack which eventually resulted in his death.

76. Included in the *Yün-ch'ou Kang-mu* subsection on "Chü-kao Tsung-shui" in his "Shui Chan" and cited in illustration of rain aiding an amphibious attack in the *T'ou-pi Fu-t'an,* "T'ien Ching."

77. Textual reports of this famous incident are extremely sparse. In the *San-kuo Chih,* the "Wu Ti Chi" makes no mention of deliberately blocking the river's outlets; Yü Chin's biography states the water was several *chang* deep and mentions Kuan Yü's attack by boat; while Kuan Yü's own biography just mentions that the seven armies drowned. However, according to the "Wu Chu Chuan" some 30,000 were reportedly also captured, suggesting somewhat more than half Wei's strength perished.

78. *Yün-ch'ou Kang-mu,* "Shui Chan." Dating to A.D. 897, the incident is taken almost verbatim from the *Chiu Wu-tai-shih, chüan* 21 (P'ang Shih-ku's biography). Part of a more complex sequence of events, the surviving soldiers apparently were immobilized by the mud and easily decimated.

79. "Cavalry in Battle," *Liu-t'ao.*

80. "Ni-yung Ti-hsing."

81. "Liao Shui."

82. "Marshes in Warfare."

83. Also cited in the earlier *T'ung Tien, chüan* 151.

84. The late Sung *Ts'ui-wei Pei-cheng-lu,* in a chapter devoted to discerning gaps in the enemy, advised attacking troops caught in floods, particularly if the men and horses have suffered casualties, or encamping on low lying terrain during the wet sea-

son, especially if the troops have cast aside their armor ("Kuan Hsin" or "Observing Rifts").

85. "Li Ying."

86. The *Fang-shou Chi-ch'eng* (in "Yin Cheng") contains an example of a commander using flags to shape the battlefield (in classic fashion) before breaking embankments open to flood the enemy. In another incident at the end of the T'ang, government forces were cut off when the Pien River was used to flood the terrain. (*Tzu-chih T'ung-chien, T'ang Chi* 67, Hsien-t'ung 9, A.D. 868.)

87. "Unorthodox Army," *Liu-t'ao*.

88. "The Tao of the General."

89. *Hu-ch'ien Ching*, "Ni-yung Ti-hsing."

90. "Maneuvering the Army."

91. For example, see Hua Yüeh's "Chi Chü" ("Urgent Occupation") in the *Ts'ui-wei Pei-cheng-lu*. (In "Te Ti" he also accepts the normal view on exploitation.)

92. "Maneuvering the Army."

93. For example, in A.D. 251 the Yangtze flooded the city gates.

94. *Tzu-chih T'ung-chien, Han Chi* 57, Chien-an 12, A.D. 207.

## CHAPTER 9

1. "Ping" 10," *chüan* 157.

2. *Tzu-chih T'ung-chien, Han Chi* 31. This victory brought Liu into prominence for the first time and made the Han restoration possible.

3. "Strategic Military Power." In "Ch'i Fa," the *Kuan-tzu* likens the army's power to a flood.

4. "Incendiary Warfare." Virtually every subsequent military text cites this assertion. In "Ta Shu" the *T'ou-pi Fu-t'an* asserts that using water to flood capitals and cities is exploiting natural power to achieve military purposes while in "Wu Lüeh" it emphasizes that as water can either be blocked or led, it can assist an attack, but not constitute the sole means of assault.

5. *Military Methods*, 16, "Ten Deployments."

6. "Martial Plans." For further discussion of the relationship between what has traditionally been regarded as Taoist thought and military action, see the introductions to our *Tao of War* (Westview) and the single-volume *Six Secret Teachings* (Shambhala).

7. This account is as preserved in the *Hsü Tzu-chih T'ung-chien* for A.D. 969. However, T'ien's biography in the *Sung Shih* merely states that he advised flooding be employed, but not what was said. Moreover, there is no indication of it in the other extended Sung record of this battle, the "Pei Han Liu-shih Lieh-chuan" or the T'ai-tsu's own annals, so this may well be an embellishment. A sort of precursor occurs at the very start of the Later Han when the emperor, battling the Red Eyebrows, was advised to break the embankments and flood the area east of the Yellow River, turning the rebel mass of a million into fish, though he didn't implement the advice. (Cited under "Chüeh Shui" in the *Ping-ch'ou Lei-yao*. However, there is no mention of the fish as originally found in the *Hou-Han Shu* ["Ti Chi 1"] or the *Tzu-chih T'ung-chien* [*Han Chi* 31, Keng-shih 1, A.D. 23], only the *Hsü Han-shu* [according to comments in the *Tzu-chih T'ung-chien*].)

8. The *Ping-ch'ou Lei-yao*, "Chüeh Shui," cites the comments of the Khitan ambassador within the city: "Wang Shih channeled the water to inundate the city. If he had first flooded them then dried them out, they wouldn't have had any posterity." Also cited in the *Wu-ching Tsung-yao*, "Yin-shui Kuan-ch'eng" and *Wu Pien*, "Shui."

9. *Wu-ching Tsung-yao,* "Shui-kung."

10. "Vacuity and Substance." This downward tendency is noted in such subsequent texts as the *T'ou-pi Fu-t'an,* "Wu Lüeh," as well as several martial chapters in the Chou dynasty *Yi Chou-shu,* including "Ta-ming Wu," "Ta-chü Chieh," and "T'ien Yu Shih."

11. For an extensive discussion of China's hydraulic engineering, including dams and water works, see Joseph Needham, *Science and Civilisation in China,* Vol. IV, Part 3, *Civil Engineering and Nautics* (Cambridge: University Press, 1971).

12. "Offices, I."

13. "Shui-kung-chü." Whether verbatim or condensed, the chapter and illustrations are reproduced in such manuals as the *Wu-ching Tsung-yao, Ping Ching, Wu-pei Chih, Teng-t'an Pi-chou,* and *Wu Pien.* Its role and importance are also discussed by Joseph Needham in volume 3, "Mathematics and the Methods and Sciences of the Heavens and the Earth," pp. 569ff.

14. As always, *ch'eng*—here appropriately translated as city—always retains a connotation of "walls" and "fortifications."

15. Alternatively, "relying upon" (another primary meaning for the character *yin*) since the current's power is used, though the second case doesn't specify how. However, "according with" better matches the parallelism of the other terms.

16. Repeated verbatim in the *Ping Ching,* "Kung Shou."

17. The actual sentence, from a passage in "Vacuity and Substance," in using the analogy of water to describe the generation of strategic power, concludes more simply: "Water configures its flow in accord with the terrain." (The *Wu-ching Tsung-yao* explanation strongly implies that the editors were reading the second line as a continuous quote.)

18. "Chüeh Shui" or "Breaking Open Rivers."

19. "Sheng Yün" or "Sparing Transport."

20. "Te Ti."

21. "Aquatic Warfare."

22. The subsection appears in "Occupying Heights and Releasing Water."

23. The *Wu-pei Chih* includes three *chüan* on water encompassing every aspect from aquatic attacks to boats, rivers, and riverine warfare, essentially all drawn from earlier works with minimal introduction or commentary by Mao Yüan-yi. For example, it adopts the *Hu-ch'ien Ching's* theory of the advantages of water and its description of the water level.

24. For example, see "Shou," *Wu Pien.*

25. Among the more interesting and effective being the flooding of Chin-yung near Luoyang in A.D. 318 (*Tzu-chih T'ung-chien, Chin Chi* 12, T'ai-hsing 1) and Chin-k'ang in A.D. 328 (*Tzu-chih T'ung-chien, Chin Chi* 16, Hsien-ho 3), both with the Luo River.

26. "Han Kao-tsu Pen-chi," *Shih Chi; Tzu-chih T'ung-chien, Han Chi* 1, Kao-ti 2; also cited in the *Ping-ch'ou Lei-yao* ("Chüeh Shui"), among others.

27. *Tzu-chih T'ung-chien, Han Chi* 8, Ching Ti ch'ien 1.

28. According to the *Tzu-chih T'ung-chien,* in A.D. 204 he diverted the water from the Ch'i River into the Pai Canal and in A.D. 206 had two canals excavated, the P'ing-lu-chü and Ch'üan-chou-chü. However, he was not alone among Three Kingdoms commanders who readily resorted to canals and other massive works projects to divert and manipulate water levels. For example, Chiang Chi opened several channels

to raise the water level sufficiently to float Wei's fleet and allow it to proceed to the Huai River. (See the *Wei Shu, chüan* 14.)

29. *Tzu-chih T'ung-chien, Han Chi,* 5, Chien-an 3. Also cited as an example of "Chüeh Shui" in the *Ping-ch'ou Lei-yao* and "Shui Kung" in the *T'ung Tien.*

30. The immense size of the moat, in comparison with a city of that era, suggests that the historical records are either in error—perhaps 10 *li* or some other smaller number was intended, or that the water was channeled some 40 *li* from the Chang River. However, the latter is ruled out by the proximity of the city to the Chang. Moreover, distance would be necessary for any clandestine digging to deepen and broaden it at night to go relatively undetected. (The incident is preserved in *Wei Shu, chüan* 6, the *San-kuo Chih,* and cited as an example of "Yin-shui Kuan-ch'eng" in the *Wu-ching Tsung-yao.*)

31. *Tzu-chih T'ung-chien, Liang Chi* 2, T'ien-chien 5, A.D. 506. Also cited as an illustration of "Yin-shui Kuan-ch'eng" in the *Wu-ching Tsung-yao.*

32. A synthesized account is contained in the *Tzu-chih T'ung-chien* (*Liang-chi* 17 and 18, Wu-ti *T'ai-ch'ing* 2nd and 3rd years), and the major events in the biographies of the various participants, particularly Wang Ssu-cheng's in the *Chou Shu.* The T'ang dynasty *T'ung Tien* devotes two pages of *chüan* 161 to the siege which preserve a few additional points (such as the use of incendiary assault wagons early on), and it is cited as an illustration in "Shou," the *Wu Pien,* and "Chüeh Shui" in the *Ping-ch'ou Lei-yao.* Fragments appear in the *T'ai-p'ing Yü-lan,* sections 318, 321, and 328. Benjamin Wallacker has also reconstructed the siege and discussed the textual basis in "Studies in Medieval Chinese Siegecraft: The Siege of Ying-ch'uan, A.D. 548–549," *Journal of Asian Studies* 30:3 (May 1971), pp. 611–622.

33. Why they didn't implement ancillary scorched-earth measures as well, or simply adopt a policy of complete denial, remains puzzling.

34. Several *Ming Shih* biographies record aspects of the conflict, including *chüan* 228 (Wei Hsüeh-hui and Yeh Meng-hsiung), 238 (Ma Kui, Li Ju-sung), 239 (Hsiao Ju-hsün and Tung Yi-yüan), and 20 ("Shen-tsung Pen-chi, 1"), while battlefield reports are contained in *Ming Shih-lüeh Lei-tsuan* (Wuhan: Wuhan Ch'u-pan-she, 1993), pp. 671–673. (However, none of these record the construction of the 1,700-*chang* wall discussed in the secondary literature and *The Ming Dynasty.*) The three campaigns are also discussed in *The Cambridge History of China: The Ming Dynasty, 1368–1644,* Part I, pp. 563–567.

35. Interpretations vary, with official accounts tending to attribute leadership of the revolt to Pübei rather than Li, but it was Li who assumed and clearly exercised overall command, with Pübei's son as his one of his chief subordinates. See *The Ming Dynasty,* p. 566, for a brief discussion.

36. The highly conducive terrain was well known for its sluices and ditches. (See *Ming Shih, chüan* 93, "Ping Chih, 4.")

37. See Wei's report for chi-wei, ninth month, *Ming Shih-lu Lei-tsuan,* p. 674.

38. Li's "Chieh-lü Shou-pien Erh-chih" may be conveniently found in Chu Lu's 1853 compendia on city defense entitled *Fang-shou Chi-ch'eng* as well as the *Ssu-k'u Ch'uan-shu.* The siege and its historical context are also briefly discussed in the *Chung-kuo Li-tai Chan-cheng-shih,* Vol. 14, *Ming-tai,* pp. 503–510, while Kao Ming-heng and Li Tzu-ch'eng's *Ming Shih* biographies, *chüan* 267 and 309 respectively, provide additional information.

Unfortunately, there are serious discrepancies in the dates, roles played by various commanders, and the events themselves that require far more detailed study to reconcile. The account synthesized here necessarily focuses on the question of aquatic warfare, particularly the sequence preceding the flooding which devastated the city, and generally adopts the chronicle's dates. (Apart from the dates, among the chief questions is who shot Li Tzu-ch'eng in the eye, whether the event ended the first siege or began the second, and if the defenders attempted to drown the rebel army, as Kao's biography suggests, or Li's forces tried to inundate them twice.)

39. Both Kao and Li's biographies indicate he was hit in the eye while reconnoitering the defenses at the beginning of the second siege, prior to actually attacking, whereas the chronicle assigns the event to the end of the first siege.

40. See Kao Ming-heng's biography.

41. The conflicts are recorded in the *Tzu-chih T'ung-chien, Han Chi* 34, Chienwu 8th year, and several *Hou Han Shu* biographies, including those of Wei Ao, Lai Hsi, and Ts'en P'eng, *chüan* 13, 15, and 17 respectively.

42. *Tzu-chih T'ung-chien, Chin Chi* 27, T'ai-yüan 9.

43. *Tzu-chih T'ung-chien, Liang-chi* 3 and 4, T'ien-chien 13–15 (A.D. 514–516). The episode and its background are also briefly discussed in the *Chung-kuo Li-tai Chan-cheng-shih*, Vol. 6, pp. 309–314 and several individual biographies.

44. *Tzu-chih T'ung-chien, Liang-chi* 3, T'ien-chien 12, A.D. 513.

45. Multiple references to various effects extending a 100 *li* are of course nominal, basically a convenient integer for suggesting something far greater than 10 *li*, though certainly at least forty or fifty. There are also interesting questions of technology buried within these reports because the normal method would be to use piles of rocks lashed together with bamboo, precluding the need to build these piers to stabilize the foundation.

46. *Tzu-chih T'ung-chien, Liang Chi* 6, P'u-t'ung 6th & 7th, A.D. 525–526.

47. *Tzu-chih T'ung-chien, Liang Chi* 6, P'u-t'ung 6 to Ta-t'ung 2, A.D. 528.

48. *Tzu-chih T'ung-chien, Liang Chi* 16, T'ai-ch'ing 1, 547 AD.

49. *Tzu-chih T'ung-chien, Ch'en Chi* 8, T'ai-chien 12. (Also found in Tou-lu Chi's biography in the *Sui Shu, chüan* 39, and as an illustration for "Chüeh Shui" in the *Ping-ch'ou Lei-yao*.)

50. *Tzu-chih T'ung-chien, T'ang Chi* 36, Kan-yüan 2.

51. *Hsü Tzu-Chih T'ung-chien*, A.D. 1232.

52. The *Pao Yüeh Lu*, attributed to Hsü Mien-chih, is an unusual text in that it gives the viewpoint of the ultimately vanquished. Although the text has undergone slight revisions, it hasn't been consistently sanitized and the aggressors, the Ming armies, are generally referred to as "brigands." Moreover, it preserves accounts of Ming atrocities dramatically at odds with the traditional depiction of Chu Yüan-chang's early armies eschewing brutality, being disciplined and constrained. (*Pai-pu Ts'ung-shu Chi-ch'eng*, Yen Yi-p'ing, general editor, Taipei, Yi-wen Yin-shu-kuan.)

53. *Hsü Tzu-chih T'ung-chien*, Chih-cheng, 19th year (1359).

54. *Tzu-chih T'ung-chien, Han Chi* 47, Yen-hsi 8.

55. *Tzu-chih T'ung-chien, Ch'en Chi* 4, T'ai-chien 2.

56. *Tzu-chih T'ung-chien, Ch'en Chi* 7, T'ai-chien 10, A.D. 578, originally described in the biographies of both commanders, *chüan* 9 and 40 of the *Chou Shu*, and cited as an example under "Tuan Chou-lu" in the *Wu-ching Tsung-yao* and "Chou" in the *Wu Pien*. (Wu Ming-ch'e had previously flooded Shou-ch'un with the Fei River.)

57. Some accounts suggest the Hsi Hsia found a way to redirect the flood waters onto them, possibly through the irrigation canal, but support is lacking in Genghis

Khan's chronicles in the two Chinese-language Yüan histories, the *Yüan Shih* ("T'ai-tsu Pen-chi," *chüan* 1) and *Hsi Yüan Shih* ("T'ai-tsu Pen-chi," *chüan* 3).

58. Found first in Han Hsin's biography, "The Marquis of Huai-yin," in the *Shih Chi*, it is also reprised in the *Tzu-chih T'ung-chien* (*Han Chi* 2, Kao-ti 4th year, 203 B.C.) and cited in numerous military manuals, including the *T'ung Tien*, "Shui Kung"; *Wu-ching Tsung-yao*, "Yung-shui Wu-ti"; *Hundred Unorthodox Strategies*, "Rivers"; *Chüeh-sheng Kang-mu*, "Shui Chan"; and *Wu Pien*, "Tu Shui."

59. *Yün-ch'ou Kang-mu*, "Chü-kao Tsung-shui" in "Shui Chan."

60. Both quotes are from Sun-tzu's "Initial Estimations."

61. Sun-tzu, "Maneuvering the Army."

62. "Analyzing Rivers." Also found in the *Wu-pei Chih*, "Chi Shui."

63. No doubt prompted by its inclusion in the *Wu-ching Tsung-yao*, "Yin-shui Kuan-ch'eng," but certainly based upon the account found in the *Nan Shih*, *chüan* 25. (Also see the *Tzu-chih T'ung-chien*, *Ch'i Chi* 1, Chien-yüan 2 or A.D. 480, which preserves a discussion about the difficulty of banking the Fei River, and arguments that they should just withdraw to the security of the inner citadel, both discarded.) Huan has a biography in the *Wei Shu*, *chüan* 59, though there is no mention of this battle.

64. Shun-yang in the *Tzu-chih T'ung-chien*, Shou-yang in the *Fang-shou Chi-ch'eng* ("Yin Cheng").

65. *Tzu-chih T'ung-chien*, *T'ang Chi* 6, Wu Te 5. Presumably the T'ang forces had been forewarned and managed to escape the tidal wave, though this remains undiscussed. (The river is called the Ming and the town Ming-chou in the *Yün-ch'ou Kang-mu* account.) Also cited in the *Wu-ching Tsung-yao*, "Yung-sui Wu-ti," and *Wu Pien*, "Tu Shui."

66. "Shen-ta-lan."

67. *Hu-ch'ien Ching*, "Shui Li."

68. *Tzu-chih T'ung-chien*, *Sung Chi* 8, Yüan-chia 28, A.D. 451.

69. *Hsü Tzu-chih T'ung-chien*, A.D. 1206 (K'ai-hsi, 2nd year). The *Hsü Tzu-chih T'ung-chien* is drawn primarily from Pi's biography in the *Sung Shih*, *chüan* 402.

70. *Tzu-chih T'ung-chien*, *Chin Chi* 1, T'ai-shih 8, and also an illustration for "Yen Chan" in the *Ts'ai-lü Ching-lüeh*.

71. *Tzu-chih T'ung-chien*, *Ch'i Chi* 7, Yung-t'ai 1st, A.D. 498. (Also see Wang's biography in the *Pei Shih*.)

## CHAPTER 10

1. "Liao Shui."

2. Hua Yüeh obviously considered denying water to the enemy fundamental for he mentioned it several times, including in the sections entitled "Ma Cheng," "Hsien Ch'i," and "Te Ti."

3. *Art of War*, "Maneuvering the Army."

4. *Art of War*, "Maneuvering the Army."

5. "Ni-yung Ti-hsing," *Hu-ch'ien Ching*.

6. "Mountain Warfare."

7. "Crow and Cloud Formation in the Mountains." King Wu's original query posited even more dire conditions: "Suppose we have led the army deep into the territory of the feudal lords where we encounter high mountains with large, flat rock outcroppings on top of which are numerous peaks, all devoid of grass and trees. We are surrounded on all four sides by the enemy." (Conversely and symmetrically, the *Liu-*

*t'ao* continues by stating, "When they hold the land below the mountain, they are imprisoned by the forces above them.")

8. "Evaluating Enemy Encampments." However, armies well encamped with dispersed troops and good access to water could not be treated lightly.

9. Also cited as an illustration in "Shui," the *Wu Pien*.

10. In "Planning Offensives" Sun-tzu states: "Subjugating the enemy's army without fighting is the true pinnacle of excellence."

11. The *Tzu-chih T'ung-chien* account (*Wei Chi*, 3) integrates fragments from four *San-kuo Chih* biographies: Chang Ko's, *chüan* 17; Chu-ko Liang's, *chüan* 35; Ma Liang's, *chüan* 39; and Wang P'ing's, *chüan* 43. (Also found as an illustration for "Hunger and Thirst" in the *Wu Pien*).

12. One of Tu Yu's illustrations for "Severing Supply Lines and Baggage Trains" in the *T'ung Tien* (*chüan* 160, "Ping" 13), the basic account (which Tu closely follows) is found in Ch'en T'ai's biography in the *San-kuo Chih*, *chüan* 22. (The incident is also mentioned in *chüan* 26, 28, and 44, though only minimally in Chiang Wei's biography; summarized in the *Tzu-chih T'ung-chien*, *chüan* 75, *Wei Chi* 7, for A.D. 249; and cited in illustration in "Liang Tao," the *Wu Pien*.)

13. *Tzu-chih T'ung-chien*, *Chin Chi* 16, Hsien-ho 3, A.D. 328.

14. *Tzu-chih T'ung-chien*, *Chin Chi* 30, T'ai-yüan 19, A.D. 394.

15. *Tzu-chih T'ung-chien*, *Chin Chi* 40, Yi-hsi 14, A.D. 418. In A.D. 428, Northern Wei's reckless campaign into Kansu under Hsi Chin was defeated by the Hu Hsia because they lacked both provisions and water. (*Tzu-chih T'ung-chien*, *Sung Chi* 3, Yüan-chia 5.)

16. *Tzu-chih T'ung-chien*, *Sung Chi* 3, Yüan-chia 7.

17. *Tzu-chih T'ung-chien*, *Sung Chi* 1, Ching-p'ing 1st year. The siege of Hu-lao, which was located just south of the Yellow River in Honan near modern Jung-yang, is also described in the defensive commander's biography in the *Pei Shih*.

18. Ho-lou's biography appears in *chüan* 53 of the *Sui Shu* and the incident is cited as an illustration for "Hunger and Thirst" in the *Wu Pien*.

19. These and other incidents in Liu Po-po's rise to power are preserved in his biography found in the *Chin Shu* (*Chin-shu Chiao-chu*, *chüan* 130). For context, also see Yao Hsing's lengthy biography, *Chin-shu Chiao-chu*, *chüan* 117 and 118. (Also cited as an illustration in "Shui," the *Wu Pien*.)

20. *Tzu-chih T'ung-chien*, *T'ang Chi* 3, Wu-te 2, A.D. 619.

21. *Hsü Tzu-chih T'ung-chien*, A.D. 1219. (Another example, an attack on Sung forces in Kansu, is found for A.D. 1236.)

22. The incident is extensively discussed in all the secondary military histories, *The Ming Dynasty* (in the *Cambridge History of China* series), and Frederick W. Mote's chapter, entitled "The T'u-mu Incident of 1449" in *Chinese Ways of Warfare*, Frank A. Kierman, Jr., editor (Cambridge: Harvard University Press, 1974), pp. 242–272.

23. *Tzu-chih T'ung-chien*, *Han Chi* 22, Ho-p'ing 2.

24. *Tzu-chih T'ung-chien*, *Han Chi* 13, T'ai-ch'u, 3rd year, 102 B.C. The primary account is found in the *Shih Chi*, *chüan* 123, "Ta-yüan." (For a translation of "Ta Yüan," see Burton Watson, *Records of the Grand Historian of China*, Vol. II, pp. 280–288.)

25. *Tzu-chih T'ung-chien*, *Han Chi* 37, Yung-p'ing 18. (A remarkably similar story is told about Chung Shih-heng of the Sung in the Wu Pien section entitled "Shui.")

26. The background and campaign are discussed in detail in the *Hsü Tzu-chih T'ung-chien*, A.D. 1082, with further information found in the biographies in the Sung dynastic histories.

27. An example of relying upon melted snow is found in the Three Kingdoms period for 249 when one of Chiang Wei's subcommanders, Kou An, was encircled by Wei forces which deliberately refused to engage in battle in order to deplete their resources. Kou's forces managed to survive for a period but finally surrendered when Chiang proved unable to rescue them. (*Tzu-chih T'ung-chien, Wei Chi* 7, Chia-p'ing 1.)

28. *Tzu-chih T'ung-chien, Chin Chi* 27, T'ai-yüan 9, A.D. 384.

29. *Tzu-chih T'ung-chien, Sung Chi* 3, Yüan-chia 5.

30. *Tzu-chih T'ung-chien, Liang Chi* 10, Ta-t'ung 2.

31. *Tso Chuan*, Duke Hsiang, 14th year. It numbers among the few examples included in Tu Yu's *T'ung Tien* (*chüan* 161, "Ping" 14) under the rubric "yin chi she ch'üan or "in accord with the subtle crux establish a tactical imbalance of power." It is also cited by T'ang Shun in his very brief, two-item section on poison ("Tu") in the *Wu Pien*. (For a detailed account of the battle and its context, see our *History of Warfare in China: The Ancient Period*.)

32. *Tzu-chih T'ung-chien, Chin Chi* 24, T'ai-ho 4. Huan had originally thought to supply the campaign by boat but the water was too shallow, so he had a 300-*li* canal undertaken to bring the Wen and Ch'ing rivers together, and later redirected the Sui into the Yellow River showing such apparently ambitious schemes were not regarded as insurmountable.

33. Ch'ang-sun Sheng's biography appears as part of *chüan* 22, the *Pei Shih*. In his precipitous rise to power An Lu-shan also poisoned the Turks, but for personal gain rather than as part of tactical maneuvering, inviting thousands to drinking festivities and then giving them poisoned wine made from a local herb. He then claimed the casualties were part of his suppression achievements and was duly rewarded by the emperor. (*Tzu-chih T'ung-chien, T'ang Chi* 32, T'ien-pao 9, A.D. 751.)

34. The clash is extensively discussed in all the secondary military histories and summarized in the *Hsü Tzu-chih T'ung-chien* for A.D. 1140, but the primary source is Liu Ch'i's biography in the *Sung Shih, chüan* 366. (Not surprisingly, Wu Shu's biography in the *Chin Shu, chüan* 77, hardly mentions the defeat.)

35. Subsequently found in the *Wu Pien's* section on poison; included in the *Yün-ch'ou Kang-mu*, "Chu Ch'i" under the rubric of poison; and also the *Ch'eng-shou Ch'ou-lüeh*, which provides a few formula.

36. *Yün-ch'ou Kang-mu*, "Ch'u Ch'i." However, there is no mention of poison in conjunction with provisions in either P'eng Yüeh's or Liu Pang's biography in the *Shih Chi*.

37. *Yün-ch'ou Kang-mu*, "Ch'u Ch'i."

38. For example, the late Ming dynasty *Ch'e-ying Pai-pa Ta*, entry 89, advises poisoning the external water sources of citadels too well secured to be attacked.

39. The first such instructions appear in such *T'ai-pai Yin-ching* chapters as "Ch'ien Mao Hou Tien" and "Ching Ch'üan Pien," emphasizing reconnaissance and the use of local guides to find sources of water and grass, as well as locate any opposition forces in the vicinity. (Also see "Hsing Tao" and, in the *Hu-ch'ien Ching*, "Ti Shih.") The same admonitions appear in the *T'ung Tien, chüan* 157, "Ping" 10 which even includes a subsection entitled "First Occupy Essential Terrain and Water and

Grass." The *Wu-ching Tsung-yao* ("Hsing-chün Yüeh-shu") and *T'ou-pi Fu-t'an* ("Wu Lüeh") both note that towns and cities need to be located near ample water supplies.

40. For example, the *Teng-t'an Pi-chiu*, "Shou Ch'eng," advises that additional wells should be done in cities whenever other affairs are not pressing in order to ensure an adequate supply of water. Even the *Mo-tzu* refers to pools and ponds used to protect against incendiaries, and many of the military texts discuss the deployment of water resources atop the walls.

41. *T'ai-pai Yin-ching*, "Ching Ch'üan Pien," repeated thereafter in the *T'ung Tien, chüan* 157, "Ping" 10, and *Wu-ching Tsung-yao*, "Hsün-shui Ch'üan-fa." (Most *T'ai-pai Yin-ching* texts have "yellow cows," though "yellow sheep" appears as an erroneous variant, and it is in fact picked up by the *T'ung Tien.*) A briefer form which appears as "Hsün Shui Mo" in the *Hu-ch'ien Ching* is notable for substituting "manure" for evidence of animal tracks when trying to find water.

42. *T'ai-pai Yin-ching*, "Ching Ch'üan Pien," repeated thereafter in the *T'ung Tien, chüan* 157, "Ping," 10 and *Wu-ching Tsung-yao*, "Hsün-shui Ch'üan-fa."

43. First seen in the *Wu-ching Tsung-yao*, "Hsün-shui Ch'üan-fa."

44. *Wu-ching Tsung-yao*, "Hsün-shui Ch'üan-fa." (Li Ling's remnant troops set off with pieces of ice to slake their thirst.)

45. First seen in the *T'ung tien, chüan* 157, showing how the earlier section is being accretionally expanded, subsequently in the *Wu-ching Tsung-yao*, "Hsia-ying Che-ti-fa" and *Ts'ui-wei Pei-cheng-lu*, "Shou Ti."

46. *T'ung tien, chüan* 157, and *Wu-ching Tsung-yao*, "Hsia-ying Che-ti-fa." (The *T'ung Tien* section entitled "First Occupy Essential Terrain together with Water and Grass" somewhat surprisingly begins by quoting *Wu-tzu* since Tu Yu is so closely associated with Sun-tzu's *Art of War.*)

47. *Wu-ching Tsung-yao*, "Hsia-ying Che-ti-fa."

48. *Military Methods*, "Male and Female Cities." The T'ang dynasty *T'ung Tien* includes an admonition not to drink "stagnant (dead) water" in the subsection on encamping the army in *chüan* 157, "Ping" 10, and numerous other military writings concur, such as the *Wu Pien* ("Ying Chih") which defines "dead" water simply as water that doesn't flow rather than showing any characteristics of pollution or poison.

49. "Analyzing Rivers." In "Ti Shih" Hsü emphasizes the need to establish encampments near flowing water, especially water that flows eastward, and not deploy contrary to the flow.

50. Two of Hua Yüeh's forty-two secret methods for attacking cities preserved in his early thirteenth century *Ts'ui-wei Pei-cheng-lu* ("Te Ti") are sprinkling poison and employing windblown drugs.

51. See, for example, *Teng-t'an Pi-chou*, "Shou Ch'eng."

CHAPTER 11

1. Additional examples may be found in Yates, "Early Poliorcetics," and a brief overview (together with another view of several of our examples) in Herbert Franke's "Siege and Defense of Towns in Medieval China" in *Chinese Ways in Warfare*, pp. 151–201.

2. The siege is employed as an illustration in the subsection "Yin-chi She-ch'üan" in *chüan* 161 (*Ping*, 14) of the *T'ung Tien* as well as "Shou" in the *Wu Pien* and "Chüeh Shui" in the *Ping-ch'ou Lei-yao*, and discussed at length by Benjamin A. Wallacker, "Studies in Medieval Chinese Siegecraft: The Siege of Yü-pi, AD 546" in *Journal of Asian Studies* 28:4 (1969), pp. 789–802. The ongoing struggle between

Eastern and Western Wei is analyzed and reprised in "Tung Hsi Wei chih Chan" in the *Chung-kuo Li-tai Chan-cheng-shih*, Vol. 6, pp. 375–414, though the focus is upon the earlier clashes and Yü-pi itself only receives brief coverage.

3. *Tzu-chih T'ung-chien, Liang-chi* 14, Ta-t'ung 8. Kao Huan also personally commanded this incursion into Western Wei.

4. *Tzu-chih T'ung-chien, Liang-chi* 15, Chung-ta-t'ung 1, and Wei Hsiao-kuan's biography, *Pei-shih, chüan* 64, and *Chou Shu*, chüan 31.

5. For a brief discussion, see Wallacker, pp. 794–796.

6. *Pei-shih, chüan* 64 (Wei Hsiao-kuan's biography).

7. *Pei-shih, chüan* 64 (Wei Hsiao-kuan's biography), *T'ung Tien,* and *Pei-shih, chüan* 6 all agree that twenty-one tunnels were excavated, but the latter says they were all dug on the eastern side of the citadel. However, see Wallacker, p. 798 for further speculation.

8. The *Tzu-chih T'ung-chien* includes the 70,000 man figure, the *Pei-shih, chüan* 64 (Wei Hsiao-kuan's biography) simply states 40 to 50 percent against an unspecified force size, but possibly as high as 200,000 men.

9. Some hundred pages of the *Tzu-chih T'ung-chien—Liang-chi* 16 through 20—record aspects of the campaign and siege. Hou Ching and Yang K'an have key biographies; aspects of the assault and counter-assault are briefly depicted in the *T'ung Tien* (under "Yin-chi She-ch'üan"), *Wu-ching Tsung-yao* ("Huo Kung"), and *Wu Pien* ("Shou"); a fragment is included in the *T'ai-p'ing Yü-lan* (*chüan* 319); and Benjamin Wallacker numbers it among his three illustrative sieges of the period ("Studies in Medieval Chinese Siegecraft: The Siege of Chien-k'ang, A.D. 548–549," *Journal of Asian History,* 5:1 [1971], 35–54).

10. See, for example, Yü Chin's analysis, *Liang-chi* 16, *Tzu-chih T'ung-chien.* (This campaign has previously been discussed.)

11. Eighty to 90 percent constantly recurs as a casualty figure in these extended sieges. While it may simply be a general estimate or literary device for expressing severe losses, it certainly is a figure at which resistance would become impossible.

12. Hou Ching even had to purify the city by burning all the bodies, yet illness continued.

13. Even though similar populist attacks were raised at the start of many rebellions throughout China's stormy history, they were rarely recorded.

14. This surely ranks as one of the great, unimaginable obstinacies in history.

15. The *Tzu-chih T'ung-chien* asserts they were steeped in lard and wax, the *T'ung Tien* that they were impregnated with oil and had iron arrowheads affixed.

16. Hou astutely employed psychological warfare measures throughout, though space precludes their discussion here.

17. *Tzu-chih T'ung-chien, T'ang-chi* 68, Hsien-t'ung 11.

18. A succinct account, preserved in the *Hsü Tzu-chih T'ung-chien* for A.D. 1126, is also reproduced in the *Chung-kuo Li-tai Chan-cheng-shih,* Vol. 12, pp. 76–77 and the late Ming *Wu Pien* includes it among the few illustrations appended to its section on "Defense."

19. "Ching-k'ang Ch'ao-yeh Chien-yen Hou-hsü."

20. "Shou-ch'eng Chi-yao."

21. Ch'en Kuei's biography in the *Sung Shih* (*chüan* 377) reprises some aspects of the siege at Te-an, but the most important is the reference to their sallying forth with *huo ch'iang* (fire lances) to burn the enemy's Heavenly Bridge and having bolstered the attack with (straw) fire oxen.

22. For further discussion and an assessment of the historical importance, see Joseph Needham, "The Gunpowder Epic," p. 23.

23. The *K'ai-hsi Te-an Shou-ch'eng Lu* was compiled by Wang Chih-yüan, son of the defensive commander Wang Yün-ch'u. (*Ts'ung-shu Chi-ch'eng Hsü-pien*, Vol. 23, *Shih Pu*, Shanghai Shu-tien.)

24. On 12/5, 12/6, and 1/7.

25. Chao Wan-nien, *Hsiang-yang Shou-ch'eng-lu*, Yen Yi-p'ing, general editor, *Ao-yang-t'ang Ts'ung-shu*, Taipei, Yi-wen Yin-shu-kuan. (Chao Wan-nien, who also played an active though subordinate command role, was Chao Ch'un's son.) This siege should be distinguished from the famous, subsequent one mounted by the Mongols from 1268 to 1273 which was finally ended by the use of giant earth-shaking catapults constructed with the assistance of Persian engineers. Incendiary measures played an important but not decisive role, especially being employed to destroy the Sung's fleet.

26. See, for example, *Hsü Tzu-chih T'ung-chien*, K'ai-hsi 2nd and 3rd years. (The chronicle indicates Jurchen forces first appeared at the city several days earlier.) Despite his outstanding leadership and tactical mastery, Chao Ch'un is otherwise unknown. His burning of Fan-ch'eng, the companion city just across the river on the northern bank—perhaps because it was indefensible or as part of a scorched earth policy—before retreating to Hsiang-yang has caused commentators to doubt the chronicle's veracity and question his ability to direct such a successful defense. However, others believe the account to be valid or assume that much of the credit should probably accrue to his generals and advisers, including Chao Wan-nien, the chronology's author.

27. As always, the lack of mention doesn't necessarily mean they were not used.

# Bibliography of Chinese Materials

## ORIGINAL SERIES

二十五史
八陣合變圖說，龍正
十七史百將傳，張預
十大經
三十六計
三國志
三略，黃石公
大同鎮兵車操法，俞大猷
王氏新書，王基
火攻挈要，焦勗
火器略說，黃達權、王韜
火龍神器陣法
太平條規
太平軍目
太平御覽
太白陰經，李筌
六韜
公羊傳
史記
司馬法
戊笈談兵，汪紱
左傳
北洋海軍章程
古今圖書集成
老子
自強軍創制公言，沈敦和
自強軍西法類編，沈敦和
百將傳續編，何喬新
守城錄，陳規、湯君寶
行軍總要
永樂大典
兵法，魏禧
兵法史略學，陳慶年
兵法百言，揭暄
兵要四則，
兵跡，魏禧

兵謀，魏禧
兵學新書，徐建寅
兵略對，俞大猷
兵鏡，吳惟順、吳鳴球、吳若禮編輯
兵機要訣，徐光啟
兵矗？，尹賓商
兵籌類要，慕崇禮
何博士備論，何去非
宋本十一家注孫子
投筆膚談，何守法
決勝綱目，葉夢熊
吳子
李衛公兵法輯本，李靖
防守集成，朱璐
呂氏春秋
言兵事書，晁錯
車營叩答合編，孫承宗（鹿善繼、茅元儀、杜應芳）
尚書
武侯八陣兵法輯略
武備志，茅元儀
武經七書直解
武經七書匯解，朱墉
武經總要
武編，唐順之
孟子
虎鈐經，許洞
明實錄類纂，武漢出版社
長江水師全案，
長短經，趙蕤
直隸練軍馬步營制章程
美芹十論，辛棄疾
風后握奇經
施氏七書講義，施子美
荀子
春秋

城守籌略，錢栴
草廬經略
紀效新書，戚繼光
洋防說略，徐稚蓀
訓練操法詳晰圖說，袁世凱、段祺瑞、馮國璋、王世珍
海防要覽，丁日昌、李鴻章
海防圖論，胡宗憲
海國圖志，魏源
陣紀，何良臣
鬼谷子
素書，黃石公
孫子
孫子書校解引類，趙本學
孫子參同，李贄
孫臏兵法
尉繚子
唐太宗李衛公問對，李靖
射經，王琚
淮南子，劉安
淮軍武毅各軍課程，聶士成
救命書，呂坤
乾坤大略，王餘佑
國語
商君書
曾文正公水陸行軍練兵誌，王定安
曾胡治兵語錄，蔡鍔
登壇必究，王鳴鶴
鄉約，尹耕
運籌綱目，葉夢熊
道德經論兵要義述，王真
道藏
塞語，尹耕
經法
詩經
新書
新建陸軍兵略錄存，袁世凱
資治通鑑
道德經
逸周書

稱
說苑
廣西選鋒兵操法，俞大猷
翠微北征錄，華岳
管子
閫外春秋，李筌
墨子
潛夫論，王符
練兵實紀，戚繼光
練勇芻言，王璞山
選練條格，徐光啟
諸葛忠武候文集
歷代兵制，陳傅良
戰國策
戰略，司馬彪
魏武帝集
韓非子
韓詩外傳
籌洋芻議，薛福成
籌海圖編，鄭若曾
鶡冠子
權書，蘇洵
續武經總要，趙本學
續資治通鑑

Key Secondary Studies

中國軍事史，解放軍出版社
中國軍事通史，軍事科學出版社
中國歷代戰爭史，黎明文化事業股份有限公司
劉旭，中國古代火炮史，上海人民出版社，1989.
張鐵牛、高曉星，中國古代海軍史，八一出版社，1993.
王兆春，中國火器史，軍事科學出版社，1991.
席龍飛，中國造船史，湖北教育出版社，2000.

# SUGGESTED FURTHER READING

Further discussion of the topics raised by Sun-tzu's *Art of War* and many other focal subjects in Chinese military and intelligence history may be found in the following Westview Press books, translated and authored by Ralph D. Sawyer.

## The Tao of War
*The Martial Tao Te Ching*
0–8133–4081–0, $15.95/$25.00 CAN, paper

Wang Chen, a ninth-century military commander, was sickened by the carnage that had plagued the glorious T'ang dynasty for decades. "All within the seas were poisoned," he wrote, "and pain and disaster was rife throughout the land." Wang Chen wondered, how can we end conflicts before they begin? How can we explain and understand the dynamics of conflict? For the answer he turned to a remarkable source—the *Tao Te Ching*. Here is Wang Chen's own rendering of and commentary on the ancient text, insightfully expanded and amplified by translator Ralph D. Sawyer, a leading scholar of Chinese military history. Although the *Tao* long influenced Chinese military doctrine, Wang Chen's interpretations produced the first reading of it as a martial text—a "tao of war." Like Sun-tzu's *Art of War*, certainly the most famous study of strategy ever written, the Tao provides lessons for the struggles of contemporary life. In the way that the ancient *Art of War* provides inspiration and advice on how to succeed in competitive situations of all kinds, even in today's world, Wang Chen's *The Tao of War* uncovers action plans for managing conflict and promoting peace.

A book to put on the shelf next to *Art of War*, Wang Chen's *The Tao of War* is a reference of equally compelling and practical advice.

## Sun Tzu: Art of War
0–8133–1951-X, $15.95/$25.00 CAN, paper

"The *Art of War* has become so accepted as a 'must read' book. . . that it need no further justification. . . . The most accurate, concise, and usable English-language translation available."— *Military Review*

The *Art of War* is almost certainly the most famous study of strategy ever written and has had an extraordinary influence on the history of warfare. The principles Sun-tzu expounded were utilized brilliantly by such great

Asian war leaders as Mao Tse-tung, Giap, and Yamamoto. First translated two hundred years ago by a French missionary, Sun Tzu's *Art of War* has been credited with influencing Napoleon, the German General Staff, and even the planning for Desert Storm. Many Japanese companies make this book required reading for their key executives. And increasingly, Western businesspeople and others are turning to the *Art of War* for inspiration and advice on how to succeed in competitive situations of all kinds.

Ralph Sawyer places this classic work of strategy in its proper historical context. Sawyer supplies a portrait of Sun-tzu's era and outlines several battles of the period that may have either influenced Sun-tzu or been conducted by him. While appreciative of the philosophical richness of the *Art of War*, his edition addresses Sun-tzu's practical origins and presents a translation that is both accurate and accessible.

### The Complete Art of War
Sun-tzu Sun Pin
ISBN 0–8133–3085–8, $35.00/$52.95 CAN, cloth

"The combination of a. . . clear translation with an informative commentary makes this an essential element in the study of Chinese martial philosophy. . . . An excellent [book]."—*Military & Naval History Journal*

The only single-volume edition available of the classic essays on strategy by the great Sun-tzu and his descendant, Sun Pin. With Sawyer's thoughtful chapter-by-chapter commentaries, *The Complete Art of War* is designed to guide the reader to new insights into the nature of human conflict and a greater understanding of every field of human activity—from playing the game of politics to building a successful marriage, from closing a deal to managing a large organization, and even from making war to making peace.

### The Seven Military Classics of Ancient China
ISBN 0–8133–1228–0, $37.50/$56.50 CAN, cloth

*The Seven Military Classics* is one of the most profound studies of warfare ever written. Here translated in their entirety for the first time, the seven separate essays in this volume (written between 500 B.C. and A.D. 700) include Sun-tzu's famous *Art of War*. This is the definitive English-language edition of a unique contribution to the military literature.

### Sun Pin
*Military Methods*
ISBN 0–8133–8888–0, $32.00/$47.95 CAN, paper

"Sawyer's translation. . . further adds in an important way to our knowledge of the place of warfare in classical Chinese civilization."—John Keegan

In addition to translating this "eighth military classic," Sawyer has prepared insightful chapter-by-chapter commentaries and a vivid general introduction that describes Sun Pin's life and times, analyzes in detail Sun Pin's tactics in important battles, and compares Sun-tzu's strategic thinking with Sun Pin's.

## One Hundred Unorthodox Strategies
*Battle and Tactics of Chinese Warfare*
ISBN 0–8133–2861–6, $22.00/$32.95 CAN, paper

"Not only insightful, but impeccable."—*War in History*

"Sawyer's commentary, written in language understandable to both soldiers and businessmen, is useful beyond its application to the study of military theory. . . . Enjoyable and enlightening."—*Military Review*

Beginning with Sun-tzu's Art of War, the anonymous author of this Sung dynasty military manual abstracted the one hundred generally paired tactical principles—such as fast/slow, unorthodox/orthodox—he felt to be essential to battlefield analysis and martial conceptualization before appending a similar number of historical examples.

## The Tao of Spycraft
*Intelligence Theory and Practice in Traditional China*
ISBN 0–8133–3303–2, $35.00/$52.95 CAN, cloth

"Ralph Sawyer has once again written a text which combines the virtues of scholarly integrity, shrewd analysis, and plain fun. This book is not only for those interested in the history and theory of intelligence, but for those simply intent on a good read."—Robert L. O'Connell, author of *Ride of the Second Horseman*

In *The Tao of Spycraft*, for the first time anywhere Ralph Sawyer unfolds the long and venerable tradition of spycraft and intelligence work in traditional China, revealing a vast array of theoretical materials and astounding historical developments.

# Index

A-shih-na Ssu-mou, 105,
106
A-shih-te-wen, 270
A-shu, 211
Accelerant, 7, 11, 12, 33,
62, 65, 91, 113, 128,
191, 364, 371
Accord, 86–88, 91, 281,
318
Advance, 46, 157, 166, 167,
196, 266, 268, 269,
273, 310, 314
Advantage, 17, 21, 41, 43,
47, 82, 83, 88, 79,
99–101, 106, 132,
140, 141, 195, 196,
282–284, 318, 319,
340, 344, 346, 349
Agent, 3, 19, 20, 21, 26, 61,
81, 110, 111, 116,
171, 204, 221, 231,
300, 337, 351, 352,
355, 366, 369, 370
Aggressor, 4, 26, 28, 58, 94,
105, 144, 149, 155,
158, 164, 165, 175,
178, 179, 181, 187,
188, 191, 193, 228,
234, 252, 253, 285,
288, 290, 301, 302,
306, 307, 317, 336,
344, 347, 351, 363,
369
Agriculture, 243, 315, 343
Air, 34
All under Heaven, 42, 262,
263
Alliance, 42, 43, 50, 53, 67,
68, 116, 222, 261,
326, 345
Altar, 44
Ambush, 13, 38, 39, 50, 54,
62, 64, 65, 74, 90, 93,
97, 100, 131, 156,
157, 167, 173, 312,

327, 333, 336, 337,
364
An Chíing-hs,, 74, 302
An Lu-shan, 67, 71–75,
189, 190, 250, 302
An-chíing, 218, 222
An-yi, 263, 280, 282, 284
Anger, 10, 12, 17, 41, 66
Anhui, 157, 159, 189, 218,
287
Animals, 25, 27, 44, 78, 91,
96, 109, 115, 118,
120, 122–125, 127,
131, 174, 175, 187,
198, 204, 242, 275,
290, 299, 317, 328,
331, 340, 342, 347,
353, 370
Annam, 358
Ant, 340
Antiquity, XX 45, 75, 87,
93, 96, 99, 103, 122,
123, 133, 167, 168,
202, 241, 284, 289,
293, 350
Archer, 56, 63, 129–131,
195, 200, 208, 211,
213, 217, 224, 278,
289–291, 336, 337
Armor, 52, 80, 132, 145,
147, 186, 218, 231,
254, 255, 259, 301,
314, 337
Armory, 6, 16, 119, 259,
358
Army, 17, 18, 35, 38, 39,
41–44, 46, 53, 59, 60,
68, 72, 74, 78, 87, 88,
92, 94–96, 103, 104,
106, 107, 115, 117,
120, 137, 153–157,
160, 162, 163, 165,
167, 170, 171, 177,
195–197, 202, 212,
214, 218, 219, 222,

226, 228–230, 248,
249, 251–253, 258,
260–263, 265, 273,
275, 280, 283, 284,
286–288, 292, 294,
297, 308–312, 315,
318, 321, 324, 326,
328, 330, 332–334,
341, 345–347, 353,
354, 357, 359, 371
Arrogance, 55, 68, 115,
117, 138, 161–163,
309
Arrow, 3, 7, 18, 19, 29–31,
36, 40, 63, 74, 87, 91,
109, 113, 121, 127,
129, 132, 147, 153,
154, 166, 173, 175,
180, 181, 187–188,
190, 200, 204,
206–208, 213, 214,
232, 235, 259, 277,
289, 291, 294, 314,
159, 362–264, 371
incendiary, 3, 19, 29, 20,
63, 128, 130–133,
141, 153–154, 159,
175, 176, 180, 181,
183, 184, 201, 204,
206, 211, 217, 251,
362, 364, 365, 368,
371
whip 133
*Art of War,* 12, 15, 21, 22,
43, 54, 71, 77–79, 83,
84, 86, 103, 110, 155,
199, 200, 202, 204,
270, 272, 280, 283,
289, 319, 338, 357
Assault, 4, 13, 17, 19, 29,
30, 71, 73, 110, 131,
136, 140, 151, 158,
161, 163, 165, 170,
177, 192, 227, 229,
254, 255, 257, 276,

289, 305, 311, 318, 323, 333, 337, 344–349, 351, 357, 358, 360, 361, 363, 364, 371
amphibious, 52, 81, 82, 133, 161, 195, 200, 216, 217, 229–232, 235, 255, 277, 287, 288, 294, 302, 304, 367
cart 99, 362
Assessment (evaluation), 156, 160, 161, 347, 353
Attack
aquatic, 16, 253, 254, 256, 271, 275, 276, 278–286, 288, 290, 291, 295, 297, 299, 301, 306, 357, 359
follow-on, 19, 41, 62, 103, 139, 144, 147, 164, 193, 210, 214, 224, 357, 370
incendiary, 3, 15, 16, 22, 35, 37, 41, 45, 46, 49–51, 55, 56, 59, 62, 64, 66, 67, 70, 74, 75, 78–80, 83, 85, 86, 89, 90, 92–97, 100, 102, 103, 107, 109, 110, 118, 147, 149, 151, 153, 155–157, 159, 161, 162, 164, 165, 172, 173, 177, 185, 188, 190, 200, 201, 208, 210–217, 220, 223, 225, 229, 235, 254, 280, 293, 365, 370
surprise (sudden), 54, 80, 84, 88, 90, 141, 151, 152, 155, 157, 167, 168, 171, 177, 179, 205, 216, 250, 313, 337
Authority, 71, 72, 289, 291, 312, 344, 360
Autumn, 75, 137, 225, 226, 267, 273, 308, 321, 363
Axe, 234, 338

Backfire, 37–40, 58, 70, 84, 95, 177

Ball (sphere), 8, 125, 126, 134, 142, 180, 181, 193, 371
Bamboo, 7–9, 14, 20, 52, 78, 81, 93, 97, 121, 126, 132, 143, 145, 155, 163, 166, 168, 173–175, 182, 186, 188, 193, 197, 199, 205, 207, 210, 224, 233–235, 237, 267, 338, 340, 363–365, 368, 369
fire chicken, 181–183
*Bamboo Annals,* 249
Banner, 24, 54
Barrel, 209, 210
Barrier, 46, 90, 97, 100, 107, 136, 164, 176, 183, 184, 201, 202, 221, 229, 232, 235, 237, 252, 279, 281, 300, 307, 335, 347
Basket, 181, 329
Battle, 7, 89, 96, 153, 156, 189, 196, 202, 210, 212, 219, 225, 265, 346
Beam, 33, 34, 176, 191, 213, 338, 341
Bellows, 32, 35, 192, 350, 361
Benevolence, 44, 47, 89, 99
Bird, 47, 65, 91, 116, 122–125, 210, 242, 340
Black powder. *See* gunpowder
Blade, 173, 187, 350
Blinded, 149, 168, 181, 186, 213
Blood, 213
Bomb, 9, 183, 188, 201, 209
Boat, 51, 52, 55, 56, 59, 60, 62, 63, 65, 67, 82, 85, 86, 88, 89, 91, 97, 104, 107, 109, 126, 132–134, 142, 143, 151, 153–155, 159–162, 173, 176, 184–186, 195–215, 217–219, 221–225, 230, 232–237, 247, 249, 251, 252, 254–256, 265, 266, 272, 273, 277, 279, 281, 284, 288, 290,

291, 294, 296, 298, 301, 307, 313, 315, 334, 336, 354, 368
Boiling water, 30
Bolt, 181, 363
Border, 26, 39, 40, 72, 80, 81, 91, 92, 94, 95, 97, 104, 105, 117, 130, 173, 248, 270, 273, 292, 293, 320, 324–329, 335, 343, 345–347
Bow, 27, 52, 83, 106, 113, 129, 141, 159, 181, 204, 220, 234, 255
Bridge, 69, 70, 162, 163, 171, 189, 197, 199, 211, 223, 224, 227–230, 234–237, 244, 249–251, 265, 266, 305, 347, 354, 355, 357, 363–366, 368, 369
Brigand, 46, 87, 88, 97, 135, 157, 158, 173, 208, 222, 339
Bronze, 140, 184, 186
Brush, 14, 88, 113, 171, 184, 201, 252
Bucket, 174, 175, 235, 319, 369
Buddhist, 119, 354
Building, 29, 44, 49, 78, 107, 125, 132, 264, 278, 336, 355
Bullet, 141

Caltrops, 27, 134, 142–144, 147, 178, 188, 347, 371
Camel, 340
Campaign, 17, 41, 44, 50, 52, 53, 55, 58, 59, 61, 64, 66, 67, 71, 80, 96, 102, 107, 115, 119, 135, 153, 171, 197, 200, 201, 214, 215, 225, 230, 232, 252, 265, 268, 270, 277, 278, 286, 291, 292, 301, 303, 319, 320, 324–326, 330–334, 351, 358, 363, 367
punitive, 44, 151, 161, 169, 203, 222, 223, 327–329
Canal, 52, 71, 173, 253, 265, 269, 276, 277,

279, 280, 283, 285, 286, 300, 302, 313, 315, 349, 361
Cannon, 9, 45, 91, 131, 132, 140, 141, 165, 187, 188, 204, 206, 208, 218, 220, 229, 364, 369
Capital, 46, 135, 215, 279, 285, 294, 296, 328, 343, 353, 385
Cart, 113, 127
Casualties, 6, 13, 40, 42–44, 50, 55, 56, 62, 63, 69–73, 75, 86, 94, 99, 103, 105, 116, 120, 121, 125, 131, 136, 157, 158, 160–162, 171, 185, 189, 191, 201, 211, 212, 214, 218, 221, 223, 227, 228, 230, 233, 267, 268, 271, 288–292, 294, 300, 301, 308, 311, 322, 324, 325, 327, 331–335, 337, 338, 344, 345, 351–353, 355–357, 359, 360, 362, 370, 371
Catapult, 218, 220, 363
Cavalry, 27, 36, 38, 40, 51, 53–55, 65, 69–71, 73–75, 85, 89, 102, 105, 106, 111, 135–137, 153, 156, 158, 160, 169–171, 177, 216, 225, 227, 234, 252, 258, 265, 266, 269, 271, 273, 289, 295, 303, 307, 312, 313, 324, 327, 329, 332, 335, 337, 364, 367, 369, 370
Chaff, 165, 181, 193
Chains, 69, 181, 183, 211, 220, 224, 225, 230–236, 307
*Chan-kuo Tsie*, 257, 262, 263
Chían River, 69, 244
Chang Fei, 62
Chang Han, 49, 50, 285
Chang Hsiu, 53
Chang Hs‚-tío, 137, 138
Chang Hs‚n, 189–191
Chang Juo, 325
Chang Ko, 319, 320

Chang Meng-tían, 258–262
Chang River, 297, 298
Chang Shih-chíeng, 303, 306
Chang Tíing-tuan, 331, 332
Chang Yi, 263, 264
Chíang-an, 73–75, 160, 172, 190, 214, 215, 247, 320, 324, 358
Chíang-chou, 162
Chíang-píing, 45
Chíang-sheh, 157
Chíang-sun Sheng, 334, 335
Change, 16, 19, 96, 100, 141, 157, 167, 311
Channel. *See* Canal
Chao (state), 46, 115, 116, 249, 257–262, 264, 285
Chao, King, 115, 116
Chao Chia, 258, 261, 262
Chao Chíun, 154, 367, 368–371
Chao Hsin, 6
Chao Wan-nien, 366
Chao Y‚, 120, 121
Chao Y‚n, 312
Chíao Tsío, 97
Chíao-hu, Lake
Chíao-ko, 10
Chaos, 3, 18, 19, 28, 33, 41, 54, 62, 65, 72, 74, 75, 84, 88, 90, 94, 100, 112, 121, 130, 131, 136–139, 141, 143, 157, 158, 161, 177, 213, 214, 229, 294, 313, 330, 332, 337, 355
Charcoal, 8, 27, 30–32, 209, 234
Chariot, 14, 18, 38, 51, 52, 55, 75, 204, 224, 258, 263, 265, 266, 268, 269, 271
Chechiang, 304
Chíen, 79–83, 103, 158, 160, 161, 169, 306, 307
Chíen Chíeng-hao, 277
Chíen Chi, 92, 202
Chíen Kuei, 361
Chíen Lung-chih, 119
Chíen Pa-hsien, 107, 211
Chíen Tíang, 50, 51
Chíen Tsíai 321
Chíen-tíou-hsieh, 75

Chíen-tsíang Gorge, 49, 62, 97
Chíen Yu-liang, 217–221, 303
Cheng, 6, 12, 13, 15, 256
Cheng-chou, 10, 13, 235
Chíeng Ho, 267
Chíeng-chou
Chíeng-píu 18,
Chíeng-tíou-shan, 245
Chíeng-tu, 119, 169, 180, 246, 343, 347–359
Chíeng-yang, 310
*Chevaux-de-frise*, 37, 188, 333, 369
Chi River, 54, 116, 242, 282
*Chi-li huo-chíiu*, 143, 178, 192
Chi-ming-chíeng, 246
Chi-mo, 115- 119
Chíi (state), 13–15, 35, 96, 115, 116, 118, 169, 200, 226, 247, 264, 266, 308, 309, 315
Northern, 129, 130, 158, 211
Chíi Chi-kuang, 89, 139, 203
Chíi Chieh, 116
Chíi Chíung-li, 85, 283, 284
Chi-fu, 18
Chia-ling River, 302
Chiang River, 263, 284
Chiang Wei, 65, 98, 321
Chiang Yu, 121, 122
Chiang-ling, 306, 315
Chíiang, 66, 96, 121, 248, 319
Chíiang River, 307
Chianghsi, 218
Chiangsu, 157, 161, 213, 304, 321
Chiao, Mt., 211
Chíiao-chou, 354
Chicken, 78, 121–123, 134, 208
Chieh-hsiu, 325
Chien-chou, 138
Chien-kíang, 66, 82, 153, 211, 227, 351–357
Chien-píing, 230
Chíien Chíuan-chí‚an, 213
Chih Kuo, 261, 262
Chih Po, 257–264, 279, 282, 294
Chih River, 275
*Chih-hu y‚an-píao*, 143
Chíih Pi. *See* Red Cliffs

Chíih Yu, 164
Children, 295, 352
Chin, 6, 10–14, 79, 107,
   115, 116, 121, 171,
   212, 216, 230–233,
   249, 257, 315, 321,
   322, 334
   Eastern, 66
   Later, 66
   Western, 332
Chin River, 248, 280
Chin-yang, 102, 257–262,
   264, 270, 279, 294,
   307, 348, 349
Chin-yung, 6
Chíin 10, 12, 13, 23, 35, 52,
   102, 115, 116, 200,
   249, 263–265, 285,
   333, 334, 347
   Former, 102, 103, 160,
   297, 322
   Later, 322, 324, 332
   Northern, 107
Chíin-chou, 14
Chíin-huai River, 354
China, 3, 4, 43, 51–53, 65,
   79, 80, 93, 107, 170,
   172, 175, 186, 195,
   216, 218, 225, 226,
   241–244, 252, 275,
   279, 294, 298,
   324–326, 328, 334,
   340, 343, 359, 361
Ching, 55, 58, 313
Ching Lake, 151
Ching River, 333, 334
Ching Yang, 266
Ching-chiang, 249
Ching-chou, 59, 61, 245,
   301
Ching-ling, 60
Chíing, 101, 188
Chíing Tao, 217
Chíing-hai, 105
Chou (state, dynasty),
   10–13, 18, 37, 52, 245,
   246, 343, 344
   Northern, 79, 129, 160,
   302, 306
   Western, 197, 199
Chou, King, 10
Chou Y,, 56, 57, 97
Chu Chi, 264
Chu-chia-sai-kíou, 295
Chu Chíuan-chung, 95, 161,
   162
Chu Ch,n, 157, 158
Chu Hs,an, 95

Chu Lu, 188
Chu River, 247
Chu Tíao, 70, 71
Chu Tsíu, 70, 190
Chu Tzíu, 70
Chu Chíen-hao, 221–223
Chu Wen-cheng, 218, 219
Chu Yi, 353, 354
Chu Y,an-chang, 217–223,
   303, 326
Chu-a, 137
Chu-ko Liang, 16, 45, 59,
   62–65, 997, 310–312,
   314, 320, 333, 339
*Chu-ko Liang Ping-fa, 63*
Chíu, 11, 13, 15, 23, 24, 35,
   96, 115, 116, 118,
   119, 200, 202, 204,
   214, 249, 256, 257,
   266, 267, 308–310,
   339
Chíu River, 248
Chíu-chou, 216
Chí, Chen, 330
Chí,, Mount, 321
Chí,-wo, 10, 11
Chíuan-tíang, 31
Chuang, Duke,
   *Chíun Chíiu,* 11
*Chí,n-feng-píao,* 144
Chung-han, 257
*Chung-lei-píao* (Colliding
   Thunder Bomb) 142
Chung-li, 226–229, 343
Chung-shan, 116, 136
Citadel, 13, 17, 23, 33, 41,
   84, 130, 131, 136,
   138, 149, 162, 163,
   172, 181, 225–227,
   232, 233, 236, 246,
   249, 256, 263, 265,
   277, 284, 287, 288,
   290, 292, 298, 302,
   304, 313, 314,
   320–323, 326, 330,
   334, 337–351,
   354–357, 359
City, 3, 5, 6, 12, 13, 17, 18,
   20, 25–27, 33–35, 41,
   42, 50, 52, 63, 66, 67,
   70, 83, 88, 92, 96, 98,
   100, 102, 104, 107,
   110–112, 115–117,
   120, 123–125,
   129–131, 139,
   143–145, 157, 158,
   163, 165, 166, 170,
   173, 188–190, 192,

   201, 215, 218, 219,
   222, 235, 243–251,
   254, 256, 258, 260,
   263, 264, 272,
   276–278, 280,
   282–285, 287–292,
   294, 296, 297,
   299–303, 306–309,
   311–314, 327–332,
   338, 339, 343–347,
   352, 354, 356, 358,
   361, 362, 364, 366,
   367, 369–371
Clay, 147, 173, 185, 209,
   371
Climate, 51, 52, 57, 80, 81,
   92, 241, 306
Cloth, 14, 63, 84, 125, 350,
   351, 356
Clothes, 142, 145, 147, 190
Cloud, ZZ 47, 150, 167,
   171, 181, 213
Coast, 52, 200, 203, 208,
   215, 223
Cold, 52, 80, 105, 106, 136,
   167, 195, 250, 251,
   273, 286, 290, 292,
   295, 301, 332, 348
Color, 168, 341, 342
Combat, 4, 42, 93, 151,
   163, 166, 170, 176,
   195, 202
Combustion, 6–9, 113, 149,
   151, 155, 156
Command, 24, 53, 62, 72,
   74, 304
Commander, 3, 37, 55, 61,
   65, 66, 71, 79, 85, 90,
   99, 102, 103, 112,
   129, 130, 139, 151,
   156–159, 161, 162,
   167, 170, 172, 173,
   175, 177, 189, 197,
   203, 215, 216, 220,
   227, 230, 231, 249,
   253, 266, 268, 271,
   279, 284, 290, 291,
   297, 301, 302, 306,
   307, 315, 322–325,
   327–329, 334, 335,
   337, 341, 349, 354,
   358, 359, 364
Conceal (Obfuscate), 149,
   154, 164–169, 171,
   181, 217, 314
Conflagration, 3, 6–8, 16,
   19, 41, 56, 58, 86, 95,
   110, 151, 164, 191,

201, 212, 220, 223, 230, 234, 371
Confucian, 24, 56
Confusion, 14, 31, 38, 50, 70, 71, 90, 96, 110–112, 117, 118, 120, 121, 124, 125, 137, 138, 142, 146, 147, 161, 162, 164, 167, 169, 210, 213, 216, 224, 230, 289, 327
Contrary, 87, 281, 313
Cooking, 4, 5, 29, 282, 290
Copper, 52, 260
Corner, 191, 192
Counter-attack, 68, 71, 163, 229, 251, 264, 322, 328, 332, 337, 361
Courage, 4, 58, 66, 67, 85, 110, 111, 140, 141, 161, 287, 301, 309, 333, 338
Credibility, 99
Crossbow, 29, 38, 40, 50–52, 113, 120, 121, 129–131, 133, 141, 153, 159, 170, 181, 201, 202, 212, 220, 229, 254, 255, 362, 368–371
Current (flow), 57, 58, 69, 88, 91, 98, 109, 151, 153, 163, 196, 197, 200, 202, 204, 206, 212, 213, 223–225, 230, 231, 233, 236, 241, 244, 247, 249, 265, 278, 279, 281, 283, 285, 290, 296, 298, 313, 340, 341

Dam, 69, 237, 242, 248, 249, 264, 267, 271, 276, 278, 279, 281, 283, 288, 290, 298, 300, 302, 310–313, 315, 318, 361
Darkness, 3, 39, 50, 92, 97, 110, 131, 134, 154, 181, 204, 313, 338, 363
Day, 16, 60, 92, 154, 229
Death, 42, 340, 341
Debilitate, 21, 81, 101, 103, 105, 324, 331, 333, 346

Deception, 14, 49, 54, 56, 60, 69–71, 82, 85, 90, 95, 117, 169, 171, 198, 283, 287, 289, 337, 366
Deck, 176, 201, 206, 208, 210
Deer, 78, 122, 136
Defeat, 49, 58, 74, 75, 95, 117, 120, 138, 153, 154, 156, 158, 162, 172, 214, 218, 222, 223, 230, 273, 292, 308, 310, 320, 323, 332, 333, 347, 358, 360
Defector, 170, 215, 216, 226, 286, 298, 333, 356, 357
Defenders, 28, 63, 112, 113, 116, 120, 145, 162, 166, 170, 171, 186, 190, 193, 195, 224, 228, 229, 232, 234, 235, 252, 255, 277, 285, 287–289, 293, 294, 297, 298, 305, 306, 323, 326, 330–332, 335, 345–347, 349, 351, 355, 360–362, 364, 367, 370
Defense, 6, 19, 27, 29, 37, 61, 62, 70, 74, 80, 82, 86, 90–93, 97, 114, 120, 127, 134, 138–140, 143, 144, 147, 154, 160, 161, 165, 168, 169, 172, 176–179, 181, 184, 187, 189, 201–203, 217, 218, 244, 245, 247–249, 253, 256, 304, 305, 308, 318, 320, 324, 326, 338, 347, 354, 361, 362, 369
Denial (policy of), 91, 95, 104, 106, 172, 173, 215, 314, 317–333, 336, 370
Deployment, 11, 17, 126, 167, 160, 200
Deprivation, 11, 64, 84, 286, 293, 294, 297, 298, 303, 309, 320, 322, 324, 327, 333, 346, 355, 356, 361

Desert, 106
Destruction, 42, 43
Detection, 191
Detonation, 93, 208, 209
Difficult, 88
Dike, 5, 202, 242, 249, 254, 256, 262–264, 270, 276, 279, 282, 283, 293, 294, 297, 298, 306, 308, 311
Discipline, 19, 26, 27, 71, 96, 315, 367
Disguise, 110, 111, 125, 139
Disorder, 44, 171
Dispirit, 18, 54, 55, 61, 62, 67, 70, 136, 139, 163, 191, 221, 229, 232, 271, 286, 290, 327, 347, 359
Dissension, 82, 85, 119, 135, 136, 158, 209, 217, 221, 291, 294, 298, 306, 334, 335, 346, 347, 351, 360
Distant, 156, 199, 209
Ditch, 25, 37, 113, 180, 182, 244, 247, 249, 152, 154, 255, 269, 270, 281, 287, 295, 349, 362, 364, 367–369
Divination, 27, 77, 202, 349
Dog, 237, 341, 366, 371
Donkey, 18, 189, 351, 355, 363–366, 370
Doubt, 39, 97, 100, 116, 167, 168, 171, 196, 220, 336
Downstream, 57, 58, 62, 88, 91, 154, 159, 160, 163, 223, 237, 2778, 281, 297, 300, 307, 312, 351
Dragon boat, 127, 128, 206, 210
Drain, 249, 252, 254, 256, 300 See also ditch
Dream, 352
Dredge, 242
Drought, 162, 250, 253, 332
Drowning, 70, 71, 74, 160, 161, 195, 201, 210, 230, 251, 267, 271, 275, 278, 291, 296, 300, 311–313, 337, 365

**INDEX    431**

Drum, 32, 36, 39, 50, 70, 75, 90, 117, 158, 167, 215, 253, 281, 289, 314

Dry (dryness), 5, 8, 18, 22, 37–39, 62, 78, 90, 92, 93, 129, 155, 161, 162, 190, 268, 272, 273, 329, 368

Duck, 208, 210

Dummy, 14, 92, 98, 126–128, 220, 314

Dusk, 39, 74, 78, 128, 213, 221, 271, 313

Dust, 75, 83, 87, 88, 92, 120, 154, 165, 171, 181, 213

Earth, 38, 47, 63, 69, 93, 97–100, 117, 189, 190, 227, 237, 244, 253–255, 264, 276, 278, 281, 287, 289, 291, 296, 299, 303, 306, 329, 344, 349, 350, 351, 356, 360, 365, 368, 370

Earthworks, 18, 36, 44

Easy, 88

East, 51–54, 68, 74, 75, 105, 138, 223, 228, 233, 248, 300, 304, 307, 311, 312, 337, 348, 356, 357, 360

Egg, 208, 210

Elephant, 96, 119, 122

Embankment, 5, 27, 98, 200, 225, 228, 248, 249, 253, 255, 260, 262, 264–266, 268, 270, 275, 276, 279, 283–285, 288, 290–292, 295, 296, 299, 302, 304–307, 311, 320, 345, 360, 369, 370

Emperor, 46, 61, 70, 72, 73, 84, 86, 105, 137, 158, 163, 190, 215, 230, 232, 242, 277, 302, 322, 324, 326, 327, 329, 333, 335, 52–354, 360

Encampment, 3, 6, 17, 18, 20, 36, 39, 46, 50, 56, 59, 62, 64, 69, 71, 78, 84, 89–91, 94, 96, 100, 104, 109–111, 115,

118, 121, 122, 124–127, 130, 131, 136–139, 142, 143, 145–147, 149, 151, 152, 155, 157, 158, 160, 161, 165, 167, 169, 176, 177, 192, 201, 223, 228–230, 235, 249, 252, 262, 266, 267, 270, 271, 278, 280, 284, 306, 312, 313, 325, 332–334, 337, 339, 341, 349, 350, 369

Enemy, 4, 19, 24, 25, 32, 36, 39, 42, 44, 72, 73, 78, 82, 84, 88, 90, 91, 93–102, 109, 114, 125–130, 132, 133, 136–138, 142–147, 149, 151–158, 160–162, 165–168, 172, 175, 177, 179, 182–185, 188, 192, 193, 196, 198, 200, 206, 208, 213, 215, 219, 223, 224, 228, 233, 235, 248, 249, 256, 263, 268–273, 276, 278, 280–283, 287, 294, 305, 307, 311, 314, 318, 319, 323, 330, 332, 333, 335, 338–341, 344, 346, 347, 350, 356, 357, 360, 362, 364–366, 368, 370, 371

Equipment, 16, 19, 84, 92, 101, 103, 113, 136, 140, 141, 154, 55, 173, 186, 195, 197, 202, 206, 208, 247, 259, 260, 276, 278, 345, 362, 364–366, 368–370

Error, 54–56, 59, 60, 162, 257, 320

Eruptors, 92, 100, 128, 132, 140, 165, 169, 186–188, 362, 365, 369

Escape, 169, 212, 215, 216, 221, 223, 249, 286, 307, 322, 333

Esen, 326, 327

Exhaustion, 58, 62, 105, 106, 157, 169, 226,

260, 297, 328, 337, 347

Exploit, 6, 19, 20, 29, 31, 33, 50, 58, 62, 70, 78, 80, 84, 86–88, 90, 94–98, 101, 110–112, 117, 120, 124, 130, 137, 1146, 151, 152, 154–159, 162, 200–204, 214, 216, 220, 224, 233, 245, 248, 278, 279, 281, 286, 291, 298, 338

Explosion, 8, 9, 101

Explosives, 8, 94, 125–127, 130–134, 141–145, 165, 191, 204, 209, 210, 295

Extinction, 42, 54, 59, 162, 189, 257, 262, 265, 362

Evil, 44

Eyes, 323

Fa-huo, 93

Family, 255, 257, 258, 262

Fan, 151, 152, 193, 257

Fan Yang, 15

Fan-chíeng, 59, 60, 266, 267, 367

Fan-yang, 73

Fang Kuan, 75

*Fang-shou Chi-chíeng,* 182, 188

Farmer, 13

Fear, 3, 39, 41, 50, 152, 161, 215, 247, 262, 288, 323, 327, 330, 332, 334, 338, 352, 354, 356

Feather, 132

Fei River, 297, 311

Fei-chou, 285

*Fei-huo,* 93

*Fei-huo chiang-mo-chíui,* 143

*Fei-yen-chíiu* (Flying Swallow Bomb) 142

Fen River, 248, 263, 277, 280, 284, 287, 348, 349

Feng Hung, 96

Feng Yen-po, 311

*Feng-lei huo-kun,* 145

Feng-tíien, 190

Ferghana, 328

Feudal Lords, 25, 38, 334

Feudal States, 10, 11, 344, 347

Field, 5, 36, 51, 91, 151, 184, 249, 256, 263, 266, 269, 272, 304, 305
Fire bed, 178
Fire Dragon, 207, 210
Fire fighting, 4–6, 14, 174, 177, 188, 339, 354, 364, 367
Fire lance, (*huo-chíiang*) 217, 363
Fire ox, 35, 83, 91, 96, 115, 118–120, 122–126, 182, 184, 257, 365
Fire ship (boat), 62, 90, 91, 97, 109, 204–207, 220, 221, 223–225, 229, 230, 235–237, 368
Fires, signal, 26, 231
Firewood, 25, 31, 34, 36, 37, 65, 74, 84, 110, 113, 154, 165, 166, 174, 180, 188–193, 206, 223, 233, 281, 303, 349, 354, 360–364, 368, 370
Fish, 282, 353
Fish Mountain, 161
Five Dynasties, 138, 162, 213, 214, 268
Flag, 14, 24, 26, 27, 66, 90, 162, 169, 202, 289, 330
Flail, 175
Flames, 5, 36, 190, 205, 208
Flame thrower, 92, 128, 145, 184, 185, 201
Flank, 62, 167
Flood, 6,21, 30, 34, 71, 85, 98, 241, 242, 247, 249, 251, 253–257, 260, 262–268, 270, 271, 273, 275–280, 283–285, 287, 289, 291–293, 295–307, 313–315, 340, 342, 351, 357
Flying Bridge, 197
Flying River, 197
Fodder, 84, 91, 102, 104, 106, 130, 155, 173, 177, 335, 353
Fog, 164, 168, 169
Foodstuffs, 25, 26, 84, 101, 259, 260, 293, 341, 353, 355, 356
Forage, 234

Forces, elite, 38, 167, 229, 289, 294, 356, 359
Forces, naval, 55, 57, 59, 87, 154, 158–160, 163, 213, 216, 218, 220, 224, 231–233, 287
Ford, 88, 171, 195, 196, 198, 199, 203, 230, 272, 283, 309–311, 330, 347, 354
Forest, 25, 40, 44–46, 62, 89, 97, 100, 142, 155, 163, 173, 269, 272, 318
Forge, 17
Fork, 97, 185, 188, 235, 254, 255
Formation, 16, 18, 84, 88, 89, 125, 127, 128, 141, 147, 153, 161, 314
Formless, 98
Fortifications, 27–30, 33, 69, 96, 98, 138, 166, 172, 184, 186, 188, 191, 228, 229, 242, 245, 251, 252, 265, 266, 277, 278, 285, 288, 289, 291, 292, 294, 295, 298, 301, 329, 345–347, 349, 358, 359, 362, 371
Fou, Mount, 299
Front, 74, 95, 177
Fu Chíai, 13
Fu Chien, 102, 160, 297, 332
Fu Píi, 298
Fu Teng, 322
Fu Yung, 96
Fu-chou, 66
*Fu-tíi-lei-píi-li*, 92
Fuse, 93, 125–127, 168, 208–210

Gas, 7, 8, 28, 30, 32, 34, 35, 84, 115, 128, 132, 140, 143–146, 165, 170, 184, 186, 192, 193, 349, 350, 356
Gate, 12–14, 28–30, 32, 33, 35, 110, 112, 114, 115, 119, 154, 155, 163, 174, 175, 187, 190, 219, 242, 252, 254–256, 261, 264, 287, 295, 312, 328, 333, 337, 338, 349,

354, 355, 359, 362, 363, 366
General, 17, 29, 65, 67, 68, 79, 85, 88, 93, 117, 141, 150, 154, 156, 167, 203, 212, 221, 226, 227, 247, 252, 263, 273, 280, 288, 297, 298, 314, 315, 319, 320, 331, 346, 347
Genghis Khan, 308
Geophone, 33, 34, 191–193
Ghost, 47
Gobi, 105
God of War, 59, 61
Gods, 44, 59, 127, 296
Gourd (*hu-lu*), 9, 122–124, 130, 131, 145, 146, 186, 187
Grain, 11, 25, 44, 51, 78, 81, 107, 242, 258, 259, 339, 341, 347, 353, 356
Grass, 25, 36, 38, 39, 62, 64, 74, 78, 83, 90, 91, 95, 101, 104–107, 122–124, 142, 145, 151, 155, 165, 166, 173, 177, 182, 189, 206, 223, 229, 242, 266, 269, 319, 338, 339, 341, 360, 361, 363, 364
Grave, 25, 44, 116
Granary, 5
Guerrillas, 104, 215, 216, 292
Gunpowder, 7–9, 41, 45, 84, 89, 91, 94, 100, 110, 123, 126, 127, 129–133, 139–147, 165, 166, 181, 182, 184, 186, 188, 191, 193, 200, 204, 208–210, 217, 219, 304, 363–365, 371

Hai-chou, 216
Hai-ling 216
Hail, 87
Halberd, 204
Han, 29, 40, 49, 51, 52, 116, 186, 200, 201, 247, 257–262,266, 267, 275, 280, 285, 297, 309, 320, 327, 328, 339

Former 177, 308
Later 120, 134, 157, 169, 223, 306, 329
Northern 277, 278
Southern 162–164, 172, 173
Han-chao, 171, 172
Han-chou, 119, 164
*Han Fei-tzu*, 4, 5, 257, 262
Han Hsin, 49, 86, 97, 198, 280, 282, 308, 310, 311
Han River, 60, 242, 250, 267, 367
Han Shih-chung, 215, 335
Han Sui, 248
Han-chung, 59,
Han-shan, 302
Han-tan, 68, 69, 285
Hang-chou, 215, 216, 284, 304
Hanoi, 358, 359
Hao Chao, 63
Hard, 243
Harvest, 80
Hate, 12, 20, 25, 41,
Head, 65, 123, 124, 127, 139, 141, 206, 210, 237, 262, 266
Heat, 7, 8, 41, 52, 62, 129, 155, 306, 317, 322, 337
Heaven, 5, 42, 66, 86, 92, 93, 97, 99, 100, 105, 117, 137, 141, 190, 203, 242, 253, 332, 335, 349
Heavenís:
Fissure, 272
Jail, 272
Net, 272
Pit, 22, 272
Well, 22, 272
Heavenly Float, 197
Hegemon, 15, 256
Heights, 87, 100, 170, 196, 254, 266–270, 279, 283, 284, 311, 318–320, 327
Hemp, 4, 14, 121, 173, 175, 190, 201, 235, 350, 362
Hero, 59, 66, 93, 233, 301, 312, 324
Ho Huai, 97
Ho Huan, 233
Ho Juo-pi, 169, 170

Ho Liang-chíen 39, 92, 94, 202, 203
Ho-fei, 228, 287, 288, 353
Ho-lien Chíang, 322
Ho-lien Po-po, 320, 324
Ho-lu Tzu-wan, 324
Ho-l¸, 202, 256, 257
Ho-yang, 235
Honan, 232, 235, 244, 275, 301, 312, 322
Hook, 178, 206,234, 291
Hopei, 6, 135, 312
Horses, 38, 50–52, 64, 87, 90, 95, 97, 105, 110, 115, 120, 122–124, 127, 132, 133, 143, 144, 151, 154, 167–170, 174, 204, 229, 231, 268, 272, 281, 303, 312, 319, 322, 328, 329, 335, 338, 340, 353, 354, 371
Hou Chen, 159
Hou Chi, 243
Hou Ching, 288–291, 301, 302, 351–357
Hsi Hsia, 291, 292, 307, 308, 329, 330, 331
Hsi Kíang-sheng, 169
Hsi-cheng, 297
Hsi-juo-luo, 105
Hsia, 10, 241, 243, 244
Hsia Kuei, 331
Hsia-píi, 282, 286, 306
Hsia-yang, 198
Hsiang, Earl (of Chao), 258–262
Hsiang Liang, 249
Hsiang Y¸, 10, 35, 49–51, 102, 198, 249, 285, 308
Hsiang Y¸eh, 91, 173, 174
Hsiang-chíeng, 289
Hsiang-yang, 60, 173, 267, 335, 343, 363, 364, 366–371
*Hsiang-yang Shou-chíeng Lu*, 366
Hsiao Cheng-te, 353, 354
Hsiao Pao-ying, 226–228
Hsiao-chien, 136
Hsieh-yen-tío, 105, 106
Hsien Yang, 10, 35
Hsien-chíiu, 11, 85
Hsien-ling, 134, 248
Hsien-pei, 102, 169, 226, 322

Hsin-chíeng, 153
Hsin-chiang, 329
Hsin-yeh, 312
Hsing Luan, 226
Hsing-chou, 68, 69,
Hsing-jen, 81
Hsiung-nu, 40, 50,250, 324, 329
Hs¸ Hsi, 329–331
Hs¸ Mien-chih, 304
Hs¸ Tung, 51, 83, 155, 156, 271, 272, 281, 318
*Hs¸ Wu-ching Tsung-yao*, 155
Hs¸ Yu, 96
Hs¸-chíang, 53
Hs¸-chou, 306, 307
Hs¸an, Earl (of Wei), 258
Hs¸an, Emperor, 74
Hs¸an-fu, 326, 327
Hs¸an-wu, 357
Hu, 52, 248
Hu Hsia, 322, 324
Hu Ta-hai, 304, 306
Hu-chíien Ching, *83, 87, 155, 156, 191, 256, 270, 280, 281, 311, 317, 319, 341*
Hu-hsiao, Mt., 331
Hu-lao, 323
Hu-tíuo River, 135
Hua Y¸eh, 86, 87, 252, 283
Hua-kíou-chíuan, 267
Hua-tíai, 43
Huai River, 215, 223, 226, 227, 236, 242, 275, 287–290, 303, 307, 335, 336, 352
Huan Chíung, 311
Huan, Duke, 256
Huan Hs¸an, 66, 67, 212
Huan River, 69
Huan Shu, 10, 11
Huan Tsung-tsu, 284
Huan Wen, 334
Huang Kai, 56–58
Huang-fu Sung, 95, 157, 158
Hui, King, 264
Hui River, 51, 84
Humane, 45, 46
Humidity, 45, 52, 57
Hung Bridge, 154
Hunger, 11, 103, 104, 253, 321, 338, 348, 353, 361
Hunting, 11, 66, 353
*Huo-hung Shan-píao*, 92

*Huo-lung Shen-chíi Chíen-fa*, 63
*Huo-tan*, 145
Huo-tsu, 31
*Huo-yao*, 145
Hupei, 245
Hut, 5, 6, 28, 29, 44, 45, 49, 64, 78, 81, 112, 120, 123, 155, 176, 282, 370

Ice, 250, 251, 340
Ignition, 209
Illness, 18, 42, 56, 60, 260, 264, 271, 277, 2778, 286, 291, 296, 301, 306, 318, 324, 339, 341, 344, 350, 351, 353, 367
Imbalance (tactical), 87
Incendiaries, 3, 29, 63, 129, 132, 145, 175, 189, 210, 220, 228, 281, 283, 289, 351, 354, 357, 359, 360, 362, 364
Incendiary cart (wagon), 69, 74, 90, 109, 113–115, 163, 174, 190, 204, 293, 356
Incendiary ball (sphere, bomb), 134, 181, 207, 208
Incendiary thief, 3, 110, 111, 138, 164
Incursion, 26, 82,104, 105, 335, 359
Infantry, 21, 40, 51, 53, 65, 75, 102, 105, 136, 153, 154, 156, 170, 171, 202, 216, 224, 229, 265, 268, 289, 303, 329, 332, 363, 367
Inner Mongolia, 171, 250
Interior, 16, 19, 27, 29, 34, 109, 181, 206, 228, 245, 252, 254, 269, 281, 287, 311, 313, 330, 369
Invaders, 30, 101, 104, 196, 248, 292, 309, 314, 317
Invasion, 38, 52, 63, 81–83, 85, 115, 153, 200, 215–217, 230–232, 247, 249, 264, 315,

324, 335, 338, 346, 348, 359
Iron, 9, 31, 52, 69, 97, 140, 144, 160, 174, 178, 179, 181, 183, 211, 218, 224, 230, 234, 235, 299, 307, 354
Iron bed, 182, 183
Iron-beaked fire chicken 181, 182
Iron-beaked fire goose, 65
Irrigation, 243, 253, 276, 279, 285, 304
Isolated, 62, 228, 286, 287, 301, 313, 320, 321, 327, 355, 364

Japan, 203, 292
Jars, 33, 179, 192, 197–199, 208, 233, 241
Jen Chang, 262
Ju River, 242
Jurchen, 4, 42, 85, 86, 171, 173, 175, 215–217, 247, 303, 307, 314, 336–339, 359–366

Kíai-feng, 163, 170, 188, 294, 295, 343, 362
Kan River, 219
Kan-chou, 105
Kan-tsíao, 170
Kíang, Earl (of Han), 258
Kíang-lang, Mount, 219
Kansu, 105, 321, 326, 332, 333
Kao Chíeng, 291
Kao Chiung, 80–82
Kao Chung-mi, 236
Kao Huan, 236, 288, 348–351
Kao Lang, 258
Kao Y̨eh, 289, 291
Kao-li, 153, 154
Keng Kung, 329, 331
Khitan, 72, 105, 153, 170, 171, 186, 277, 331
King, 46, 103, 116, 163, 212, 215, 328
Kite, 125
Ko-shu Han, 72–74
Kío-luo-hai, 324
Kou Chien, 4, 304
Korea, 72, 153, 154, 200, 292
Ku River, 297
Ku-liang, *85, 253*
Ku-su, 13

Kíuai Tíung, 308
Kíuai-chi, 304
Kíuai-kai, 310
Kuan Y̨, 59–61, 68, 267, 284, 312
Kuan-tu, 52–55, 86, 102, 103
*Kuan-tzu*, 15
Kuang, King, 308–310
Kuang-tung, 65
Kun, 242
Kíun-yang, 275
Kung-shan-tíai, 325
*Kung-yang*, 85
*Kuo Y̨,* 15

Ladder, 30, 31, 38, 63, 121, 190, 191, 289, 358, 363, 368, 370
Lake, 19, 51, 52, 57, 65, 151, 195, 201, 213, 218, 219, 221, 243, 244, 248, 265, 272, 283, 285, 286, 290, 295, 300, 304, 314, 340, 342, 343
Lang-chou, 251
Lard, 7, 33, 113, 114, 117, 121, 128, 181, 183, 188, 355
Laxity, 68, 82, 90, 117, 138, 216, 219, 273, 289, 332, 336
Leader, 44, 72, 328
Leather, 6, 33, 160, 166, 173–176, 178, 180, 186, 192, 193, 197, 201, 207, 233, 331, 362
Legalism, 257
*Lei-tía*, 30, 31
Li Cheng-yi, 68
Li Chien-chi, 97
Li Chih-chi, 106
Li Chíng, 79, 107
Li Ching-yeh, 161
Li Chí̦an, 77–79, 84, 122, 123, 280
Li Chung, 163
Li Chung-chíen, 68
Li Hei-tía (Liu Hei-tía), 311, 312
Li Hsiao-yi, 96, 161
Li Hsiung, 112
Li Huai-kuang, 71
Li Kuang-li, 328
Li Kuang-pi, 72, 74, 235
Li Kuang-tien, 294

Li Ling, 40, 95, 177
Li Ling-yao, 68
Li Mi, 275
Li Nao, 68, 69
Li Pao, 216
Li Pao-chíen, 68, 70
Li Sheng, 308
Li Shen-fu, 212, 213
Li Shih-chi, 106
Li Shih-ku, 268
Li Te, 6
Li Tsai, 93
Li Tung-yang, 292
Li Tzu-chíeng, 170, 193, 294–296
Li Tzu-tíung, 138
Li Wei-y̦eh, 68–70
Li Yu, 3
Li Y̦an, 172
Li-chou, 302
Li-yang, 53, 54, 354
Liang, 107, 225–232, 288, 298–301, 351–357,
  king of, 173
  Later, 160, 213, 225, 233
  Northern, 332
  Southern, 136, 287, 288, 301
Liao, 359
Liao-tung, 153, 326
Li-chih-píao, 144
Licorice, 193
Lieh-huo, 93
Lien Fan, 95
Life, 42, 47, 340
Lighting, 7, 29, 69, 181, 182
Lightning, 5, 47, 338
Lime, 120, 165, 181, 193, 208, 213
Lin-chin, 198
Lin-chíiu, 13
Lin-ming, 68, 69
Lin-tzu, 15, 35,
Ling-chíang, 250
Ling-chou, 293
Ling-ling, 120
Liu Chíang, 311
Liu Chíi, 216, 223, 334, 336–339
Liu Chou-wen, 172
Liu Feng-sheng, 289, 291
Liu Ho, 314
Liu Hsiu, 297
Liu Nan, 14
Liu Pei, 54, 55, 57–59, 61, 62, 64, 223, 320

Liu Pang, 6, 10, 49, 80, 198, 249, 285, 308, 318
Liu Piao, 53, 57
Liu-tíao, 19, 37, 40, 44, 79, 84, 156, 197, 253, 265, 268, 269, 271, 315, 318
Liu Wu-chou, 325
Liu Yen-tao, 214
Liu Yi, 67, 96, 212
Liu Y̦, 66, 67, 153, 212, 226
Local Guide, 50
Log, 74, 146, 178, 281, 307
Logistics, 17, 18, 22, 52, 53, 64, 86, 103, 107, 211, 276, 279, 283, 286, 289, 292, 315, 328
Lord Shang, Book of (Shang-ch̦n Shu), 23, 24
Loyalty, 26, 57, 73,
Lu (state), 11, 85, 247
Lu Hșn, 60–62, 65, 68, 97, 153, 212
Lu Ming-y̦eh, 137
Lu Wen-chi, 170
Lu-chou, 102
Lu-pu, 365
L̦ Chen, 304–306
L̦ Meng, 60, 61
L̦ Pu, 280, 282, 283, 286
L̦ Shang. See Tíai-kung
L̦-shih Chíun-chíiu, 313
L̦eh-yang, 297
Lung Ch̦, 49, 282, 309, 310
Lung River, 306
Lungshan, 242, 244
Luo River, 247
Luo Shang, 112
Luo-shuo, 312
Luo-yang (Loyang), 6, 10, 73, 226, 236, 247, 348

Ma Hsi-kuang, 214, 215
Ma Hsi-oh, 214, 215
Ma Su, 319, 320, 321
Ma Sui, 67–71, 248
Ma Y̦an, 96, 134, 319
Ma-chia-kíou, 296
Male, 346
Man, 99
Man Chíung, 96, 152
Man-ai-ti Tao-luo, 333
Manchu, 294
Maneuver, 11, 22, 104, 200, 219, 305, 314, 335

Mang-pao, 365
Manipulation, 69, 73, 74, 82, 102, 103, 137, 138, 155, 167, 171, 172, 183, 222, 271, 310, 312, 314, 322, 333, 338
Manure, 190, 303, 322, 329, 341
Ma Te-tsu, 323
Mao Y̦an-yi, 47, 98, 131, 140, 150
Market, 12, 25, 36
Marsh, 25, 36, 40, 46, 51, 163, 177, 184, 213, 232, 242, 244, 248, 264–266, 269–271, 304, 319, 340
Mat, 30, 178, 190
Materials, 17, 41, 43, 133, 347, 368, 379, 371
Mei-chou, 214
Mencius, 97
Meng Huo, 64
Meng-chin, 53, 204
Meng-sung River, 171
Metal, 27, 65, 98, 168, 173, 178, 179, 180, 181, 189, 231, 254, 259, 304, 337, 352
Meteor, 161
Military Governor, 67, 72, 73, 161, 212
Military intelligence, 58, 162, 216, 230, 231, 307, 337, 366, 369, 370
Military Methods, 227, 281
Military writings, 16, 24, 35, 43, 49, 50, 77–79, 83–85, 88, 89, 94, 98, 99, 101, 110, 111, 114, 122, 123, 130, 149, 155, 1556, 164, 165, 172, 177, 179, 188, 197, 198, 201, 203, 204, 232, 252, 254, 256, 257, 268, 271, 279, 280, 342, 347, 348, 359, 361, 369
Milky Way, 150
Min, 115, 116, 138
Mines (mining), 23, 30, 33–35, 143, 164, 181, 191–193, 350
  counter-mining 191–193

Mines (explosive), 64, 93, 140

Ming (dynasty), 39, 45, 63, 89, 91, 94, 98, 99, 101, 104, 110, 115, 123, 130, 131, 133, 134, 139, 141, 165, 166, 168, 170, 181, 182, 185, 191, 202–205, 219–221, 249, 271, 292–296, 303–306, 318, 325–327, 339

Ming Kuo, 96

Ming River, 250, 251

Ming-chou, 215, 251

Missile, 41, 110, 115, 220, 234

Mo-ho, 153

Moat, 25, 30, 33, 37, 113, 133, 164, 181, 182, 196, 226, 227, 244–249, 251, 252, 254, 270, 271, 287, 304, 305, 312, 344, 355, 356, 360, 364, 366–368, 370

Mobility, 36, 91, 104, 136, 170, 173, 175, 176, 201, 203, 204, 220, 234, 235, 269, 326, 330

Mohists, 20, 23, 24, 26, 28, 30, 34, 164, 172, 191, 254, 255, 317

Moisture, 173

Mongols, 42, 85, 86, 89, 91, 119, 134, 141, 211, 217, 292–294, 303, 307, 325–327, 331, 367

Monkey, 121, 122

Moon, 16, 78, 79, 93, 150, 188

Mo-tzu, 21, 23, 25, 31, 33, 110, 133, 166, 172, 176, 177, 184, 287, 370

Mo-tzu, 25, 172, 177, 192, 254, 256, 361

Morning, 337

Mound, 33, 46, 63, 119, 176, 189, 237, 270, 277, 287, 289, 291, 302, 346, 349, 351, 356, 357, 365, 368, 371

Mountain, 25, 40, 50, 62, 66, 73, 74, 87, 102, 120, 121, 136, 156, 170, 211, 214, 228, 231, 236, 242, 256, 257, 263, 267, 269, 272, 275, 277, 282, 297, 300, 305, 318, 319, 325, 327, 331, 333, 334, 340, 357, 370

Mouth, 166, 208, 213, 221, 264, 332

Movement, 151, 167, 169

Moxa, 32, 35, 122–124, 142, 165, 166, 192

Mu-jung Chíui, 297, 298

Mu-jung Chung, 160

Mu-jung Hui, 134

Mu-jung Pao, 135, 136

Mu-jung Píing, 96

Mu-jung Shao-tsung, 289, 291

Mu-yeh, 10

Mud, 4, 6, 28–32, 34, 160, 173–176, 178, 181, 208, 217, 235, 252, 254, 269, 272, 304, 315, 342, 370, 371

Musket, 91, 141, 143, 187

Naptha, 133, 184

Nan-chao, 358, 359

Nan-chíang, 218, 219, 222

Nan-ching, 107, 211, 222, 303

Nan-y.eh, 213

Naval Clash, 82

Near, 156, 199, 209

Needham, 140, 141

Neolithic, 199, 244, 343

Night, 3, 16, 50, 54, 56, 60, 62, 64, 69, 82, 88, 95–97, 102, 107, 112, 117, 119, 123, 125, 130, 131, 134–136, 138, 139, 142, 152, 157–159, 162, 164, 169, 189, 193, 197, 211, 217, 221, 229, 230, 234, 251, 252, 267, 270, 271, 287, 293, 303, 309, 312, 332, 333, 335, 337, 338, 346, 355, 356, 363–366, 369

Nine Rivers, 242

Ning-hsia, 292–294

Nitrates, 8, 9, 92, 130

Noise, 36, 69, 70, 90, 97, 117, 121, 138, 158, 197, 281

Nomads, 91

North, 51–53, 57, 60, 62, 64, 65, 67, 73–75, 85, 120, 135, 136, 154, 159, 161, 162, 216–219, 225, 227, 229, 234, 236, 289, 290, 292, 294, 298, 300, 305, 311, 312, 320, 321, 329, 333, 335, 336, 349, 357, 367, 368

Northeast, 348, 367

Northwest, 292, 311, 324, 329

Oar, 51, 52, 60, 198–201, 204, 207, 218, 266

Objective, 6,7, 15–17, 21, 32, 44, 78, 82, 104, 199, 209, 263, 278, 286, 353, 363, 367

Ocean, 52, 188, 200, 204, 216, 217, 242, 300, 304

Offensive, 43

Officers, 84

Officials, 25, 73, 74, 259, 260, 320, 330

Oh-chou, 212

Oil, 9, 29, 33, 56, 91–93, 110, 113, 114, 131, 133, 166, 174, 176, 178, 179, 181, 188, 189, 191, 206, 210, 217, 233, 309, 350, 359, 361, 364, 368

fierce incendiary, 184–186, 191

sesame, 7, 9, 65, 128, 206, 231

tíung, 168, 210

Oirat, 326, 327

Omen, 6, 27, 116, 161

Orders, 24, 99, 330

Ordos, 195, 250, 293

Orthodox, 22, 96

Outnumbered, 3, 57, 66, 67, 144, 169, 189, 214, 220, 221, 248, 249, 277, 289, 305, 306, 310, 323, 330, 332, 335, 337, 338, 367

Oxen, 64, 75, 105, 115,
117, 118, 144, 169,
174, 185, 288, 328,
340, 366, 370
Oxygen, 7–9, 33, 65, 149

Pai Chíi, 35, 45, 46
Pai River, 267, 312
*Pai-chan Chíi-l,eh,* 85, 88,
101, 103, 1511, 152,
155, 196, 198, 201,
270, 308, 318, 319
Pai-ma, 54, 264
Palace, 5, 12, 35, 44, 110,
112, 355
Palisade, 28, 31, 32, 37, 64,
69, 90, 100, 110, 120,
121, 136–139, 162,
164, 170, 173, 177,
184, 186, 202, 218,
224, 227, 229, 232,
244, 251, 278, 293,
305, 306, 320, 331,
333, 350, 362, 366,
367, 369
Pan Chíao, 50
Pan-pío, 244
Pían Mei, 97, 164, 224
Pían-lung-chíeng, 246
Pían-she-ku, 97
Píang Te, 267
Pao Chíe, 133
Pao-ku, 305
Pao-y,eh Lu, *304, 305*
Paper, 142–145, 166, 182,
209
Particles, 7
Pass, 73, 86, 92, 170, 173,
216, 319
Passageway, 28, 100, 191
Píeng-chíeng, 49, 302
*Pei-cheng Lu,* 91
*Pei-ching,* 137, 273, 296
Pei-chou, 119
*Pei-hai Chi,* 85
Píei Chi, 325
Píei Hsing-chien, 270, 271
Píeng Y,eh, 102, 339
Pennant, 154, 202
People, 45, 46, 52, 66, 242.
*See also* populace.
Phases, Five, 8, 45
Pi, Battle of, 18
Pi Tsai-y,, 314
*Pi-li huo-chíiu,* 143, 192,
368, 371
Píi, 112
Píi Man, 192, 193

Pien-ching, 193, 294
Pien-chou, 68, 73, 235
Pig, 78, 122, 174, 341
Pigeon, 125
Pin-lang, 170
Pine, 183, 350
*Ping Ching,* 99, 149, 150
*Ping-chíou Lei-yao,* 85, 283
Ping-fa Pai-yen, *101*
Píing-kuang pu-chan sui-ti-
kun, *146*
Píing-liang-tíai, 244
Píing-yang, 263, 280, 282,
284
Pirate, 293, 208
Plan, 42, 43, 46, 47, 73, 97,
141, 260, 296, 345
Plains, 51, 195, 294, 315
Plunder, 10, 17, 43, 46, 71,
72. 100, 105, 160,
214, 215, 295, 324,
355, 357, 363
Po Tsíai, 157, 158
Po-ku-chíeng, 129
Pío-yang Lake, 203,
217–223
Poison, 24, 28, 30, 32, 34,
35, 84, 88, 128, 134,
140, 142, 143, 145,
147, 151, 164–166,
168, 170, 181, 186,
193, 206, 281, 283,
317, 333–342, 366,
371
Pole, 97, 145, 175, 179,
189, 197, 223, 225,
233–236, 331, 340,
350, 353, 362, 363,
368
Populace, 5, 13, 24, 25, 42,
61, 72, 99, 101, 112,
115, 116, 160, 172,
253, 259, 260, 278,
279, 290, 301, 303,
309, 321, 324, 325,
328, 333, 336,
343–346, 351, 353,
355, 356, 358, 359
Post, 33, 34, 191
Power, 4, 36, 37, 46, 66, 68,
71, 72, 82, 87, 88, 92,
100, 106, 116, 136,
149, 150, 152, 154,
155, 158, 201, 202,
208, 221, 232, 241,
256, 257, 265, 276,
277, 280, 283, 286,

299, 309, 312, 313,
321, 336, 344, 347
Pray, 6, 44,
Preparation, 19, 60, 90, 92,
93, 200, 231, 257,
347, 352, 353, 358
Preservation, 17, 42,
Pressure, 8, 242, 251–255,
264, 278, 290, 293,
300, 304
Prisoner, 13, 44, 50, 60, 61,
103, 116, 119, 213,
214, 250, 295, 303,
307, 328, 336, 337,
339, 366, 369
Profit. *See* advantage 41, 43
Prohibitions, 5, 24, 45–47,
111
Projectile, 187, 218
Prolonged, 21, 104, 256
Provisions, 3, 7, 10, 16–18,
20–23, 25–28, 41, 42,
49, 53, 60, 62, 63, 65,
78, 81, 84, 86, 88, 93,
95, 98, 100–104, 106,
107, 111, 124,
130–132, 134, 136,
139, 142, 143, 145,
151, 155, 173, 177,
182, 188, 197, 215,
219, 221, 222, 227,
232, 260, 278, 279,
282, 286, 287, 292,
313, 315, 317, 334,
339, 344, 347, 362,
367, 368, 370, 371
Provocation, 69
Pu Luo, 120
P,bei, 293
Píu-yang, 249
Pump, 174
Punishment, 25, 26, 28, 44,
45, 99, 105, 321, 328,
347

*Questions and Replies,* 79

Raft, 90, 97, 113, 163, 184,
199, 204, 206, 224,
231, 237, 249, 252,
256, 265, 267, 290,
294
Raid, 52, 53, 106, 107
Raiders, 101, 104, 105, 134,
136, 137, 139, 164,
173, 225, 250, 252,
270 287, 319, 339,
368

Rain, 58, 59, 64, 150, 171, 182, 202, 228, 234, 242, 250, 264–269, 271–273, 275, 278, 291, 299, 304, 305, 308, 327, 331, 332, 335, 337, 338, 342

Ram, 29, 86, 159, 160, 200, 201, 206, 208, 225, 236, 250, 278–280, 308–314, 350

Ramp, 30, 189

Rampart, 37, 92, 289, 314, 336

Raspberry, 165, 166

Ravine, 74, 87, 88, 156, 269, 271, 305, 319, 327

Rear, 38, 46, 50, 53, 62, 65, 74, 87, 95, 104, 159, 171, 177, 266, 269, 272, 307, 319

Rebellion, 26, 28, 46, 65–75, 87, 119–121, 136, 137, 153, 157, 161, 163, 164, 169, 170, 172, 189, 190, 217, 222, 223, 230, 235, 236, 261, 270, 285, 292–294, 302, 303, 306, 312, 325, 332, 348, 351–357

Reconnaissance, 26, 33, 65, 82, 106, 121, 136, 177, 229, 267, 279, 313, 336, 339, 340, 369, 370

*Records of City Defense,* 348

Red Cliffs (Chʻih Pi), 55–59, 63, 85, 86, 176, 177, 204, 205, 211, 266, 286

Red Turbans, 217

Reeds, 39, 43, 62, 64, 65, 78, 81, 90, 98, 110, 114, 117, 121, 137, 155, 164, 170, 177–179, 181, 182, 189, 199, 205, 206, 224, 250, 251, 259, 289, 340, 359, 363

Reinforcements, 69, 71 *see* rescue

Rescue, 25, 58, 63, 92, 97, 170, 171, 191, 219, 222, 227, 228, 233, 253, 262, 286, 290, 293, 294, 297, 301,

302, 306, 307, 309, 321, 322, 327, 328, 330, 332, 346, 347, 357, 358, 360, 362, 367

Resin, 142, 166

Rest, 87

Restraint, 44, 83

Retreat, 18, 37, 39, 46, 54, 60, 63, 65, 70, 71, 92, 95, 98, 103, 106, 136, 137, 153, 157, 163, 168, 188, 230, 266, 269, 288, 302, 334, 365, 371

Rewards, 4, 22, 25, 41, 57, 99, 136, 170, 233, 350, 359

Rice, 81, 245

Righteous, 44, 45, 66, 99, 102, 312, 337

River, 5, 19, 33, 46, 51, 52, 58–60, 65, 69, 71, 74, 80, 85, 87, 88, 90, 91, 98, 100–102, 105, 134, 136, 139, 151–153, 158, 159, 161, 164, 167, 171, 184, 195–201, 203, 204, 211–213, 216–218, 225, 229, 232–235, 237, 241, 243–245, 247, 249, 250, 252, 253, 255, 256, 260, 264, 266–268, 271–273, 275–277, 279, 281, 283–286, 290, 298–300, 304, 307, 309–313, 320, 323–325, 328, 330, 331, 338, 340, 341, 343, 348, 365, 367, 368, 371

Road, 58, 173, 190, 204, 269, 270, 272, 273, 282, 320, 346

Rocket, 126, 132, 133, 141, 142, 201, 206

Roof, 5, 176, 178, 303, 355

Rope, 30, 31, 63, 92, 112, 121, 198, 225, 233, 250, 323

Ruler, 25, 42, 82, 158, 257, 261, 332

Rumor, 27

Ruse, 14, 56, 88, 112, 117, 137, 168, 169, 189, 219, 302, 309–312,

314, 320, 327, 332, 333, 352, 353, 357

Sack, 69, 114, 136, 167, 168, 174, 180, 190, 278, 281, 282, 309, 310

Sage, 44, 46

Sails, 57, 58, 126, 132, 141, 144, 173, 200, 216, 217

Sailor, 57, 60, 200, 203, 213, 216, 223, 236, 368

Sally, 31, 355, 359, 362, 368

San-hsia, 311

San-hsing-tui, 246, 343

*San-kuo Chih,* 58, 273

Sand, 6, 27, 30, 31, 88, 129, 144, 147, 150, 154, 165, 175, 176, 195, 201, 202, 209, 213, 282, 290, 299, 309, 310, 311, 331, 341, 342

Sawdust, 168

Season, 5, 16, 19, 78, 90, 92, 96, 97, 100, 215, 219, 225, 229, 241, 250, 253, 264, 266, 272, 273, 276, 280, 296, 322, 342

Secret, 93

Security, 17, 42, 94, 260, 299, 336, 344

Seize, 16, 21, 257, 263, 280, 317

Sever, to 16, 21, 257, 280–282, 331

Shaanhsi, 322, 329

Shan-shan, 50

Shan-y,,40, 273

Shang (dynasty), 10, 18, 37, 127, 199, 245, 246, 275, 343, 344

Shang Yang (Lord Shang), 23

Shanhsi, 107, 277, 321, 325, 348

Shantung, 137, 275, 322

Shao Chʻing

Shao-hsing, 154, 303–305

*Shao-tʻien meng-huo wu-lan-pʻiao,* 143

*Shen huo,* 93, 146, 147, 168

Shen-chʻih, 15

*Shen-huo yen-chʻiu,* 143

Sheep, 288, 340
Shield, 34, 127, 141, 154, 166, 175, 180, 187, 192, 345, 350, 356, 359, 365, 368, 370
*Shih Chi,* 117, 308
Shih Juo, 14
Shih Ssu-ming, 73, 74, 235, 303
Shih-tíou-chíeng, 107, 211
Shore (bank), 195, 196, 204, 206,221, 224, 225, 227, 230, 236, 266, 299, 309, 330, 368
*Shou-chíeng Lu,* 361
Shou-chíun, 311
Shou-yang, 227, 299, 300, 301, 352, 354
Shu, 59–64, 87, 200, 230, 312, 320, 321
Shui-luo, 333
Shun, 241, 242
Shun-chíang, 334, 339
Siege, 25, 27, 29, 42, 43, 68, 69, 74, 116–119, 133, 139, 154, 157, 158, 163, 165, 170, 173, 186, 188, 190, 191, 218, 219, 226, 227, 252, 256, 257, 260, 261, 277–279, 284, 286–291, 294, 296–298, 301–304, 306, 312, 322, 323, 328, 329, 331, 336–339, 342–371
engines 92, 113, 139, 154, 164, 173–176, 178, 179, 181, 186, 188, 189, 228, 289, 304, 323, 345, 347, 356, 357, 359, 360, 362, 364, 365, 370
Silence, 11, 39, 69, 90, 95, 110, 167
Six Dynasties, 225
*Six Secret Teachings. See Liu-tíao*
Smoke, 5, 19, 34, 35, 38, 66, 74, 83, 88, 89, 91, 100, 115, 125, 127, 128, 134, 137, 140, 142, 143, 145–147, 149, 151, 164–172, 184, 188, 192, 193, 206, 224, 350, 362

ball 166, 168
spiritual (*shen-yen*), 168
Snake, 342
Snow, 105, 106, 136, 242, 290, 295, 321, 332, 348
Soft, 243, 277
Sogdia, 73
Soldiers. *See* troops
South, 51, 52, 54, 57, 59, 60, 64, 65, 72, 73, 75, 78, 79, 81, 87, 106, 119, 135, 138, 154, 161, 163, 197, 200, 204, 216–219, 225–227, 229, 230, 248, 285, 289, 290, 298–300, 311, 312, 329, 333, 336, 349, 367
Southeast, 356, 364
Southeast Asia, 200, 336
Southwest, 292, 357, 358
Sparrow, 78, 123, 144
Spear, 34, 106, 120, 123, 125, 134, 141, 187, 197, 199, 204, 219, 254, 355
Special Operations, 50, 83, 121, 134–139, 189, 225, 230, 304, 368
Speed, 200, 229, 231, 276, 314
Spike, 146, 178, 224, 231, 235
Spirit (*chíi,* morale), 43, 53, 73, 81, 102, 116, 140, 163, 220, 272, 290,318, 330, 331, 335–338, 355, 359, 367, 371
Spirits, 116
Spring, 41, 159, 225, 226, 228, 273, 297, 304, 334
Springs, 47, 66, 254, 255, 318, 319, 328, 335, 340
Spring and Autumn, 11, 12, 14, 15, 17, 18, 35, 42, 110, 156, 199, 200, 202, 204, 246, 253, 256, 265, 304, 330, 344
Spring and Autumn Annals, *253, 256*
Spycraft, 15

Ssu River, 242, 282, 286, 302
*Ssu-ma Fa,* 99
Ssu-ma Yi, 64
Standoff (Stalemate), 54, 73, 83, 102, 159, 161, 165, 233, 285, 286, 293, 296, 301, 357
Starvation, 18, 26, 29, 42, 53, 189, 287, 294, 296, 303, 346
State, 42
Steppe, 10, 40, 51, 72, 89, 91, 105, 170, 173, 291, 307, 319, 330, 347
incursions
peoples, 12, 41, 50, 51, 95, 104, 153, 171, 186, 214, 217, 225, 226, 249, 291, 292, 306, 311, 324, 326, 333, 334, 344, 358
threat, 73, 83
Stockpiles, 17, 28,
Stone, 27, 30, 31, 50, 63, 74, 87, 92, 113, 121, 133, 134, 150, 154, 166, 175, 178, 182, 190, 207, 224, 225, 235, 252, 255, 276, 278, 281, 299, 307, 309. 344, 355, 359, 363, 371
Stopping, 151, 266, 268
Storehouse (warehouse), 5, 14, 17, 49, 60, 84, 112, 124, 258, 259, 344
Stores, 3, 25, 36, 130, 142, 177, 282
Stove, 5, 27, 28, 32, 35, 178, 180, 359
Strategy, 42, 43
Strategist, 59, 79, 96, 231, 261, 328
Straw, 7, 19, 130, 157, 163, 164, 173, 174, 178, 180, 182, 184, 185, 189, 231, 277, 314, 361–366, 368, 370
Stream, 51, 93, 138, 145, 184, 195, 197, 323, 237, 247, 253, 255, 257, 271, 272, 275, 297, 304, 318, 327, 329, 333, 340–342
Strong, 243

Strongpoint, 13, 135, 177, 227, 229, 232, 247, 279, 299, 320, 326, 329, 342, 345, 359, 367
Su Chïin, 279
Su Ch.n, 321, 322
Su-chou, 303
Su-tsung, Emperor, 74
Substance, 88, 131, 165, 166
Suburbs, 13, 25
Subversion, 26, 28, 54, 80, 83, 110, 111, 116, 160, 162, 243, 287, 293, 332, 333, 347, 351, 355, 357, 358, 367, 369
Suffering, 42, 45, 46, 99, 101, 146, 226, 260, 265, 271, 277, 278, 286, 301, 302, 308, 332, 353, 357
Sui (dynasty), 79, 81, 82, 103, 137, 153, 157, 169, 247, 275, 324, 334, 335, 348
Sui River, 119
Sui Shih, 79
Sui-chou, 95
Sui-yang, 189
Sulfur, 8, 9, 92, 166
Summer, 85, 87, 226, 322, 332, 337, 342
Sun, 150
Sun Pin, 36, 37, 39, 70, 133, 195, 200, 227, 265, 276, 279, 322, 340
Sun Chí.an, 55, 59–61, 248
Sun Tsíe, 53
Sun-tzu, 12, 13, 15, 17, 21, 22, 29, 31, 33, 36, 37, 42, 43, 54, 56, 77–79, 81–85, 87, 89, 90, 93–96, 98, 101, 103, 110, 119, 131, 150, 156, 196, 203, 204, 222, 227, 256, 257, 262, 265, 271, 272, 276, 279, 280, 283, 298, 310, 317–319, 340, 345, 355
Sung (dynasty), 9, 12, 13, 24, 41, 65, 83, 114, 115, 119–121, 129, 131, 133–135, 140, 141, 162–165, 171,

173, 174, 178, 181, 184–186, 191, 192, 196, 197, 200, 201, 205, 211, 212, 223, 226, 256, 271, 277, 280, 288, 291, 292, 294, 313, 314, 325, 330–332, 336, 341, 359–361
Southern 43, 66, 84–86, 88, 103, 153, 164, 175, 183, 212, 215–217, 247, 252, 283, 322–339, 348, 361–366
Sung Chin-kang, 325
Supplies, 18, 44, 49, 55, 62, 73, 78, 86, 100, 104, 131, 182, 199, 226, 286, 292, 295, 297, 307, 318, 321, 328, 331, 336, 339, 350, 352, 355, 360, 368
Supply line (train), 16, 17, 71, 84, 95, 96, 101, 104, 107, 224, 278, 293, 313, 319, 321
Surprise, 18, 60, 67, 82, 234
Superiority, 55, 66
Surrender, 44, 46, 56–59, 116, 117, 134, 218, 219, 232, 285, 291, 294, 309, 310, 319, 321, 325, 327, 339, 347, 350, 370
Survival, 42
Swimmer, 209, 224, 231–233, 249, 252, 368
Sword, 6, 204, 214, 254–256
Szechuan, 10, 74, 120, 122, 136, 164, 169, 175, 180, 216, 223, 230, 302, 331, 358, 359

Tía River, 242
Ta-feng-kío, 147
Ta-huo-chiiu (Great Fireball), 142
Ta-li, 358
Ta-liang, 264, 265, 282
Ta-tu-sheh, 105, 106
Ta-tíung, 326, 327
Ta-yeh, 322
Ta-y.an, 328, 343, 348
Tactics, 71, 79, 89, 100, 151, 156, 162, 167,

183, 195, 203, 285, 320, 330, 343, 347
Tai, 250
Tai-chou, 95
Tíai Kung 37, 38, 95
Tíai-pai Yin-ching, 24, 77, 79, 83, 110, 111, 122–124, 130, 131, 133, 173, 174, 176, 178, 191, 192, 197, 205, 252, 279–282, 288
Tíai-ping, 218
Tíai-y.an, 74, 85, 277, 325, 359–361
Tail, 65, 123, 125, 127, 144, 178, 182, 210
Tan-yang (Nan-ching), 138
Tíang, 3, 16, 24, 36, 51, 67–75, 77, 79, 91, 101, 103–105, 107, 122, 129, 130, 138, 153, 155, 157, 161, 163, 172, 174, 176, 178–180, 188–193, 212, 247, 248, 250, 252, 270, 279, 302, 303, 312, 313, 321, 325, 335, 358, 359
Later, 170, 171, 225
Southern, 162, 185, 223
Tíang Shun, 91, 115
Tíang Tíai-tsu, 277, 278
Tíang Tíai-tsung, 105, 107, 172, 310–313
Tíang Tao, 216
Tao 17, 42, 46, 85, 94, 106, 156, 157, 281, 283
Tao Tè Ching, 5, 243, 277
Tarda, 324, 335
Targets, 3, 12, 38, 52, 84, 89, 109, 110, 132, 204, 223, 265, 326
Taxes, 5
Tears, 168
Temple, 5, 12, 28, 35, 46, 190, 336
Te-an, 361–366, 367
Tè-an Shou-y, Lu, 362
Te-sheng, 232, 234
Teng Ai, 65, 97
Teng-tían Pi-chiu, 89, 104, 111, 123–125, 134, 165, 191, 203, 205
Tent, 177
Terrain, 25, 46, 81, 85, 86, 90, 91, 100, 101, 177, 242, 245, 247, 265,

269, 280, 282, 283,
286, 287, 305, 310,
315, 346
accessible (open), 22, 89,
156, 177, 183, 349
configuration of, 22, 97,
156, 244, 265, 269,
271, 272, 276, 279,
281, 282, 306, 313,
318, 340
constricted, 22, 73, 129,
130, 156
difficult, 175, 176, 320,
321
enmiring, 268, 271
fatal, 330, 355
low 87, 265–268, 271,
272, 278, 318
Territory, 72, 116, 341, 346,
352
Terror, 38, 41, 84, 121,
122, 127, 132, 136,
145, 155, 162, 195,
275, 219, 313, 358
Tíang Shou, 361, 362
Theft (of water), 281, 314
*Thirty-six Strategems*, 118,
251
Thirst, 103, 284, 317,
319–322, 327, 340
Three Kingdoms, 16, 45,
52, 59, 62, 68, 77,
151, 157, 169, 200,
230, 233, 234, 247,
285, 311, 320, 367
Thunder, 47, 271
*Ti Shu* (Earth Rats), 142,
147
Tíieh-le, 105
Tíien Chíeng-ssu, 67–72
Tíien Chíou, 273
Tíien Ch,n, 212, 213
Tíien Tan, 35, 86, 97, 115,
117, 127, 157, 257
Tíien Y,, 269
Tíien Y,eh, 67–71, 248
*Tíien-chui-píao,* 142
Tibet, 358
Tiger, 128
Timing, 16, 18, 19, 47, 87,
93, 96, 99, 100, 150,
208–210, 280
Tomb, 35, 46
Topography, 51, 52, 156,
218, 225, 230, 231,
366
Torch, 19, 29, 63, 95, 97,
98, 109, 110, 117,

119, 127, 144, 158,
159, 164, 178, 181,
183, 188, 191, 207,
213, 223, 231, 332,
350, 362, 363, 365
pheasant-tail, 65, 355, 357
swallowís tail, 65, 176,
178, 179, 188
Tou Chien-te, 312
*Tíou-fu Pi-tían,* 157
Tower, 25, 38, 119, 131,
164, 174, 175, 186,
278, 281, 296, 301,
349, 350, 355, 356,
363–366
Town, 5, 13, 23, 29, 40–43,
52, 73, 104, 135, 164,
215, 232, 234,
244–246, 279, 295,
301, 302, 322–324,
327, 329, 336, 343,
345, 346
Training, 11, 56, 57, 82,
203, 286
Transformation, 47, 96, 311
Transport, 97, 224, 285,
286, 304, 315, 348,
354
Trap, 23, 24, 31, 32, 40, 49,
64, 95, 144, 157, 168,
177, 184, 195, 272,
318, 338, 366
Treasury, 258, 259
Treaty, 80
Trebuchet, 29, 31, 63, 83,
93, 109, 113, 131,
133–135, 141, 144,
153, 159, 166,
181–183, 188, 201,
204, 234, 351, 361,
366, 368
Trees, 14, 45, 52, 83, 90,
101, 106, 164, 242,
244, 248, 266, 269,
282, 300, 303, 319,
339, 342
Trench, 63, 181
Troops, 6, 16, 18, 22, 24,
38, 39, 46, 51, 54–56,
59–63, 65, 66, 69, 74,
78, 80–82, 84, 85,
87–90, 95, 96, 102,
105, 110, 116, 119,
120, 125, 133, 136,
139, 140, 143–146,
153, 154, 159,
162–164, 167, 168,
171, 180, 182, 185,

189, 192, 195–197,
199, 201, 209, 212,
214, 217, 221, 225,
228–232, 235, 250,
253, 257, 265, 267,
271, 277, 279,
285–287, 293–296,
299, 300, 305–307,
309–311, 313,
319–323, 326–332,
334, 337–340,
344–349, 351, 352,
354–356, 358, 359,
364, 366–369
elite, 90, 323
Tsíai, 13, 258
Tsíai-shih, 217, 354
Tsíang-wu, 97
Tsíao Chen, 63
Tsíao Chíing, 96
Tsíao Jen, 54, 267
Tsíao Tsíao, 16, 53–61, 85,
86, 97, 102, 103, 158,
222, 251, 266, 267,
273, 280, 282, 283,
285–287, 322
Tsíao Ching-tsung, 227–229
*Tsíao-l, Ching-l,e,* 39, 45,
89, 103, 104, 111,
112, 166–168, 177,
203, 235, 271
Tsíen Píeng, 223, 297
*Tso Chuan,* 5, 14, 15, 156,
256
Tso-ma-kíu, 59
Tso-ma-ling, 245
Tsui Chíien-yu, 73
*Tsíui-wei Pei-cheng-lu,*
85–87, 103, 104, 201,
283, 317
Tsíui Yen-po, 236
Tu Fu-wei, 157
Tu Yu, 78, 79, 103, 130,
280
Tíu River, 249
Tu-huo, 93
*Tíu-men* (Sally Port), 31,
139
Tíu-mu, 325–329
Tuan Kuei, 257, 258, 261
Tuan Shao, 129
Tube, 9, 93, 94, 100, 132,
141, 146, 168, 186,
304, 338
Tíun-kíou, 160
*Tíung Tien,* 36, 78, 79, 83,
103, 130, 158, 172,

174, 175, 191–193, 275, 2800, 288, 340
Tung Cheng, 164
Tung Chuo, 248, 249
Tung Kuan-y,, 258–260
Tíung River, 332
Tíung-kuan, 73, 234
Tung-tíing, Lake, 214, 245
Tunnel, 23, 34, 35, 63, 102, 119, 139, 143, 151, 164, 166, 170, 175, 181, 187, 188, 190–193, 287, 295, 298, 323, 328, 349, 350, 356, 366
Turfan (Tíu-fang), 105, 107
Turks, 73, 80, 105, 106, 172, 270, 320, 324, 325, 334, 335
*Twenty-five Histories,* 366
Tzu Chían, 6
*Tzu-chih Tíung-chien* 158, 348, 351
Tzu-kan, 320

Unorthodox, 13, 22, 46, 62, 65, 96, 97, 99, 117, 136, 139, 146, 152, 157, 167, 168, 198, 266, 284, 287, 311, 338
Upstream, 57, 67, 87, 151, 201, 202, 211, 221, 224, 230, 234, 236, 237, 256, 264, 278, 279, 281–283, 299, 309–311, 334, 341

Vacuity, 88, 131, 165–167, 175, 199, 347
Valley, 22, 40, 64, 65, 170, 267, 271, 272, 319, 327
Vegetation, 8, 22, 31, 36, 37, 39, 40, 62, 70, 78, 89, 92, 95, 104, 106, 129, 155, 157, 161, 162, 177, 214, 244, 272, 304
Vengeance 10, 35, 41, 61
Victory, 4, 16, 42, 51, 55, 64, 85, 90, 99, 104, 120, 139, 140, 143, 146, 150, 154, 156, 158, 161–163, 169, 171, 202, 203, 213, 214, 218, 266, 283, 285, 297, 301, 311,

318, 319, 332, 335, 338, 353, 354, 358
Vietnam, 65
Village, 46, 57
Virtue, 44, 47, 115, 241

Wagon, 18, 31, 53, 54, 63, 69, 74, 104, 113, 120, 176, 224, 229, 236, 237, 273, 289, 293, 307, 315, 336, 339, 345, 350, 365
Wall, 6, 12, 14, 17, 25, 27, 29–31, 33, 45, 51, 63, 69, 105, 106, 112, 113, 115, 117, 121, 137, 139, 143, 158, 164–166, 170, 175, 176, 178, 179, 181, 183, 184, 187–189, 191, 192, 205, 218, 226, 228, 233, 242, 244–251, 253–256, 258, 259, 264–266, 277, 278, 285, 288–291, 293–295, 297, 299, 301, 302, 305–307, 309, 329, 331, 333, 336, 337, 342, 344, 345, 347, 349, 350, 355–357, 359–361, 363, 364, 366–371
Walnut, 123, 124
*Wan-huo fei-sha shen-píao,* 147
Wang Chen, 326, 327
Wang Chien-chi, 233
Wang Chíien-hsiu, 251
Wang Chin-tían, 96
Wang Ching-hsien, 322
Wang Ching-tse 315
Wang Chíing-y,n, 333
Wang Ch,n-chíuo 105
Wang Chung-cheng, 292
Wang Hsi, 320, 324
Wang Hsiung-tían, 138
Wang Hs,an-mo, 43
Wang Hun, 107
Wang Kuei 307
Wang Kíuei 119
Wang Lin, 86, 158–160
Wang Mang, 275
Wang Meng, 96, 102
Wang Ming-ho, 131, 203, 204, 207, 209
Wang Pen, 265
Wang Shih, 85

Wang Shih-chíung, 137, 138
Wang Shou-jen, 222, 223
Wang Ssu-cheng, 289–291, 351
Wang Te, 96
Wang Tse, 96, 97, 119, 120
Wang Tsu, 298, 299
Wang Wu-ch,n, 70, 71
Wang Yen-chang, 233, 234
Wang Yen-cheng, 138, 139
Warfare, 42, 85, 89, 246, 247, 283, 319, 344, 345, 366
  aquatic, 203, 313, 339
  riverine, 51, 52, 66, 100, 107, 126, 132, 133, 140, 141, 143–145, 151, 169, 176, 183, 185, 195–237, 286
Warring States, 4, 7, 10, 19, 21, 23–47, 52, 77, 129, 172, 177, 179, 191, 243, 246, 252, 254, 257, 263, 266, 270, 271, 276, 279, 315, 318, 340, 344–347
Warriors, 33, 34, 59, 97, 102, 112, 167, 168, 171, 202, 233, 254, 255, 281, 324, 329, 335, 338, 353
Water
  level 69, 159, 163, 224, 229, 244, 249, 250, 254, 267, 272, 273, 289, 281, 283, 287, 288, 294, 299, 302, 304, 307, 308, 311, 312, 315, 360
  supply 70, 244, 245, 247, 263, 264, 281, 283, 314, 317–333, 342, 344, 349, 365–368
Weak, 243, 277
Weapons, 3, 6, 7, 13, 17, 29, 43, 45, 52, 94, 98–100, 109, 113, 122–125, 127, 132, 136, 137, 139, 149, 165, 184, 186, 188, 190, 200, 201, 203, 206–208, 217, 219, 231, 256, 259, 277, 297, 304, 314, 315, 318, 352, 363, 369
Weather, 42, 78, 136, 150, 155, 228, 268, 275, 295, 306, 326, 357

Wei, 57, 59, 61, 63, 87,
116, 151, 169, 230,
248, 257–267, 314,
320
Eastern 6, 236, 288–291,
301, 302, 348–352
King Pao of 198
Later 339
Northern, 43, 135, 136,
169, 225–232, 250,
287, 288, 298–301,
311, 322–324,
333–348
Western 6, 236, 288–290,
348–351
Wei Ao, 297
Wei Hsiao-kuan, 349
Wei Hs̟eh-hui, 294
Wei Jui, 228, 229, 287, 288
*Wei Liao-tzu*, 24, 277, 346,
347
Wei River, 64, 282, 290,
309, 310
Wei-chou, 69–71, 248
Well:
water, 27, 143, 192, 254,
256, 273, 299, 303,
317, 318, 323,
327–329, 332, 334,
340, 341, 367
listening, 33–35, 191, 192
Well Sweep, 134
Wen Chiao, 321
West, 51, 52, 75, 186, 215,
277, 304, 305, 311,
326, 337, 338, 348,
356
West Lake, 284
Western Region, 50, 51
Wet, 6, 8, 80, 180, 195, 268
Wetlands, 265, 266, 268,
270, 271, 305, 306,
318
Wheel, 31, 32, 183, 190,
207, 224, 236, 237,
266, 307, 368
Wheelbarrow, 31, 64
Wind, 5, 7–9, 16, 18, 19,
22, 36–39, 46, 50, 58,
62, 66, 70, 78, 81, 83,
87, 88–94, 96, 109,
120, 126, 129, 136,
138, 143, 149–171,
174, 177, 182, 184,
185, 189–191,
200–202, 204, 206,
212–214, 216, 220,
223, 234, 236, 271,

272, 281, 290, 291,
322, 362, 364, 365
downwind, 16, 19, 36,
151, 160
upwind, 16, 38–40, 83,
100, 157, 166, 171,
177, 201, 213, 236
Wine, 26, 175, 308, 339,
341
Wing, 126
Winter, 5, 163, 215, 250,
251, 273, 322, 340,
368
Wood, 12, 27, 28, 30, 37,
98, 134, 136, 164,
173–176, 178, 180,
188, 190, 197, 201,
207, 209, 234, 251,
278, 289, 306, 350,
361–363, 366, 370
Women, 336, 352, 362
Worthy, 46
Worthy King of the Left,
250
Wu, 4, 13, 56, 59–62, 79,
83, 118, 119, 162,
200, 202, 204, 212,
213, 224, 230,
231–233, 248, 256,
257
Duke, 11
Eastern, 107, 315
Emperor, 161, 163, 357
King, 38, 204
Wu Chían, 230, 231
Wu Chíi, 36, 42, 266, 268,
280
Wu Kuo-kung, 303
Wu Li, 151
Wu Lin, 175, 216, 335
Wu Ming-chíe, 307
*Wu Pien*, 89, 91, 123, 130,
134, 149, 165, 184,
318, 342
Wu Shu, 215, 216, 336–339
Wu-chíang, 158
*Wu-ching Tsung-yao*, 24, 65,
83, 84, 91, 111, 113,
114, 118, 123, 124,
131, 133–135, 151,
152, 156, 165, 166,
176, 178, 179,
182–185, 197–199,
205, 232, 256, 282,
339–341
*Wu-han*, 160
Wu-hsi, 214
Wu-hu, 159

*Wu-pei Chih*, 45, 89, 98, 99,
123, 125–128, 131,
132, 139, 144–147,
150, 151, 168, 180,
184, 187, 206, 207,
210, 284
Wu-ting River, 330
Wu-tsung, 221,221
*Wu-tzu*, 36, 44, 79, 95, 152,
153, 196, 266, 271,
340
Wu-y̟eh, 162, 213, 214

*Yang*, 77, 318
Yang Gate, 15
Yang Chien, 79, 80
Yang Hsing-mi, 284
Yang Hs̟an, 97, 120, 165
Yang Hu, 14
Yang Kían, 302, 321,
354–356
Yang Kuei-fei, 73
Yang Su, 136
Yang Ta-yen, 227, 229, 230
Yang-chou, 159, 216
Yangshao, 244
Yangtze River, 51, 52,
55–57, 59, 61, 62, 65,
72, 80–82, 84, 120,
139, 153, 158–160,
173, 185, 206,
211–213, 215,
217–219, 221, 223,
230–232, 242,
245–247, 250, 275,
315, 321, 353, 354
Yao, 18, 242
Yao Hsiang, 221
Yao Hsing, 324
Yates, Robin 140
Yeh Ling-sheng, 258
Yeh Meng-hsiung, 62, 94,
104, 155, 267, 268,
284, 293, 310, 311,
319, 320, 324, 333,
339
Yeh-chíeng, 247, 287, 297,
298, 302
Yellow Emperor, 164
Yellow River, 51, 53, 74,
195, 230, 232, 233,
235, 236, 241, 245,
249, 250, 265, 275,
276, 282, 285, 288,
289, 292–295, 303,
308, 322, 323, 348,
351
Yellow Turbans, 49, 95, 157

**444    INDEX**

Yen, 52, 115–118, 266
  Former, 102, 103, 334
  Later, 135, 136, 250, 298
  Southern, 66
  Western, 160
Yen-shih, 246
Yi, 11, 59, 242, 247, 282, 286
*Yi Chou-shu*, 247, 263
Yi-ling, 60
*Yin*, 318
Yin Keng, 91, 92, 173
Yin River, 336
Yin To, 258
Yin Tzu-chiI, 189
Yin-hsiang-chíeng, 245
Ying, 77, 119, 264

Ying-chíuan, 282, 288, 289, 302, 351
Ying-tsung, 326, 327
Ying-yang, 339
Ying-tíien, 219
Yu-chou, 170, 171, 186
Y̧, 241–243, 253
Y̧ Chin, 59, 267
Y̧ Y̧n-wen, 217
Y̧-lin, 334, 340
Y̧-pi, 288, 289, 348–351
Y̧an (dynasty), 191
Y̧an, Duke, 15
Y̧an River, 139, 214, 251
Y̧an Shao, 53–55, 86, 96, 273
Y̧an Shu, 286

Y̧an Ying, 226–232
Y̧eh, 4, 13, 162, 200, 304, 306
Y̧eh Fei, 215, 335, 336, 338
Y̧eh Yi, 35, 116
Y̧eh-tu 332
Y̧n-chung, 95
*Y̧n-chíou Kang-mu*, 65, 94, 251, 284, 293, 319, 324, 333, 339
Y̧n-nan, 357
Yung Gate, 14
Yung River, 313
Yung-chíiu, 189
Yung-chou, 321
Yung-lo, 326, 329